LORCA IN TUNE WITH FALLA

Lorca in Tune with Falla

Literary and Musical Interludes

NELSON R. ORRINGER

UNIVERSITY OF TORONTO PRESS
Toronto Buffalo London

© University of Toronto Press 2014
Toronto Buffalo London
www.utppublishing.com
Printed in Canada

ISBN 978-1-4426-4729-9

Printed on acid-free, 100% post-consumer recycled paper with vegetable-based inks.

Library and Archives Canada Cataloguing in Publication

Orringer, Nelson R., author
Lorca in tune with Falla : literary and musical interludes / Nelson R. Orringer.

(Toronto Iberic)
Includes bibliographical references and index.
ISBN 978-1-4426-4729-9 (bound)

1. García Lorca, Federico, 1998–1936 – Influence.   2. García Lorca, Federico, 1898–1936 – Criticism and interpretation.   3. Falla, Manuel de, 1876–1946 – Influence.   4. Falla, Manuel de, 1876–1946 – Criticism and interpretation.   5. Music and literature – Spain – History – 20th century   I. Title.   II. Series: Toronto Iberic

PQ6613.A763Z874 2014   861'.62   C2013-903762-4

University of Toronto Press acknowledges the financial assistance to its publishing program of the Canada Council for the Arts and the Ontario Arts Council.

  Canada Council   Conseil des Arts
for the Arts   du Canada

University of Toronto Press acknowledges the financial support of the Government of Canada through the Canada Book Fund for its publishing activities.

In memory of my mother, Alta M. Orringer,
a consummate pianist

Table of Contents

Illustrations and Musical Examples

I. Illustrations

II. Musical Examples

Preface

The ear perceives and processes a richer gamut of sensations than the eye. For philosopher of music Juan David García Bacca, the eyes see a space that is lit, but not the process of its becoming illuminated, while the ears actually hear Beethoven's *Ninth Symphony* coming into being. Luminous reality, conceived as vibrations of an electromagnetic field, emerges too fast for the eyes to perceive its production, while symphonies allow auditory perception of their emergence (*Filosofía de la música* 478–88). Since the natural state of the universe is the fusion and confusion of everything in everything else (474), the senses act as universal selectors and organizers. Faced with the wealth of potential sounds to be selected and organized out of the primordial chaos of sounds, the composer Manuel de Falla (1876–1946) and the poet Federico García Lorca (1898–1936) have often chosen and structured like sounds for their respective arts: they lived in the same portion of the audible universe, Granada, Spain, for sixteen years, from 1920 to 1936. There Falla and Lorca became friends in 1920, and the poet's family swept up the composer and his sister María Carmen into its daily life during the sixteen most productive years of Falla's and Lorca's careers.

When reading a Falla score or a Lorca poem, the reader with a well-tuned mental ear can detect analogous sounds emerging from the artworks. In a word, the artist Lorca lived in tune with Falla, and Falla in tune with Lorca. Recognition of this harmony increases knowledge and appreciation of both artists. Unfortunately, with few exceptions, specialists in music and poetry have failed to sense the active, ongoing connection between the arts of both creators. To begin to correct the omission, produced by a division of knowledge contrary to the art of both Falla and Lorca, is the purpose of the present book. To clarify Lorca by applying the analogous sound system of Falla is the method. To discipline the application with the scientific and ontological philosophy of music of García Bacca – a source never before exploited in this fashion – is to sensitize the process. Neither Falla nor Lorca would have disapproved such sensitization: Falla often resorted to philosophy of music – specifically, that of Louis Lucas, which was well known to Lorca – for greater precision in his composition process, and some of Lucas's ideas helped structure Lorca's best-known poetry. Therefore, the well-tuned critic can try to reconstruct the composition process of the music and poetry, enabling both to re-emerge before the mental ear of the listener or the reader.

The following pages have something new to say to scholars of Falla, experts in Lorca, admirers of Hispanic culture, comparatists in modernist European culture, and lovers of music, music philosophy, and poetry in general. To remove barriers to knowledge, a musical glossary will appear at the start of this book. Hispanists will recognize terms in Spanish music not familiar to most musicologists while reacquainting themselves with basic musicological terms. Falla and Lorca both read scores as well as literature. Whenever scores appear in my text, they come with clear explanations for those who may not read music; whenever quotations from Lorca's verse appear, they are accompanied by my English translations. The novelty of the approach and the vastness of the subject may cause me to miss many aspects of the Falla-Lorca artistic relationship, or perhaps even to misidentify the music affecting the poet. Nevertheless, I will at least have accomplished the mission of attuning the cerebral ear of future critics, capable of correcting me, to similar sound waves emerging from both authors. My objective in the pages that follow is to open new pathways to intuitive and conceptual enjoyment of Lorca's production – and through the newness and rigour of my approach, of Falla's as well.

Nelson R. Orringer
Storrs, Connecticut
29 February 2012

Acknowledgments

How grateful I am to have enjoyed the aid of two of the most disciplined and innovative researchers of Falla's life and art: Michael Christoforidis, Senior Lecturer at the Melbourne Conservatorium of Music, and Carol L. Hess, Professor of Musicology at Michigan State University! The first scholar, learned in Spanish musicology, literature, and guitar, sent me his valuable offprints on Falla's music, which are otherwise difficult to obtain, along with some of his unpublished lectures on Falla. The second scholar answered my all too numerous queries on Falla in rapid, enthusiastic responses by e-mail. Both thinkers enabled me to confirm my hypothesis that archival research in Manuel de Falla's library collection could clarify hidden aspects of García Lorca's writings, for both Falla and Lorca drew from common printed and musical sources of knowledge.

At the University of Connecticut, Lana Babij of Interlibrary Loans diligently pursued for me microfilms of Falla's articles in Western European periodicals. Professor Glen Stanley of the Music Department graciously responded to my questions on water music in Falla.

While writing, I realized that I needed to understand Falla and Lorca with the immediacy and depth I hoped to convey to readers in Hispanic literature and music history and theory. Therefore, I followed in the footsteps of specialists Christoforidis and Hess by going straight to the archives of Falla and Lorca and examining documents on their artistic relationship. In May 2011 I visited both the Archivo Manuel de Falla (Granada) and the Fundación Federico García Lorca (Madrid). The wealth of information garnered at both would fill several books. The holdings of the Falla archive in particular, imported from Argentina, had suffered fewer losses than the Lorca collection, which was decimated during the years of the Spanish Civil War.

How can I adequately thank the staff at the Archivo Manuel de Falla? Elena García Paredes de Falla (Agent), Diego Martínez (Head Archivist), and Concha Chinchilla (Archivist) educated me in twentieth-century European culture that shaped and was shaped by Falla. E. García Paredes de Falla gave me access to published copies of Falla's personal notes on Andalusian deep song, which were influential on Lorca's poetry and theatre. C. Chinchilla placed in my hands Falla's handwritten notebooks on composition. She also made available to me unpublished material.

Photocopies of Falla's and Lorca's correspondence became obtainable for me, with Falla's musical notations, unnoticed or overlooked by previous critics. I found out that Falla and Lorca often communicated by alluding to music well known to both. Lorca would write poetry and theatre to be read especially by Falla, and this factor largely explains Lorca's literary musicality. I consulted scores by Falla's and Lorca's favourite composers, with Falla's marginal notes. Not only could I record Falla's annotations in his preferred readings on musical and on non-musical themes (like magic and Gypsy life, intriguing to Lorca), but I also read obscure article clippings on the Falla-Lorca relationship. Major information unexpectedly emerged from concert programs in which Falla's music appeared, analysed by the composer himself. In sum, the Archivo Manuel de Falla is a valuable resource tool for understanding Lorca.

In the Fundación Federico García Lorca I supplemented information on the Lorca-Falla relationship obtained in Granada. Helpful staff members Rosa María Illán and Sonia González copied for me photographs of Falla and Lorca on the road, in theatres, and at banquets; and those archivists provided documents about Lorca before he befriended Falla. Moreover, in the Fundación, autographed copies of scores by Falla, dedicated by him to Lorca and to his sister Concha, allowed perception of new connections between the two artists.

How right was my friend Ricardo Quiñones, an author with the University of Toronto Press, to recommend that press to me for its traditional scholarly rigour! To Richard Ratzlaff, its Humanities Editor, I am indebted for supporting this publication and for encouraging me at each step through the painstaking process of peer review and revision. No one could have received more exacting, sensitive, and better-informed manuscript readers than I. Their suggestions for improving my book were invaluable.

To the fertile imagination of my daughter Elise, I owe the main title of this book and the idea for the cover design. Finally, I am grateful to my dear wife Stephanie for her love and support. To all here mentioned go my deepest thanks. The errors I commit in the following pages stem solely from my mind, not theirs.

Musical Glossary

Andalusianism: style of composition incorporating melodies, harmonies, and rhythms typical of folkloric Andalusian music into the European canon. This incorporation especially includes flamenco dance and *cante jondo* ("deep song") vocals and guitar pieces. Musical nationalism motivated Falla's cultivation of this style between 1904 and 1919. Main works in this style are *La vida breve, Andaluza, Noches en los jardines de España, El amor brujo, El sombrero de tres picos,* and *Fantasía bætica.*

Appoggiatura: a grace note that delays the next note of the melody, taking half or more of its written time value:[1]

Arabesque: a musical piece of interlacing themes, autonomous though melodically related, repeated several times, and integrated in suggestive ways throughout the work. A melodic line seems to determine its own progressions and thereby to acquire melodic quality in itself. Examples are *Noches en los jardines de España* and, by analogy, Lorca's *Poema del cante jondo,* an arabesque made of words, ideas, sounds, and rhythms.

Arpeggio: the successive playing of each of the notes forming a chord.

Bulería: a rapid, twelve-beat flamenco rhythm combining ternary and
  binary patterns.

Cantaor: a singer of deep song.

Cante jondo: "deep song," which for Falla is a generic term for the
  oldest, purest songs of Andalusian tradition. Derived, according to his
  vision, from layers of influence – plainchant, Moorish rhythms, Gypsy
  music with its Indian substratum – *cante jondo* includes many genres,
  characterized by adorned melodies, with numerous repetitions of
  single notes (related by Falla to old magical rites), a range rarely
  transcending the sixth and enharmonic modes. Falla's detractors
  regarded this folk music as merely a trivial musical by-product
  of taverns and brothels. This notion, without the necessarily negative
  connotations, is gaining adherents today.

Caprice: an instrumental piece more or less free of formal rules, written
  in a lively tempo and composed to display virtuosity.

Coda: a cadence of varying complexity and length used to conclude
  a musical movement.

Copla: a term denoting both the couplet of a song and a popular poem
  sung to an improvised tune.

Enharmonism: a term coined by Falla to translate Louis Lucas's French
  word "enharmonisme."It signifies the alteration of musical scales
  or their divisions into ever smaller intervals in harmony with the
  demands of the voice. In deep song, the voice modulates the scale
  with microtones.

Flamenco: a set of Andalusian folk melodies and dances derived for Falla
  from older, more serious deep-song forms and identified with regions
  of their origin: hence, *granadinas* from Granada, *malagueñas* from
  Malaga, or *rondeñas* from Ronda.

Flatten: to play or sing a note half an interval lower than the normal
  expected pitch. Flattening occurs in Arabic-Andalusian music and
  in deep song.

Glissando: a rapid sliding over successive chords or keys.

Hemiola: in folk music, a metric pattern in which two successive measures in ternary time (3/4 or 3/2) join one another as if they were three
  measures in binary time (2/4 or 2/2). They are counted, "One-and-two-
  and-three-and- / one-and-two-and-three-and." "Danza lejana," second
  nocturne of *Noches en los jardines de España*, exemplifies such a rhythm.

Hold (or fermata): the suspension of motion in a melody. The sign for a
  hold, placed above a note, is a semicircle facing downward with a dot
  in the middle.

r a single syllable of
    text. Melisma is usually employed in the exclamation "¡ay!" beginning
    pieces of deep song and in portamentos (q.v.) with which they close.
Mode: the ordering of sounds to form a scale. The modes of greatest
    interest to Falla are the Phrygian, the Lydian, and the Doric. The
    Phrygian, according to Falla's personal jottings, contains the notes
    E–F#–G–A–C#–D. The Lydian includes F–G–A–Bb–C–E. The Doric
    holds D–E–F–B–C–E. The Phrygian is the most frequent mode used
    in flamenco and deep song and often appears in classical Arabic music.
Modulation: the transposition of a melody from one key to another.
Neoclassicism: a musical trend rising in the 1920s when composers like
    Stravinsky, Hindemith, and Vaughn Williams created compositions
    using styles and forms derived from the seventeenth and eighteenth
    centuries. Chamber orchestras playing humorous or ironic passages
    mocked the orchestral excesses of romanticism. Falla's neoclassicism
    includes *El retablo de maese Pedro* and the *Harpsichord Concerto*.
Pavane: a slow, stately dance for couples, created in sixteenth-century
    Europe.
Portamento: a musical adornment in which the voice slides through
    infinitesimal gradations of keys in a short time. A portamento appears
    towards the end of the *soleá* in the final scene of *La vida breve*.
Recitative: a style of singing that imitates declamation. Most of the
    trujamán or interpreter's song in *El retablo de maese Pedro* exemplifies
    recitative.
Reprise: a return to the first part of a piece following an intervening
    different section. Reprises abound in Falla and also in the poetry
    of Lorca.

Rubato: the abandonment of strict rhythmic time for a while in the performance of a musical passage to convey spontaneity or emotion.

Saeta: a brief "arrow" or unaccompanied strophe of deep song aimed from a balcony toward the image of the Virgin or Christ crucified in the procession below during Holy Week (sometimes during Corpus Christi as well). *Saetas* also entered the cries of Andalusian street vendors hawking their wares. Falla incorporates *saetas* into the lines of Maese Pedro and the *trujamán* or interpreter in *El retablo de maese Pedro*.

Seguidilla: a quick Andalusian dance in ternary time, probably of Castilian or Manchegan origin, with roots in the sixteenth century. *Seguidilla serrana* is a provincial species of seguidilla, derived, for instance, from Seguro de la Sierra in Jaen province (eastern Andalusia).

Siguiriya gitana: for Falla, the prototypical deep-song genre, the one closest to the "primigenious Andalusian spirit," purest, most ancient, and most fertile, producing other genres like the *serrana*, the *caña*, the *polo*, the *martinete*, and the *soleá*. These four, in turn, engender flamenco genres (according to Falla) including *rondeñas*, *malagueñas*, and *peteneras* (after a legendary songstress from Paterna, Cadiz). The typical siguiriya has a free-flowing rhythm following four descending chords, endlessly repeated with variations.

Soleá: a plaintive song of *cante jondo* composed of three octosyllables with lines 1 and 3 rhyming in assonance. The *cantaor* in *La vida breve* sings a soleá in act 2. Candelas's theme in *El amor brujo* is a soleá. The word in Andalusian dialect denotes solitude, aloneness.

Tempered scale: the diatonic scale, a set of seven full steps between notes used in a major or minor key and present in almost all Western music since the baroque. The rising tempered scale, based on C major, includes C–D–E–F–G–A–B. Falla and Louis Lucas find the scale rigid and limited as distinguished from enharmonism (q.v.) with its microtones.

Tocaor: a deep-song instrumentalist, usually a guitarist.

Zarzuela: a light musical comedy of regionalist character close to operetta. The zarzuela contains spoken dialogues, songs, duets, and choral pieces. Though dating back to the sixteenth century, this genre came into its own in the second half of the nineteenth and maintained high popularity at least until Falla's times.

Lorca In Tune with Falla

Si les digo que este poeta y músico es uno de mis mejores amigos granadinos es sólo la mitad de la verdad, pues es también, por muchos conceptos, uno de mis discípulos que más estimo en todo orden, y es también, refiriéndose a lo popular español, un excelente colaborador.

Cuando quiere Dios que se logre un artista de tal calidad, no sólo capaz de asimilar en lo técnico lo necesario para su trabajo, sino de superar lo que la técnica tiene de mero oficio (y éste es el caso de García Lorca en sus armonizaciones del folklore español), es cuando comprendemos la enorme diferencia entre lo que es producto de enseñanza y lo que surge por obra de la creación personal, ayudado por esta enseñanza.

[If I tell you that this poet and musician is one of my best friends from Granada, that is only half the truth, since he is also in many respects one of my close students whom I most value in every sense, and he is also an excellent collaborator in everything related to Spanish folklore.

When God wills the self-attainment of an artist of such quality, able not only to absorb technically what is needed for his work, but also to surmount mere tools of the trade in technique (and this is García Lorca's case in his harmonizing of Spanish folk songs), that is when we understand the enormous difference between what a product of training is and what arises by virtue of personal creativity, aided by that training.]

Manuel de Falla, Granada, March 1930, Letter to Antonio Quevedo and his wife, Falla's former music student María Muñoz, in Havana, Cuba[2]

Introduction:
The Intersection of Two Artists' Lives

Seldom does chance bring together two artists in different media with decisive impact on each other's works. When that mutual influence occurs, epoch-making creation emerges. The friendship that developed between Manuel de Falla and Federico García Lorca while both resided in Granada led to some of their most celebrated writings. Both approached art between the two poles of music and letters, though from different directions. Falla, one of the most performed twentieth-century Spanish composers, wrote music often inspired by literature. Federico García Lorca, one of the most published twentieth-century Spanish poets, penned verse often stimulated by music. As a pre-adolescent, Falla considered a career in letters, yet at age seventeen felt divinely called to create music (Hess, *Passions* 14). Lorca as a teenager hoped to become a classical pianist, yet shortly after the death of his piano teacher Antonio Segura Mesa in 1916, he answered instead a calling to write poetry.[1] The friendship between composer and poet remained constant from 1920, peaked in 1923 during their collaboration on a comic opera, underwent a crisis early in 1929, then steadied into somewhat distant yet genuine affection until Lorca's assassination seven years later.[2]

The musical quality of Lorca's poetry transcends the literary world and enthrals composers and musicologists. For Falla biographer Carol Hess, Lorca's lyric "exudes musicality in imagery, rhythm, and subject matter; the fact that he 'supplies constant cues for music in his writing,' as critic Alex Ross points out, is certainly part of Lorca's appeal to composers."[3] Music historian Michael Christoforidis uses Falla's own words in calling Lorca his "musical disciple" ("Folksong models" 16), but their relationship arose from mutual admiration (Persia, "Lorca, Falla" 74). They first met in Granada in the fall of 1919 when Lorca was introduced to Falla as a "town curiosity, as a 'precocious child of poetry'" (Gibson, *Life* 92). The Cadiz-born Falla was then considering moving to Granada with the encouragement of his friend Granadan guitarist Ángel Barrios and with awareness of the composers Debussy's and Albéniz's musical attraction to that city (García Montero, "Introducción," in García Lorca, *Poema del cante jondo* 30). Once Falla settled there in September 1920, he and Lorca often visited one another's homes. They exchanged letters when either was away, shared aesthetic affinities, developed multivalent conceptions of poetry and music, blurred boundaries between the two arts, influenced each others' production, and collaborated on artistic projects. They played piano duets together, composed together arrangements for medieval Spanish songs, and hiked together through the countryside in search of folk music (Zapke, "Presentación," in *Falla y Lorca* 3; Orozco, *Falla* 150). Often invited with his brother to Falla's house to hear him perform on the piano (Francisco García Lorca, *Federico y su mundo* 157), Lorca also played for Falla his own musical compositions, earning Falla's polite praise (Mora Guarnido, *Lorca* 159).

Lorca exported Falla's ideas on music to his college for talented Spanish youth, the Residencia de Estudiantes (Madrid), which he attended from 1919 to 1928 (García Lorca, *Obras completas* 3:1092). There he played Falla's pieces on the piano and helped stage his ballet *El amor brujo* [Love, the Magician] (3:1100; Persia, "Lorca, Falla" 80). Lorca accorded Falla a high ranking, together with Isaac Albéniz and Enrique Granados, in the history of Spanish music. For his compositions Albéniz mined the treasure of Andalusian folk song; and Falla also filled his music, Lorca thought, with "our pure and beautiful musical themes in his distant, ghostly form."[4] From Falla, as well as from avant-garde poets (see ch. 1), Lorca learned distance for his own works. With Falla he regarded Andalusian *cante jondo*, deep song, as a "pure, ever-renewing source,"[5] always regenerating musical creativity. Already by 1920 Falla and Lorca had explored together the Gypsy caves of Sacromonte (Granada), befriending and applauding the singers and guitarists living there (Gibson, *Life* 106).

Falla developed his controversial conception of deep song in a milieu of artistic primitivism, cultivated by his admired fellow composer Igor Stravinsky and the Ballets Russes. This troupe had received a warm welcome into Spain in spring 1916 from the Madrid press and the public (Hess, *Modernism* 96). In 1917, Falla accompanied Sergei Diaghilev, choreographer-dancer Léonide Massine, and Gypsy dancer Félix Fernández García on a tour of Spain from Zaragoza, Burgos, Salamanca, and Toledo to various cities of Andalusia in search of musical materials to stage what would eventually become the ballet *El sombrero de tres picos* [The three-cornered hat] (113–15). In 1921, Diaghelev consulted Falla about staging the May 17 performance in Paris by the Ballets Russes of *Cuadro Flamenco* [Flamenco tableau], employing a Spanish Gypsy troupe (173). With all these experiences behind him, Falla persuaded Lorca of his notions on deep song and its origins.

They collaborated with others to organize the First *Cante Jondo* Contest in Granada during Corpus Christi of 1922. Most researchers hold that the businessman Miguel Cerón Rubio, Falla's friend, first conceived the idea for the contest, while others attribute the idea to Falla or Lorca (3:109). Lorca's admiration for Falla's creativity explains his own view of Falla as originator of the idea in 1921 during a summer walk with him in Granada. The composer complained of the degeneration and scorn the old songs were suffering, viewed as the musical dross of taverns and brothels. Suddenly from a nearby window emerged an excellent rendition of deep song by an amateur guitarist accompanying someone singing. Instantly, Falla determined to organize the *cante jondo* contest for amateur performers in Granada to preserve a disappearing legacy (Maurer, *Arquitectura* 111).

Falla and Lorca defined *cante jondo* as a group of Andalusian folk songs whose genuine type resides in the Gypsy *siguiriya*, origin of others like *soleares*, *polos*, *martinetes*, and all distinguishable from the flamenco group.[6] The designation *flamenco*, they held, belongs only to more modern songs like *malagueñas*, *granadinas*, *rondeñas*, *sevillanas*, and *peteneras*, derived from the older ones previously mentioned.[7] Falla's musical theories and practice clarify Lorca's prose and poetry on *cante jondo*, such as in lectures titled "El cante jondo. Primitivo canto andaluz" [Deep song. Primitive Andalusian song, 1922] (*Obras completas* 3:195–216), and "Arquitectura del cante jondo" [Architecture of deep song, 1931] (Maurer, "Arquitectura" 109–61), and in the poetic anthology *Poema del cante jondo* [Poem of deep song, 1931].[8]

This anthology, mostly dating from fall 1921 and winter 1922, has strong links to Falla. In a letter dated 1 January 1922 to his friend Adolfo Salazar, Lorca identifies Falla as his first reader. This verse, remarked Lorca, was full of "Andalusian suggestions," its rhythm stylized folklore. It featured legendary Andalusian folk singers and the full range of their musical fantasies, including Death personified. It was puppet theatre; it was also "an American puzzle, understand? The poem begins with a motionless twilight; and the *siguiriya*, the *soleá*, the *saeta*, and the *petenera* parade through it. The poem is full of Gypsies, oil lamps, forges, and it even has allusions to Zoroaster. It is the first thing to come out of a different direction of mine, and I do not yet know what to tell you about it … but it sure is something novel! The only one who knows it is Falla, and he is enthusiastic." [9]

No record exists of Lorca's words to Falla or of explanations for Falla's enthusiasm. For C.B. Morris, Lorca's word "puzzle" means that readers must arrange the individual pieces. "American" denotes an "alien quality which diversifies and modulates the Andalusian basis of the work." Its stylized folk rhythm may refer to "a phonic quality having less to do with meter and form than with a mode of stylization he found exemplified in the music of Falla. Luis García Montero has rightly pointed out that the 'psychic purification' Lorca achieved in *PCJ* had the musical precedent of Falla close at hand" (Morris 184). Falla wished to stylize Andalusian folk music by restoring its essence, lost through artificial absorption of Italianate elements. He filtered it through old Spanish learned and folk conventions and French impressionist music able, in his opinion, to capture Andalusian being. Analogously, in literature Lorca aspired to cleanse Andalusian lyric of the slavish imitation of popular anonymous verse by modern Andalusian poets. He imitated in poetry what Falla attempted in music by passing folk images through the filters of new avant-garde metaphors seeking the essences of their referents. He even transferred some of Falla's musical conceptions to his verse. "The liking of both for folk culture and the idea that it is possible to find in it the essences that allow them to build their own language (…) lead them to labor on works in common."[10]

However, Falla's and Lorca's aims differed. "Throughout his career," writes Christoforidis, "Manuel de Falla sought to create a Spanish identity in music, and until 1920 foregrounded his Andalusian origins in order to achieve this" ("Falla, flamenco" 230). He justified his Andalusianism by maintaining that folk music from the region captured the primordial experience so striking for non-Spanish composers. Lorca, however, aimed directly for original human experience through verse imitating the lyrics of *cante jondo*. Lorca and Falla could say with Russian composer Igor Stravinsky, admired by both (Armero, *Manuel de Falla* 93; Francisco García Lorca, *Federico y su mundo* 425), and sharing Falla's love of Eastern strains in Andalusian music, "Some Andalusian folksongs (…) arouse atavistic reminiscences within me."[11] Both Falla and Lorca sought to reach Andalusia's essence, which Falla hoped would lead him to the essence of Spain, and which Lorca regarded as a purified way to savour the bitterness of unfulfilled love and the terror of mortality, the "first lament and the first kiss" originating deep song.[12]

1. Lorca's Impact on Falla

PCJ, not published until 1931, was one of the lasting results that the First *Cante Jondo* Contest had yielded. Another was the psychological fallout of the contest on Falla, focusing his creativity on the musical possibilities of puppetry, religious music in general, and *autos sacramentales*, or sacred one-act allegorical dramas usually staged for Corpus Christi. The effort of helping to organize the deep-song competition left Falla fatigued and exasperated with the indifference or hostility of many Granadans towards their musical heritage.[13] Perhaps to console or distract him, Lorca proposed that they revive the old Andalusian Punch and Judy tradition. Already in the summer of 1921 Lorca had written to Salazar that he was scouring his Andalusian vacation town of Asquerosa (today Valderrubio) for information about the hand puppets. Although the puppets had vanished, older village folk recalled hilarious details about the shows (*Epistolario* 1:38). Lorca told Salazar that he aimed to involve Falla in the puppetry on the Andalusian Punch-and-Judy theme that he was writing (43). By January 1922, Falla had committed himself to setting the shows, and he hoped to encourage Stravinsky and Maurice Ravel to contribute their art too (50). Lorca and Falla would tour Europe and the Americas with their theatre, to be called "Los títeres de Cachiporra de Granada" [The Punch-and-Judy puppets of Granada] (51).

This ambitious dream ended up as a single performance of that puppet theatre for Lorca's twelve-year-old sister Isabel and her friends on Epiphany, 6 January 1923, at Lorca's home. At the time, under contract since 1918 to Princess Edmond de Polignac to compose a short concert piece with limited ensemble (Hess, *Modernism* 199), Falla was writing a marionette opera, *El retablo de maese Pedro* [The puppet-theatre of Master Peter], on a Cervantine theme. He feared that a corpulent tenor or baritone would not do visual justice to lanky, spiritual Don Quixote in part 2, chapter 26 of Cervantes' novel. Falla hoped to set to music the hero's reaction to a puppet show on a chivalric tale as the visionary knight, caught up in the illusion, takes it as real life and destroys the enemy puppets – and the whole show. In Ortega y Gasset's words, "Don Quixote's soul, weightless as thistledown, as a dry leaf,"[14] had been sucked into the fantasy world. Therefore Falla conceived the solution of a double puppet show with characters of two different sizes: doll-sized puppets for Master Peter's and life-sized (or larger) puppets for Don Quixote and other spectators. To test the plan, it was Lorca who proposed staging a hand-puppet show for children during Epiphany of 1923 in his own home (Mora Guarnido, *Lorca* 164–5), and it was later Lorca and other friends who helped Falla arrange the libretto for the *Retablo* (158; see ch. 9, n. 36 below).

Meanwhile, Falla, Lorca, and set designer/craftsman Hermenegildo Lanz prepared the performance for Epiphany. They decided to interpret three works: the one-act farce *Los dos habladores* [The two chatterers], then attributed to Cervantes; Lorca's adaptation of an Andalusian folk tale, *La niña que riega la albahaca y el príncipe preguntón* [The girl who sprinkles the sweet basil and Prince Ask-a-Lot]; and, in honour of Three Kings' Day, the *auto sacramental Misterio de los reyes magos* [Mystery play of the Three Wise Men].

For background music, Falla selected Stravinsky's "The Devil's Dance" and "Waltz" from *L'Histoire du soldat* [The soldier's story] for *Los dos habladores*. By employing the Russian composer's version for clarinet, violin, and piano, he performed part of a prominent modern work for the first time in Spain,[15] nine years before its formal debut there. As Eckhard Weber explains ("Titeres" 118, 130), *L'Histoire du soldat* was a key work for twentieth-century musical theatre, radically departing from nineteenth-century realism and introducing declamation in addition to song. As incidental music for Lorca's version of *La niña que riega la albahaca*, Falla chose Debussy's "Serenade for the Doll" (1906) from the *Children's Corner* (1906); excerpts from Albéniz's piano solo *La vega* [The Granadan lowland] (1897); Ravel's *Berceuse sur le nom de Gabriel Fauré* [Lullaby on the name of Gabriel Fauré] (1922) for piano and violin; and the anonymous Spanish seventeenth-century dance, *Españoleta y paso y medio*. As music for the *auto sacramental*, he arranged King Alfonso X the Wise's Cantigas no. 60 and 65 for clarinet, violin, lute, and harpsichord, together with the invitatories "Laudemos Virginem" [Let us praise the Virgin] and "Splendes ceptigera" [Splendid ruler], from the anonymous *Llibre Vermell* [Red book of Montserrat]. Finally, he set to voice and the same instrumental ensemble the Catalan Christmas carol *Cançó de Nadal* (Nommick, "Día de reyes" 62). With no harpsichord available, he simulated one by stuffing newspapers under the strings of the Lorca family piano (Pahissa, *Falla* 127).

This experiment influenced Falla's subsequent musical development. In retrospect, Lorca himself remained puzzled and not completely aware of its full impact on Falla. Three days before the show, when the poet came knocking at Falla's door, the composer was absorbed in practising the Albéniz on the piano. Lorca entered Falla's house on his own, enquired what he was doing, and received the response, "Well, I am preparing for the concert of your theatre." With astonishment ten years later, Lorca praised him as a perfectionist, even when amusing merely a group of children![16] Yet he was looking ahead toward future projects. He even had a concert program printed and mailed to distinguished artists about his Andalusian puppet theatre. Indeed, he sent the program to Maurice Ravel as if to announce a performance of great consequence (see figure 1). Falla viewed his eventual puppet tour of Europe with Lorca as a real possibility. The puppet Punch (Cristobica) announces the program from the puppet-theatre window, giving the title of each play presented and naming the accompanying music with title and composer. The program closes by asking the children to hush for the play to begin precisely at three p.m. (see figure 2).

Hermenildo Lanz remarks that the performance at Lorca's residence "turned out to be a prolegomenon of what was about to debut the same year in Paris under the name of *El retablo de maese Pedro*,"[17] for the work "takes for its inspiration the *guiñol* (hand-puppet theater) associated with southern Spain" (Hess, *Modernism* 198). Weber shows that Stravinsky's *Histoire du soldat*, present in the Three Kings' Day concert, influenced the innermost musical and theatrical structure of *Retablo* ("Titeres" 131, 134–5).[18] Further, the simulated harpsichord may have reinforced the stimulus on Falla of his long-time friend, harpsichordist Wanda Landowska, during a 1922 concert visit to Granada, to expand the role of the harpsichord in the *Retablo*. She played in its 1923 Parisian debut, with puppets and scenery designed by Lanz and Manuel Ángel Ortiz (Hess, *Modernism* 201, *Passions* 146). Envisioning new possibilities for that instrument, Falla wrote his *Harpsichord Concerto* (1923–6) in Landowska's honour (Hess, *Modernism* 234). His contact with the *auto sacramental Misterio de los Reyes Magos* in 1923 encouraged him in 1927 to set to music *El gran teatro del mundo* [The great world theatre], Calderón de la Barca's famous *auto sacramental* (269).[19] The acclaim achieved by the arrangement, with set design by Lanz, elicited Lorca's enthusiastic congratulatory note to Falla sent from Catalonia (Hess, *Passions* 157). Possibly the religious music that Falla had researched while arranging the puppet theatre at the Lorcas' prompted him eventually to compose his own ambitious religious work, the unfinished *Atlàntida*, which he alternately called a "scenic cantata" and a "mystery play for voices and orchestra." D. Breisemeister and E. Weber have shown the proximity of the work to Calderón's *autos sacramentales* (Weber, "Misterio" 914).[20] Falla began the composition in 1926 (Hess, *Passions* 277), played segments for Lorca in 1932 (Orozco, *Falla* 186), sporadically composed additions while in self-exile in Argentina (1939–46), and his student Ernesto Halffter had to complete the work after his death

TITERES DE CACHIPORRA

(CRISTOBICA)

Figure 1   Program cover "For Maurice Ravel, whom I admire and love despite his forgetfulness of old friendships. Manuel de Falla. Granada, 1/23." Reproduced with gracious permission of the Archivo Manuel de Falla (Granada)

OIGAN SEÑORES el programa de esta Fiesta para los niños, que yo pregono desde la ventanita del Guiñol, ante la frente del mundo.

PRIMERO: Se representará el entremés de nuestro Cervantes titulado

LOS DOS HABLADORES

(Con la aparición final del pícaro Cristóbica.)

La música que oirán ustedes es original de Strawinsky.

a) Danza del Diablo (de La Historia del Soldado.)
b) Vals

Arreglo del autor para clarinete, violín y piano.

SEGUNDO: Verán ustedes el viejo cuento andaluz en tres estampas y un cromo.

LA NIÑA QUE RIEGA LA ALBAHACA Y EL PRINCIPE PREGUNTON

Dialogado y adaptado al Teatro Cachiporra Andaluz por Federico García Lorca.

a) La Vega de Granada, (fragmento) . . . . . Albéniz.
b) . . . . . (piano y violín)
c) . Berceuse . . . . Ravel.
     (piano y violín)
d) . Españoleta, Paso y medio (anónimo español del siglo XVII, trascrito por . . . . . . Pedrell.

Las cabecitas de los personajes de ambas obras han sido talladas por el aguafuertista Hermenegildo Lanz.

Las decoraciones pintadas por el poeta Federico García Lorca.

ATENCION

¡AHORA VIENE LO GRANDE!.

Vamos a representar el

MISTERIO de los REYES MAGOS

(Siglo XIII)

(Teatro pianista)
MUSICA

Cantiga «Ave et Eva»
Cantiga LXV (Del códice de Alfonso el Sabio), trascritas y armonizadas por . . . . . . Pedrell.
Dos Invitatorios (del códice de Montserrat, «Llivre Vermell»)
Cançó de Nadal (Antiguo villancico de los Tres Reyes de Oriente) Armonizada por . . . . . . P. Luis Romeu

Decoraciones y figuras pintadas y talladas por Hermenegildo Lanz.
La música de esta última parte ha sido instrumentada para Cémbalo, Violín, Clarinete y Laud por Manuel de Falla.

La música de todo el programa será ejecutada por:

Manuel de Falla . . . . Piano y cémbalo.
José Gómez . . . . Violín.
Alfredo Baldrés . . . . Clarinete.
José Molina . . . . Laud.

Cantarán: el Invitatorio primero y el Villancico de los tres Reyes de Oriente, las niñas Isabelita García Lorca y Laurita de los Rios Giner.

Adiós, señores... Buenas tardes y estad calladitos que va a empezar muy pronto.

El Dueño del Teatrillo

Una vez comenzada la representación se cierran las puertas y ya no se permite la entrada.

La función empieza a las TRES en punto de la tarde del día de los Reyes Magos.

AÑO 1926. . . . . GRANADA

Figure 2   Semi-transparent Program, Three Kings' Day Puppet Show. Reproduced with gracious permission of the Archivo Manuel de Falla (Granada)

(Hess, *Passions* 304). To summarize, without Lorca's influence and enthusiasm, Falla's musical career might have taken a different turn.

Lorca influenced not only Falla's major musical projects, but also minor ones, some completed, others not. After Falla broke in 1921 with his librettists Gregorio and María Martínez Sierra (Hess, *Modernism* 182), Lorca tried in vain to take their place. In 1922 and 1923, he began writing a libretto, *Lola, la comedianta* [Lola the actress], for a comic opera. Falla provided musical suggestions in notations on the manuscript, which Lorca never finished (Menarini). In 1924, Falla unsuccessfully attempted to elicit the aid, first of Federico and subsequently of his brother Francisco García Lorca, to translate from French to Spanish Jean-Aubry's brief poem "Psyché," which Falla had set to music.[21] Another endeavour, the musical arrangement of Góngora's sonnet "A Córdoba" [To Cordoba], had positive results. While promoting the tercentennial celebration of Cordoban poet Luis de Góngora (1561–1627), Lorca persuaded Falla to reread and re-evaluate that writer. He convinced him to set Góngora's sonnet to music (Pahissa, *Falla* 155). The resulting piece for voice and harp follows a tradition of "declamation, supported by strong, rich chords," derived from vocal parts of old *vihuela*-players like Luis Milán, Alonso de Mudarra, and Miguel de Fuenllana (Chase, *Music of Spain* 196). For Carol Hess (*Passions* 157), Falla's musical tribute to Góngora displays "the composer's increasing attraction to starkness, economy, and 'pure music,'" in keeping with the unsentimental aestheticism recommended by Lorca in his famous 1926 lecture "La imagen poética de don Luis de Góngora" [The poetic image of D. Luis de Góngora] (3:228–9).

2. Falla's Impact on Lorca

After surveying Falla's debt to Lorca, we need a full appreciation of Lorca's deeper indebtedness to Falla. Each fed off stimuli provided by the other, so that one would serve a stimulus like a tennis ball to the other, and the other would lob his own stimulus back over the net. We already saw that Falla had encouraged Lorca to research folk song, that this research led to Lorca's *PCJ* (1921+), and that Lorca, in turn, had stimulated Falla to introduce Andalusian folkloric hand-puppetry into R*etablo* (1923). In the same folkloric vein, Falla's *El amor brujo* aroused Lorca's interest in Gypsy themes around 1924. In a 1933 interview, Lorca informed a reporter that "friendship with Falla while imbibing the warm air of Granada's villas dictated to [Lorca] the verses of *Romancero gitano* [Gypsy ballads],"[22] the poet's best-selling work. He venerated no one more than Falla for his industriousness and perfectionism. He quoted Falla as having scolded him for working too little: "That poem about Andalusia, which it is up to you to write, must be beautiful and great. Work ... Work ... When you've died, you'll be sorry you didn't."[23] Lorca aspired to give *Romancero gitano* the stature Falla would have wished. During a lecture-recital Lorca affirmed that the word "gitano" denoted the most elevated values of Andalusia (3:340). He conceived the Gypsy as deep song personified, the bearer of all virtues ascribed by Falla to that music. How these qualities permeate Lorca's best-known anthology and express his personal concerns of unfulfilled love and death will receive detailed study in the chapters to follow.

Falla's presence in Lorca extends from his speeches on deep song and his Andalusianist poetry to his theatre. The farce *La zapatera prodigiosa* [The prodigious shoemaker's wife] displays the influence of *Retablo*. Lorca's tragic farce *El amor de Don Perlimplín con Belisa en su jardín* [The love of Don Perlimplín for Belisa in his garden] owes much to Falla's *Harpsichord Concerto*. Let us review criticism on the artistic relationship between the two artists.

3. Critical Opinions on the Falla-Lorca Relationship

Critics show little continuity in considering the connection between Lorca and Falla. References to their aesthetic bonds appear in biographies of both artists, studies of Falla's music, and analyses of Lorca's writings. Falla historians and musicologists are acquainted with biographies of Lorca, though few with his poetry, theatre, and literary criticism on both figures.[24] Lorca researchers display little knowledge of Falla's scores, and less of Falla scholarship and biographies. Yet Lorca read Falla's scores and tried to play his music.[25] Literary Hispanists touching on Falla fear venturing beyond the libretti with their often weak plots into the music itself, where the essence of his art lies. For example, Dennis Klein summarizes his 1976 article "The Influence of Manuel de Falla on García Lorca: A Note" by concluding that "the composer and the poet were more than just social friends (...)[26] Falla had a decisive influence on Lorca's artistic activities."[27] However convincing this statement may be, and however ingenious Klein's conception of comparing a musical work with a play, his proof does not rise to the height of his hypothesis. He makes tenuous comparisons between the plots of Falla's ballet *El sombrero de tres picos* and *La zapatera prodigiosa*. Might not Lorca have gleaned the plot just as easily from Falla's source novella, Alarcón's *El sombrero de tres picos*? In another article, Klein likens the plot of Falla's early opera *La vida breve* to plots of additional Lorca plays, *Bodas de sangre* [Blood weddings], *Doña Rosita la soltera* [Doña Rosita the spinster], and *La casa de Bernarda Alba* [The house of Bernarda Alba]. Use of foreshadowing in opera and plays, coincidences between literary metaphorical topoi like floral symbolism, and similarity of urban setting do not completely convince.

A more recent article, "Parallel Trajectories in the Careers of Falla and Lorca" by D. Gareth Walters, without referring to Klein, reaches opposite conclusions: the friendship between Falla and Lorca was "warm but never close," and they showed an odd "lack of artistic collaboration," with "no more than traces of influence between the two." Falla, writes Walters, was "austere" and "unpityingly religious" (*pace* Stravinsky), whereas Lorca was "gregarious and hedonistic" (93). Whatever "unpityingly religious" means, Falla was generous to a fault, with a childlike humour[28] and willingness to risk his own life to save Lorca from the fascists in August 1936 (Mora Guarnido, *Lorca* 199, 203). Moreover, a reliable eyewitness, Lorca's younger sister Isabel, reports, "The union and identification in ideas and sentiments of Don Manuel [de Falla] with Federico was very deep, and together they explored many towns to gather folk songs."[29] The composer's niece María Isabel de Falla writes of the warmth and collaboration between him and Lorca as she reviews their common projects: "In Granada is born and developed a friendship, a deep affection and mutual respect between two personalities so distant but at the same time so close in their way of seeing and understanding art, in their form of creating." Together, specifies María Isabel, they participated in many daily discussions in the *Rinconcillo* or "Little Corner" of the Café Alameda (Granada) and in many soirées devoted to music or poetry at Falla's home or at Federico's. Together they arranged with enthusiasm and care the Epiphany puppet show at García Lorca's home. Together they travelled through the mountains of Granada seeking the roots of musical folklore. Together they organized with childlike zeal the First Deep Song Contest. María Isabel even admits that together they worked on undertakings yielding no results. Yet this does not negate the warmth of their togetherness.[30]

Falla's "austerity" mentioned by Walters did not exclude gregariousness. In the *tertulia* or conversation group of the *Rinconcillo*, the composer participated as a respected "senior member" and "spiritual guide" (Hess, *Passions* 156). Stravinsky met Falla only sporadically, whereas Lorca spent many days in his company and saw his multiple sides, just as Falla savored manifold aspects of his young and talented friend. Lorca's liberty to enter Falla's rented home at will speaks volumes about their cordiality. So does their practice of travelling together throughout Andalusia.[31]

Walters not only perceives Falla and Lorca in black and white, presenting them as caricatures of themselves, but also overlooks their mutual influence. He understates the proven connection of Lorca's Three Kings'
Day puppet show to the staging of *Retablo*.[32] He makes Falla's priggish-
ness about the restless Spain of the 1930s the cause for his flagging interest in *Lola* after 1923.[33] He proposes far-fetched comparisons between
Lorca's earliest, mimetic, Andalusian-style poetry and Falla's mature, elab-
orately structured *Noches en los jardines de España* [Nights in the gardens
of Spain]: both were supposedly influenced by the sensuality of Rubén
Darío.[34] Can this factor account for Falla's attraction to Darío? In pages to
follow, we document that the attraction obeyed deeper existential needs.
Yet, Walters intelligently brings forth Falla's piano solo *Fantasía bætica*
(1919) [Andalusian fantasy] for comparison to Lorca. While analysing its
structure as a whole, he likens its occasional discords to isolated clangs and
hoofbeats in *Romancero gitano* (Walters 100). There should exist a way to
compare a complete musical piece of Falla's to a total poetic unit of Lorca's,
either an individual poem or an entire section of poetry. As García Bacca
writes, "the original form of every musical work (…) is heard as a block as
far as the number and qualities of its notes are concerned. For that reason
it is perceived as real; and it is through such a block of reality that one
notes that real music is really being heard."[35] The same perception is applicable to verbal artworks, for García Bacca calls a poem – for instance,
the *Divine Comedy* – "verbal music" (*Filosofía de la música* 12). In the
present book, whenever possible, I compare "blocks" of musical reality
composed by Falla to "blocks" of poetic reality by Lorca.

The Falla-Lorca relationship in the history of Spanish culture receives
scholarly consecration in the book *Falla y Lorca. Entre la tradición y la
vanguardia* [Falla and Lorca. Between tradition and the avant-garde,
1999]. Here the musicologist Susana Zapke has gathered six speeches offered at a 1998 colloquium on Falla and Lorca at the University of Cologne.
While some of the six deal either with Falla or with Lorca individually and
only marginally with their relationship, nearly all offer pertinent background material valuable to us.[36]

A useful overview of the Falla-Lorca relationship appears in Jorge de
Persia's "Lorca, Falla y la música. Una coincidencia intergeneracional"
[Lorca, Falla, and music. An intergenerational coincidence]. Persia argues
the importance of the Falla-Lorca relationship for the development of
Spanish avant-garde music and literature ("Lorca, Falla" 68). From earliest
youth, music occupied a major part in Lorca's life. As an eighteen-year-old

music and poetry lover and pianist, even in his *tertulia*, or discussion circle, of the *Rinconcillo* he was known as the musician. The few original scores by Lorca still preserved, one titled "Pensamiento poético – Canción de Invierno" [Poetic thought – winter song], the other "Granada," show inexperience, romanticist aims, and "technical deficiencies" (68; Maurer, "Lorca y las formas" 249–50). Persia underscores that even Lorca's turn in 1916 or 1917 to literature does not displace the presence of music in his writing. A "musician in essence," with no advanced training, but with a surprising ability for musical expression, he joined Falla in savouring Chopin and in appreciating folk song ("Falla, Lorca" 69). Musical imagery pervades Lorca's first published work, *Impresiones y paisajes* [Impressions and landscapes, 1918] (70–1).

It surprises Persia that the only text by Lorca on musical aesthetics dates to 1917, the year in which he became a writer. He published in the *Diario* [Daily] of Burgos the brief essay "Divagación: Las reglas de la música" [Digression: The rules in music]. Persia marvels at Lorca's rare knowledge of the then avant-garde composers like Debussy and Ravel, and also shows the closeness of Lorca's views to Falla's as of 1915 on the latest music. Such views were available to Lorca in local Granadan journalism on arts and letters. In the essay, Lorca equates music to "impassionedness" [apasionamiento]. Such art transcends words. As in other arts, including poetry, the impassioned genius, Lorca finds, needs no rules. Study of them constitutes an apprenticeship, but once the artist transcends them, truth lies outside them in the works themselves (Persia 71–2). These ideas seem to Persia to coincide with Falla's as formulated in 1915 and published in 1917: dogmatists in art err and even damage the art they feign to protect. The new art aims to produce emotion, attained without awareness. Technical training is a prerequisite, yet innovation is to be found in the works, not the handbooks of techniques (72).

Persia hypothesizes that Lorca may have had an early first glimpse of Falla in person. Despite the impoverished state of early twentieth-century Granadan philharmonic life, the music lover Lorca may have attended the 26 June 1916 concert at Charles V's palace adjoining the Alhambra. There, accompanied by the Madrid Symphony Orchestra, Falla played *Noches en los jardines de España*, musically alluding to the Alhambra (73). Even had Lorca not attended that concert, his second personal meeting with Falla, occurring in 1920, meant much for both and for new Spanish culture about to gestate. Persia finds "mutual influences" between the two, which generated their mutual "admiration and friendship." Persia values the First *Cante*

Jondo Contest as a call on the part of Spain's most famous thinkers and artists to re-evaluate a cultural expression socially sidelined and debased in cafés at the whim of the market.

Parallel to this rekindling of interest in deep song, Persia appreciates the new generation's introduction of Spanish guitar into the concert hall after years of disdain by the "cultured" class.[37] Around the same time as Debussy, Albéniz incorporated guitaristic passages into his pieces. Guitarists Ángel Barrios, Falla's friend, and Regino Sainz de la Maza, Lorca's friend, offered virtuoso concerts. Falla's 1920 *Homenaje* [Tribute] in memory of Debussy became one of the favourite classical guitar pieces of the twentieth century, paving the way for younger virtuosi like Andrés Segovia and Miguel Llobet. Lorca loved the instrument, learned to play it from two Granadan Gypsies and possibly from an aunt as well, and mythicized it in his poetry (76). His and Falla's independent but converging interests in folk song (balladry and songbooks) also affect members of Lorca's generation (79).

With Mario Hernández, who alludes to the totality of Lorca's farces, Persia does not think it excessive to speak of "a whole developmental phase ruled by Falla's influence on the theatrical production of the poet" (75). Hernández's "Introducción" to his 1982 critical edition of Lorca's *La zapatera prodigiosa* develops the important thesis of this influence. After the failure of Lorca's first play *El maleficio de la mariposa* [The butterfly's curse, debuting 22 March 1920], he tried his hand at minor theatrical genres like the Punch-and-Judy puppet farce, comic opera, the theatre of *aleluyas* or small popular prints, and the one-act farce or *entremés*. The *Tragicomedia de Don Cristóbal y la señá Rosita* [Tragicomedy of Don Cristóbal and Missy Rosita] illustrates the Andalusian Punch-and-Judy folk farce he cultivated in collaboration with Manuel de Falla. *Lola* (1923), as already mentioned, is the unfinished comic opera libretto written with Falla's musical suggestions. *La zapatera prodigiosa* (1930, 1933) stems from a tragic modification of the traditional *entremés* or interlude, whereas *El amor de Don Perlimplín con Belisa en su jardín*, debuted in 1933, has the subtitle of "erotic popular print in a prologue and three scenes." The poet remakes this genre into a tragic farce with a subtlety and dramatic wisdom attributed to him by Hernández (13–14).

He maintains that Falla provided Lorca the example in two musical works, *El corregidor y la molinera* [The corregidor and the miller's wife (1917)], self-defined as a "mimed farce inspired on some incidents of Alarcón's novel *El sombrero de tres picos*," and the revision of this farce into the ballet (debuted in London, 1919) originally under the French title *Le tricorne* [The three-cornered hat]. Hernández does not delve into specifics of Falla's influence other than to mention that the cast of characters of *El corregidor y la molinera* is "pre-Lorcan" in a broad sense. Moreover, the sketches made by Picasso for the stage decoration of Falla's ballet, adds Hernández (14–15), influenced the sketches of the first edition of Lorca's romantic drama *Mariana Pineda* (1928), as well as the scenery and costuming of *La zapatera prodigiosa* at its 1930 debut. Hernández could have gone further by affirming that Picasso revolutionized scenery painting in Spain of the 1920s and exercised enormous influence on Lorca's entire generation.[38]

Further, Hernández affirms the impact of Falla's *Retablo* on Lorca's farce *La zapatera prodigiosa*. The learned critic limits himself to showing the influence on Lorca of Cervantes's *Don Quixote*, part 2, chapter 26, the Maese Pedro episode, a source to which Falla had presumably led the poet. Hernández's minute Cervantes-Lorca comparisons delve into the substance of *La zapatera prodigiosa*. What is missing is the study of the scores, libretti, and performances of *El corregidor y la molinera*, of the ballet *Sombrero* and the puppet opera *Retablo*, as well as of other compositions by Falla present in Lorca's theatre. He regarded *Retablo* as an autonomous artwork with respect to Cervantes's *Don Quixote*: the Granadan poet himself, we already saw, had helped Falla with the libretto and with puppetry techniques. Indeed, as I have shown in an article, "Married Temptresses in Falla and Lorca" (2011), Lorca depends as much on Falla's music as on Cervantes's novel for the expression of his own concerns on freedom of imagination in the elaboration of *La zapatera prodigiosa*.

Falla's librettist María Lejárraga foregrounded feminine imagination while reading Pedro Antonio de Alarcón's *Sombrero de tres picos* jointly with the composer.[39] Female fantasy dominated Falla's pantomime *El corregidor y la molinera* (1916–17) and the revised version, the ballet *El sombrero de tres picos* [The three-cornered hat, 1917–19]. This work, which Lorca admired for its childlike humour and ingenious orchestration (Francisco García Lorca, *Federico y su mundo* 122), helped generate his own comic opera libretto *Lola la comedianta* [Lola the actress, 1923], on an imaginative married thespian. Yet Lorca's opera plot, I have argued in my 2011 article (Orringer, "Married Temptresses"), eventually seemed too derivative to Falla, too dependent on the plot and use of musical techniques in his own ballet *El sombrero de tres picos* to sustain his interest. However, Lorca more skilfully absorbed techniques from Falla's ballet for his ballad "La casada infiel" [The faithless wife, 1926], also influenced by a salacious ballad rejected by Falla but modified by Alarcón, "El molinero de Arcos" [The miller of Arcos]. Falla's neoclassicism leaves its mark on

Lorca's farce, *La zapatera prodigiosa* (1930, revised 1933). Here a coquett-
ish wife displays an imagination similar to Don Quixote's in Falla's neo-
classic puppet opera *El retablo de maese Pedro* (1919–23). She idealizes her
husband in his absence, just as Don Quixote idealizes Dulcinea, yet she
finds him abhorrent in her presence. Like Falla in *Sombrero*, Lorca employs folk-music to characterize the protagonists of *Zapatera*. However,
whereas Falla used tunes to type characters by their native regions, Lorca
makes use of folk melodies to *individualize* the shoemaker and his wife.[40]

Falla's impact on Lorca's theatre does not stop here. Eckart Weber maintains that Falla's manipulation of aesthetic distance and closeness to the
event staged in *Retablo* reveals his kinship to the playwright Lorca. The
"polarization between illusion and reality," Weber writes, becomes a
central motif of his avant-garde theatre of the early 1930s, particularly in
El Público [The public] and *Comedia sin título* [Untitled play]. Wilma
Newberry, who has influenced Weber's thinking, holds that in *El Público*
the author focuses on "the destruction of poetic illusion wrought by the
breakdown of aesthetic distance caused by theater-within-the-theater techniques in their extreme form." The audience aggressively takes part in the
drama and, like Don Quixote with Maese Pedro's puppets, destroys everyone onstage creating the dramatic illusion.[41]

4. The Relationship of Falla's Music to Lorca's Lyric

Every piece of music has a general conception or structure that the composer aspires to convey to the listener's mental ear through a performance,
actual or virtual. By attending a concert, perceiving it on television or com-
puter screen, or reading a score, the listener apprehends the structure and
thereby takes part in the performance. Lorca, in addition, translated Falla's
musical structures by analogy into his own literary structures. He converted the reader into a performer not only of the music but also of the
play or poem thus analogized. According to Roberta Ann Quance, "just
as a piece of music only fully becomes a work of art when it is performed,
so, too, for Lorca does a poem only become a poem when it is read." She
adds that in *PCJ*, "the poems themselves are conceived by analogy to a
musical score" (*Contradiction* 140). In the case of the poetry we examine,
the majority of the scores came from the pen of Falla. In an objective sense,
therefore, Lorca wrote much poetry and theatre "in the style of" Falla.

He filled his analogies to Falla's musical structures with affects consistently found in his own writing, yet seldom seen in Falla: unfulfilled love,
fear of dying, fascination with death, the freedom and discipline of fantasy,

illness at ease with fixed gender roles, and a sense of personal insufficiency in the universe. For example, a Falla piece in polyphony could generate a series of multiple metaphors in Lorca, whereby each trope is a multilevel connection between two or more unlike objects with surprising emotional repercussions on each level. A contrast between two musical motives in Falla could lead to a contrast between the characters of two cities in Lorca, following the same general pattern of phrasing, but never with mechanical, phrase-by-phrase correspondence. His literary translations of Falla's music are never literal.

Although the poet's skill consisted of drawing verbal analogies with the music, he always added to the analogy an individual flourish, as a rubric is added to a document to individualise the signer. That unique flourish could be a plastic sensation rendered with painterly vision, for what Ralph Waldo Emerson said of Goethe – "He seems to see out of every pore of his skin" (*Representative Men*) – applies as well to Lorca. Not only a flair for visual sensation, but also a talent for staging dramatic situations or dialogues both in lyric and theatre characterized Lorca's writing. Or else he left his mark on a musical analogy by offering a sexual impression provoked by a subtle swish of a ballet skirt. Falla's blending of multiple sources in music to exalt human fantasy (*Retablo*) led Lorca to combine many literary sources to express ribald humour ("Preciosa y el aire" [Preciosa and the air]). Or Falla's arrangement of sacred melody furnished Lorca with images of childlike reverence as he tried to recapture the lost faith of his earliest years ("Oda al Santísimo Sacramento del altar").

In face-to-face conversation, music, and essays, Falla provided Lorca an idea of Andalusia as its essence or cultural spirit (*Volksgeist*), based on musical contradictions of moods and tempos. However, Lorca projected over that idea his own sense of individual deficiency, fear of death, and wonder at the mystery of creativity – traits he originally attributed to himself, yet later saw as defining the entire region from which he and Falla hailed.

5. A New Way of Conceptualizing Falla's and Lorca's Art: García Bacca's Philosophy of Music

Falla and Lorca sought what Maurer calls a "synthesis of all the arts" in every medium or genre they cultivate.[42] A conceptual way to approach both music and literature seems necessary in view of Lorca's admitted indebtedness to classical composition in general.[43] An overarching theoretical work embracing both music and letters can throw light on the production of Falla and Lorca. Juan David García Bacca's *Filosofía de la música*

[Philosophy of Music, 1990], a book "conceived in integral realism,"[44] has a scientific foundation, since music is subject to the laws of physics. For García Bacca, music expresses philosophy; and poetry conveys music, with its philosophy as well.[45] Music employs a type of language, composed of notes, and it uses organs of expression, the instruments. In the same way, literature, including philosophy and poetry, makes use of words and of conventional syntax (11–12). García Bacca conceives a musical motif as a discrete phrase that moves virtually on its own towards a more complete one and finally towards the perfected theme (212). A structure, whether in music or letters, forms a framework of relationships that yield a text. That framework, along with the plots filling those relationships, produces a context. The text is a tissue or framework giving rise to a context (209). In music and in theory of being, form becomes structure and changes its matter into material. A form may transform into a superstructure when something new is added with its own laws. The superstructure, or advent of novelties, does not destroy the structure and reality of the previous form, but preserves it and rearranges it with the relationship between inferior and superior forms co-implicated or co-internalized (210–11). In music or in ontology form may change into a superstructure. When such change occurs, the material changes into a new body with new organs (319).

Following García Bacca, who uses musical scores and poetic texts alike by way of illustration, let us employ his terms to analyse Falla's *Noches* and a thematic analogue, Lorca's poem "Danza. En el huerto de la Petenera" [Dance. In the garden of the Petenera]. Falla's set of three nocturnes is a complex body of melody based, by the composer's own analysis, on five motives, one in the first movement and two each in the second and third (see musical example 1). The entire work merely varies the five motives, complicating them, inverting them, transposing them.

The work as a whole develops out of the mysterious motif initiating the first movement, "En el Generalife" [In the Generalife Palace gardens]. Falla employs a melody possibly heard by him in remote childhood from an old *zorongo,* or Gypsy dance in ternary rhythm, played by a blind fiddler outside his window.[46] Written in *allegretto tranquillo e misterioso,* this initial melody unfolds in a soft vibrato, indicated on Falla's score by brief parallel horizontal lines on the staff of each note. The strings give an eerie vagueness to the melody,[47] which the piano, upon entering, simply inverts with a liquid sound recalling water. Michael Christoforidis observes of "En el Generalife" that "the movement is (...) indebted to an extended lineage of water music (from Liszt to Debussy and Ravel) to evoke the fountains of the Alhambra"[48] (see figure 3).

1 The five motifs of *Noches en los jardines de Espana* (Falla's analysis). Reproduced from the program "Festival Manuel de Falla," Nov. 5, 1926, Associació de música "Da camera" de Barcelona, 2nd. Concert, 1926–7. With gracious permission of the Archivo Manuel de Falla (Granada).

Figure 3   Generalife garden, Alhambra, Granada, Spain. Photo by Peter Lorber, 22 June 2006.

In this evocation of the Generalife gardens near the Alhambra Palace, irrigated by artistic fountains, parallel tremolos of strings and of liquid, lapping, legato piano sounds, rising then falling, may express parallel arches of trembling streams of water as in the *Patio de la Acequia* [Canal patio], with "crystalline textures reminiscent of Ravel's *Jeux d'eaux*" (Hess, *Passions* 92). Since for García Bacca music has a plot, Falla recognizes that the contemplation of beauty alleviates the existential angst produced by mystery in the universe. In "En el Generalife," remarks Molina Fajardo, "over the nostalgic orchestral background, the piano evokes the strings of the Andalusian instrument [the guitar], tracing lines of a mathematical abstractness, originating and generating themselves *within* themselves. When they seem to initiate a second musical theme, they come back linked to the first theme or to one of its variations."[49]

The second nocturne, "Danza lejana" [Distant dance], shows structural interlacing like the first. When the first musical motive undergoes a variation, a second motive emerges. This new motive, transformed, passes without pause into the initial motive of the third nocturne. The second nocturne, like the first, resembles water music and traces a soft vertical fall. Falla calls for playing twelve measures in 3/4 time *sordamente, senza espressione* [dully, without expression] while the piano's rapid six triplets per measure contrast with the few quarter notes rendered *pizzicato* and *piano* by violin, cello, and contrabass, as if to emulate a plucked dripping (Falla, *Noches*, score, rehearsals 14–16, pp. 49–51). An aqueous texture forms between the first and second movements, a weaving pattern of waters linking the two. Falla's conception of "Danza lejana" in terms of physical space shows that, like García Bacca, he found music subject to the laws of physics. At his home one day on Calle de Antequeruela Alta, situated on a hillside, when asked about the placement of the "Danza lejana," he responded that it was as if a dance resounded about 100 metres up the hill in the Field of Martyrs, and as if he and his interlocutor heard it from Falla's home (Nommick, *Jardines* 38). Further up the hill beyond Martyrs lie the grounds of the Alhambra itself, where Falla in all likelihood conceived the dance as taking place.

The first and second nocturnes, therefore, present Granada's Moorish palaces from different viewpoints, first nearness, next remoteness. The second nocturne, moreover, is akin to the third: both share the air of a faraway dance (Pahissa, *Falla* 101). The first motif of "Danza lejana" begins *pianissimo* (see music example 1, above), like the softness of music heard from afar. The first motif of "En los jardines de la Sierra de Córdoba" [In the gardens of the Cordoban Sierra] starts with an exotic dance, resembling flamenco and remote from everyday reality. In García Bacca's terms, superstructures link to form a body with its own members. Orozco informs that the third nocturne paints the mountain passes of Cordoba at early dawn in Sierra Morena (*Falla* 80). To complete the sensation of an arabesque, symmetry exists between nocturnes 1 and 3: both incorporate two different *zorongos*. The second one, a variation on the *petenera* forming the fifth motif of *Noches* (see musical example 2), turns into an echo of what would later become Lorca's favourite folk tune, the Gypsy *Zorongo*, recorded by him at the piano (see musical example 3).[50] Dance rhythms in nocturnes 2 and 3 have a regularity that causes them to approach poetry without words.

The mysteriousness conveyed by Falla's piano performance has impressed Lorca and others. In 1933 he remarked that the *cantaor* Manuel Torre, an illiterate whom Lorca called "the man of greatest [Andalusian] culture in his blood that I have ever known, uttered this splendid opinion while listening to Falla himself play his 'En el Generalife' [in 1922]: 'Everything having black sounds has the spirit of the earth'."[51] Lorca defines black sounds as "the mystery, the roots driven into the loam that we

2   Falla, "In the Gardens of the Sierra of Cordoba," measure 39. *Noches en los jar-dines de España. Nuits dans les jardins d'Espagne. Impressions symphoniques pour piano et orchestee en trois parties.* París: Max Eschig et Cie. Editeurs, 1922. Reproduced with gracious permission of the Archivo Manuel de Falla (Granada)

all know so well but never heed, yet from which comes to us whatever is of substance in art."[52] Falla's nocturne, if Lorca's metaphors are trustworthy, is rooted in the collective Andalusian subconscious. The subsoil of the southern Spanish region nurtures its inhabitants with concern for the mystery of life, which for Lorca personally can only mean the mystery of mortality. "Our people hold their arms in the shape of a cross while looking at the stars, and will wait in vain for the sign of salvation," because "Death (...) is the question of all questions."[53] This mystery is what Falla's initial motif seeks to communicate. Darío is present here, though not the superficial, erotically sensuous Darío that Walters has in mind, but a Darío fraught with existential anguish (Acereda and Guevara, *Modernidad en Darío* 31), the crisis of religious belief prevalent in post-Darwinian letters. In his anthology *Cantos de vida y esperanza* [Songs of life and hope], Darío, who helped revitalize early twentieth-century Hispanic poetry, included two poems titled "Nocturnos" and a third with the same title in *El canto errante* [The wandering song], all expressing an insomniac's awareness of time passing, fear of dying, and a vague illusion of salvation after

3 Zorongo, harmonized by Lorca (2:1174), with words from *La zapatera prodigiosa*. Reproduced with gracious permission of the heirs of Federico García Lorca.

death (*Obras completas* 5:899–900, 931–2, 1018). To this list of three could be added the poem "La dulzura del Ángelus" [The sweetness of the Angelus], with the same theme (Acereda and Guevara 136). This fourth has exercised direct influence on the author of *Poema del cante jondo*.[54] Falla had originally intended to write a suite of four nocturnes (Hess, *Passions* 49), which he had at first wanted to title "Nocturnos" like Darío's poems (Pahissa, *Falla* 81).

Falla's librettist María Lejárraga discovers a spiritual crisis in the early Falla comparable to the spiritual dryness of mystics (*Gregorio y yo* 123). Francisco García Lorca reveals, and his brother Federico confirms, that Falla had always seen his musical endowments as a "gratuitous gift, a grace,"[55] conferred on him by God. Yet while living in Paris, informs Lejárraga, he suffered a creative block for months. This paralysis of his creativity may have struck him as a fall from grace. He wandered the Parisian streets in despair. At last he greeted the discovery of a book in a shop window as providential. After buying and reading *Granada. Guía emocional* [Granada. Affective guide] (1911), authored by Lejárraga herself, under the name of her husband Gregorio Martínez Sierra, he reached a solution to his crisis in a chapter titled "En el Generalife," which became the title of the first movement of *Noches*.[56] Out of spiritual chaos Falla could create order through beauty. The musical sequence forms the super-structure into which he integrates the various structures gradually emerging out of the initial enigmatic motif.

Hence, García Bacca's terms apply to Falla's nocturnes. They also serve for grasping Lorca's poem "Danza. En el huerto de la Petenera" from *Poema del cante jondo*. The Petenera, a seductive flamenco singer probably from the town of Paterna (Cadiz), lies dying. A guitar laments her, its six white strings likened to dancing Gypsies:

En la noche del huerto,
seis gitanas,
vestidas de blanco,
bailan.

En la noche del huerto,
coronadas,
con rosas de papel
y biznagas.

En la noche del huerto,
sus dientes de nácar,

escriben la sombra
quemada.

Y en la noche del huerto,
sus sombras se alargan,
y llegan hasta el cielo
moradas.

[At night in the garden,
six Gypsies,
dressed in white,
dance.

At night in the garden,
crowned
with paper roses
and sprigs.

At night in the garden,
Their nacreous teeth
Write down the burnt
shadow,

And at night in the garden,
Their shadows lengthen,
And reach the sky
Deep purple.]   (*PCJ* 164; reproduced with gracious permission
                                     of the heirs of F. García Lorca)

For its rhythmic and pictorial values, the critic Ángel del Río describes
this poem as "a haunting nocturne" [*un nocturno encantado*] (*Federico
García Lorca* 35). Any of Falla's three nocturnes of *Noches* could have
inspired it. Lorca does not imitate Falla with words, but rather adopts his
artistic perspective.[57] Just as Falla reiterates with variations the blind
man's enigmatic theme, the initial motive of Lorca's nocturnal garden
repeats four times, each time deepening the mystery of the darkness.
García Bacca likens words to musical instruments, and Lorca employs his
verbal tools as such. While Falla's stringed instruments convey a mysterious air, sounds of Lorca's well-chosen words do the same, with vivid accompanying visions. The first line of each strophe stresses the darkness by
accenting the sombre word *noche* [night]. Through anaphora, the deep,

dark vowel ó, set off against the resonating nasal -n-, seems to toll softly. The repetition of the word sombra [shadow] has a like effect, with dark vowel ó resonated by bilabial nasal -m-.[58] Contrast, rhythmically produced, sets off the mysterious blackness against the whiteness of the dancers' dresses, of their paper roses, of their nacreous teeth. Hence, the initial motif of night develops into the theme of the sombre dance, evolving into the structure of choreographed mournfulness.

As in Falla's Nocturnes 2 and 3, depicting dancing, here sounds music within music. In "Danza lejana" the orchestra plays a muted version of what imaginary dancers would be hearing at full volume, and in Lorca's "Danza," a rhythmic recitation of music is differently audible to the dancers within the poem. Falla's and Lorca's "Danzas" both prove García Bacca's assertion that "the same musical work can be undergoing performance (...) in distant places (...) simultaneously."[59] In Falla's and Lorca's compositions, simultaneity becomes the superstructure subtended by its structures (individual performances). Lorca adds a further visible and audible structure – music within music within music – with reader awareness that the six dancing Gypsies may symbolize the six rhythmically strummed guitar strings. Analogously, in Falla, an informed concertgoer hears a full-fledged orchestra imitating a guitar. In Lorca, however, as distinguished from Falla, the strings behave like creators, poets, inspired by pain. The Gypsy dancers "write" the darkness as they recreate through their movements a woman "burned" (*quemada*) by passion. The musicality of this hot anguish emerges through frequent juxtaposition of the open vowel **a** to the nasal **n**, vibrant and resonant like the guitar: *la noche* (four times), *gitanas, blanco, coronadas, biznagas, nácar* (see n. 58, above). The heat of passion burns even shadows. The reader refers the poem to its context in the anthology to determine that the subject of the passion, a once impetuous singer, is expiring. Her agony becomes pantomimed by dancers mimicked, in turn, by a guitarist's fingers, whose virtuosity an implied poet-reciter's moving mouth and larynx reproduce. Superstructures acquire a total body with many members.

The shadows projected by the guitarist's agile fingers acquire such universality, and the music such depth, with structure upon structure of meaning, that the shadows extend skyward transmuted into purple, a vague light illuminating the night. Purple was the colour that Paul Drouot, one of Falla's favourite poets, associated with his sad departure from the Alhambra during "Un soir de pleurs et de Novembre, / Un soir de pourpre et de regrets" [An evening of laments and November, / An evening of purple and yearnings].[60] In Lorca, the Petenera takes her leave from life while

Gypsy music pervades the night sky. No metaphysical mystery attains solution, but from start to finish aesthetic enjoyment intensifies thanks to the posing of the problem of dying, expressed by direct imagery, like Falla's musical plasticity, and thanks as well to unvarying strophic parallelism. In Lorca and Falla an elaborate maze appears with no exit, its totality inserted into a greater arabesque which is the entire work itself.

6. *Volksgeist* Theory in Falla and Lorca

The application of García Bacca's philosophy of music to Falla and Lorca cannot conclude without our recalling that both music and poetry imply philosophy. A common philosophy underlies the musicality of both artists. Both rely on an Andalusian variation on nineteenth-century *Volksgeist* theory as a point of departure for their own highly individual arts.[61] According to Nathan Rotenstreich, cultural spirit or *Volksgeist* signifies the "productive principle of a spiritual or psychic character, operating in different national entities" and showing up in "creations like language, folklore, mores, and legal order" (*Volksgeist* 490–1). Montesquieu wrote of the "general spirit of nations," referring to a result of religion, laws, morals, and customs, but he also married the principle of nature as a norm with the principle of a people's genius as a standard of government. This union of principles led to the idea of a German national spirit, an idea appearing in Friedrich Carl von Moser (1765) and later influencing Johann Gottfried von Herder. Herder, never using the term *Volksgeist*, though he used similar expressions, refers to the "spirit of the times" impressed on the soul and best understood through folklore, daily speech, and popular poetry. He viewed "national character" as an innate idea, indestructible and perpetual. Yet he paradoxically feared the disappearance of the distinction between national traits during the Enlightenment and urged study of them before they vanished (Rotenstreich 490–1). This paradox passes through many other minds until reaching Falla's and Lorca's, deeming the Andalusian national soul perpetual but perishable!

Nationalism in nineteenth-century European music developed through the application of *Volksgeist* theory to that art. According to Niemöller, politically and culturally, the idea of the nation state determined the consciousness of European peoples. In music, he continues, Italy, Germany, and France enjoyed hegemony, according their composers utmost respect, while performers dominated stage and concert hall. Combining Herder's theory with early nineteenth-century Romantic folklore theory, composers attempted to re-evaluate and revitalize the heritage of their "peoples" by incorporating folk themes. This revitalization became politicized as of 1848, with nationalist revolts against the Austrian Empire. In Czechoslovakia, Smetana's and Dvořak's music defied Austria; the Pole Chopin and much later the Finn Sibelius challenged Russia. Musical strivings for emancipation inspired descriptions of the life of the people, their land, and their nature; historical reminiscences of the nation; inclusion of folk music through melodies, dances, and typical instruments; and retrospection on the ancient music of the land as a buried tradition (Niemöller, "Gedank einer nationalen Musik" 25, 29).

In 1891, Felipe Pedrell, composer and teacher of Albéniz, Granados, and Falla, applied *Volksgeist* theory to Spain in his manifesto *Por nuestra música*. He used the word *nación* to mean the common people as well as the creative entity of a culture. Pedrell held that the national character of any music lay in folk song, in the untutored music of primitive eras, and in works of genius of the great epochs of art. "National" art presupposed uninterrupted musical tradition, whose characteristics persist through time and reappear in the most varied works (9). Composers needed to borrow native forms (38).

Falla appreciated Pedrell as a theorist, but criticized him for his antiquarian practice as a composer (Trend, *Falla* 14). In Europe following the First World War, Falla modified Pedrell under the influence of his friend, French music critic Georges Jean-Aubry (1882–1950). Together with the avant-garde circle of artists and performers known in Paris as *les Apaches*, with whom Falla associated, Jean-Aubry disputed German claims to musical hegemony. He held in 1915 that victory in the Great War would hopefully make French artists understand their racial purity and nobility, for French music sprung from a "race française" (Hess, *Modernism* 65). Hence, while unwilling to underestimate Wagner's genius, Jean-Aubry adhered to the "truths" of Debussy's early essays against Wagner, decried excessive foreign influences on French music, and favoured the innovative select minorities of composers. Hess finds that Falla applied this thinking to Spanish music. The First World War seemed to him to re-establish ethnic boundaries that had been vanishing, along with ethnic values worthy of preserving as sacred. Such values reflected the "autonomous spirit of each nation" (67). The liberal, anti-German Falla deplored academicians in Spain who obliged students to write like Mendelssohn, alien to the "special music implicit in our Spanish scene, in the gait and speech of our folk, in the outline of our hills."[62]

Falla lauded Debussy as leader of a select minority who renationalized music as against the Germans Beethoven and Wagner, whom he saw as excessively universalistic. Falla regarded himself and true Spanish composers as members of a Latin brotherhood, part of an "invincible stock" to which Debussy also belonged (Hess, *Modernism* 72). He admired Debussy for admitting modes, cadences, chord progressions, rhythms, even melodic phrases from *cante jondo* into the European musical canon (Falla, *Escritos* 69–70). Hence, in pieces like *Noches* among others, Falla filtered Andalusian-style melodies through chords and progressions frequent in Debussy (Demarquez 94). Moreover, he became focused on *cante jondo* in 1921 when he seemed to see pure Andalusian music values threatened by extinction:

> The solemn, sacred song of yesteryear has degenerated into the ridiculous flamenco culture of today. Into this its essential elements have become adulterated and modernized – what a fright! The sobre modulation of the voice – the natural inflections of song called forth by the division and subdivision of the sounds of the gamut – have been transformed into the artificial decoration of the musical phrase belonging rather to the decadentism of the bad Italian age than to the primitive songs of the East only to which ours can be compared when they are pure.[63]

Purity in Falla signifies the essence of Andalusia. Thus, we cannot read as mere rhetoric the following warnings of García Lorca in his 1922 lecture on *cante jondo*: "Ladies and gentlemen, the musical soul of the people is in gravest danger! The artistic treasure of our whole [Andalusian] stock is on the road to oblivion!"[64] Mora Guarnido, belonging to Falla's and Lorca's daily discussion circle, clarifies that "the First *Cante Jondo* Contest was in fact a kind of artistic crusade for the salvation, if it still were possible, of a rich vein of natural folk music."[65] In Lorca's musical inspiration, Quance discovers "an essentially nostalgic, Romantic desire for a natural model in poetry. According to Lorca's 1922 lecture, which is heavily indebted to Manuel de Falla, ""deep song" originates in a source so remote in time and place that for the poet it appears to communicate with nature itself.' Invoking the song, his poetry gestures towards the natural – as if proximity to music were capable of communicating some of its primordiality – and in the same motion it confesses its secondary, fallen status with regard to the other art" (*Contradiction* 140–1).

7. Structure of This Book

Volksgeist philosophy underlies *PCJ* and *Romancero gitano*, both of which are attempting to preserve a heritage threatened with extinction, yet both of which are responding in Lorca's highly personal way to that heritage. The objective of this book is to contribute to clarifying Lorca's multidimensional relationship to Falla in his works, especially in the two poetry books here named. Before the Falla-Lorca relationship could exist, Lorca needed artistic preparation. The first chapter sketches his musically poetic art prior to Falla as grounding for Falla's entrance into his existence. Next comes an eight-chapter study of *Falla* in *PCJ*, followed by an examination of Falla in *Romancero gitano*.

The chapters on *PCJ* start from the critic Christian de Paepe's premise that Falla's theories on the history of deep song structure four of the original segments of Lorca's book. These chapters attempt to show that Falla's musical compositions influenced all segments of the anthology while enabling the poet to voice his personal concerns. Chapter 1 examines Lorca's self-training in making analogies between music and literature before meeting Falla in 1920. Chapter 2 argues the probable impact of *Fantasía bætica*, Falla's most synthetic Andalusian-style piece, on the structure of "Baladilla de los tres ríos" [Little ballad of three rivers], Lorca's most synthetic poem of *PCJ*. Chapters 3 through 6 relate Falla's music to each of the four divisions of this anthology named for a different genre of folk song: the Gypsy siguiriya (chapter 3), the soleá (chapter 4), the saeta (chapter 5) and the petenera (chapter 6).

The remaining four original divisions of *PCJ* enrich and round out the previous four.[66] Chapter 7 concerns Spanish creativity in the face of death, seen in the divisions of *PCJ* titled "Viñetas flamencas" [Flamenco vignettes] and "Tres ciudades" [Three cities], examined together. "Viñetas flamencas" exalts great deep-song artists well-known to both Falla and Lorca as immortals subject to mortality. "Tres ciudades" offer Lorca's musical characterizations, with the help of Albéniz and Falla, of three Andalusian communities coping with death. Chapter 8 treats the segment of *PCJ* titled "Seis caprichos" [Six caprices], in Lorca's musical sense of caprice, a quick, surprising show of virtuosity. Falla's music enters this poetry in different, humorous ways, originally meant to serve as a witty end to Lorca's work.[67]

Falla considerably influences *Romancero gitano*. Chapter 9 presents his musical theory and practice with regard to deep song as an agglutinative force in this anthology. His music suggests to Lorca ways to bring together poetic elements in a fashion distinguishing our poet from others of his Generation of 1927. Chapter 10 considers Falla's theory of the Andalusian *Volksgeist* or "cultural spirit" and Lorca's creative modifications of that notion in the "historical ballads" of *Romancero gitano* and in the three ballads on the archangels Raphael, Michael, and Gabriel. Chapter 11 deals with Lorca's three artistic tributes to Falla through the years in an attempt to chart the changing relationship between the two artists. The "Postlude and Coda" offers a synthesis of findings in this book; an interpretation of Lorca's elegy to a bullfighter *Llanto de Ignacio Sánchez Mejías* as a compendium of Falla's Andalusianist music in his poetry; and an account of Falla's conduct during Lorca's final days. Contrary to Walters' opinion and in harmony with Maurer's, Falla's presence in Lorca has so many facets that no single study can encompass them all.

1

Music in the Letters of Lorca
before Meeting Falla

García Lorca's brother Francisco puzzles over his first published book, *Impresiones y paisajes* [Impressions and landscapes, 1918]. These travel essays appear dedicated to the memory of the author's former music professor, Don Antonio Segura Mesa, deceased two years earlier. Under his direction, Federico had studied Beethoven, Mendelssohn, Schumann, Schubert, Chopin, Glinka, Liszt, Wagner, Strauss, Debussy, and Ravel. Francisco thinks that Federico should instead have dedicated the book to Don Martín Domínguez Berrueta, his art history professor, who organized excursions to study artworks and monuments throughout Andalusia and Castile while encouraging students to keep a journal of their impressions. From such trips Federico gleaned the journal that became *Impresiones y paisajes*. He could have foreseen Domínguez Berrueta's sense of betrayal for receiving so little recognition, prompting him to suspend his friendship with Federico. The dedication to Segura Mesa fills a whole page at the beginning of the book, while Domínguez Berrueta gets consigned to a final page, titled merely "Envío" [Envoi], like the end of old poems. Here he hardly deserves mention beside the five students travelling with him and Federico. No allusion appears to the purpose of the trips, or to their initiation by Domínguez Berrueta (Francisco García Lorca, *Federico y su mundo* 90–3; Maurer, "Introduction," in Lorca, *Prosa inédita* 17–18).

The explanation does not lie in indifference towards or disrespect for Domínguez Berrueta, but in Lorca's religious reverence for Segura Mesa. He dedicates the book to his "veneranda memoria" [venerated memory]. The piano teacher "suffered his old passions, conjured up by a Beethoven sonata. He was a saint!"[1] Stressing his religious solemnity, Lorca ends with the following words: "With all the piety of my devotion" [Con toda la piedad de mi devoción] (3:4). Segura Mesa's role in Lorca's adolescence passed to Falla in his youth and maturity. In a 1933 newspaper interview, Lorca asserted, "Falla is a saint ... a mystic. I venerate no one like Falla." He praised Falla's perfectionism, his indifference to material gain and fame, and his "only wish to be better each day and to leave behind an opus."[2] Given the loftiness of these two "saints" in Lorca's religion of music, we understand why, when justifying his use of piano for musical examples in a lecture on Granada's musicality, Federico affirmed, "It is because I am a musician before anything else."[3]

To account for his cult of music, critics offer various explanations. Eutimio Martín furnishes a psychological one. In Lorca's earliest manuscripts, Martín discovers signs of a sexual crisis of adolescence, to which he relates music in general. Around 1917, he feels sullied by erotic guilt, and music transferred to literature offers him cleansing – a purgative tendency later to assume collective form as deep song in 1921 in *PCJ*. Meanwhile, in 1918 he confesses in an autobiographical fragment, "Pierrot. Poema íntimo" [Pierrot. Intimate poem], "I sing with the lyre, with the flute, with the guitar, with the lute, with the castanet, with Verlaine's panpipes, with the rare bassoon of Baudelaire, with the splendid trumpet of Rubén Darío. I may not play them well, that much I know, but I hope that these bad strophies will be litanies that save me from the temptation of evil."[4] The new poet, though attracted at the beginning to the opposite sex, one day, with a suddenness that he afterwards viewed as a tragic fate, found himself governed, in Martín's words, by a "bisexualism unable to cope with the determining weight of [his] homosexuality."[5] Subsequently threatened by social opprobrium, Lorca opposed all orthodoxy as cruel. He replaced Roman Catholicism, dogmatic and exclusivist, with a personal religion of art, pan-erotic, intimate, and high-minded. Hence the religious veneration he felt for his old piano teacher and eventually for Falla.

Christopher Maurer offers a different explanation: at puberty Lorca suddenly felt a "desire for the impossible," a wish lacking a specific object and permeating his early writings and, in fact, all his works. Such would explain his attraction to the musical or literary ideal to fill the void of what he desired and to transport him above crass carnality.[6] Desire, Roberta Quance reminds, is experienced as a lack, as recognized in Plato's *Symposium* 200 e ("Trouble" 398). The poet feels what she calls "gender malaise," uneasiness about the male role assigned by society (401), with aggressive courtship, marriage, and procreation. Hence, in posthumously published allegorical poetry given the musical name of *Suites* (1922), his poetic voice issues a warning to stay away from the gardens of wounding swords (*espadas*) and roses (*rosas*), the conventional phallic role and the conventional feminine role (403–4).

To the explanations of Martín and Maurer/Quance we add a third, complementary one: by serendipity, in the early twentieth century, Lorca found modernism in vogue in Spain, born from the clash between traditional faith and Darwinian scientific reason. The young poet channelled his psychological needs and lacks into the cultural outlets provided him. The weakening of the old religion in Europe made way for a religion of personal or professional creativity. In Lorca's case, the saints of his artistic faith included not only his teacher Segura Mesa, but also Baudelaire, Verlaine, Darío, and, at base, the composer Richard Wagner. Wagner held that art, especially his music, could present total reality. He advocated the synthesis of all arts – the musical, the plastic, the literary. In France, Wagner's prioritization of music among the arts convinced Baudelaire, forerunner of Parnassianism and Symbolism, and after him the Parnassian Catulle Mendès and the Symbolists Villiers de l'Isle Adam, Verlaine, Mallarmé, René Ghil, and Henri de Régnier (Barzun, *Darwin* 188–9). In his sonnet "Correspondances," Baudelaire presented nature as a temple of enigmatic harmonies, filled with symbols of the true reality, like a forest of lights, perfumes, colours, and sounds corresponding among themselves. In the same fashion, the mind corresponds with objects (Baudelaire, *Fleurs du mal* 7). Verlaine affirmed, "Music before everything else" [De la musique avant tous choses]. In his "Art poétique" he valued the sound of poetry, its vagueness and weightlessness, over what is heavy and stolid (*Œuvres* 206). Lyric verse arises in contact with the music of ideas before consciousness resolves to think. French poets, born in a chaotic world, sought order through esoteric doctrines of a world harmony obedient to hidden laws.

Learned in Symbolist poetry, Parnassian verse, and the esoteric ideas underlying them, Rubén Darío shared Verlaine's predilection for music before all else. He wrote, "Just as every word has a soul, there is in every verse an ideal melody besides verbal harmony. Music only belongs to the idea, very often."[7] For Darío, the ideal melody of verses captured the harmony of archetypes, the true reality. Therefore at the start of Darío's anthology *Prosas profanas* [Profane prose] come the melodic and harmonious verses of "Era un aire suave" [It was a soft air]," a festival for the senses, especially hearing. The Marquise Eulalia, an archetypal figure, belongs to all epochs, not one alone. Slow music dominates these lines, with orchestrated dance in a rococo garden. Such verses alone might have given Lorca enough stimuli and metaphorical paradigms to fill his poetry with "ideal

music." A call to faith in ideal music sounds in Lorca's words: "To penetrate into the musical delights that make our soul give out sound, it is especially necessary to have faith in the concept of music without sounds,
that is, sounds of ideas, (...) melody of ideas being born that sweep away
like sea waves."[8]

García Bacca distinguishes between talking about [*tratar de*] music and
dealing with [*tratar con*] music (*Filosofía de la música* 339). The essence of
music lies in the hearing alone, even when this sensation takes place in the
mind (Darío 5:358). Analogously, we cannot capture the essence of Darío's
poem "Era un aire suave ..." merely by saying or reading its title; we must
instead let the words of the poem resound within us.

Throughout his literary career, Lorca experimented with analogies between poetry and music in verse and prose. The plainest examples consist
of the presence of lyrical writings titled "waltzes" [valses] both in his juvenilia (1917–18) and again in his mature *Poeta en Nueva York* (1929). All
these verses are easily readable in a ternary rhythm, although in the more
mature, more finished verse, typographical distribution of few words per
line makes the text a kind of visual poem, whose sight rhythms set up
rhythmic readings.[9] The poetry of adolescence imitates Darío in seeking
ideal music, the harmony of ideas or archetypes, with classical music as a
symbol of that harmony and with the read musicality of verse as an entry-
way. In this mimetic phase of a new poet, he *speaks* about music, but rarely
makes it. Musical landscapes appear to be modelled after those of the poet
Antonio Machado, and amorous sentimentality with piano background
mimics the poet Juan Ramón Jiménez. Guided by the French Symbolists,
Darío, and Segura Mesa towards Central European music, the teenage
Lorca, as he himself admits at the time, forces musicality onto his verses.
He seeks every opportunity to introduce into them (1) mentions of musical genres, (2) allusions to orchestral instruments, (3) references to musical
tempos, and (4) mentions of composers' names. In these four poetic us-
ages, tantamount to writing *about* music, but not to writing verbal music
itself, he poorly imitates the Rubén Darío of *Prosas profanas*. He admires
Rubén as an emulator of Théophile Gautier's "Symphonie en blanc ma-
yeur" [Symphony in white major] and shows familiarity with Darío's
"Sinfonía de gris mayor" [Symphony in grey major], his "Bouquet," a
poetic symphony in white, and his "Sonatina" in verse, endowed with high
musical value.

This imitation explains the omnipresence in young Lorca of musical
genres ("aria," "romance," "rigadoon," "sonatas," "pavane," "gavotte"),
following Darío's poetic practice in lines like "gallant pavanes, gavottes on

fleeting foot/[that] sweet violins of Hungary would sing."[10] In Darío's
"Era un aire suave ..." are heard "sobs of violoncellos" [sollozos de vio-
loncelos] (Darío 5:765); and in "Sinfonía en gris mayor," natural creatures
play instruments: "The old cicada/rehearses its hoarse and hoary guitar,/and the cricket, a prelude, monotonous solo/on the lone string of its
violin."[11] Hence, on Lorca's poetic landscapes appear "violin, tambourine,
bugle, and sistrum/which Father Sun announces clearly."[12] The sounds of
cicadas find their way into Lorca's verses as "Crazy violins asleep/on an
unconscious note/that ends with a moan."[13]

Symbolist synesthesia in Lorca's poem "Mediodía" [Noontime] mixes
sensations perceived by different sense organs and expressed with instruments playing a melody in a specific key. The symbolic sense of that key
remains obscure even for the most discerning music-loving reader: "Oh
potent sun, disquieting quiets of fire./Eddies of lights and singing of cicadas./Rare tones of F on enormous trumpets."[14] Here the echo of Antonio
Machado, more moderate, is in evidence: "Toward a brilliant sunset/the
summer sun made its way,/and amidst clouds of fire, it was a giant trumpet."[15] Glimpses of the original, sensualist poet that Lorca will eventually
become appear in a plastic as well as auditory, riverside vision that he offers
of frogs as "green flutes" [flautas verdes] from the waters (Poesía inédita
386). Poplars on the banks are "flowering cellos/animated by the wind"
blowing through their branches (365). In the water, the fatal dream of
Shakespeare's drowned Ophelia is accompanied by "clavichords that cry
impossible sonatas" (422).

Composers' names, scarce in Darío's verse, overpopulate the immature
Lorca's as if to commemorate his piano teacher Segura Mesa. Mozart, for
his distance of 150 years, reminds the poet of autumn with its "clavichord
soul" (although Mozart composed for piano). The romanticist Berlioz symbolizes for Lorca unfulfilled carnal passion. Schumann embodies the grace
of a flower with which the poetic subject would throw himself at the feet
of his beloved.[16] Yet of all composers loved by young Lorca, he preferred
Chopin. The speaker's agony, produced by frustrated love, is "wounded
by Chopin and piano."[17] The image recalls a clearer one of Juan Ramón
Jiménez: "The grey-faced moon was born, and Beethoven was weeping,
/beneath the white hand and inside her piano."[18] In another of young
Lorca's poems, the beloved wonders if a certain nocturne played on a
grand piano is Chopin's; she at once assents, and wounds the poetic subject by disdainfully – and inexplicably – leaving his presence (Poesía inédita 263). In "Cielo azul lleno de tarde" (Blue sky full of evening), Lorca

takes poetic advantage of his knowledge of Chopin. To express nostalgia for the impossible and to tinge it with erotic yearning, vague as Verlaine would prefer, yet sensuous and played on the piano with a soft, crystalline touch, Lorca offers a lovely allusion to the Polish composer: "The whole soul of Chopin/Pulsates in the black piano./Chopin of mist and crystal,/Perplexing, carnal, vague."[19]

The young poet, entranced with Central European music, follows Darío in sprinkling his verse with Italian terms for tempos. In the ballad on Chopin already mentioned, "Cielo azul lleno de tarde " the tempo *allegro ma non tanto* [rapid but not so much], repeated at beginning and end, seems forced. In Lorca it does not mean *allegro* as in Darío and "hasty" as in music in general, but "merry," though somewhat tempered by disheartening memories (*Poesía inédita* 330–1). In another poem (388), Lorca introduces musical terms (here italicized by us) in the description of the Granadan countryside: "The lonely garden beds. The restless lowlands, /Full of depth and one *measure* long,/*tempo rubato* of silver and mist /with full *fortes* of sunlight."[20] The young poet here wishes to retard the pace to convey with emotion visual impressions of clouds that half hide the sun. In music, the *rubato*, skilfully used, gives the impression of spontaneity, but the insertion of the term "rubato" into Lorca's poetic text has the opposite effect. The reason lies in the distinction between dealing with music and merely speaking of it in the artificial language of musical scores (García Bacca, *Filosofía de la música* 15). Lorca's frequent insertion of unnatural language, found in scores, gives his lines an unwanted artificiality. No, the musical references in the earliest poetry of Lorca lack the subtlety and depth visible in his verses after he meets Falla.

In his prose poetry, the stripling poet goes to ludicrous extremes in trying to transform poems into musical scores. Maurer observes that in Lorca's prose poem "Sonata que es una fantasía" [Sonnet which is a fantasy], orchestral instruments – violins, oboe, horns, piano – dialogue with a youth unlucky in love (Lorca, *Prosa inédita* 19, 275–7). Further, Maurer identifies the presence here of Beethoven's *Moonlight Sonata*, titled by him *Sonata quasi una fantasia* (op. 27, no. 2). Some of the many tempos indicated in Lorca's poem come directly from Beethoven's score (Maurer, "Lorca y las formas" 242). Yet the poem misses the mark because not only does a score employ an artificial language, but instruments serve merely as organs of musical expression (García Bacca, *Filosofía de la música* 11). Therefore, a second level of artificiality enters young Lorca's poem. The work is neither music nor strictly poetry, but lies somewhere in between a text in current language and a score. It resembles macaronic poetry, comic Latin verse form in which words from the vernacular receive absurd formal Latin endings. The Lorca poem, though, is meant to be deadly serious.

Lorca's early artistic prose takes greater liberties with analogies between literature and music than does the poetry. The young prose writer does not feel as constrained by convention as in verse. In the prose of Darío's *Azul ...* [Blue ...], it is true, little separates poetry from prose, but in Lorca the treatment of music differs. We have seen how his essay "Divagación: Las reglas de la música" [Digression: The rules of music] represents a call to freedom vis-à-vis classical rules. These norms, he holds, serve only as points of departure for the final conception of music, using them as a means to reach artistic heights. With Verlaine, Lorca writes that "music is art by nature."[21] He finds the rules necessary for the "initiation" into the artistic rite.[22] Yet since Lorca defines music as "impassionedness and vagueness" [apasionamiento y vaguedad] (3:370) – passion is the lesson of Segura Mesa, vagueness that of Verlaine – he maintains that in "dramatic, deep" instants of existence, the musician oversteps all the rules and alarms the purists. The rules do not help genial composers, but only mediocre ones, incapable of feeling. To clarify, Lorca does not mention a composer, but rather his then-favourite poet: "Ruben Darío 'the Magnificent' arrived, and on seeing him, away fled the everlasting sonnetists by profession who are the academicians."[23] Lorca perceives Rubén as a rule breaker, but with his own heartfelt ideas and spirit (3:370). Great composers, the essayist feels, do the same. If they overstep measured time "with love, with fire" [con amor, con fuego] and if they manage to express "a rare thought" [un raro pensamiento], Lorca thinks it necessary to welcome them (3:371). In this fashion he will shortly accept into *PCJ* the vast musical conceptions that he will consider exceptional in Falla.

Meanwhile, in his first published book, *Impresiones y paisajes* (1918), with its modernist travel descriptions, it is possible to find tributes to A. Machado and to Darío – the Andalusian sun that "begins to sing songs of fire,"[24] or the harvest flies of the lowlands that "tune their violins to become drunk at noon."[25] Yet in general Lorca alludes to concrete musical compositions with visual associations. The most memorable examples prepare his ear to hear, less than five years afterwards, similarities in the musical theory and practice of Falla and to emulate them in poetry on deep song. One incident associated with music stands out most, overleaping every literary convention: Lorca describes his first true experience of plainchant.

García Bacca, originally a member of the Claretian Order, offers a precise description of Gregorian chant, clarifying Lorca's impressionistic characterization. This form of sacred song lacks quantity, which vanished from Latin prose and verse as of the fourth century. Instruments remain excluded, as well as all instrumental music. Only what can be sung by mouth, unmindful of quantity, is permissible. Measure and rhythm also are eliminated. The music must adjust to the words, not words to music. The number of words corresponds to the number of notes, but the quantity of notes depends on the number of words (held to be divine). The verbal text governs the music because of its superior antiquity, its divine provenance, its theological or legal stature. Faith or belief determines musical forms. The liturgy guides the coadjustment of musical forms, proved with works of public and official worship. Finally, the performance of such song takes place within a divine atmosphere of coexistence between God and human beings (García Bacca, *Filosofía de la música* 66). The intervention of any secularism constitutes mere tourism.

In the church of the convent of Saint Dominic of Silos, when the monks sing mass in plainchant, the young tourist Lorca's essayistic voice hears a song that overshoots rhythmic regularity and the Western tempered scale. "The melody," he writes, "like an enormous column of black marble that got waylaid in the clouds, has no resolution. It is undulating and smooth, deep and with a vague inner sentiment. The voices go passing over all the tonal melancholies throughout the fantastic world of keys."[26] The young listener, inclined towards sentimentality, feels alien to the otherworldliness of this music. The song seeks elevation "above all existing things,"[27] and the canticles of praise, remoteness from the "tragedy of the heart."[28] The individual notes "flee from emotional points. There are enormous pantings in which one syllable goes passing over notes and notes without the expected resolution."[29] Concretely, the essayist comments on an *Agnus Dei* "with a very rare and archaic melody."[30] Here we can understand Lorca's predisposition to accept Falla's guidance, several years later, to appreciate the Gypsy siguiriya. This genre, largely rooted in Byzantine liturgical chant, has an ancient melody extending to the infinite without resolution, while adorned only with enharmonic *paramentos* (Lorca 3:198–200, 218).

Lorca's musical experience in Saint Dominic of Silos takes an unexpected direction, also pertinent to *PCJ* and underscoring his secular orientation. For someone like the youthful essayist/visitor, for whom secular Eastern European classical music constitutes a religion, it seems inconceivable that a certain monk has renounced the world to the extreme of ignoring the "immortal name" of Beethoven.[31] On the organ, the narrator plays the first chord in the famous second movement (Allegretto) of Beethoven's Seventh Symphony (opus 92). He next enters the "anguished hiccup [of this piece] with its constant, nightmarish rhythm."[32] Such is Lorca's semi-lyrical, semi-comic description of this pavane in A minor in 2/4 time, with its initial theme of eight measures, with ceaselessly recurring rhythm and a melody undergoing many variations to the end (see musical example 4).[33] The "nightmarish rhythm" consists of what Beethoven in his time regarded as a stately dance step. In the score he indicates as much with many staccato notes. If we repeat Lorca's words, "nightmarish rhythm," in an eight-measure unit while stressing only every first, fourth, and fifth beat, and if we pronounce the other syllables staccato, we receive an exact idea of the rhythm of each of the measures.

This music affects the listening monk so much, that he covers the eyes of the young organist to stop him from playing. The monk's admission makes us aware that he is an alter ego of the author. Eutimio Martín has hypothesized that Lorca immersed himself in a religion of music to avoid a life of lust. The monk, on the other hand, to avoid a life of spiritual "lust" [lujuria], has avoided secular music, which he feels makes him bestial. Therefore he has limited himself to singing plainchant (3:55). Although Lorca never follows the monk's example, his subsequent acquaintance with Falla and with the study of deep song will enable him to harmonize his taste for secular music with his fascination for the melodic and modal flexibility peculiar to Gregorian chant.

The direction in which Lorca moves appears in the poem in prose "Un pregón en la tarde" [A cry to buy wares in the evening]. Here he describes a street vendor's cry heard in the Andalusian city of Baeza and filling a summer evening with a "painful scream" [grito doloroso], an artistic complaint.[34] In every cry to buy merchandise, Lorca finds the repetition several times of a single note, usually sung in a minor key in Andalusia. However, he thinks it especially noteworthy that a particular cry in Baeza has a "quality found in Wagnerian song."[35] We cannot determine whether Lorca has a specific song of Wagner's in mind, because he does not supply enough details. Still, the description endows this cry with enough specificity to individualize it. It began on "a plaintive, sung note that vibrated like a bell in a very brilliant major tone, repeated in an *andante maestoso* [slow majestic tempo] and made a pause. Afterwards, it uttered the same theme again, now more quietly, and, finally, as a resolution, the voice took on a guttural pitch, modulated to the minor note, and striking a very elevated

4   Beethoven, *Allegretto*, Symphony No. 7, Opening.

one, fell languidly back onto the initial note. The cry sounded swooning and loud like a horn phrase of the great Wagner."[36] Interestingly, Lorca is close in sensibility to Falla without having yet met him personally. Certain of Falla's Andalusian-style pieces, like *La vida breve* and *Noches en los jardines de España*, employ climactic points borrowed from Wagner to help introduce such music into the European canon.[37] Moreover, in the puppet opera *El retablo de maese Pedro*, the puppet master himself sounds an operatic cry to attract an audience, a cry derived from Andalusian *pregones*.[38]

In the prose poem "Romanza de Mendelssohn" [Mendelssohn's song without words], also from *Impresiones y paisajes*, Lorca supplies words for that piece. His book title "Impressions and Landscapes" indicates a will to cultivate impressionism. Psychology of that period, applied to painting, holds that pictorial impressionism eliminates tactile elements belonging to close-range vision and prefers to render long-range vision, stressing purely visual sensation (Jaensch 470–4). Lorca, guided by other impressionist essayists like "Azorín,"[39] keeps his distance from the objects he represents – here, a *Song without Words* by Mendelssohn. He wishes to present with words an artwork that resists verbalization. To that end, removing himself from the aesthetic object itself, he devotes nothing less than half the essay to the pictorial setting of this music. He begins with the silence preceding the sweet auditory experience, and he selects a port, perhaps for its similarity, observed by impressionist composers, of the piano keyboard to the sounds of water.[40] He describes the sea as "sweet honey" [miel dulce] to prepare the reader's ear to savour the Romantic sweetness of Mendelssohn. In addition, he weaves a dreamy atmosphere like that preferred by impressionist poets like A. Machado, author of "Ensueño" (Daydream),[41] and impressionist pianists like Debussy, author of "Reverie."[42] Hence, he depicts "barges [that] bob drowsily."[43] He focuses the eyes and ears of the reader on the horizon: "In the distance are seen the towers of the city and the rocky slopes of the hill."[44] Noonday light enables tactile vision of objects, while filtered light hinders perception of their depth. For that reason, the essayist prefers the "twilight hour," when "lights of the boats and the houses start to be lit."[45] Impressionism favours indefinite forms, avoiding what is tangible and preferring vision, like the aquatic paintings of Claude Monet, Gustave Caillebotte, Berthe Morisot, and Alfred Sisley with painted reflections of the Seine. Lorca offers a twilight pictorial panorama of "groups of houses turned upside down in the waters amidst the golden, trembling zigzags of the reflections."[46] What is nearby holds little interest. Therefore the essayist populates the foreground with two "large men dressed in blue that speak heatedly" and turn attention away from themselves.[47]

Projected to the distance, the reader's consciousness reaps the sweet prize: "From a faraway piano came the *Song without Words*."[48] The essayist underscores the historical distance of the piece, fruit of the "Romantic spirit of 1830" [espíritu romántico del 1830]. He describes what the ear attuned to distance can devise: "It began slowly with a delightful rubato tune and entered afterwards with a song overflowing with impassionedness. At times the melody would hush while the bass played some soft, solemn chords."[49] There exist numerous pieces under the title *Songs without Words* by Mendelssohn. Let us select one that seems to approach the description supplied by Lorca. Of the *Lieder* [Songs], opus 85, number 1, an "*andante espressivo*" [expressive flowing tempo] begins in a slow 2/4, with a medium loud introductory measure, which in view of its slowness could be interpreted with a *rubato*. In the second measure begins an impassioned melody, while the bass plays ceaseless arpeggios. Their notes, if rendered simultaneously, could form chords as soft and solemn as the two with which the brief piece ends. The song overflows with passion in the measures with crescendos. It ends with diminuendos and measures played very softly.[50]

How to describe the cumulative effect of the slowness, the rubato, the melodic passion, the softness, and the circumspection? In Lorca's words, "over the port came music enveloping everything in an enchantment of sentimental sound."[51] A musical atmosphere is born, projecting itself over the pier. The steep and narrow waves of the shore "were falling as they voluptuously licked the steps of the wharf,"[52] as if to imitate the liquid, soft, and savoury waves of piano music. While the song continues to sound, the light completely disappears and reduces the impression of tactility to a minimum. If close-range vision intensifies the sense of reality, solidity, and bodiliness, far-range vision lessens it, and seems to derealize objects (Jaensch 470). Hence, "to the slow rhythm of the oars" – which seems to follow the rhythm of the music – a visual "phantom" [fantasma] emerges, a white barge appearing in a mysterious sensation with which Lorca ends his essay, as if with a diminuendo (Lorca 3:120).

From this description we may gather multiple tendencies of the emerging lyric art of Lorca. As here, in *PCJ* aesthetic impressionism prevails, imitating pictorial and musical techniques of artists belonging to that current. Just as Falla was described as the only immediate descendent of the impressionist Debussy, Lorca, who learned Debussy from Segura Mesa, found himself open to the music of Falla before meeting him in person. Like Falla, he would cultivate an art distant from the objects he depicted.

Just as he put distance as an essayist from the *Songs without Words* of Mendelssohn, so he would take a faraway stance with respect to the deep song of which he writes in his poetry, but not without experiencing catharsis through stylization of that art form in his special fashion. Moreover, he would appreciate the silence that precedes the music as an essential element of the work. His reverence towards that music would not exclude a certain humour that is apparent, though infrequent, in his juvenilia. He would take care to sketch the setting of that music before anything else. With impressionist brushstrokes and sounds he would describe the ambiance in which the song is performed. The descriptive technique to follow, whether applied to sight or sound, had an inductive character. It accumulated a series of concrete objects and derived from them a general idea, conception, or atmosphere. Lorca's writing would easily slide between verbalization, visualization, and suggestions of music, while sometimes superimposing them. Just as in *Impresiones y paisajes* he felt free of burdensome conventions for verse, in *PCJ* metric and melodic freedom of folkloric song would also pass into his lyric, which in form if not content often approaches prose. Finally, whereas in *Impresiones y paisajes* the piano imitated water, in *PCJ*, guided by Falla's appreciation of guitar, Lorca would play water music on his verbal guitar.

Lorca passed from modernism to Falla over the bridge of the avant-garde, whose influence sharpened the poet's skills in musical metaphor. In spring 1919, members of the *Rinconcillo* then in Madrid took Lorca to the Ateneo or Arts Club to meet the poets Guillermo de Torre, Pedro Salinas, and Gerardo Diego, among others. Torre was spearheading the Spanish avant-garde movement known as *ultraísmo*, and Diego, after his initial affiliation with the *ultraístas*, joined the Chilean Vicente Huidobro and the Spaniard Juan Larrea in their emerging movement called *creacionismo*. *Ultraísmo* and *creacionismo* absorbed aesthetic innovations in France championed by Apollinaire, Reverdy, Cocteau, Picasso, Juan Gris, and Sergei Diaghilev (Gibson, *Life* 84), and in Spain promoted by Gómez de la Serna, Cansinos Asséns, and Ortega y Gasset. At the same time, the *ultraístas* and *creacionistas* espoused stylistic principles of Italian Futurism, which also had a decisive impact on Lorca's literary style (Bonaddio, *Poetics of Self-Consciousness* 49). Manuel Durán synthesizes the stylistic traits of Futurism as follows: preference for the brief sentence, omission of adjectives, suppression of transitions and conjunctions, verbal economy, simplification of syntax and even of punctuation, loss of everything discursive, descriptive, and accidental, and contraction of poetic language to metaphor ("Lorca" 765–7). To this list Bonaddio correctly adds "eradication of excessive sentimentality and emotionalism," with the displacement of

the first person, the lyric "I." While Durán (766) finds isolated examples
of the new writing style in Lorca's first published anthology *Libro de poemas* [Book of poems], Bonaddio notes stylistic simplification as a general
rule, despite some reservations, in Lorca's *Suites* (*Poetics of Self-Consciousness* 50). Let us examine one of the exceptional poems on music
from *Libro de poemas* before focusing on poetry from *Suites*, written almost contemporaneously with *PCJ*.

The poem "El concierto interrumpido" [The interrupted concert, 1920]
from *Libro de poemas* rejects the modernist style of creating music previously exaggerated by Lorca. Music scores belong to an artificial world. To
introduce their signs into a natural setting, as Lorca attempted in his earliest verse, is to denaturalize that setting. He dedicates "El concierto interrumpido" to his friend, the music critic Adolfo Salazar, aware that in a
score, the suspension of motion of a melody appears in the staff as a semicircle with printed points downward and with a period in the middle. This
sign, denoted a hold or fermata (see musical example 5), is comparable in
nature to a half moon with cusps pointing downward:

5   Hold.

If nature outside art operates in harmony with universal laws, as
Parnassianism and Symbolism maintain, then a hold borrowed from a musical score and appearing in the natural order can stop all movement, all
sound in the universe. The hold creates a new, superficial world order by
paralysing the universe; hence, the title "The interrupted concert." Even
the verse form points to the unnaturalness introduced by the crescent moon
that forms the hold (in Spanish, *calderón*). A classical verse form is the silva,
a flexible combination of seven- and eleven-syllable lines (Navarro Tomás,
Arte 165). Insert a six-syllable line, and the usual harmony of the *silva*
vanishes. The following verses from the poem show two heptasyllables
and one hendecasyllable followed by an unexpected hexasyllable constituting the fourth line:

Ha roto la armonía
de la noche profunda
el calderón helado y soñoliento
de la media luna.

[The harmony belonging
To deep night has been broken
By the frigid and sleep-inducing hold
Of the crescent moon.]   [Lorca, *Obras completas* 1:104]

The jocose narrative continues uninterruptedly with seven- and eleven-
syllable lines until the end. The rest of the poem recounts the imagined
(un)natural effects of the hold. The irrigation channels, reduced to silence,
"protest deafly" [protestan sordamente]. The frogs, which generally call
their brethren under the half moon – symbol of Islam – like "muezzins of
the shadow,/have kept completely mute."[53] In land and sky, silence prevails. The tavern interrupts its "sad music" [triste música], and the oldest
star "has placed a damper on its edge"[54] to keep from producing the music
of the spheres. The wind ceases to move, sitting down in the depressions
of the mountain. The poem ends by comparing a poplar tree to Pythagoras,
cosmic mathematician, supposed author of the doctrine of the harmony
of the spheres – the notion that the heavens move in accordance with nu-
merical proportions, and produce silent music on spinning in their orbits
(García Bacca, *Filosofía de la música* 129; Huffman, "Pythagoras" 761).
The poplar, old and wise like Pythagoras, wishes to punish the subversive
satellite that has interrupted the cosmic concert: "It wants to take its hun-
dred-year-old hand/and give the moon a punch."[55] The poem, with its
revolutionary stance towards poetic tradition, seems to augur a break
with Darío-style modernism, steeped in Pythagoreanism.[56]
    Passing now from *Book of Poems* to *Suites*, we find this collection of
two hundred brief poems a training ground for what would later become
Lorca's more finished anthologies, *Canciones* (Songs, 1924) and *PCJ*
(1931). André Belamich dates *Suites* from the end of 1920 to July 1923
(Lorca, *Suites*, cit. in Bonaddio, *Poetics of Self-Consciousness* 9) and sees the
work as the "laboratory for the *Poem of Deep Song*" (49). Although these
verses show traces of Juan Ramón Jiménez's modernism while rejecting
Torres' *ultraísta* materialism and cult of speed, they constitute "independent poems in line with the precepts of the avant-garde" (Bonaddio, *Poetics
of Self-Consciousness* 49). Lorca never rushed to publish his books, because
his poetry circulated in journals, letters, and readings with friends. At last

in 1926, he determined to publish *Suites, Canciones,* and *PCJ* all at once. Although only *Canciones* came out in 1927, Roberta Quance argues the interrelationship of all three by theme and structure (*Contradiction* 2–3).[57] *Suites* furnished "just under half of the poems published in *Canciones*" (Dinverno, "Lorca's *Suites*" 306n5), and given the problematic state of its manuscripts, its definitive version has yet to be established (312). Quance summarizes some of its main themes as unrealizable ideals (*Contradiction* 14), problems of selfhood (12), uneasiness about established gender roles (4), and a struggle between modernism and avant-garde aesthetics (29–31).

Considering how many of the poems from *Suites* generate those of *Canciones,* we can only wonder whether Lorca had selected his poetry of the later collection for its superior musicality and its closeness to poetic *creacionismo.* He regarded this movement as "one of the most formidable efforts to construct lyric upon purely aesthetic substance."[58] He remarked that "Juan Larrea and his student Gerardo Diego build poems grounded on poetic facts linked together, with ever purer imagery and crystalline loftiness."[59] Of all the members of Lorca's Generation of 1927, Gerardo Diego seemed most committed to music, performance, and musicology. Between 1921 and 39, he maintained correspondence and friendship with Falla.[60] On 12 February 1921, Diego sent Falla, whom he had not yet met personally, an avant-garde poem entitled "Estética" [Aesthetic], dedicated to the composer himself. The verses, he explained to Falla, were "a direct consequence of Debussy's 'Mouvement' [*Images,* Bk. 1] and certain measures of *El amor brujo*" ("Gerardo Diego en apuntes" 34). Accordingly, when Lorca began writing *PCJ* in November, he might have found the groundwork lain for drawing analogies between entire pieces of Falla and complete emerging poems of his own.[61]

2

Fantasía Bætica and
"Baladilla de los tres ríos":
Two Searches for Andalusian Wellsprings

"Alhambrism," as defined by Michael Christoforidis, denotes "the Romantic construction of Granada as the last European refuge of Arab culture." This stylized nostalgia originated in Ginés Pérez de Hita's *Historia de las guerras civiles de Granada* [Civil wars of Granada, 1595].[1] A historical novel on the feuds between noble families in Granada, the Zegri and the Abencerage factions, the work originated the prototype of the Moor as "brave, spirited, courtly, and chivalric." The idealization affected Spanish Golden Age and Enlightenment authors and spread abroad to Romanticists F.-R. Chateaubriand, Victor Hugo, Washington Irving, and Théophile Gautier (Haboucha, "Pérez de Hita" 1260).

By the end of the nineteenth century, Christoforidis informs, Alhambrism assumed a connection to Andalusian nationalism. Moreover, French Symbolists helped introduce into literature and painting the commonplaces of gardens, twilight, arabesques, and the final Moorish king Boabdil's sigh as he surrendered his kingdom of Granada to Isabella and Ferdinand (Christoforidis, "Moor's Last Sigh" 1). In music, cross-fertilization of the theme took place between Isaac Albéniz, Claude Debussy, and Manuel de Falla. Falla knew much music associated with Granada and in 1904 had considered basing a composition on Irving's *Tales of the Alhambra*. In November 1913, in a Paris concert with the theme of Granada, Falla played his own pieces as well as those by Albéniz and Debussy along with readings of Alhambrist poetry from Gautier and Hugo. As for Alhambrism in Falla's own music, Christoforidis mentions the intermezzo in *La vida breve*, set in Granada, which moved Debussy when Falla played it on the piano; and a Wagnerian sigh like the musical ones heard at the start of the Prelude to *Tristan und Isolde* and echoed in "En el Generalife,"[2] thereby imitating Boabdil's sigh.

Alhambrism appeared in Lorca's writings before he met Falla and acquired subtlety once he underwent Falla's influence in *PCJ*. The change measures the quality and depth of Falla's impact on the younger artist. The early poem "El Dauro y el Genil" [The Darro and the Genil rivers], composed 17 June 1918, contains raw material for the later, more sophisticated "Baladilla de los tres ríos" [Little ballad of the three rivers]. Both poems contrast rivers, attributing to them the characters of the Andalusians inhabiting their banks. Further, Mario Hernández, in his edition of *PCJ*, mentions Lorca's passing allusion in the "Baladilla" to the will-o'-the-wisp as a tribute to Manuel de Falla for his song *Canción del fuego fatuo* (Will-o'-the-wisp song) in the ballet *El amor brujo*, as well as for a three-act comic opera, never performed and titled *Fuego fatuo* [Will-o'-the-wisp, 1918].[3] However, the present chapter will show that Falla's influence runs deeper, affecting the structure of the "Baladilla." An examination of "El Dauro y el Genil" will come first, followed by a comparison of Falla's and Lorca's aesthetics on adapting folk material to the European canon in nationalistic music, and finally the application of that aesthetics to Falla's piano solo *Fantasía bætica* [Andalusian fantasy] (1919) and to "Baladilla de los tres ríos" (1922?).

Lorca's "El Dauro y el Genil" contains echoes of Victor Hugo's "Grenade." Hugo's paean to Granada alternates series of hexasyllables with alexandrines (129–33). Young Lorca's verse mostly does as well, although, being more flexible, it also introduces dactylic lines in imitation of Darío and A. Machado. The first lines offer an idea of the tenor of the poem:

¡Ríos de Granada!,
Con agua de nieve,
Viejos consagrados
Que saben leyendas de cruz y de luna
De harem y de altar,
Hermanos de agua con almas distintas.
Madre tierra os salve antes que las cintas
De vuestras corrientes
Vayan al mar.

[Rivers of Granada
With water from snow,
Revered old men,
Knowers of legends of cross and of crescent.

Of harem and altar,
Brothers made of water with different souls.
May Mother Earth save you long before the ribbons
Of your currents
Pass to the sea.]   (Poesía inédita 306)

The poem has five parts: (1) a preface praising the two rivers of Granada, the Darro and its tributary the Genil; (2) a panegyric to the Darro as a "río aljamiado" [Hispano-Arabic river], nostalgic for past Moorish glory; (3) a contrasting section on the Genil as a "Christian river," focused, unlike the past-facing Darro, on the present and the future; (4) a "consecration" [consagración], glorifying both rivers for the melancholy, idealistic poets of the Darro and the robust farmers to be raised by the Genil; and last, (5) a "Gloria final," which consists of a repetition of the preface verbatim, though enclosed between a rhetorical question preceding and following that repetition, and enquiring, What does death matter? The poem ends with the tolerant command to the rivers to teach the legends they know about crescent and cross (306–12).

Each river personifies one of the opposing sides of the Granadan provincial character, with the Darro oriented towards passive, contemplative resignation and the Genil towards future agricultural dynamism. The Darro faces the cemetery cypress, the Genil the strong guardian poplar. The poetic voice associates the first attitude with the Moors that lost the Granadan Wars, resulting in their cession of the city to the Catholic Monarchs in 1492. This treatment of the Darro illustrates what Christoforidis defines as Alhambrism. The Darro nostalgically emerges as a river of "tristezas antiguas y moras" [ancient, Moorish sadnesses: l. 20]. The literary topos of the noble Moor appears. The lyric voice calls the Darro the "trovador eterno / del pueblo admirable que tanto lo amó" [the eternal troubadour / of the admirable people that cherished it so much: ll. 36–7]. In the "ardent strophe" [copla ardiente] of that watery troubadour can be heard the "sigh of the Moor" [suspiro del moro], King Boadbil, on departing from Granada (l. 127).

The hackneyed Alhambrism of this early poem all but disappears in "Baladilla de los tres rios," written four years later in 1922. The poetic subject's awe before picturesque Granada diminishes in order to encompass all Andalusia. Into Lorca's verse will enter new depth in fluvial imagery thanks to the discovery of his own voice and to Falla's conceptualization of Andalusian history, together with the synthetic quality of his mature Andalusian music. Falla and Lorca feel torn between their attraction to the beauty of Granada and their aversion to what is merely picturesque about it. Falla seeks to avoid the musical commonplaces of Emilio Arrieta's famous zarzuela *La conquista de Granada* [The conquest of Granada], with showy melodies, Oriental-style orchestration, Andalusian modal scales, and local dance rhythms. In his article "Nuestra música" [Our music], he remarks that Spanish composers have purported to create national music, but have failed. Andalusianist zarzuelas chose Spanish themes, yet developed them with musical techniques borrowed from Italian opera. With his teacher Felipe Pedrell, Falla believes in an essence, a creative genius of the people that composers, when handling traditional music, need to incorporate into their own works. Falla seeks a happy medium between zarzuela composers and Pedrell in practice, for his teacher seems to him to introduce into his composing too many non-essential elements: fragments of the Spanish classics as well as folk songs in their consecrated forms. Falla specifies what new composers should seek:

> In folk song, the spirit matters more than the letter. The rhythm, the modality, and the melodic intervals that determine its undulations and cadences constitute what is essential in those songs … I oppose that music which takes genuine folkloric documents for its basis. On the contrary, I think it is necessary to start from the natural, living sources and utilize sonorities and rhythms in their substance, not in the outward aspect.[4]

Composing with traditional melodies presents challenges that starting from zero would not. Falla deems the procedure one of the most difficult chores. He finds himself constrained, on the one hand, by the uniqueness of the melody and, on the other, by its affiliation to a particular genre of folk music.[5] Hence, his works like *La vida breve* and *Noches* dwell on the beauty of Granada in folkloric passages, yet bring them down to earth with echoes of non-Spanish composers.

In Lorca appear parallel claims, applied to lyric poetry with a folkloric basis. The result is no longer poetry that merely speaks of music, but verse that aspires to *be* verbal music, to engage the reader in performing it. Where Falla criticizes the zarzuela and Pedrell, Lorca disapproves the practice of Salvador Rueda, Ventura Ruiz Aguilera, and Manuel Machado: "What a notable difference between the verses of these poets and those that the people create: the difference that there is between a paper rose and one from nature!"[6] Straightaway, Lorca offers an explanation that may well refer to the "natural, living sources," the Andalusian essences venerated by Falla: "Poets that compose folkloric lays muddy the clear waters of the genuine heart; and how easy it is to note in their verses the secure, ugly pace of the man who knows his grammar! One should take from the people nothing but the ultimate essences and an occasional trill for colour, but never make a docile imitation of its ineffable modulations."[7] C. Brian Morris, while unaware of Falla's probable presence in this thinking and of the musical references in Lorca's metaphors ("lay," "trill," "modulations"), does recognize that his words describe his practice in *PCJ*. For Morris, Lorca's praxis reflects disdain for Manuel Machado's shallow glibness, whose anthology *Cante hondo* slavishly adheres to folkloric strophes, abounds in contrived phrasings, and accumulates italicized Andalusian dialectalisms (192). While surpassing Machado by simply avoiding his poetic habits in *PCJ* and later in *Romancero gitano*, Lorca also outdoes him by drawing analogies between Falla's music and his own verse and by adding his own experiences of Andalusia. From the start of Falla's Andalusian style in the opera *La vida breve* (1905) to its culmination in the piano solo *Fantasía bœtica* (1919), he builds carefully crafted structures, coherent musical arabesques, which seek the primordial depths of Andalusia. Similarly, in *PCJ*, Lorca stylizes the folk lyrics of his native region to delve to its emotional origins without losing sight of his personal concerns.

Of all Falla's music in the Andalusian idiom, the *Fantasía bœtica* can claim greatest depth. This piano solo represents a "return to the sources" of Andalusia (Demarquez 117). The regress applies not so much to its Latinate title, representing the Roman heritage of the Spanish south,[8] as to Falla's summing up and surpassing of all that he had attempted previously in his Andalusian musical idiom. For Christoforidis, Falla here displays his deepest inspiration in flamenco forms, "translating and synthesizing into a modern language the musical traits of the folkloric singers and dancers, the ornamental, rhythmic phrases of the guitar, and the simulation of microtonal modulations and scales of cante jondo."[9] If by a "modern language" we understand an artistic idiom of Western origin, then Lorca understandably affirms in his 1931 lecture on deep song that the drama of Andalusia in general, symbolized by the guitar that westernized *cante jondo*, consists of "West and East in combat, making the Baetica an island of culture."[10]

In *PCJ*, the introductory poem, "Baladilla de los tres ríos," displays much in common with Falla's *Fantasía bœtica*. Lorca's ballad establishes a structural basis for everything preceding its composition in the anthology. Like Falla's synthesizing solo in relation to his other Andalusianist music, the "Baladilla" came into being late (around 1922) with respect to most of the other poetry, written in November 1921 (though sporadically revised until 1931, publication date of *PCJ*). As a felicitous afterthought in 1931, Lorca decided to use the ballad as a poetic prologue (de Paepe, *PCJ* 16–19, 37). By then, the *Fantasia bœtica* had existed for nine years under its established title, signifying Latin-Andalusian roots; and Lorca's three rivers, taken together, make up what he understands as the Andalusian "cultural spirit," the creative principle of southern Spanish culture. The "Baladilla de los tres ríos," a mix of East and West, has the traditional form of Castilian *coplas,* quatrains in assonance, alternating with very terse refrains, perhaps corresponding to the single repeated notes seen in Eastern song and always preceded by the sighed syllable, "¡Ay!" The ballad contains avant-garde metaphors synthesizing ancient aspirations and fears – unfulfilled desire and death – expressed in all the poetry that follows in the *PCJ* (and paramount in Lorca's lyric):

El río Guadalquivir
va entre naranjos y olivos.
Los dos ríos de Granada
bajan de la nieve al trigo.

¡Ay, amor
que se fue y no vino!

El río Guadalquivir
tiene las barbas granates.
Los dos ríos de Granada
Uno llanto y otro sangre.

¡Ay, amor
que se fue por el aire!

Para los barcos de vela
Sevilla tiene un camino;
por el agua de Granada
sólo reman los suspiros.

¡Ay, amor
que se fue y no vino!

Guadalquivir, alta torre
y viento en los naranjales.
Dauro y Genil, torrecillas
muertas sobre los estanques.

¡Ay, amor

que se fue por el aire!

¡Quién dirá que el agua lleva
un fuego fatuo de gritos!

¡Ay, amor
que se fue y no vino!

Lleva azahar, lleva olivas,
Andalucía, a tus mares.

¡Ay, amor
que se fue por el aire!

[The river Guadalquivir
Passes between orange and olive trees.
The two rivers of Granada
Flow down from the snow to the wheat.

Oh love
That left and never came back!

The river Guadalquivir
Has a pomegranate-red beard.
The two rivers of Granada,
One is tears, the other blood.

Oh, love
That fled away through the air!

For all boats with sails
Seville has a road;
Through the waters of Granada
Only sighs hold the oars.

Oh, love
That left and never came back!

Guadalquivir, high tower
And wind in the orange groves.
Darro and Genil, little towers

Dead above the ponds.

Oh love,
That fled away through the air!

Who would think the water carries
A will-o'-the-wisp of screams!

Oh, love   .
That left and never came back!

Remove the orange blossoms, the olives,
Andalusia, to your seas.

Oh love,
That fled away through the air!]   (PCJ 150–3; reproduced with gracious
                                            permission of the heirs of F. García Lorca)

Lorca may have composed this poem after the style of Falla's piece, although the affects expressed in the verse typify Lorca's writing. Let us analyse the Falla solo first, then the Lorca ballad. Bætica, Roman name of Andalusia, comprised that part of Hispania irrigated by the river Bætis, today called the Guadalquivir. By extension, the river came to denote the entire region of Andalusia (Demarquez 117). Falla intended the *Fantasía bætica* to be a tribute to the "Latin-Andalusian stock" (Hess, *Passions* 122). His mentor Claude Debussy, in his opinion, belonged to the "Latin" stock (84), and the piece displays a subtle influence of at least four Debussy compositions behind the much more pronounced flamenco rhythms.[11] The work has generated a number of different thematic analyses, including sonata form, large binary form, ternary structure, and rhapsody. However, the most analytical and performance-oriented breakdown stems from the pianist-scholar Nancy Lee Harper ("Interpretation of *Fantasía Baetica*"). She divides the work into Theme Block 1, Variations on Theme Block 1, Theme Block 2, Variations on earlier motifs, Intermezzo, Recapitulation of Theme Block 1, Recapitulation of Variations on Theme Block 1, Recapitulation of Variations on earlier motifs, Final Development, and Coda.

Within the theme blocks and variations, Harper does not find the development of a melody, properly speaking, but rather the swift juxtaposition of many motifs, woven into a structure that she calls a "multi-coloured carpet." With each motif she associates a deep-song guitar technique, a flamenco dance step, or a dance rhythm. Her meticulous motivic analysis enables us to identify all the stages of Falla's Andalusianism save the earliest, marked by *La vida breve* (1905), which, despite its later successful performances, he disdained as passé. Of the nine motifs enumerated by Harper in Theme Block 1 (A1, A2, B1, B2, C1, C2, C3, D1, D2), A1, composed of the first chord, is a *rasgueado* or guitar flourish played in the Hindu mode called the *sriraga*. Falla had learned this mode in Louis Lucas (*L'Acoustique nouvelle* 16–17) as an example of the flexibility of enharmonic scales.[12] The musical synthesis of Falla's Andalusianist phase therefore appropriately begins by alluding to music theory present in his personal notes on deep song that passed to his anonymous 1922 pamphlet *El "cante jondo" (canto primitivo andaluz)*. The piece starts moving with relentless flamenco rhythms as of its second motif, called A2 by Harper, with running notes, simulated guitar plucking, boleros, *bulerías*, and seguidilla. *Fantasía bætica* thereby asserts its kinship to the best known of the early *Cuatro piezas españolas* [Four Spanish Pieces] (1908), titled "Andaluza" and played "avec un sentiment sauvage" (Walters, "Parallel Trajectories" 64).[13] Falla follows an example set in *Noches en los jardines de España* (1914) in the Intermezzo of the *Fantasía bætica*, based on a *zorongo* from Isidoro Hernandez's *Flores de España* [Blossoms of Spain], a melody of the same genre as that dominating the first nocturne and the second half of the final nocturne (see Introduction, above), and submitted to many variations as these other *zorongos* are in *Noches*. Among Falla's *Siete canciones populares españolas* [Seven popular Spanish songs] (1914–15), the Andalusianist folk songs "El paño moruno" [The Moorish cloth]" and "Polo" (a deep-song dance in ternary rhythms) each feature *cante jondo* screams (¡ay!) sung at different, carefully specified lengths (see ch. 3n45). Nancy Harper informs that in motif C1 of Theme Block 1, the right hand leaps many keys on the first beat in imitation of the deep-song singer's ¡ay!, and another imitation of this scream appears in motif F-2 of Theme Block 2. Finally, numerous motifs of *Fantasía bætica* recall the choreography of the Ballets Russes in *El sombrero de tres picos*. Shoe and heelwork percussion effects (*zapateado, taconeo*) appear imitated by the piano between measures 172 and 194 and in the brilliant coda (Harper 1992).

Many analogies to the piece just analysed appear in Lorca's "Baladilla." Falla has exalted Andalusia by weaving its prominent forms of guitar, dance, and song into a musical fabric, and Lorca pays verbal and visual tribute to the ethos of Andalusia as creator of deep song within a vast geographic tapestry. Building on the traditional vision of human life as a river, he takes three Andalusian rivers together – the Guadalquivir, the Granadan Darro, and the Genil – as symbols of the ongoing creative life force of

Andalusia. Lorca's poem is predictably not as complex as Falla's piano solo: whereas Falla synthesizes eleven years of Andalusianist pieces, Lorca merely draws together barely several months of poetry. Nevertheless, while Falla offers an orderly summation of his Andalusianism, Lorca provides fives theme-groups relating to these Andalusian rivers, which we may label (1) presentation of the rivers, (2) reflection on the meanings of their depths, (3) historical uses, (4) appreciation of their values, and (5) annihilation of those values. Presenting Andalusian reality, meditating on it, appreciating it, and witnessing its destruction constitute a general pattern of the anthology original to Lorca and organizing its first four parts. In every quatrain of the "Baladilla," the first two verses concern the Guadalquivir, the last two the Darro and the Genil (always taken together as a unit). Therefore each theme-group consists of two motifs. Between all four quatrains comes a third set of semantemes, sighs of unfulfilled love in two-line refrains always beginning with the *¡ay!* heard in deep song.

Initially, Lorca presents the rich and contradictory Andalusian regional character in visual form, just as Falla has shown that entity through "changes of dynamic intensity" in motivic variants (measures 63–86, 121–49: Harper 1998). In his 1922 lecture "El cante jondo. Primitivo canto andaluz" [Deep song. Primitive Andalusian song], the atavist Lorca writes of the cultivation of deep song "from time immemorial (...) [with its] deep psalmodies that cross and define our unique, highly complicated Andalusia from the peaks of Sierra Nevada to the olive groves of Cordoba and from the Sierra Cazorla to the very merry mouth of the Guadalquivir."[14] The complexity of Andalusia takes the shape, in the visual poet Lorca, of a panoramic vista within each four-line strophe of the "Baladilla," contrasting the dynamic Guadaquivir of Seville with the languid Genil and Darro of Granada. Like the opposing rhythms of *Fantasía bætica*, Lorca's ballad proceeds by starts and stops. The Guadalquivir's potency differs from the listlessness of the Genil and the Darro. In the first quatrain, the geographic presentation of the three rivers, the Guadalquivir goes on its own momentum between orange and olive trees, whereas the two Granadan rivers descend from the snows of Sierra de la Yedra and Sierra Nevada to the wheat fields below. The second quatrain reflects on the depths, the substance, of the rivers. Falla has advanced a sedimentary conception of Andalusian history, with each culture – Roman, Byzantine, Moorish, Gypsy – depositing its own stratum on the emerging regional essence to bring deep song into being (Falla, "*Cante jondo*" 141, 146–7). Likewise, Lorca finds that Andalusia has come into being through the sedimentation of its creative past.

With his gift for painterly vision, he resorts to original pictorial mythology. The Guadalquivir, like river gods minted on ancient Greek coins, acquires a beard of pomegranate red [barbas granates], an allusion to its reddish bed, formed with fertile alluvial sediment (*PCJ* 150, l. 8). By contrast, the two rivers of Granada contain mourning [llanto] and blood [sangre], the sedimentation of tears in past wars (ll. 9–10). The Vega or lowland of Granada, where the two rivers flow, witnessed bloodshed and laments during the War of Granada (1481–92), one of the pivotal events of the Catholic Monarchs' reign. The other main happening was the discovery of the New World (Comellas, *Historia de España* 49). The third quatrain refers to this event, praising Seville for its route that takes sailboats to the sea, while Granada has only lyric sighs to row its boats. Alhambrism is present, yet underplayed and set off against personal lyric sentiment together with a positively viewed historical event, unmentioned in Lorca's adolescent poem on the rivers of Granada.

The fourth quatrain seeks appreciation of the values of the three rivers. The mighty Guadalquivir displays grandeur, making it what García-Posada calls the "great river, great king of Andalusia" [gran río, gran rey de Andalucía] of which Góngora spoke in his sonnet "A Córdoba" [To Cordoba] (152n19–22). Its architectural equivalent, the Giralda, sturdy Sevillian minaret or "high tower" [alta torre] of the poem, rises to the sky, with wind blowing amidst fertile orange groves. By contrast, the sluggish Darro and the Genil elevate "dead little towers / above the ponds."[15] Of his home city Lorca said, "Granada is like the recounting of what already happened in Seville. There is a vacuum belonging to something definitively over and done."[16] The small, towered Alhambra palace, in Lorca's opinion, has served as the aesthetic axis of all Granada. Washington Irving's *Tales of the Alhambra* (1832) helped to create the landscape inhabited by palace ghosts of valiant Moors. Falla continued the ghostly tradition in *Noches* as had the Granadan Ganivet before him and Lorca would afterwards.[17] Nevertheless, that phantasmal heritage forms a necessary part of the cultural treasure of Andalusia. Without those shadows of the past, as Lorca's poetic voice indicates, the region would lose much of its emotional legacy.

Gypsy superstition associates will-o'-the-wisps with phantoms. In the "Canción del fuego fatuo" [Song of the will-o'-the-wisp] of *El amor brujo* (1916 version), the Gypsy girl Candelas flees the ghost of her lover and sings in deep-song cadences,

> The same as will-of-the-wisp,
> Just the same it is to love.
> You flee it and it pursues you,
> You call it and it runs off.[18]

To be sure, Mario Hernández has correctly viewed Lorca's image, "a will-o'-the-wisp of screams," as a tribute to Falla,[19] and yet within this metaphor the poet expresses human vulnerability. Fragility in the universe comes across even through the strophic form, as the strophe unexpectedly breaks in half. Instead of the firm four-line stanza of the normal *copla*, the poetic voice surprisingly accords merely two verses to each of the two remaining strophes. The speaker, in the penultimate couplet, urges Andalusia to carry even the fertility and wealth of Seville out to sea.

Let us examine the configuration of the six two-line refrains following each quatrain and continuously repeated even when these *coplas* break into couplets. The first, "¡Ay, amor / que se fue y no vino!" alternates with the second, "¡Ay amor / que se fue por el aire!" in a kind of braiding pattern of a tapestry that at the end comes unravelled with despair, unlike the firmer "carpet" of music woven by Falla. The first refrain refers to Seville, where love disappears on sea-bound boats. The second refrain alludes to landlocked Granada, where love vanishes into air. Everything rhythmically passes into nothingness, from the most substantial to the most evanescent beings. We may diagram the entire pattern of the poem while designating each theme group with a descriptive label. Every reference to the Sevillian Guadalquivir will appear in bold, and every allusion to the Granadan Darro and Genil in sans serif:

Theme group 1: quatrain on presentation of the three rivers
(**Guadalquivir motif,**
Darro and Genil motif)
                    Refrain on Guadalquivir (**love disappears from Seville**)

Theme group 2: quatrain on depth of the rivers
(**Guadalquivir motif,**
Darro and Genil motif)
                    Refrain on Darro and Genil (*love disappears from Granada*)

Theme group 3: quatrain on historical uses of the rivers
(**Guadalquivir motif,**
Darro and Genil motif)
                    Refrain on Guadalquivir (**love disappears from Seville**)

Theme group 4: quatrain on values of the rivers
(**Guadalquivir motif,**
Darro and Genil motif)
                    Refrain on Darro and Genil (*love disappears from Granada*)

Theme group 5[1]: couplet on disappearance of life and worldly goods (*Darro and Genil motif*) (will-o'-the-wisp tribute to Falla)
> Refrain on Guadalquivir (**love disappears from Seville**)

Theme group 5[2]: couplet on disappearance of life and worldly goods (**Guadalquivir motif**)
> Refrain on Darro and Genil (*love disappears from Granada*)

The goods of this world have a transitory quality, as the fifteenth-century Castilian poet Jorge Manrique affirmed in a river metaphor:

Our lives are the rivers
that go off to the sea
which is our dying.
There flow the lordly fortunes
to be finished and consumed straightaway.[20]

Andalusia affirms the transience of life as the substance of art – a frequent theme of Lorca's – and transmutes this negativity into the sacred beauty of ritual.

In conclusion, seven factors make "Baladilla de los tres ríos" the synthesis of all the poetry that follows. First, it returns in synthetic fashion to the roots of *cante jondo*, like the *Fantasía bœtica* in its title and synthetic complexity. Second, like most poetry of the anthology, the "Baladilla" proceeds by *coplas* with refrains. Yet it takes formal liberties, like Falla in the *Fantasía bœtica,* to emulate the irregularities of flamenco singing and guitar playing. Third, given Lorca's love of the visual, the "Baladilla" strives for plastic evocations of the Andalusian cityscape or its rural landscape with awareness that the land affects the collective character. However, like the *Fantasía*, mawkish daughter of the earlier piece "Andaluza," the poem sometimes inserts a note of irony while underscoring human foibles. Fourth, it focuses on the Andalusian "cultural spirit" as author of universal creations, as does Falla in his 1922 pamphlet. Still, it recognizes that while Sevillian creativity gives the appearance of triumphant permanence, Granadan productivity has the look of frailty, rhythmically ritualizing tears. Lorca foregrounds Andalusian contradictoriness and human insufficiency more than Falla, yet like him avoids transitional passages between extremes of nostalgia and agitation. Fifth, melancholy, at most sporadic in Falla's *Fantasía*, pervades most of Lorca's ballad with its twin refrains on the fugacity of love. However, the poetic voice metaphorically mocks even the will-o'-the-wisp, much as scherzo-like passages in the *Fantasía bætica* contradict its underlying technical seriousness (Falla, score, measure. 29, 3). Sixth, in the ballad, East and West coexist in successive sedimentations of culture. The *Fantasía bætica* submits Indian modes and Gypsy rhythms to contemporary pianistic virtuosity, and the "Baladilla" expresses the ancient emotions of deep song with brilliant avant-garde metaphor composed of layer upon layer of meaning. Seventh, the ballad exemplifies self-conscious art at a pictorial and sentimental distance, just as do the strains of Falla's Andalusian-style compositions, among them the *Fantasía bætica*, which sets off savage rhythms and harmonies of Stravinsky and Bartók against a restrained background of Debussy and Ravel. Alambrism survives into Lorca's "Baladilla." Yet how understated and free of triteness it has become, aided by the maturing of his lyricism and by analogies with Falla's music!

3
"Poema de la siguiriya gitana": Return to the Sources of Deep Song

Falla's presence in Lorca's poetry endows it with depth, a third conceptual and intuitive dimension that it might otherwise lack. Every artistic element refers to every other. In "Poema de la siguiriya gitana" [Poem of the Gypsy siguiriya], first section of *PCJ*, Lorca develops motifs not emphasized in the introductory "Baladilla de los tres ríos," written with Falla's musical theory and practice in mind. The initial ballad offers return to the sources of deep song in the Andalusian collective character – a lesson in ethno-anthropology, poetically expressed. Awareness of the precariousness of existence, a pain without object and solution, pervades the southern Spanish ethos as viewed by Lorca, and gives rise to all genres of deep song. In his critical edition of *PCJ*, Christian de Paepe has plumbed some of its depth. From Falla's ranking of deep-song genres, he discovers that Lorca derives his first four poetic divisions, the first on the Gypsy siguiriya, the second on the soleá, the third on the saeta, and the fourth on the petenera (*PCJ* 42). Falla's historical theories on deep song, set out in personal notes, also structure the norms for the First *Cante Jondo* Contest. The siguiriya gitana, for Falla the fountainhead of all the other genres ("*Cante jondo*" 142), receives primacy in Lorca after his introductory poem "Baladilla de los tres ríos." Genres derived by Falla from the siguiriya include the soleá, to which Lorca devotes his second poetic section. The text of rules for the contest sets aside a third category, songs without guitar accompaniment, among them the saeta. De Paepe thereby explains Lorca's selection of the saeta to preside over a poetic division. Finally, since Falla distinguishes deep song from flamenco, a more recent, nineteenth-century product, and since the petenera belongs to a flamenco genre, Lorca includes a section on this song form (*PCJ* 101–2).

Still, Falla's influence extends further, covering all nine divisions of the *PCJ* and offering expressive vehicles for Lorca's own longings. He brings into play not only Falla's theory, but also his practice. If the "Baladilla" owes its main conception and inner thematic structure to an analogy with *Fantasía bætica*, similar relations to Falla's production appear in the rest of the poetry. The "Baladilla" synthesizes all units of verses coming after it, allowing unstudied relationships to and among the other poetic divisions to come to light. Andalusian life contains contradictions without transition, as reflected in its folk music. Falla's compositions often develop antitheses between longing and agitation. Analogously, in Lorca's poetry, sighs for the past, seen in Granada, clash with future-facing adventurousness, typical of Seville (see ch. 2, above). Consequently, *PCJ*, despite its depth, solves no problems and remains open-ended. Poetry on the siguiriya, the soleá, the saeta, and the petenera precedes verses about individual performers, their concerns, and the natural surroundings in which such concerns arise. With nothing resolved, the stylized exposition of the pain of living affords aesthetic enjoyment in and of itself.

Paradoxically, the enigmatic quality of Falla's and Lorca's production imparts coherence to the individual parts. To employ a visual analogy, in the mysterious Alhambra palace the eye and the mind delight in perceiving one coloured tile in the wall embellishing the Hall of the Ambassadors, echoed in another tile and still another until the whole constitutes a compact design filling the greater part of the wall enclosing the room. In a passage that Falla has copied in handwritten notes, to be found in his archive, the French poet Paul Druout, admired by him, has poetically addressed the tiles in the Alhambra as "sombres nids / De papillons et d'étincelles!" [sombre nests / of butterflies and sparks!] (121). Similarly, the seven poems on the siguiriya gitana cohere as in a nest, with the central poem focused on the dusky dancer personifying the ancient and mysterious dance. The poetic voice stresses her relationship to the Andalusian collective character, the moving force of "Baladilla de los tres ríos." This ballad, like Falla's Andalusian opera and ballet backdrops, underscores the significance of landscape in shaping the collective essence. Moreover, with Granada identified as cradle of *cante jondo*, and its most typical song said to be the siguiriya (Falla, *"Cante jondo"* 141), Lorca's section on this genre opens with a specifically Granadan landscape, embellished with the remembered warmth of Falla's company.

Miguel Cerón recounts that one night he, Lorca, and Falla climbed to a lofty outlook, the *Silla del Moro* [The Moor's chair], a hill topped with ruins behind the Alhambra. When a breeze moved olive trees in the moonlight, Lorca, with his acute powers of visual perception, exclaimed that the trees were opening and closing their branches like a fan (Gibson, *Life* 306). Likewise, in "Paisaje" [Landscape], the first poem of "Poema de la siguiriya gitana," a grove of olive trees opens and closes like a fan [abanico]. The Granadan landscape anticipates the solemn dance like a group of women fanning themselves in the circle of participating spectators. A dark sky hangs low over the olive grove, presaging the sombre rite and representing "the pregnant moments before the music actually begins" (Quance, *Contradiction* 147). Bulrushes and shadows tremble. In the olive trees overloaded with screams, a flock of birds moves long tails, perhaps resembling the *colas* or long trains of the dancers' gowns (*PCJ* 156–7). All nature augurs the event of the performance, whose hieratic character is Falla's major idea, transmitted to Lorca.

Falla influences as well the second poem of Lorca's section on the siguiriya, wherein a guitar resounds; the third, in which a scream begins the dance; and, finally, the fourth, where a contrasting silence precedes the *bailaora*'s entrance. The title of the poem "La guitarra" [The guitar] matches the subtitle of the final part of Falla's pamphlet on *cante jondo*. He esteems the instrument because "the harmonic effects that our guitarists produce *unconsciously* represent one of the wonders of natural art."[1] The performer, by surrendering himself to his skill, supposedly allows the "natural art" – the voice of the Andalusian ethos – full expression (Falla, "*Cante jondo*" 153). In lectures, Lorca confirms in more lyrical terms the desirability of such naturalness. He remarks that the Andalusian, especially the Gypsy, has a knack for purifying melody and rhythm. By eliminating what is new and superfluous, the performer can stress "what is essential" [lo esencial], the essences of the Andalusian stock so necessary to capture in cultivated art. For Lorca, the guitar has "constructed" [construido] deep song (3:221). Michael Christoforidis, an expert on guitar, comments that in Falla's judgment the instrument offers an underpinning axis for rhythm, harmony, percussion, and adornment giving direction to the genres of deep song.[2]

Lorca's poetry on the guitar strives for this orientation. For him, a good guitarist must have a "magic power to know how to sketch out or measure a siguiriya with an absolutely ageless accent."[3] In determining the accent, Lorca follows Falla's notes in presenting the siguiriya as "sung prose, destroying every sensation of metric rhythm, although in fact their literary texts are tercets or quatrains in assonant rhyme."[4] Luis García Montero concludes that in the *PCJ*, most of the poems mix rhythms and set up a melodic sequence that breaks with the number of syllables or graphic organization of the verses. A poem like "La guitarra," for example, reads like a "sung prose piece, a painfully developing monotone."[5] At most, we find cadences rhymed in assonance, following the tradition of folk music.

In "La guitarra," Lorca, amateur guitarist, imitates the sound and passion of the instrument with words. He emulates the composer Falla, following Rimsky-Korsakov, Albéniz, and Debussy, in mimicking guitar sounds with piano or other traditional orchestral instruments.[6] Renouncing metric regularity, seeking cultivated naturalness, Lorca's first four lines pair pentasyllables and heptasyllables (5–5–7–7) with assonant rhyme á-a of all even-numbered verses, each with varying syllabic lengths. Liquids, especially double trills, abound (*ll-*, *l-*, *-rr-*, *r-*, and *-r-* following *–d-*), to imitate the lambent strumming: "Empieza el *ll*anto / de *l*a guita*rr*a. / Se *r*ompen *l*as copas / de *l*a mad*r*ugada" [The guitar's lament / Is starting up. / Goblets of dawn / Break apart].

This poem, as R.A. Quance has pointed out (*Contradiction* 145), is about desire unfulfilled, a frequent theme in Lorca. However, the form this desire assumes, as Federico Bonaddio affirms, sets the yearning at a distance from the poet, under the influence of the avant-garde. The guitar transforms into "the very mouthpiece of sorrow," and through this "personification" transmits the lyric subject's insufficiency in the universe (Bonaddio, *Poetry of Self-Consciousness*, 65). Recurrence of the monotonous á-a cadence conveys the fatality of the content of the song. So does the repetition of the initial two lines of the poem, together with the parallel syntax of the third and fourth lines ("Empieza el llanto / de la guitarra. / Es inútil / callarla. / Es imposible / callarla" [The guitar's lament / Is starting up. / To silence it / is useless. / To silence it / Is impossible]). Inevitability of form matches fatality of content. Anaphora of the verb *llora* [it weeps], with its two liquids, coupled with repetition of the dark vowel *o*, produces a weeping sound that the guitar can make with soft liquid strumming and lower notes: "*Ll*o*r*a monótona / como *ll*o*r*a el agua, / como *ll*o*r*a el viento / sobre *l*a nevada" [It weeps monotony / the way water weeps, / the way wind weeps / over the snowfall] (*PCJ* 158).

Without entering into specific situations, but keeping distant, like the musical subject in Falla's "Danza lejana," while conveying Lorca's own preoccupation, the speaker translates into metaphors the content of the guitarist's song: a root sentiment of cosmic dissatisfaction. The guitar communicates impossible aspirations ("It weeps for distant things"),[7] desire for passion from the sphere of hot sterility ("Sand of the hot South / that seeks white camelias"),[8] pain without object or relief ("It weeps, an arrow without a target"),[9] a present moment of vague despair without hope for the

future ("the evening with no morning"),[10] and the death of spring reawaken-
ing to life, expressed as the first songbird in creation dead upon the branch.[11]
In other words, the guitar has the power to provide atavistic experience,
close to the beginning of time. The poem ends with a striking metaphor:
"Oh guitar!/Heart badly wounded/By five swords."[12] The instrument,
for its shape and the passion it communicates, resembles a heart injured by
five agile, well-aimed fingers. Christian de Paepe connects the swords in
the heart to primitive religious symbolism of the Virgin Mary's seven sorrows (*PCJ* 160n25–7). Underlying the symbol is the syncretic ritualism of
cante jondo, in other words, Falla's stress on deep song as a sacral rite.

A less onomatopoeic, more introspective treatment of the guitar appears in "Las seis cuerdas" [The six strings] from "Gráfico de la petenera."
Here as in "La guitarra," a prose-like irregularity prevails until mid-poem,
when ghostly hexasyllables take over. The death of a flamenco singer, the
Petenera, has inspired the elegiac guitar. The instrument, again the protagonist, "makes dreams cry,"[13] lamenting unsung songs, desires of an artist lost to the world. The "round mouth" [boca redonda] of the instrument
metamorphoses into the organ through which "the sob of lost/souls"
flees the anguish of lives lived in a daily Purgatory.[14] Translating such agitation into music might well yield Falla's "La danza del terror" (Dance of
terror) in *El amor brujo*, based on an ancient dance, the tarantula's dance,
comparable to the Italian tarantella, the jittery spider-bite dance. Yet, as
opposed to the Italian music in 6/8 time, this dance in Falla, according to
Demarquez, displays "panting repetition" [repetición jadeante] of double
eighth notes in 2/4 time, describing "the maddening of a lost soul not
knowing where to seek refuge"[15] (see musical example 6, below). Lorca's
poem, after its non-metrical beginning, ends with brief, metrically regular
lines, hexasyllables where each verse except the first contains at least two
strong accents (all written here in boldface, below). Once again, the guitar
assumes an active role, usurping the lyric "I." Like a fearful tarantula (in
Lorca's fantasy, even tarantulas spin webs), the instrument weaves a musical web, an aura vast as a star, in which to capture fleeting sighs. The sighs
float among the possibilities for liquid, dark sounds open to the instrument, the black wooden cistern of the guitar:

Y còmo la tarántula [,]
teje una gran estrella
para cazar suspiros,
que flotan en su negro
aljibe de madera.

[And just like a tarantula,
It weaves a mighty star
To capture every sigh
Afloat upon its cistern,
Night-black and made of wood.]   (*PCJ* 212)[16]

Lorca may owe Falla his appreciation not only of melodic but also of melismatic musical elements of cante jondo. Falla's pamphlet on *cante jondo* affirms that "The voices and screams with which our people encourage and excite the singers and players also originate in the custom still observed today for analogous situations in peoples of Oriental origin."[17] In *La vida breve*, the wedding guests repeatedly shout "¡Olé!" to prompt the cantaor to sing and everyone assembled to dance.[18] These calls form part of Falla's libretto and of the artwork itself.

The scream "¡Ay!" that customarily starts a cantaor's performance appears in significant works of Falla, not simply at the beginning of pieces.[19] In Lorca's "Paso de la siguiriya," two poems concern phenomena extraneous to the melody of the dance: "El grito" [The scream] and "El silencio" [The hush]. The first equates a scream with an ellipse, which de Paepe sees as a "visual depiction of the tension of the scream, an auditory phenomenon" (*PCJ* 161n1). A scream is enharmonic to an extreme. The voice rapidly slides to a high pitch and brusquely falls into silence. Here the poetic voice paints its curved geometric path in tercets without regular metre and, as in the guitar poems, gives the initiative to the sonorous agent itself: "The ellipse of a scream/Goes from hill/To hill."[20] In Lorca's lecture on deep song, following Falla, he affirms that in this art form, the musical scale emerges as a direct consequence of the range of the voice, or the "oral gamut," to employ his and Falla's words.[21] If the scream introduces a song, it expresses in music a gamut of sorrows, differing nuances of black, given metaphoric plastic form by Lorca: "The most infinitesimal gradations of Pain and Sorrow, placed at the service of the purest, most exact expression, palpitate in the tercets and quatrains of siguiriyas and their derivatives."[22] Lorca's lyric subject, guided by a love of vision, projects into the heavens a metaphorically visible musical scale, encompassing the scream and originating from the Andalusian landscape: "Coming from the olive trees/it may be a black rainbow/over the blue night sky."[23] Next appears what could be a subtle tribute to Falla. In the third movement of *Noches*, according to Suzanne Demarquez, "on p. 35, no. 1, the solemn flute sketches (...) the sway of a malagueña, stippled by the vocalization of violas."[24] Violas in Falla may imitate vibrations of vocal cords. Likewise, "El grito" compares

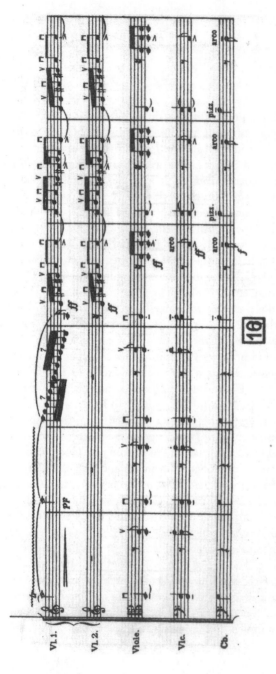

6　Falla, Tarantula's Dance, *El amor brujo*. Maestro Arbós, *Cuarto concierto de abono. Orquesta sinfónica de Madrid, año XIV*, 3rd Pt, Teatro Real, April 29, 1917, Falla's program notes. Concert program. Reproduced with gracious permission of the Archivo Manuel de Falla (Granada).

this sound to a viola player's bow, playing the wind like a vast stringed instrument. The likening of auditory to visual sensation in two references to a kind of bow – a rainbow and a musical bow – traces a vibrating rhythm on the landscape: "Like a viola bow / the scream has set long strings / of the wind aquiver."[25] Gypsies peer from their caves with passive surprise and curiosity to the scream's announcement that the siguiriya has arrived (*PCJ* 162).

A poem titled simply "¡Ay!" serves a parallel function in "Poema de la soleá," the following poetic division of *PCJ*. It prepares the arrival of the soleá, personified as a female dancer like the siguiriya. Two-line strophes on a scream alternate with two-line refrains imploring solitude for tears, perhaps modelled on the following traditional soleá:

Ar campito solo
Me boy á llorá
Como tengo yena e penas el arma
Busco soleá.

[To the lonely field
I go off to weep
since my soul is full of woes
I seek to be alone.]   (Machado y Álvarez 57)

Lorca's poetic voice sings, "Dejadme en este campo / llorando" [Leave me in this field / Weeping]. Like Falla, who stylizes Andalusian folk music by harmonizing it in accordance with contemporary European musical canons, Lorca alternates the folkloric refrain with depersonalized, avant-garde metaphors, distancing his characteristic concern with death from the first-person pronoun: "The scream leaves in the wind / the shadow of a cypress."[26] The cypress forms a synecdoche for the cemetery; the shadow stands for the essence of that funereal tree, the wind for the vehicle of that sombre essence, and the scream for the eerily autonomous stimulus that calls it forth. A similar metaphor occupies the penultimate strophe: "The unlit horizon / is bitten by bonfires."[27] In Lorca's Gypsy world of violence, lights bite the darkness, bonfires the night horizon. The central pair of verses, like an axis around which the whole poem revolves, project the problem to the cosmos and make it an impersonal expression of Lorca's sense of insufficiency. The cosmic order has failed. The scream has faded to nothingness: "All has broken down in the world / Nothing is left but silence."[28]

After a scream, absence of sound penetrates the ear in waves. If, as Protagoras holds, the human being is the measure of all things, then the human imposes a measure on sound, but also on lack of it. A rest is a measured lack of sound between notes; a silence, a lack of sound before or after a set of notes and rests that form a musical work (García Bacca 269). In "Poema de la siguiriya gitana" and in Lorca's poem "El silencio," silence receives a sacral value. Falla has taught awareness of this value in Andalusian folk music. Within Andalusian folk songs of *Siete canciones populares españolas* [Seven Spanish folk songs], rests varying in length after "¡ay!" receive careful notation by Falla in the score.[29] Similarly, Lorca's lyrical subject reveres such a hush as part of the collective ritual of *cante jondo*, fruit of the regional musical spirit: valleys and echoes move atop this silence as upon a comforting surface. The silence, as impersonal agent of the action, commands reverence, causing heads to bow. A speaker, representing the vox populi, addresses his son in verses whose irregularity approaches prose, yet whose lyricism befits the siguiriya: "Hear, my son, the silence./ It's a wavy silence,/ a silence/ in which valleys and echoes are gliding/ and which makes heads bow/ toward the ground."[30]

Falla stresses the "priestly" nature of cante jondo ("*Cante jondo*" 146n1), and Lorca's poetry presents the siguiriya as sacred. An ambiguous title heads the central poem of this section, "El paso de la siguiriya" [Passage of the siguiriya], the Andalusian genre of folk song serving as a point of reference for all others. "Paso" can signify merely the footstep of a dancer, but also a sacred image, sculpture, or acted scene representing an event in the Passion of Christ, especially during Holy Week.[31] In view of the suffering expressed by the dance and its purification through ritual, the siguiriya, personified as a dark-skinned girl bearing her pain in the form of a dagger, acquires hieratic dignity. She moves between "black butterflies,"[32] flounces of a sombre-coloured gown. Beside her slithers a "white serpent of mist,"[33] a visual poet's symbol of her sinuous movement while she struggles with the "invisible mist surrounding her,"[34] the unseen challenge she faces as a dancer to clarify the architecture of motions required by the music.

In the melody of the siguiriya gitana, Falla finds that obsessive use of a single note cancels out every sensation of metrical rhythm, despite regular versification in the text ("*Cante jondo*" 145). Lorca echoes Falla in his 1922 lecture on deep song (3:199). Therefore "El paso de la siguiriya" contains more or less octosyllabic quatrains in assonance, as well as another irregularity, the pentasyllabic refrain "Tierra de luz,/ cielo de tierra" [Land made of light/ Sky made of land]. In this refrain, Lorca's sense of cosmic insufficiency receives impersonal expression once again. Creative Andalusia, land of sunlight, is fated to an afterlife symbolized by a sky [cielo] made of earth [tierra], dust, nothingness, nullifying all endeavours (*PCJ* 164). Additional metric quirks mark these *coplas* with refrains: the first quatrain ends with a broken foot of three syllables ("junto a una blanca serpiente/ de niebla") [beside a white serpent/of mist], conveying the broken musical rhythm of the siguiriya. The second quatrain finishes with a heptasyllable, "y un puñal en la diestra" [and a dagger in her right hand], to stress a threat to the dancer's "corazón de plata" [silver heart]. As in a *paso* for Holy Week, the dancer imitates the Virgin of Sorrows, depicted in Spain with seven swords in her heart.

The poetic voice alludes to rhythmic irregularity, defying listener expectations and forming an essential attribute of the siguiriya: the dusky dancer "goes along chained to the tremor/of a rhythm that never arrives."[35] Moreover, the speaker expresses the dancer's submission to her art, her surrender of full conscious control to some larger force for which she serves as medium – Falla and Lorca often refer to an Andalusian "cultural spirit." In question form, expecting no answer to emerge from a performer in an artistic trance, the speaker asks, "Where are you going, siguiriya,/with a headless rhythm?"[36] The poem concludes with another rhetorical question, introducing a note of magic, of folk superstition, with the moon perceived as a vampire, sucking up its victim's blood – in this case, the dancer's ever-renewed pain, made of quicklime to speed decay, and of oleander to embitter the tongue: "What moon will gather up/Your pain made of quicklime and oleander?"[37] In harmony with the Gypsy practice of magic, Falla finds the siguiriya suitable for enchantments with its obsessive repetition of a single note ("*Cante jondo*" 145), here reflected in Lorca's use of terse, repetitive refrains in four out of seven poems making up this section.[38]

Two brief pieces – "Después de pasar" [After she has passed by] and "Y después" [And after that]) – show the emotional aftermath of the siguiriya. Silence follows music. Sombre after the rite, children and the sierra itself – the Andalusian nature with which they live in harmony – nostalgically contemplate a distant point. In his 1922 lecture on cante jondo, Lorca remarks that cantaores sing while dazzled by a brilliant point on the horizon (3:215), the distant object of their desire. This is the same point on which the dancer's spectators focus after her departure in the poetry. Oil lamps go out, superfluous in view of the light emitted by the distant point. Blind maidens in the dark address questions to the moon, perhaps savouring the dancer's final echoes as they look upward with eyes closed, or else, as is more likely, directing new songs skyward. Spirals of laments rise to the heavens (*PCJ* 167). Many objects invented by the *bailaora* [dancer] disappear with her, offering a sense of the futility of her art: mazes created by time – her labyrinthine movements in her temporal art; the heart, source of desire; and the futile hope for dawn and love (169). Her absence leaves a sterile desert behind, wavy like the sands and like the silence that preceded her (169).

In summary, seeking to sanctify the ancient dance, Lorca joins Falla in opposing the Germanic tendency dominating European concert halls to overlook all music treasures prior to Bach (Falla, *Escritos* 40). "Poema de la siguiriya gitana" follows a linear path like the siguiriya itself, with its "undulating, interminable melody" [melodía ondulante e inacabable] so different from the "round," repeated phrases of Bach, whose counterpoint brings back melodies in endless self-reflections. "But the melody of the siguiriya," continues Lorca, "gets lost in a horizontal direction, it slips through our hands, and we see it move into the distance toward a point of common aspiration and perfect passion from which the soul is incapable of disembarking."[39]

The point here mentioned symbolizes a painful privation, the unattainable goal of the performer's desire, ever present in Lorca's verse from the landscape of fan-waving olive trees to the scenes of nostalgia following the dancer's departure. Yet in every case, oriented by the avant-garde, he strives for impersonal expression of that desire through multiple means – personification of guitars, visualization of screams, materialization of silences, representation of pain as a dancer with a dagger, and the dematerialization of her art.

4

"Poema de la soleá": Consciousness-Raising of Pain in Lorca and Falla

"Poema de la soleá" [Poem of the soleá], the second poetic division of *PCJ*, parallels the first, "Poema de la siguiriya gitana" [Poem of the Gypsy siguiriya]. Both begin with Andalusian landscapes, offer verses on screams preceding the dance, and introduce female personifications of the dance in the central poem. In Lorca an arabesque emerges with direct links between its components. The poet remarks, perhaps with his own art in mind, "The arabesque tradition in the Alhambra palace, complicated and covering little space, weighs heavily on all the great artists of that land [Granada]."[1] In Lorca's poem, an interlocking of disparate elements occurs through repetition in the third and fourth parts as well, as in the geometry of the Alhambra and in the thematic interlacing of Falla's Andalusian-style pieces, with their limited melodic range.

However, of all parts of the *PCJ*, the one on the soleá moves not forward like the siguiriya, but inward like the human soul in the mystic poetry of Saint John of the Cross. The siguiriya presented the pain of deep song to the world, but the soleá, introverted, emphasizes becoming aware of that pain. A rare, reflective passage from Falla's ballet *El sombrero de tres picos*, marked *Tranquillo*, can clarify. The Miller's Wife, unjustly separated from her husband, contemplates her loneliness in a soleá of twelve measures with a modal legato melody that alternately rises and falls four times in a melancholy breathing rhythm.[2]

Lorca, uneasy about fixed gender roles, often translated loneliness into lyricism. Yet he knew that the pain of solitude increases in art that lacks geographical specificity. The surroundings provide company, however tenuous, to the lonely. In "Poema de la soleá," absence of a given place focuses the reader more on the sufferer, the dancer, and less on the setting.

The lonely sufferer in her selfhood stands further apart from the author as well. Unlike "Poema de la siguiriya," anchored in Granada, "Poema de la soleá" applies both to Upper and Lower Andalusia (*PCJ* 172nn5–6). Falla too wrote soleares to be performed by his characters situated anywhere in Spain.[3]

Besides avoiding geographic confines, "Poema de la soleá" leaves time unspecified. Neither the first poem of the section, an untitled one beginning "Tierra seca/tierra quieta" [Dry land/Quiet land], nor the second, titled "Pueblo" [Village], contains a finite verb (Karageorgou-Bastea, *Arquitectura* 129). The poetic subject concentrates on pain associated with the music, not on spatio-temporality. Eyes stay shut in song, dance, or audition, and only arrows of pain make themselves perceived: "Land/of death without eyes/ and [land] of arrows."[4] The manner and posture proper for listening to music consists of absorbing it with closed eyes. Listeners with "ears conscious of hearing" are behaving as "operatives and active agents of the fact that what is musical (...), audible, is being heard in the act" of performance.[5]

In Lorca's poetry, music assumes pre-eminence, shunting aside the specificity of the ambiance. The bivalent title of the poem "Pueblo," lacking concreteness, may refer in Spanish either to any typical Andalusian village or to the Andalusian people in general, needing to purge its pain creatively. Lorca moves directly to the main theme of loneliness with no introduction, just as Falla does in the orchestrated soleá of *Sombrero*. In Lorca's poem, sober and simple, expressing desolation in a less personal fashion than we find in Falla's Andalusianist art, crosses top a bald mound of earth, a *calvario* or hallowed ground denoting Christ-like pain suffered in solitude. Age-old trees irrigated by clear ditches line the fields in a typical Andalusian natural setting. Through narrow streets, men with faces hidden assert their right to be alone. The Andalusian dialectical form soleá denotes *soledad*, solitude. Atop village towers, weathervanes spin, expressing the ephemeral quality of this art form, floating in the wind, awaiting the nuance of each generation and subject to "an ideal weathervane that changes direction with the air of the Time."[6] Out of this timeless, spaceless song on loneliness emerges a collective sentiment of pain in the past (the crosses), present (the disguised men), and future (the whirling weathervanes). The poem closes with a verbal sigh inspired by collective anguish, as reflected in the hillock of crosses mentioned at the start: "Oh village [or people] lost/in the Andalusia of mourning!"[7]

Reading the intimacy of these human monads poses little challenge. Caught up in solitary pain inspiring deep song and dance, they repel one another. In the poem "Encuentro" [Encounter], its title notwithstanding, dancers of the soleá are choreographed to shun human company. Male jealousy may form the pretext. The theme comes into play in Falla's pantomime *El corregidor y la molinera*, debuted in Madrid in 1917, and revised into the ballet *El sombrero de tres picos*, with its world premiere in 1919,[8] only two years before the composition of most of *PCJ*. Although Falla's source, the novelist P.A. de Alarcón, had portrayed his jealous miller as a hunchback, the choreographer Léonide Massine of the Ballets Russes danced that character as a manly youth.[9] With his talent as a dramatist, Lorca, who knew *Sombrero* as well as Massine's art,[10] seems to stage an original, highly stylized confrontation between two ardent rivals for a woman's love. The poetic subject, like another Massine, choreographs and participates in the interaction with the enemy. The meeting produces embarrassment. In lines of assonance without regular metre, like those on the siguiriya gitana, the speaker reads his foe's intent, corresponding to his own. Although their paths have crossed before the beginning of the poem, he remarks at the start and the end, "Neither you nor I are / in a mood / to meet."[11] The reason offered shows silent communication between the two, proper to the pantomime of ballet, and mutual awareness of all that has happened before: "You … for what you know full well. / Me … I have loved her so!"[12] The addressee seems to have perpetrated some unspeakable, and unspoken, offence against the speaker involving a woman he loves. As a consequence, the offended individual, afflicted by the unfulfilled love common to so many of Lorca's dramatic plots, has had to endure Christ-like suffering, which he displays as in a ballet pantomime by holding up his hands for his adversary to see: "On my hands / I have the holes / of the nails. / Can't you see how / I am bleeding?"[13]

The speaker gives four commands, all requiring visual actions and perfectly capable of being gracefully mimed. Like Massine, he continues on, both as choreographer and lead dancer. First, he would send his rival away in a particular direction: "Follow that little path."[14] Second, he would forbid him from looking over his shoulder: "Don't dare look back".[15] Third, he would keep him on his guard by having him depart gradually in case the speaker loses his serenity and seeks vengeance: "Walk away slowly".[16] Finally, he urges him to pray to Saint Cajetan, "Father of Providence," to promote looking ahead and not behind.[17]

In several of Lorca's poems, awareness of pain, the main theme of this section, assumes the oft-repeated image of a dagger entering the heart, associated with the seven swords in the Virgin's heart. The poem "Encrucijada" [Crossroads] reduces this lyrical violence to geometric abstractness. As in

"Pueblo," the reduction entails the elimination, at least at first, of finite verbs to delete concrete temporality. At the end, a rare first-person pronoun suddenly appears to accentuate the pain:

Viento del Este;
un farol
y el puñal
en el corazón.
La calle
tiene un temblor
de cuerda
en tensión,
un temblor
de enorme moscardón.
Por todas partes
Yo
veo el puñal
en el corazón.

[East Wind;
A streetlamp
And the dagger
In the heart.
The street
Is atremble like
A string
Tensed to play,
Atremble like
A huge botfly.
Everywhere
I
see the dagger
In the heart.]   (PCJ 177–8)

The East Wind may refer to the essence of the Orient, source, according to Falla, of deep song. With precision, the gaslight marks the exact spot of the stabbing, where all roads converge, as upon the scene of a crime. Finally, the speaker may be identifying her own heart as the target of the weapon, if not someone else's: the text does not specify. Punctuating the entire poem, like open-mouthed exclamations, come rhymed cadences of deep, accented o's in the even-numbered lines: *farol, corazón, temblor, tensión, moscardón, yo, corazón* [streetlamp, heart, trembling, tension, botfly, I, heart]. Comparable in verbal intensity, and amassing stressed o's, is the anagnorisis in Falla's opera *La vida breve,* where the horrified heroine Salud discovers her lover Paco's infidelity, a revelation that costs the girl her life out of grief. As a playwright attentive to Falla's libretti,[18] Lorca may well have observed the dramatic efficacy of the rounded vowel. In a short recitative with harmonies in a minor key, the soprano playing Salud at times makes vocal leaps of an octave ("Separ**ao**" [separated, referring to faithless Paco]; "**Dios**," the invocation of God's name). Verbal denials, also with stressed **o**, are accompanied by strings balanced against woodwinds: "¡Paco! ¡Paco! ¡No! ¡No! ¡No!/ (con angustia) ¡Qué fatiga!/ ¡Qué *doló*!/ Unas veces se me para/ y **o**tras veces se dispara/como l**o**co mi coraz**ó**n" [Paco! Paco! No! No! No!/ (With anguish) How wearying!/ How painful!/ Sometimes stopping,/ Sometimes starting/ Like mad goes my heart].[19]

In Lorca's poem the whole street trembles like the string of a musical instrument, perhaps the quivering bowstring of a guitar, if not of violins in Falla's orchestrated Andalusian compositions. By restricting the aesthetic universe to a mere street intersection or crossroads ("Encrucijada"), the poetic subject concentrates great pain into a single geographic point. For its sting, persistence, mournfully low buzz, and fleshy oscillation, the trembling in the poem repels like a "huge botfly." Awareness of the pain culminates at the end, where the speaker takes the floor and sacrifices spatial precision imposed by the traumatic event to the intensity of the anguish, geographically boundless: "Everywhere/I/see the dagger/in the heart."

In another poem, "Sorpresa" [Surprise], consciousness of pain attains a new threshold. As Ortega y Gasset remarks, "To be surprised, to be astonished, is to begin to understand."[20] Awareness starts here. Accordingly, the poem begins *in medias res*, with no introduction, with a brusqueness as "usual with Falla" (Trend, *Falla* 78) as it is with Lorca: "Muerto se quedó en la calle/con un puñal en el pecho./No lo conocía nadie" [He lay dead in the street,/a dagger in his breast./He was known to no one] (*PCJ* 181). These three verses gather force through repetition at the end of the poem, with each line preceded at the end by a percussive, untranslatable conjunction "que,"[21] as if to punctuate that ending with a musically emphatic, Falla-like coda.[22] In mid-poem a spare elegiac notation of time and place, also repeated for emphasis, accompanies the shocking death: at dawn a street light trembled (as if agitated). A dream-like, nightmarish atmosphere arises, comparable less to the eeriness of the phantom's scenes in *El amor brujo* than to the defamiliarization staged by seventeenth-century playwright Pedro Calderón de la Barca in *La vida es sueño* [Life is a dream], act I, sc. 4. The surprised Clotaldo's heart advises him that Rosaura is his own child whom he has never met before, yet may have to execute. His heart, feeling like a prisoner in his breast, "va a los ojos a asomarse,/que son ventanas del pecho/por donde en lágrimas sale" [goes to look out of the eyes,/which are windows of the breast/through which it comes out in tears] (101, ll. 413–25). With a similar metaphor in poet-dramatist Lorca's poem, the witness of violence shows acute awareness of the victim's sudden and surprising loss of identity through pain: "Nadie/pudo asomarse a sus ojos/abiertos al duro aire" [Nobody/was able to look out of his eyes,/open to the harsh air] (*PCJ* 182). This "nobody" is the victim's heart.

Beginning brusquely like Falla's pieces, the following poem, "La soleá" [The soleá], brings a dancer onstage in black mourning clothes and personifying the dance of solitude itself. This poem is the centrepiece of its whole poetic section like the "Paso de la siguiriya" [Passage of the siguiriya] in the first section. Moreover, in the same way that Lorca, in search of depth, produces an echoing mosaic effect between the parts of the *Poema del cante jondo*, so he aims for rippling auditory and visual echoes within the present poem. The dancer's solemn attire receives mention four times throughout the brief, thirteen-line work to drive home her growing awareness of pain, as in deep song the melody always returns to the same note. The first line, "Vestida con mantos negros" [Dressed in black garments] (*PCJ* 183), without ever mentioning a subject, becomes detached as a refrain set between each of three three-line strophes in assonance. She loses her identity in her pain, purged through her art.

In deep song the soleá enjoys a "tremendous diversity of forms" (Miller, *Lorca's PCJ* 29). Accordingly, Lorca may well have borrowed his ternary strophic form, interrupted by brief refrains, from the cantaor's soleá, interrupted by the spectators' encouraging cries of "¡Olé!" in the wedding scene of *La vida breve* (act 2, tableau 1, sc. 1, rehearsals 103–10, 31). Falla's soleá itself stems from musical scores that he modified of popular *soleares* (García Matos, "*Vida breve*" 188–9). However, in Lorca, by contrast with Falla, every strophe presents deepening anguish. In the first strophe, linking this poem to the previous one through a common theme (in Lorca, the anguished heart), the dancer mentally compares her heart, seat of boundless pain, to the cosmos, unfeeling and hence limited: "She thinks the world is tiny/and her heart is immense."[23] Disregarding the immensity of this sorrow, the wind of the second strophe wafts away sighs and screams, as did the water in "Baladilla de los tres ríos." In the third strophe, the cosmos reacts to the anguished dancer, annihilating her. The sky enters at dawn through the open balcony and engulfs her like a river flowing to its mouth: "The balcony was left open / and through the balcony at dawn / the whole sky flowed right in."[24] Here recurs the fluvial imagery of "Baladilla de los tres ríos," where rivers symbolize the Andalusian creative principle. The dancer has surrendered her identity to the "cultural spirit" enveloping her. The river image of the present poem recalls the refrain of the parallel poem "El paso de la siguiriya," with an anguished dancer inhabiting a land of light under a "sky made of earth."[25] With her loss of identity in view, the final refrain of "La soleá" modulates as the poetic voice intercalates a prolonged scream, common, according to Falla, in Oriental music and affording the atavistic shudder of contact with elemental grief: "Ay yayayayay, / she was dressed in black garments."[26]

In Lorca the agitation of the soleá yields at times to vague nostalgia, in accordance with the two antipodes typifying Andalusian music (Pahissa 102). The poem "Cueva" [Cave] exemplifies nostalgia and the impact of Falla. The work unfolds in a cave like those of the Gypsies of *El amor brujo*. A Gypsy cantaor evokes "remote countries," which in Falla would refer to the Eastern roots of deep song. The singer concentrates on his voice, with its enharmonic intervals and broken rhythms: "Into his emotion-choked voice / go his eyes."[27] In "Surprise" the street lamp trembled as if in terror, but here the cave interior trembles nostalgically in the soft gold of candlelight. In most of the even-numbered two-lined strophes, however, a jarring series of colour contrasts comes to the fore, inserting an avant-garde note of expressionism in an otherwise traditional setting: livid against red (str. 2), black against red (str. 6), white against red (str. 8). These antitheses present in visual form, compatible with Lorca's sensitivity, the pain of living life as a contrast – the opposition between sordid present and mythic past, the confinement of the cave as opposed to the freedom of "high towers and mysterious / men" of ages gone by.[28]

The "Poema de la soleá" closes with a lyrical piece expressing catharsis, cleansing more congenial to Falla's art. Just as in *El amor brujo* the orchestra imitates joyous morning church bells at the end of a night of phantasmal horrors, so here calming bells, mentioned at the beginning and the end of the poem titled "Alba" [Dawn], ring out after the previous flood of anguish. In Falla's libretto appear the words "Las campanas del amanecer" [Bells of dawn].[29] These words and their placement at the end of Falla's ballet could well have inspired Lorca's conclusion of this division of his book: "Campanas de Córdoba / en la madrugada. / Campanas de amanecer /

en Granada" [Bells of Cordoba / in the early morning. / Bells of dawn / in Granada].[30] From the beginning to the end of the "Poema de la soleá," therefore, geographical concreteness has vanished as the dance has become a consciousness-raising exercise. The final verses on the bells present young girls from Upper and Lower Andalusia alike, uniting to mourn the tender dancer of *soleares* dressed in black. These maidens lend their moderating purity to the recent unmitigated outpouring of pain. Holding candles, with skirts lit by the flickering, feet apt for the dance, they converge at the crossroads of Andalusia: "The girls of Spain / with tiny feet / and trembling skirts / who have filled the crossroads / full of lights."[31]

The renunciation of solitude, the gathering for a religious rite as a tacit tribute to the Andalusian ethos, makes an apposite transition from "Poema de la soleá" to "Poema de la saeta." The third section of the *Poema del cante jondo*, to be examined in the next chapter, centres on the oblation of the sufferer's pain to the Virgin and her Son. The event occurs no longer in an unspecified locale of Andalusia, but in Seville during Holy Week in the form of a saeta, an arrow of song. This spontaneous artwork, unaccompanied by instruments, is aimed by a pious singer from a balcony at early dawn at an image of the Virgin passing beneath. The first poem, "Arqueros" [Archers], refers either to pilgrims on their way to Seville to aim saetas like arrows, or to Cupid-like lovers seeking mates. Their points of origin, "The remote countries of sorrow,"[32] signify distant nations like the Oriental sources of *cante jondo*. Their destination, "a maze. / Love, crystal, and stone,"[33] expresses the temporal maze formed by the music of deep song, often stemming from frustrated love, clear and simple as crystal, while hard and crushing to the heart as stone. The two-word refrains allude four times in regular intervals to the Guadalquivir, echoing "Baladilla de los tres ríos," or the expression of the grounding of deep song in the Andalusian "cultural spirit." After the first and third two-line strophes on the archer-pilgrims there appears the refrain "Guadalquivir abierto" [Open Guadalquivir], perhaps alluding to the heart of the Andalusian city in its openness to the musical arrows of love aiming towards it. Likewise, after the second and fourth couplets on the archers comes the refrain "¡Ay, Guadalquivir!" an anticipation of the pain of love as the arrow penetrates its target (*PCJ* 192–3). Hence the speaker, who has stressed the solipsism and closure of anguish in "Poema de la soleá," now focuses on its transitiveness and openness in "Poema de la saeta," as the following chapter will show.

5

"Poema de la saeta":
The Oblation of Pain in Seville

Sevillian-born modernist poet Manuel Machado ranks the saeta at the apex of deep song. The religious quality of that genre, he finds, does not deny its Gypsy roots. Unaccompanied except for street sounds of Seville on Holy Week nights, this music employs commonplaces of deep song like love, death, pain, and motherhood. However, in this festive context, Machado observes that love is divine, and the mother the Virgin.[1] To paraphrase the poet, whatever passion an individual singer experiences – a failed love, death of a loved one – that artist sublimates such passion, offering it up to honour the suffering Christ or his mother. Lorca raises the tone of the fourth poetic section of *Poema del cante jondo* to exaltation.

Still, the result must have cost him effort. Granadan journalist José Mora Guarnido reports the decadence of the saeta in the early 1920s: "Only in the mystical/profane bacchanal of Holy Week in Seville could the saeta still barely be heard, a pathetic musical lament of Christ's death, but even the saeta had suffered the influences of flamenco degeneration."[2] Falla agreed. In April 1922, during Holy Week spent in Seville with the Lorca brothers Federico and Francisco, while searching the streets for genuine old saetas, the composer told Mexican poet and historian Alfonso Reyes that in that city flamenco had corrupted the genre (Armero, *Manuel de Falla* 156). Perhaps because of its Catholic content, threatened by secularism in Seville, the devout Falla had made no mention of the saeta in his 1922 brochure El *"cante jondo" (Canto primitivo andaluz)*, although that song form does appear in the norms of the deep-song contest as an example of an unaccompanied entry.

Yet how could Lorca, a favourer of the underclasses, have neglected, for instance, the *martinete*, genre of blacksmiths and prisoners? This song type, also unaccompanied by instruments, appeared beside the saeta in the

contest rules. His preference for the saeta probably stemmed from its special link to Seville, Spain's third largest city and Andalusia's most populous
and enterprising. Lorca might have realized, as perhaps Falla had not, that
by limiting the Granadan deep-song contest to amateurs to eliminate commercialism, the organizers would have slighted professional performers
from Seville. Therefore, when composing most of his poems for *PCJ* in
November 1921 with the idea of publishing the work in time for the mid-
June 1922 competition (*Epistolario* 1:48–9), he wanted the publication to
express pan-Andalusianism. "Baladilla de los tres ríos" concerned the
Guadalquivir of Seville as well as the Darro and Genil of Granada. Falla
too recognized Seville's significance for deep song, because along with
Lorca he loved to talk about this folk music and its best-known perform-
ers in the *tertulia* held at the home of their friend Fernando Vílchez
(Gibson, *Life* 109). Further, Falla knew Lorca's pan-Andalusian aspirations: in his handwritten dedication of the 1921 score of *El amor brujo*, the
composer put, "To the Poet of the Andalusias [i.e., the Upper and the
Lower], Federico García Lorca, from his true friend, Manuel de Falla,
Granada, 28 November 1921."[3]

All participants in the *tertulia* conversed about the greatest flamenco
singers, dancers, and guitarists, and knew full well the significance of
Seville. The cantaor Silverio Franconetti (1831–89), called by Lorca "the
last Pope of *cante jondo*,"[4] had been born in Seville and died there in his
own café. The songstress Pastora Pavón (1890–1969),[5] nicknamed "the
Girl of the Combs," was also native to Seville and became a notable flamenco recording star. Manuel Torre (1878–1933), though born in Jerez de
la Frontera, resided and would die in Seville. Revered for his siguiriyas and
saetas, he was lionized by Lorca and other writers of his generation, especially Rafael Alberti and Ignacio Sánchez Mejías (Alberti, *Lorca* 124–6).
Urged at the last minute by Falla's friend, the painter Ignacio Zuloaga,
guitarist Amalio Cuenca persuaded flamenco professionals in Seville like
Torre, the well-known dancer Juana "La Macarrona," and the guitarist
Juan "El de Alonso" to perform in Granada at the *cante jondo* contest in
June (Molina Fajardo 110–11). In summary, the saeta formed Lorca's musi-
cal pretext for praising the importance of Seville in the history of deep song.

To that end, he gleaned a major idea from Falla, who had Hispanized the
French thinker Louis Lucas's philosophy of music and maintained that
deep song imitates the natural order. As an enharmonic musical genre,
whereby the voice or the instrument glides through intervals excluded by
the rigid Western tempered scale, *cante jondo* mimics "birdsong, animal
screams, and the infinite noises of matter."[6] Now, the universe as a whole

forms a hybrid of what is natural and what is artificial: "The natural universe has not been made such *by* the human being nor *for* the human being,
while the world (…) of sounds has been made, invented, *by* the human and
for the human." Therefore, the "natural" human differs from ourselves as
"supra-natural" human beings the way that the bird does from the airplane,
and thunder from the musical notation *fortissimo* (*fff*).[7] Early twentieth-
century primitivism fantasized the reconstruction of art as perceived by the
"natural" man. Stravinsky, Bartók, Falla, and other composers appreciated
atavism as a musical value, an artistic convention, and this primitivism explains Falla's interest in promoting the *cante jondo* contest in the first place.
Accordingly, Lorca converted the saeta of Seville's Holy Week into a kind
of musical return to nature. The city harmonized culture and nature. In
Lorca's metaphorical fantasy, she even became a primitivist artist herself.

   During Holy Week as portrayed by Lorca, nature and culture blend.
Instead of avoiding spatio-temporality as in "Poema de la soleá," the poet
with his keen visual powers resolved to stress concrete natural features of
Seville and of her most characteristic festival. In the poem "Noche," fireflies accompany candle and lantern lights, forming "the constellation of
the saeta," a nocturnal parade of luminous participants in the procession
that will culminate in the saeta.[8] A constellation is a human construction
that connects natural lights in the sky. The procession discovers a new closeness to nature. At dawn, human and natural lights remain in harmony:
golden windows tremble in the sunlight; crosses superimposed on the
dawn seem to rock as the participants move forward (*PCJ* 194).

   In the poem "Sevilla," art and nature fuse. The poetic voice calls Seville
a city that spies on long rhythms, entwining them like mazes – the temporal mazes of deep song seen previously – and twisting them like burning,
intoxicating stems of grapevines, a Dionysian image. Since Seville lives in
tune with nature, the turn of a melody there conforms to the spiralling of
a vine. Art emulates nature. Holy Week, a time of devotion for some in
Seville, becomes for others an occasion for carousing. The city's lifeblood
– the Guadalquivir – partakes both of nature and art: beneath the bow
[arco] of her sky, over her sun-washed plane, Seville shoots the arrow of
song, the saeta of her river. This archery makes the city herself a cantaora
with a calling for folk music. With a horizon open to boundless possibilities, into her wine she mixes the bitterness of Don Juan,[9] never-sated
human masculinity, with the perfection of the wine god Dionysus, in-
toxicated god of natural vitality. The refrain contrasting activity with passivity, "Sevilla para herir / Córdoba para morir" [Seville, apt for wounding /
Cordoba, apt for dying], insists at least four times on Seville's ability to

hit the mark (*PCJ* 195–6): no city serves better either for saeta-singing or for lovemaking.

The procession with images of the Virgin and Christ, targets of saetas, grows gradually visible in two poems, "Procesión" [Religious procession] and "Paso" (here translatable as a scene from the Passion of Christ). The lyric voice, ever seeking disguises for greater distance, assumes a child's viewpoint, a perspective consistent with Lorca's vision of Seville as a primitivist artist, a creative being naturalizing culture. The poet regards children as pieces of nature, endowed with limitless imagination.[10] Open to the emerging Spanish musical classics of his day, Lorca would have known the child's image of a festival in Seville set to music by Albéniz, famed for his suite *Iberia*. If Lorca gathered conceptions for his poetry from Falla's music, he could easily have treated Falla's forerunner and friend in the same fashion.[11] The most celebrated piano solo of Albéniz's suite *Iberia* is "Fête-Dieu à Seville" [Corpus Christi in Seville]. This piece, mostly consisting of variations on a traditional children's song, paints a festival in Seville from the standpoint of a nostalgic spectator recalling childlike impressions, if not from the viewpoint of the child himself.

The work musically describes a processional band from afar, slowly nearing, then receding. First the piano in the treble imitates three drum rolls (mm. 1–8), which could well signal the approach of the distant parade. Next the instrument in a staccato march time softly plays the child's nursery rhyme "La Tarara" (mm. 9–16: see musical example 7) – a piece which Lorca too has transcribed from oral sources (*Obras completas* 2:1181–2) (see musical example 8). The melody repeats in several different variations, each one with more use of pedal, perhaps symbolizing greater closeness to the listener. A hymn-like melody grounded on three ascending notes resounds in the base, marked fortissimo (**ffff**), with the treble retaining the continued staccato of "La Tarara" (mm. 84–5). The development of the three-note melody passes from *fortissimo* (m. 117) to *pianissimo* (m. 135), where the composer has indicated *doux, mais sonore et très vague* [sweet, but sonorous and very vague]. Perhaps a sacred image has come and gone, with the voices of devout witnesses sweetly and longingly trying to cling to it.[12] Analogously, Lorca presents a stationary spectator's reaction to a moving object of devotion as it approaches. The closer it comes, the more excitement it generates.

In Lorca's poem "Procesión," stressing visual sensations and metamorphosis, a childlike witness sprinkles ever more fanciful imaginings over an approaching religious procession. Penitents with heads covered by long pointed white hoods bear an image of Christ crucified:

7 Albéniz, "Fête-Dieu à Seville," measures 9–16.

Por la calleja vienen
extraños unicornios.
¿De qué campo,
de qué bosque mitológico?
Más cerca,
ya parecen astrónomos.
fantásticos Merlines
y el Ecce Homo,
Durandarte encantado.
Orlando furioso.

[Through the narrow street
Come odd unicorns.
From what field,
From what mythological wood?
From closer up,
They look like astronomers.
Imaginary Merlins

8 *Lorca*, transcription of *"La Tarara"* with harmonic arrangement by Emilio de Torre. Reproduced with generous permission of the Heirs of Federico García Lorca.

And the image of the Crucified,
Durandarte bewitched.
Orlando the Furious.]

(*PCJ* 197–8)

Perceived from a distance, the pointy hoods make their wearers resemble unicorns never seen in storybooks as these figures emerge from unknown fields or mythological forests. When seen from less distance, the mythical beasts change into "astrónomos," a word which de Paepe construes as Lorca's error (197n6). Could he have meant instead "astrólogos" with pointed, star-sprinkled caps? Whatever the response, a child or a naive spectator might not distinguish one difficult tetrasyllable from another while the poem gathers delicious polyvalence. With the same agile fantasy, the lyrical voice links the "astronomers" with "imaginary Merlins," sorcerors with pointed caps in tales of chivalry.

As the image of Christ appears, the childlike lyrical subject gives free reign to his natural imaginative powers. Christ becomes associated with Durandarte from chivalric romance, and Durandarte implicitly with Cervantes's Don Quixote and explicitly with Ariosto's Orlando the Furious.[13] All three, Christ, Durandarte, and Orlando, form alter egos of Don Quixote. Miguel de Unamuno, a philosopher-poet highly esteemed by Lorca, sees "Our Lord Don Quixote," with all his self-doubts, as the embodiment of the tragic soul of the Spanish people.[14] Like Unamuno's Christ – and Unamuno himself – Don Quixote suffers because of lingering doubts about his own immortality, and so do Unamuno's people (Unamuno, Sentimiento trágico 470). In Cervantes's novel, Durandarte mysteriously comes to life – resurrected like Christ – long enough to raise his own doubts about Don Quixote's heroism (Cervantes, Quijote, 2, ch. 23, 732–5). Durandante resembles Don Quixote in his powerlessness to serve his beloved Belerma, just as Don Quixote fails to do service to his lady Dulcinea.[15] Finally, Orlando the Furious is another alter ego of the Manchegan knight. Like him, he has gone mad out of love for his lady (Angelica), and like Don Quixote has fared poorly in love.[16]

The fantasies of Lorca's lyrical subject do not stop here. In the Holy Week procession poetically sketched by him, behind the image of Christ crucified comes the image of the Virgin of Solitude, borne on the shoulders of the faithful. The short poem devoted to her has the title "Paso" and parallels "El paso de la siguiriya" [Passage of the siguiriya] from Lorca's first poetic subdivision and "La soleá" from the second. However, as distinguished from the personifications of the siguiriya and the soleá, this Sevillian Virgin has strong natural symbolism, as does every main image here associated with the city. Moved by the naturalness of the city, devout Sevillians dress the Virgin in a costume that a childlike lyric subject likens to an inverted flower corolla:

Virgen con miriñaque,
Virgen de la Soledad,

abierta como un inmenso
tulipán.

[Virgin with hoopskirt,
Virgin of Solitude,
open like an immense
tulip.]   (*PCJ* 199–200)

According to Christian de Paepe, the poetic voice, on representing the
Virgin aboard a "barco de luces" [boat of lights], refers to a pedestal stand
with wax tapers, rocking on the shoulders of the devout (*PCJ* 199).
Nevertheless, navigational and marine metaphor may allude, as in the
"Baladilla de los tres ríos," to the spiritual grounding of the city in its
Andalusian cultural community, which has sanctified this Virgin. Her
"boat of lights" moves through the "high tide" of the city – waves of wor-
shippers – while crossing the "river of the street" to the "sea" of human
finality (*PCJ* 199n5) in Manrique's terms, certainly implicit here. The
community has appropriated that Virgin for its citizens to accompany
them until their last day.

In return, Sevillians dedicate saetas to her and her son. Lorca's poem
"Saeta" is an oblation of the singers' personal pain to an agonizing image
of Christ during Holy Week. Previously, the Virgin was compared to a
tulip. Here, however, the lyric subject marks Christ's passage from one
floral symbol to another. Both symbols, forming part of the folk tradition,
point to its naturalness. Both denote a different aspect of Christ's suffering. Yet the first image – the "clavel de España" [the carnation of Spain] –
more clearly designates the nationalization of his passion than the second
– the "lirio de Judea" [lily of Judea]. In popular Spanish religious devotion,
the lily of Judea, according to de Paepe, stands for Christ flagellated; the
Spanish carnation, for Christ agonizing, bloody.[17] The poetic voice stresses
the nationality of this Christ as it had in the poem "Procesión," which
implicitly linked Christ to Don Quixote. Southern Spain possesses a "cielo
limpio y oscuro" [clean, dark sky] (*PCJ* 202), one so sunlit, that even to
Andalusian poet Juan Ramón Jiménez it has appeared black: "¡Qué miedo
el azul del cielo! / ¡Negro!" [How frightful the blue of the sky! / Black!]
(171). The luminous sky produces a "scorched soil" [tierra tostada] (*PCJ*
202), where water runs slowly through riverbeds. Nature, therefore, would
call for the emergence here of an image of a Christ dusky [moreno] like
his people, with long locks burnt by the blazing sun, with cheekbones
protruding in naturalistic fashion, and pupils of dead white. The local

image-makers, products of the Andalusian soil, have performed their work while sensitized to nature in creating the spectacle that inspires the saeta. The refrain of the poem reproduces the verbal content of a traditional saeta, "¡Miradlo por donde viene!" [See it coming here!]; and the modification of this verse, "¡Miradlo por donde va!" [See it going by!], expresses the passage of the image from view (Morris, *Son of Andalusia* 205).

However, Lorca shares Falla's awareness of the contradictoriness of the Andalusian spirit. The poet, with his flair for theatre and plasticity, balances the sacred element of *cante jondo* with the profane part, close to nature. Holy Week celebrations in Seville have many pre-Christian components. Also, "Seville's capacity to attract the tourist, the devout, and the reveler, particularly during Holy Week, is legendary" (Morris, *Son of Andalusia* 247). By contrast with the solemnity of "Saeta," based on a serious image of Christ, there appears the lightly erotic poem "Balcón," with the seductive Lola singing a saeta from her balcony, surrounded by youthful admirers, like the opera heroine Carmen so artistically enticing for Falla (see ch. 7, and Pahissa, *Falla* 117–18). A barber of Seville (recalling Rossini's opera character who fascinated Falla's friend Stravinsky in 1921) derives aesthetic enjoyment from her art and follows her rhythms with his head.[18] The poem on Lola ends by unveiling a charming new aspect of her personality: however devout she may (or may not) be, she is also deliciously vain, fond of preening before her reflection in a water basin (*PCJ* 204).

The self-admiration generates a half-serious reprimand in the first word of the following poem, titled "Madrugada" [Early morning] and linked through its imagery to all that has come before, as in an arabesque. The poem begins with a surprise, an antithetical conjunction, "But," repeated at the end as part of a refrain, as if to underscore the sharp edges of this art: "But like love, the saeta-singers / are blind."[19] The first use of "Pero" [But] immerses the reader without warning into the poetic context, much as Falla loves plunging listeners swiftly into pieces.[20] In Lorca an implied criticism of open-eyed, saeta-singing Lola immediately comes across through a joke: just as love is blind, so good singers of saetas sing blindly, closing their eyes to concentrate on the arrows of song they propel through the air of early dawn (*PCJ* 204). In Lorca's 1922 lecture on *cante jondo*, he regards this art form as concentrated inward: introverted, it "shoots its arrows of gold, which stick in our hearts. Amidst the shadow it is like a formidable blue archer whose quiver is inexhaustible."[21] In the poem "Madrugada," these arrows can hit their mark as they pass through the "green night," whose colour precedes sunrise and suggests the fertility both of nature and of folk music. The saetas leave trails of "lirio / caliente" [hot lily] on the sky (*PCJ* 205), an image recalling Christ as the "lirio de Judea" [lily of Judea] and calling forth hot devotional passion. The sky at that point, through its contact with the song, acquires some of the popular Andalusian essence, symbolized by rivers in "Baladilla de los tres ríos." The crescent moon breaks through clouds tinged with purple like the keel [quilla] of a boat through water. The quivers [aljabas] from which the arrows of song have originated fill up with dew, the freshness of the approaching morning, breathed in by the singers to relieve parched throats (*PCJ* 206). Nature, essential to Sevillian piety, has a healing power.

In conclusion, Lorca has prepared an elaborate tribute to Seville, almost in spite of Falla, for her contributions to Andalusian folk music. He has depicted archers seeking love or showing devotion after travelling a long way from the mysterious "countries of sorrow" identified by Falla as the Asian origins of *cante jondo*. These pilgrims introduce themselves into the "maze of love" that is the saeta, the oblation of pain to divinity. Since deep song, according to Falla, imitates nature in the auditory world, Lorca's travellers delight in the lush visual, auditory, and gustatory experience of Sevillian culture in harmony with nature. Their eyes enjoy the naturalness with which candles, gas lamps, and fireflies go together at night during the procession of images towards the city. Their ears penetrate the labyrinth of musical rhythms, accompanied by eroticism and heady wines. Their minds apprehend the whole city as a saeta singer, endlessly propelling her river like an arrow over the Andalusian landscape. Their devotion acquires natural freshness when addressed to a Virgin dressed in a tulip of a hoop skirt, and to her Son, the lily of Judea transformed into the carnation of Spain. Though aware of Lola's delicious narcissism, they avoid her example by shutting their eyes in song and projecting torrid devotion to the Judean lily over Sevillian skies. They savour not only atavistic experiences sought both by Falla and Lorca, but also the essence of Spain, pursued by that composer in his Andalusianist music and by that poet in plastic and dramatic stylization of Andalusian folk poetry. The pious Falla would not have shared Lorca's identification of Christ crucified with Unamuno's tragic Don Quixote, symbol of the Spanish people, unable fully to believe. Yet this third part of *Poema del cante jondo* represents a summit towards which the composer himself has aesthetically aspired in all his Andalusian-style music, aiming from his native region toward the essential Spain.

6

"Gráfico de la Petenera" and Falla's Guitar Elegy to Debussy[1]

Lorca dedicated to Falla the first published version of the poetic section "Gráfico de la Petenera" [Graph of the Petenera]. With its semi-serious elegy played on an imaginary guitar, these verses offered a posthumous tribute to a fabled flamenco songstress. Because of one unrequited love, this Doña Juana, in defiance of established social gender roles – a habit that must have endeared her to Lorca – resolved to avenge herself on all men (Demarquez, *Falla* 50). The poetry first came into print in 1924 under the title "Petenera" in Jean Cassou's French translation for the review *Intentions*.[2] In August 1923, Lorca had written to Falla mentioning his guitar solo, a musical elegy to his admired mentor and friend Claude Debussy, a composition completed by Falla in Lorca's household.[3] With self-deprecating humour, Lorca recounted that his imperfect rendition of Falla's piece on the guitar had distressed his mother's ears: "You cannot imagine how I remember you when I play the guitar and wish to *squeeze out* of it by force your wonderful *Homenaje* [Tribute] to Debussy, of which I achieve nothing but the first few notes: it is truly funny! My mother gets desperate and hides the guitar in the strangest places in the house."[4] That solo, together with the ironic reaction it provoked, influenced "Gráfico de la Petenera." The poetic centrepiece "Muerte de la Petenera" [The Petenera's death] contains many parallels to Falla's guitar composition. The remainder of the poetry presents musical analogies to Falla's *El amor brujo*.

In the middle of the fourth division of *PCJ* appears "Muerte de la Petenera," whose central place corresponds to that of "El paso de la siguiriya" in the first division, to that of "La soleá" in the second, and to that of the "Paso" in the third. In every instance, the speaker honours a female figure for different reasons: for the antiquity of the siguiriya gitana, the purifying introspection of the soleá, and the oblation of the saeta. In the fourth division, what makes the Petenera worthy of memory is her reputation as a seductive artist, along with her musical genre so noteworthy for its imposing plasticity that it has outlived the performer herself. The durability of the musical creature makes the demise of the creator all the more unsettling. Lorca's fourth poetic division takes place both en route to, and at, the cemetery. Within the architectonic arabesque that is *PCJ*, and in the parallel between the Sevillian Virgin and the Petenera, anything but virginal, there lies an irony sometimes winking, sometimes grotesque, but unique to Lorca. A fall in tone, alien to Falla, has succeeded the exultation of the Sevillian part of the work. All human enterprises, however lofty, end for Lorca's poetic voice at the grave. Therefore the third part of *PCJ* has celebrated the sublimation of pain by means of religious devotion, tempered by pagan play; but the fourth, "Gráfico de la Petenera," offers different perspectives, some serious, others ironic, on the mystery of death, for which deep song as perceived by Lorca offers no solution (3:206).

In November 1921, when writing verse on the death of an artist, if only legendary, Lorca was perhaps following the example of Falla's *Homenaje: Pièce de guitare écrite pour "Le Tombeau de Debussy"* (1920). Falla had aspired to compose original music in Debussy's honour, ending with a direct quote from his piece *La soirée dans Grenade* (Pahissa, *Falla* 121). According to Falla's article "Claude Debussy y España" [Claude Debussy and Spain], the French composer sought to innovate by using exotic music, and in the process came to understand and express "the very essence of Spanish music."[5] This essence lay for Falla in the "evocation of the spell of Andalusia."[6] In *La soirée dans Grenade,* according to the impressionist Falla, Debussy "creates for us the effect of images reflected by moonlight on the pure water of the pools that fill the Alhambra."[7] Hence, in Falla's guitar elegy, there sounds a slow, solemn melody in the 4/4 rhythm of a rocking, sensuous habanera, imitating the rhythm of the *Soirée.* The brief guitar piece, composed of only seventy measures, divides into two sections, which include respectively measures 1 to 31 and measures 32 to 65, with a coda beginning with a quotation from the *Soirée* (measures 63–6) (Segal 20). The quotation is tantamount to direct contact with the deceased composer through his music.

Lorca, in his 1922 lecture on deep song, also recognized the picture-forming power of *La soirée dans Grenade.*[8] Perhaps he perceived that power as well while listening to Falla's *Homenaje* to Debussy. Its two main parts primarily employ the Phrygian mode favoured by deep song. Two contrasting melodic themes stand out. The first unfolds in the key of

E Phrygian, with the tempo *mesto e calmo* [sad and calm]. This theme is based on an obsessive oscillation between low F and E, without either predominating (Falla, *Homenaje*, score, rehearsals 1–7; Segal, "Truth" 20). The second theme, which starts in the eighth measure, passes from A major to B Phrygian (measures 12–13). In the thirteenth measure appears a C-sharp, introducing an "Oriental" variant of the Frigian mode: it repeats a B, which later flattens into B-flat and thereby follows a practice of Andalusian Arabic music (Segal, "Truth" 21; Chase, *Music of Spain* 228). The second theme shows its kinship with the first theme by shifting the order of the same rhythmic units (Singer, "Present" 75): (1) two sixteenth notes, (2) a dotted eighth note and sixteenth note, (3) two eighths, and (4) a triplet. The first theme proceeds in the order (1), (2), (3) and (4); and the second theme, in the order (2), (1), (4), (3).

According to Segal ("Truth" 22), the second half of the *Homenaje* (measures 31–62) concentrates on varying the first theme with glissandi and patterns of Phrygian scales that move with flamenco-like brusqueness. This half of the piece concludes by repeating almost literally measures 1 to 15 within measures 49 to 62. At measure 63 comes the quote from Debussy, whose Phrygian mode, Segal finds, allows the listener to identify that quote as the origin of the primary theme of the *Homenaje*. The stressed notes of the guitar tenor form the first theme, transposed half an interval higher. With subtle adjustments of the chords in measure 66, the main theme recurs, ending on E (Segal, "Truth" 22–3). In short, with all its variations and references to the same theme, ultimately derived from a single motif in Debussy, Falla has crafted yet another musical arabesque.

Falla's *Homenaje* and "Muerte de la Petenera" show similarities. Both consist of two interrelated themes and a direct quotation of an outside source. In Lorca, the main theme tells of the Petenera's passing, and the secondary one describes the synchronized prancing of one hundred ponies belonging to her dead lovers, her victims. The feminine theme opposes the masculine one, yet shares with it the submission to mortality. The quotation from an outside work comes from the prototype of *peteneras* sung and played by Andalusians:

Quien te puso petenera
no te supo poner nombre,
que debió de haberte puesto,
¡Niña de mi corazón!,
que debió de haberte puesto
la perdición de los hombres.

[When they called you Petenera,
They did not choose the right name.
They should have called you instead,
Dear little girl of my heart,
They should have called you instead
The damnation of all men.][9]

Here follows Lorca's ballad "Muerte de la Petenera":

En la casa blanca muere
la perdición de los hombres.

Cien jacas caracolean.
Sus jinetes están muertos.

Bajo las estremecidas
estrellas de los velones,
su falda de moaré tiembla
entre sus muslos de cobre.

Cien jacas caracolean.
Sus jinetes están muertos.

Largas sombras afiladas
vienen del turbio horizonte,
y el bordón de una guitarra
se rompe.

Cien jacas caracolean.
Sus jinetes están muertos.

[In the white house is dying
The damnation of all men.

A hundred ponies prance in time.
Their riders are all dead.

Under the shuddering stars
Of oil lamps she lies,

Her moiré skirt is trembling
Between her copper thighs.

A hundred ponies prance in time.
Their riders are all dead.

Lengthy shadows sharply honed
From murky horizons come,
And the bass string of a guitar
Snaps.

A hundred ponies prance in time.
Their riders are all dead.]   (*PCJ* 217–18; reproduced with gracious
                                              permission of the heirs of F. García Lorca)

Just as Debussy lends Falla the sensuous habanera rhythm and the Phrygian mode dominating the melody in the *Homenaje*, the original *petenera* has furnished Lorca the octosyllabic metre (except in a short verse on the broken guitar string) and the assonant rhyme ó-e (nombre, hombres), along with a half-fatalistic, half-ironic tone presiding over the whole and unheard in Falla and his French model. The sixth line, "The damnation of all men," underscores sexual fatalism and offers the most direct impression of the talent – and the character – of the lady herself. In Lorca she suffers the punishment metaphorically visited on her suitors – death. Just as in Falla's *Homenaje* it is impossible to determine the leading note of the main theme, so in Lorca's elegy it is undetermined whether admiration predominates – because the poetic subject seems to follow classical elegiac conventions for this heroic and talented non-conformist – or else irony towards her indifference to others' vulnerability. As Quance has so deftly put it with respect to *Suites* and *Canciones* but in a way apposite to *PCJ*, "mixed feelings and mixed codes are [Lorca's] own particular truth" (*Contradictions* 32). In addition, just as in Falla's *Homenaje* the second theme gives way to an Oriental variant, Lorca's second theme (on the ponies) sounds an Oriental tone: "Cien jacas caracolean./Sus jinetes están muertos" [A hundred ponies prance at once./Their riders are all dead] (*PCJ* 217).

The image of animals moving in synchrony out of respect for beauty has an Oriental flavour, related to deep song as Falla and Lorca conceive it. In a well-known sonnet, Uruguayan modernist Julio Herrera y Reissig praises his spouse in an exotic Indian setting, with hierophants that anoint her

9   Falla, Oriental theme, *El amor brujo*, rehearsal 11, *La vie breve. L'amour sourcier. Les Tréteaux de Maître Pierre.* París: L'Avant-Scène Opéra, Éditions Premières Loges (May–June), 1997, rehearsal 11, Example 14. Program. Reproduced with gracious permission from the Archivo Manuel de Falla (Granada).

sandal while "cien blancos elefantes / enroscaban su trompa hacia el ocaso" [a hundred white elephants / furled their trunks towards the sunset].[10] Oriental-style passages abound in the Andalusianist works of Falla. In an example from *El amor brujo*, an oboe plays an Arab, serpentine melody that keeps the protagonist Candelas in a hypnotic trance (see musical example 9).[11]

The Eastern-style couplet of the hundred ponies recurs three times in Lorca's poem like a refrain at unexpected intervals: after the first verse, with its folkloric quotation ("the damnation of all men"), next after the quatrain describing the dying artist, and third after the quatrain that projects onto nature the moment of her death (*PCJ* 217–18).

A mock elegy emerges, following classical conventions only to a degree. Like Falla in this period, who is beginning a neoclassical phase after the example of Stravinsky (Christoforidis, "Acercamiento" 15),[12] Lorca seeks the golden mean, balance, and the synthesis of contemporary stylization and traditional models. The handling of such models, concision, and a sense of proportion pervade Falla's notes to the *opera buffa* that he will begin with Lorca in 1923. Meanwhile, in these years, with his characteristic slow pace and neoclassical style, he composed his puppet opera on the *Maese Pedro* theme (1923) (Hess, *Modernism* 213). Lorca himself offered suggestions for staging the work (202), and he and Falla seemed to seek hard, concise irony. How to convey the resurrection of a dead puppet, derived from folklore? Brief, hard descriptive verses accent the natural vitality of the Petenera even in death. The illusion of naturalness describes the Virgin of Solitude and the saeta-singers in "Poema de la saeta," and

Lorca mockingly extends the same illusion to the earthier level of the Petenera.

The lament for a dead artist begins by following classical conventions of elegy, announcing the death of the acclaimed individual to be lamented and perpetuating the circumstances (Cannon, "*Llanto*" 229). With an irony towards the opposite sex that Falla would have eschewed out of a sense of chivalry (cf. Hess, *Modernism* 182), Lorca portrays his dying "heroine" as she expires like thousands of other women in a simple white house. Yet she owes her fame to her unconventional life as a *belle dame sans merci*, or in folkloric language, as "the damnation of all men." The refrain on the multitude of Andalusian ponies stresses the magnitude of this "damnation." Nature partakes in mourning in accordance with classical tradition (Cannon 230). Here, though, the stars shuddering in honour of the Petenera, instead of being natural beings, are products of culture, humble oil lamps. Between the two poles of what is heroic and what is sinister, what a rebel poet may approve and what his society dictates, there swings the apparent resurrection of the formidable singer: the skirt in which she used to sing, shining by lamp light, seems to bring her back to life as it apparently moves between her hard tan thighs, symbols of vitality and vigour. The hundredfold equine prancing extends the tribute by nature to hyperbolic proportions. Foreboding shadows approach from horizons as murky as the performer's past. The murkiness receives reinforcement from the final repetition of the refrain, preceded by the snap of the bass string corresponding to the low strings prevailing in Falla's elegy to Debussy. Perhaps at this breaking point she dies.

Ironically, the poem "Falsete" [Falsetto], absent from the original French translation, but following "Death of the Petenera" in all editions of *Poema del cante jondo*, has the same ambivalence as the preceding poem.[13] Aware that Falla has helped organize the contest among singers in order to preserve the deep-song heritage, Lorca would like to perpetuate the art of the falsetto as part of this legacy. Vocalization in an anatomical position relatively high in the head makes the upper vocal strings vibrate to produce a sound abnormally high for the individual cantaor. Viewing music as an artificial stratagem to make reality take place in an orderly succession of durations, García Bacca deems it a human invention for "certain men, against anatomy and physiology, [to assume] the instrumental function of soprano, alto, tenor, bass."[14] It is only necessary to think of the extreme example, hovering in García Bacca's mind, but not emerging on his page – the castrato. Interested in the score of Verdi's *Falstaff*, with its ironic protagonist, Falla finds falsetto a resource to express irony. In the manuscript of the incomplete *Lola la comedianta* [Lola the actress], which Falla and Lorca began to write in 1923, the composer mentioned that one of the main characters, a poet disguised as a coachman, should use an almost spoken falsetto to parody his own wife, the actress, about to feign a flirtation with the empty-headed marquis (*Lola* 119). The folkloric figure of the Petenera, the avenger a hundred times over of a single amorous mishap, ostensibly seems to form an excellent target for irony, mocking an excessive reaction to personal misfortune.

"Falsete," a half-ironic commentary, takes an ambivalent stance towards undoing much of the seriousness in the Petenera's demise. The poem seemingly accents the retributive justice deserved for a dissolute life. A contrast arises here between the "niñas / buenas" [good / girls] absent from the seductress's burial and the "gente / siniestra" [people / of ill repute] actually present, "Gente con el corazón / en la cabeza" [people with their hearts / in their heads]. Yet the virtuous maidens receive a stereotyped description: they offer their tresses to Christ crucified and wear white mantillas on festive days. Such models of virtue, it can be recalled, attended the funeral of the dead dancer at the end of "Poema de la soleá." In the present poem, so that the speaker incurs no blame for divulging others' sins, the disreputable folk receive no description whatsoever, despite their presence at the funeral rites for the Petenera. If they shed false tears, they think but do not feel when following the coffin through the street. Were a skilled falsetto to sing this Lorca poem, he would perform it with his "heart in his head," so to speak, by handling his voice in an unnatural way. Would he sing by imitating the feigned sadness of the unrespectable mourners? Or would he act with greater virtue, moved by sympathy for the posthumous coldness to which the Petenera has fallen victim? The disjunctive remains ironically without resolution in the two lines, full of pitiful "¡ay!"'s that open and close the poem: "¡Ay, petenera gitana! / ¡Yayay petenera!" [Ay, Gypsy Petenera! / Ay, ay, ay, Petenera!] (*PCJ* 219–20). The very indecision points to Lorca's insecurity about conventional gender roles, which the Petenera has rejected in her wayward style of living, possibly admirable for the poet despite everything.

More than the problematic virtuous/disreputable opposition, in "Gráfico de la Petenera" the masculine/feminine antithesis governs, largely associated with death, Lorca's obsession. This contrast has appeared in "Death of the Petenera," where femininity occupies the main verses in the person of the Petenera herself, and where masculinity takes over the refrains on the dead riders. Falla exploits the musical potential of the sexual opposition in *El amor brujo*, with its two contrasting leitmotivs of the phantom lover and Candelas. The male motif, *allegro furioso* [fast and ferocious], fiercely played with flute, oboe, and piano (see musical example 10),

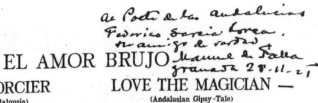

10   Falla, Phantom's motif, *El amor brujo*. From Concert VIII, Year II (1915–1916), Sociedad Nacional de Música, Madrid, March 28, 1916, Program, analysis by Adolfo Salazar, p. 10. Autographed to García Lorca. Reproduced with gracious permission from the Archivo Manuel de Falla (Granada).

11   Falla, Candelas's soleá, *El amor brujo*. From Concert VIII, Year II (1915.1916), Sociedad Nacional de Música, Madrid, March 28, 1916. Program, analysis of Adolfo Salazar, p. 11. Reproduced with gracious permission from the Archivo Manuel de Falla (Granada).

opposes a feminine soleá, sad and nasal, based on four ascending notes rendered *con dolce espressione* [with sweet expressiveness] (see musical example 11).[15] Nonetheless, Falla varies the moods with which these motifs are played, and Lorca does the same.

Falla's masculine motif, at first affirmed with ferocity, weakens at the end in defeat; and the soleá of the female character, a motif largely resembling sobbing, at the finale develops, transposed upwards, into an ascending melody of four notes, played in triumph to the accompaniment of morning bells.[16] Lorca's poem "Camino" [Road], near the beginning of "Gráfico de la Petenera," shows the hundred horsemen mounted while the poetic voice enquires into their destiny both in the first and the last quatrains. In the second quatrain, the lyrical "I" discards concrete cities – Cordoba, Seville, Granada – as the destination in question, because the world of the poem is a cemetery. At the midpoint, the third quartet asserts that the horses will transport their dead riders to the "maze of crosses / where the song is trembling" (*PCJ* 211), with the song referring to the Petenera, also in her death-throes. That the maze stands for the cemetery receives confirmation in "'De profundis,'" the penultimate poem in the series on the Petenera. Here the hundred horsemen, previously in motion, now lie still as "a hundred lovers" who "sleep forever" (221).

"Gráfico de la Petenera" ends with a grim assertion of the feminine principle. In "Clamor," the final poem of the section, there sound bells of Death, personified as a cantaora. In *El amor brujo*, Falla experiments twice with bells, once at the beginning by having them sound twelve times at midnight, an hour propitious for witchcraft, and second by causing them to peel at the end at dawn to coincide with Candelas's victory over her lover. Lorca, on the other hand, concerned about dying, employs bells twice, both as a sign of death. At the start of "Campana," they toll for someone not yet identified, because the poem bears the subtitle "Bordón," the lowest string of the guitar. Yet, in "Clamor," Death triumphs over her 101 victims, the Petenera and her suitors. In "Campana" as in *El amor brujo*, one bell rings in one tower; in "Clamor" as in the conclusion of *El amor brujo*, multiple bells sound, although in Lorca, as distinguished from Falla, they sound a death knell in many towers, covering with their lugubrious sound more Andalusian space (*PCJ* 208, 222–3). In *El amor brujo* the plot passes from an adverse situation to its resolution, while in "Gráfico de la Petenera" the poetic voice exposes a catastrophe of ever-deepening proportions.

Asymmetry prevails in this subtle, ironic poetic section of *PCJ*, undoing the neoclassical balance elsewhere so carefully expressed. Any symmetry that this section may seem to convey – with two poems on ringing bells at beginning and end, two poems on the hundred cemetery-bound lovers at second and penultimate place, two poems in the Petenera's honour in third and fourth place, and two poems on her death in the middle – is sucked up into the verses on Death at the end. In the middle of the final poem "Clamor" come two strophes dominated by Death and lacking parallels in "Campana." Since all eight poems refer to death, if we were to visualize a graph of "Gráfico de la Petenera," as the visually oriented Lorca advises, and if we phonetically employed a flat arch to trace the recited pitch of each strophe,[17] then we could present skew arches of ever-diminishing radius, one under another (see figure 4), beginning as a line segment running the length of each poem and ending at the centre, the point, of the final poem.

In this concluding poem, Death, crowned with orange blossoms like a bride,[18] although ironically the flowers have withered, goes up a road while performing her art: "Canta y canta / una canción / en su vihuela blanca, / y canta y canta y canta [She sings and sings / A song / on her white *vihuela*, / And sings and sings and sings] (*PCJ* 223). A cantaora like the deceased Petenera, Death follows the bell-ringing with a comical insistence. The repetition of the hard stops c-t, set off against multiple open a's, imitates the sonorous percussion.[19] The *vihuela*, a stringed instrument of the fifteenth century, plucked with a plectrum, parodies the ubiquitous guitar of deep song, generally strummed. Falla, when he composed his *Retablo*, followed for the time being the advice of music critic Cecilio de Roda and rejected the antiquated music of the *vihuela* as excessively Italianate, not typically Spanish. Instead, he pored over the classical masters of the Spanish guitar (García Matos, "Folklore II," 36–7). With

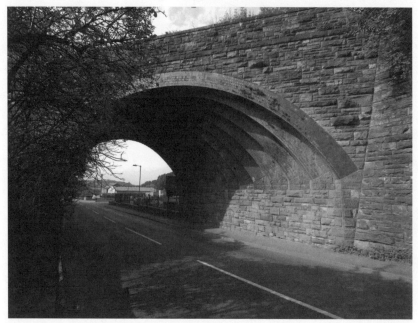

Figure 4   An example of a skew arch bridge

biting humour, therefore, Lorca portrays Death as an inferior cantaora, anachronistic inversion of the Petenera. Death is also alien to the popular spirit of Andalusian music, subject always for Lorca to the changes of every epoch.

   In conclusion, in view of Falla's music, Lorca's dedication of the French translation to him has received a possible explanation. Leaving aside the wild-sounding, difficultly restrained *peteneras* composed by Falla himself and Lorca's and his father's enjoyment of that genre of folk song,[20] the legendary femme fatale reinvented by Lorca enabled him to cultivate the elegiac style towards which he had leaned since his earliest verses. The central poem of this section proceeds in the style of Falla's elegy, the *Homenaje* to Debussy, although Lorca took advantage of the ambiguity of the melody, oscillating between F and E, in a way the composer would never have dreamed. The poetic voice vacillates between "heroine" worship and awareness of the Petenera's mortality. "Falsete" makes a fitting companion piece, with its own subtle irony undercutting its apparent strait-laced attitude towards gender roles. The other poems treat themes associated with the two sexes in a way more or less parallel to Falla's treatment in *El amor brujo* until an overriding concern with death takes over in Lorca. Neither in Falla nor in Lorca does a clear separation of styles exist between impressionism and neoclassicism. Hence, while writing the mainly neoclassical *Retablo de maese Pedro*, Falla can also pen his guitar solo in memory of Debussy's impressionist language (though within a tight, astringent neoclassical framework). At the same time, Lorca peppers echoes of the impressionist *El amor brujo* throughout "Gráfico de la Petenera." Admirer of both Falla and Stravinsky, each fond of puppet dramas – the Russian composer with his ballets *Petrushka* and *Pulcinella*, the Spanish maestro with his *Maese Pedro* – Lorca keeps a tight grip on the strings with which he moves his highly stylized figures. All one hundred suitors behave in the same way; the femme fatale Petenera stays seductive, dead or alive; and Death, dressed as a bride, represents a comic parody of a flamenco songstress. All act in a tableau of phantoms offering a grotesque, otherworldly dimension to *Poema del cante jondo*.

7

Openness to Death in Flamenco Artists and in Southern Cities

In a 1933 lecture, Lorca presented Spain as a "country open to death" [país abierto a la muerte] (*Obras completas* 3:312), chief obsession of the poet himself. The nation, he felt, derives creative energies from its reactions to dying. Two sections of poems in *PCJ* illustrate this attitude: "Viñetas flamencas" [Flamenco vignettes] and "Tres ciudades" [Three cities]. While arranging in 1931 the publication of *PCJ*, Lorca must have sensed their relatedness (*PCJ* 39), although he subsequently separated them (*PCJ* 43). On a written fold of paper enclosing the manuscript passed to his friend Rafael Martínez Nadal, he grouped them all in a single section, along with the poems today appearing under the title "Caprichos" [Caprices]. He titled the entire section "Estampas" (*PCJ* 39), perhaps, as Christopher Maurer has remarked, from Debussy's *Estampes* [Engravings, 1903], a set of three pieces appreciated by Falla for their pictorial value (Maurer, "Lorca y las formas" 243). At the same time, the word in Lorca connotes lithographs, or retrospective views. His play *Mariana Pineda*, on a Granadan folk heroine, bears the nostalgic subtitle *Romance popular en tres estampas* [Folk ballad in three engravings].[1] Some of the verse collected under the title *Estampas* in *PCJ* concerns legendary figures of more recent vintage than Mariana or Andalusian cities that have embellished death. Outstanding flamenco singers from bygone eras capture centre stage in "Viñetas flamencas," while three poetic Southern communities facing death with flamenco rhythms emerge in "Tres ciudades."

Late nineteenth-century flamenco performers livened up conversation of Falla's and Lorca's daily discussion circle in Granada (Molina Fajardo, *Falla* 45–7). In verse, Lorca treated them as Falla did Debussy in his guitar *Homenaje*, reconstructing their artistic brilliance by putting readers in touch with their music. A direct quote from a song about a legendary cantaora appears in "Muerte de la Petenera" (see ch. 6, above), essentially a verbal puppet show with the artist controlling the strings. In "Viñetas flamencas," however, his poetic voice relinquishes control to let the collectivity speak through the performers. This way of thinking harmonizes with Falla's 1922 pamphlet on *cante jondo*, deeming deep song a creation of the Andalusian collective spirit (142). His music links characters to the spirits of their native regions. In his ballet *El sombrero de tres picos*, the Murcian miller Lucas dances to Murcian folk songs, and his Navarrese wife to a *jota*, or northern dance (Hess, *Modernism* 92–4). In the background, nostalgia lingers for a simpler, bygone era, closer to the roots of existence.[2] Similar nostalgia tinges Lorca's "Retrato de Silverio Franconetti" [Portrait of Silverio Franconetti] and his sketch in "Juan Breva." These are retrospectives on legendary cantaores whom he never knew personally, archetypal Andalusians who used to unleash their voices with savage energy. If, as Pahissa maintains (*Falla* 102), Andalusian music oscillates between insecure nostalgia and harsh, exciting rhythms, then Lorca here encloses the striking rhythms of those artists within a nostalgic framework.

He remarks that the Andalusian stock utilizes deep singers to externalize its grief and tell its story. Calling those musicians "simple mediums" (3:215), he regards them as "interpreters of the soul of the people that wrecked their own souls amidst the storms of sentiment."[3] He exalts them as martyrs for producing their own cardiac arrests with their singing. All this poetic exaltation serves a preservationist aim like Falla's vis-a-vis the old folk music, and should be read in this sense when atavistic sensations are idealized in deep song. Accordingly, "Viñetas flamencas" begins with a dedication to the much-admired cantaor Manuel Torre, connoisseur of the "black sounds" of Falla's nocturne "En el Generalife." Lorca's fellow poet Rafael Alberti informs that Lorca applauded Torre's mysterious dictum, "In *cante jondo* ... what always has to be sought until it is found, is the black trunk of Pharaoh."[4] Good deep-song performers, according to this statement, must delve to the obscure roots of their Gypsy stock. Falla too showed fascination with the Gypsies' need to adhere to remotest tradition. In his personal copy of Louis Lucas, he indicated with pen the observation that Egyptian bayadères or dancing girls – supposed ancestors of the Gypsies – always followed the age-old custom of setting to music all the circumstances of amorous incidents through erotic pantomime and enharmonic modes (Lucas, *L'Acoustique* 31, n.), received from India (23n1).

From Falla, Lorca learned the sacral function of *cante jondo* performers and approached them with reverence. In his words, each cantaor sings with a "profound religious sense":[5] he celebrates a "solemn rite, calls forth old dormant essences [of the Andalusian cultural spirit], and hurls them, wrapped in his voice, to the wind."[6] With respect, in the "Retrato de Silverio Franconetti," the speaker renounces his omniscience: he poses the question as to how Silverio sang, since he never knew him personally. Perhaps with Falla's technique in mind of distinguishing folk characters with ethnic motifs, Lorca individualized his word painting of Silverio by contrasting two collective essences. His voice melds Italian and flamenco traits, inherited from an Italian father and an Andalusian mother (*PCJ* 232n1). Life in Italy, for Lorca cloyingly sweet, has little in common with life in Andalusia, sour when not downright bitter, as seen in Lorca's personification of that quality in his Andalusian character El Amargo [the Bitter One] (3:345). Lorca's lyric voice, with typical sensuality, characterizes Franconetti though the mixture of lemon and natural honey he may have sipped before singing: "The dense honey of Italy / mixed in with our lemon / went into the deep lament / of the siguiriya singer."[7]

Just as Falla valued deep-song screams and silences, Lorca stressed the fame of Silverio's screams and the subsequent hushes. Molina Fajardo (*Falla y "Cante jondo"* 46–7), who belonged with Falla and Lorca to Fernando Vílchez's *tertulia*, recalls that Lorca was only a youth when a fellow conversationalist, considerably older, recounted that old Silverio tore apart the mercury in mirrors with his song. Lorca could come no closer than through this time-honoured testimonial to the immediate experience of Silverio's singing – not to the voice, but to its impact on matter, the signature of a powerful singer; not to the singer himself, but to a respected listener. Even so, the lyric voice strives where possible for impersonal expression: "His scream was fearful. / The old folks / say the hairs rose / on their heads, and the mercury would open / in mirrors."[8] According to de Paepe, Falla, following Lucas, lauded the enharmonic practices of deep song for tonal flexibility. Hence Lorca's poetic subject praised Silverio for his skill in causing his voice to glide in this fashion: "He passed through the tones / without breaking them."[9] In addition, just as Falla composed with such silences and vocal glissandi, so Lorca, an expert verbal painter, invented imaginary geography to praise Silverio as a creator of plazas for silence in the garden of sounds. However, the poem ends with another impersonal note when the fatalistic lyric voice describes Silverio's melody as sleeping among its echoes, its final traces (*PCJ* 234).

Another celebrated cantaor, Juan Breva from Vélez-Málaga, exemplified for Lorca one of those singers visited by the Andalusian collective spirit to externalize its sorrow (3:212; *PCJ* 235n6). In this fashion de Paepe interprets the lines, "He was pain itself / singing / behind a smile."[10] In other words, for de Paepe, Breva becomes one with Andalusian sorrow, the essence of Andalusian artistic creativity. Like Franconetti, Breva attains individuality in Lorca's writing through ethnic heritage. He hails from the centre of an agricultural area barely five miles from the sea. In the poem, attributes of that land pass into his art. The speaker refers to the peace of the zone, the marine saltiness entering Breva's lament, and familiar surroundings he nostalgically recalls: "He evokes groves of lemon trees / Of sleeping Malaga / And in his lament / Are traces of sea salt."[11] As a high flamenco tenor, he excelled in sweetness of timbre, for which the poetic voice, fond of underscoring the overstepping of traditional gender roles, contrasts the "little girl's voice" [voz de niña] of Breva with his "giant's body" [cuerpo de gigante] (*PCJ* 235; 3:215). Because he must have closed his eyes to produce such sweetness, the lyric voice compares him to blind Homer. His voice had "something of the unlit sea / and of a squeezed orange": born of the sea while blind to the light of day, the sweet, golden sound emerged with effort from the throat of its author (*PCJ* 326). Yet his songs were anything but unnatural. Following Falla and Lucas, Lorca's lyric voice remarks that *cante jondo* approaches the "trill of a bird" [trino del pájaro] (3:218); and this description applies to Lorca's Juan Breva, with his surprisingly high voice: "Nothing matched his trill" [Nada como su trino] (*PCJ* 235).

Lorca's tributes to past *cante jondo* performers effortlessly enter the elegiac mode always obsessing him and dominating the remainder of "Viñetas flamencas." The transitional poem, "Café cantante" [Café for singing], foregrounds Dolores la Parrala, acclaimed nineteenth-century cantaora, while she engages in a dialogue with death during her performance. She calls death, but the ultimate negation does not respond. The audience "breathes in" her sobs as naturally as the air, as she provides an atavistic sensation of experiencing the ultimate mystery. Allusions to green mirrors of a café frame the poem at start and finish, establishing a murky and mysterious atmosphere loved by Lorca and by the composer of *En el Generalife* (*PCJ* 237–8; Falla, score, I, 3).

Like the Andalusianist Falla, Lorca in his poem "Lamentación de la muerte" [Lament on death] – originally called "Lamentación de Juan Breva" – brought death into the open. Breva's and Falla's music exemplify the culture of Spain as a "country open to death." *El amor brujo* focuses on pantomimed communication between a spectre and his beloved. Likewise, Lorca incorporated into the lament of Juan Breva imagery recast from a cherished Spanish ballad about a conversation with a deceased beloved:

Si tú eres mi linda amiga,
¿cómo no me miras, di?
Ojos con que te miraba
a la sombra se los di.

["If you are my pretty friend,
Cast your eyes on me, I pray."
"Eyes with which I looked at you
To the dark I gave away"]   (3:313)

How similar are two verses from "Lamentación de la muerte": "Vine
a este mundo con ojos / y me voy sin ellos" [I came into this world with
eyes / And I'm leaving it without them"] (*PCJ* 239)! Breva, an artist of
the people, taught the transitory condition of everything human. However, Falla had advised consulting folk musicians for ideas on composing,
not views on living. Their authority on deeper themes was a lesson in-
grained in Lorca by his family. One of his uncles relayed to him the
outlook of Juan Breva, once wealthy, but impoverished in his final years,
and disillusioned with the fugacity of material success. Everyone, no
matter how exalted, Breva concluded, ends up dying "with an oil lamp
and a blanket on the ground" (Francisco García Lorca, *Federico y su
mundo* 41). This notion came as close as Lorca could to Breva's voice.
Disenchantment with living constitutes the poetic substance of the central strophe of the poem: "I wished to reach / where the best people
reach. / And I have reached, dear God! ... / But very soon, / an oil lamp
and a blanket / on the ground."[12] The last three lines here, quoted without a verb to stress finality, undergo only slight transitional variations as
they repeat in the two strophes that follow as echoes of disenchantment
with worldly pursuits.

The first of the two strophes begins with the folk image of a lemon
thrown, as if by a beloved, to the poetic subject, yet missing the mark
(Morris, *Son of Andalusia* 215). The action is tantamount to tossing lemons to the wind and could constitute good advice in a world where effort
comes to naught. Recalling that Juan Breva comes from a land of lemon
trees, Lorca, as if to imitate him, expressed that advice with citric imagery:
"Little yellow lemon, / lemon tree. / Throw your little lemons / to the
wind."[13] Everything, even love, is transitory, ending with "an oil lamp and
a blanket on the ground."

However, does some power exist to master destiny? The final two poems of "Viñetas flamencas" affirm the triumph of life, an attitude more

compatible with Falla's art than with the fatalism of the previous poetry. In Falla's 1915 version of *El amor brujo*, Candelas resorts to magic to conjure up the lover who has abandoned her. Two young Gypsy girls perform their conjuration [conjuro]. At midnight they recite a spell (Falla, score, rehearsal 9, 63). Candelas prays to God to bring her to a new day through a fortunate path. She performs the ritual fire dance to mark the end of the day. She tosses into an oil lamp a fistful of holy incense while wishing good in and evil out (rehearsal 12, 64). In the poem "Conjuro" Lorca, a painterly observer, represents the hand of a Gypsy dancer as a symbol of her power. In the first strophe the clenched hand moves like a jellyfish, opening suddenly to propel itself forward.[14] Its movement to quash the oil-lamp flame by tossing holy incense onto it resembles blinding the aching eye of that weak light. Above the white smoke, the hand in its digging descent resembles a mole, and in its fluttering a butterfly. All – jellyfish, mole, and butterfly – are creatures of nature, pointing to the closeness of deep song to the natural order. The spell functions well: the hand grasps an invisible heart – that of the spirit it has conjured up – an airy heart reflected in the wind, subtle and fleeting. Three times, as if to suggest a magic number, a mysterious couplet sounds: "Ace of clubs. / Scissors in a cross."[15] As in *El amor brujo*, playing cards offer knowledge of the unknown [*L'amour sorcier* (1915), score, rehearsal 6, 63]. Scissors in the form of a cross, de Paepe explains, also signal belief in magic (*PCJ* 241n6).

Since primitives believe in magic, understood as a human power to affect events, the individual can assert ascendancy of life over death. The self-affirmation takes place in Lorca's poem "Memento," equivalent to *memento mori*. The poem has the tercet structure with assonance of the soleá while repeating every fourth line the first verse, "Cuando yo me muera" [When I die], a line found, for example, in a well-known Gypsy siguiriya: "When I die, take care / to do this chore just right: / With a hank of your black hair, / bind my hands real tight."[16] Frequent and regular repetition of "Cuando yo me muera" – even prior to the poetic testamentary requests made to survivors – causes the line to suggest the tolling of a bell. At each tolling, though, Lorca's poetic voice, like Falla's Candelas in *El amor brujo*,[17] affirms life over death, although in this poem an artist's life receives consideration. First, the speaker requests burial with his guitar, as if to assert the identity of his person and his art; second, he yearns to situate himself at death amidst the freshness and fertility of Andalusian orange trees and mint plants; and finally, he seeks burial in a weathervane, symbol of openness to the changing air of the times, like the responsiveness of Andalusian song to historical variation (*PCJ* 243).

While select artists as seen by Lorca can commune through music with the spirit of the Andalusian people, so, in his opinion, do whole communities. He expresses this communication in "Poema de la saeta," concerning Seville. In "Tres ciudades," he displays his pan-Andalusianism by associating music with Malaga, Cordoba, and Seville. Long before Lorca, Enrique Granados had set a pattern in *Twelve Spanish Dances* (1890) followed by Isaac Albéniz in his suite *Iberia* (1906–9), with its twelve "impressions" for piano, musical sketches of cities throughout Spain, of which ten depict Andalusian locales.[18] In his 1921 lecture on deep song, Lorca attributed to Pedrell the initiative for incorporating Spanish folk song into classical music, "but it was Isaac Albéniz who genially hit the mark by using the lyrical stock of Andalusian songs in his work."[19] The work to which Lorca referred probably includes *La Vega* [The Granadan lowland], used by Falla in 1923 as background music for the Epiphany Andalusian folk-puppet production held at the Lorca home (Mora Guarnido, *Lorca* 165), and it certainly encompasses as well the better-known *Iberia*. Already the impact of the most famous Andalusian-based piece from that suite, "Fête-Dieu à Seville," has been noted in ch. 5, on "Poema de la saeta."

Within Albéniz's suite, composed of four notebooks (*cahiers*) with three piano solos apiece, French music critic Henri Collet regards the fourth as a treasure chest, containing "the most beautiful jewels of the collection" (cit. Chase, *Music of Spain* 158). Perhaps Lorca had this notebook in mind when arranging in 1931 the juxtaposition of the three poems of "Tres ciudades" [Three cities], titled, in order, "Malagueña," "Barrio de Córdoba" [District of Cordoba] and "Baile" [Dance].[20] Norman C. Miller defines the *malagueña* as a genre of flamenco music from Malaga with lyrics about the sea and sailors. For Miller, Lorca's "Malagueña" constitutes a "poetic transcription" of that music (*Lorca's PCJ* 109). Why, then, could "Barrio de Córdoba" and "Baile" not also be transcriptions of music? Albéniz's *Cahier* IV contains the pieces "Málaga," "Jerez," and "Eritaña." Chase informs that "Jerez," named for the sherry-producing city, uses a soleá model and a modal melody with *cante jondo* adornments; and "Eritaña," with its sevillana rhythm, evokes a tavern outside Seville (*Music of Spain* 158–9). Lorca situates his "Malagueña" in a seaside tavern of Malaga. His "Barrio de Córdoba," named after districts of cities like Albéniz's pieces from *Iberia*, "El Albaicín" (Granada), "Triana" (Seville), and "Lavapiés" (Madrid), may translate Albéniz's nocturne *Córdoba* to poetry. Finally, Lorca's third poem, "Baile," unfolds in Seville and shows the syllabic regularity and ternary rhythm of a *sevillana*.

What distinguishes Lorca's works from Albéniz's is the poet's concern with death. Since Lorca saw Spain as a country "open to death," used as a point of departure for cultural creation, "Malagueña" calls for the reader's collaboration in a distant vision of mortality. "Barrio de Córdoba," contrariwise, offers an immediate view of it. "Baile" provides a mock elegiac approach to it, as did "Muerte de la Petenera." Musical clues in each poem, some borrowed from Albéniz, others from Falla, furnish these variations on a single grim theme.

Albéniz's piano solo "Málaga," one of the briefest of his suite, has a tripartite structure, A-B-A, unfolding in a quick and lively *allegro vivo* in 3/4 time. The first theme, "expressif et rêveur" [expressive and dreamy], to employ the composer's notation, may well evoke the Malagan Mediterranean glimpsed in dreams from Paris, where Albéniz was composing. This theme, written in B-flat minor, opens in F Phrygian (Clark, *Isaac Albéniz* 243), a mode common in *cante jondo* and Arabic music, and undergoes modulation time and again in four units of three measures (e.g., 4–6, 7–9, 10–12, 13–16) (Albéniz, *Iberia for Piano*, score 1), perhaps imitating the march of sea waves. The units follow parallel but unequal paths. They keep the same general melodic pattern, which rises and falls three times, before undergoing multiple variations attaining ever higher tones, like a set of waves climbing to unexpected heights. Once a high B-flat has been attained, a second theme appears in measure 58, a Malagan *jota* less mysterious and modally exotic, more lyrical than the first theme and played in B major. The composer wrote in the text that this melody requires a playing at once sonorous, expressive, and sweet. The second theme occupies eleven measures and often modulates into different keys just as the first theme had. Finally, the original motive in B minor returns once again (measure 118). Here it acquires greater force (*marcatissimo*) than at the beginning (score 5), carrying behind it the lyrical theme in a reprise, which eventually falls to a soft coda, ending with two loud chords, as if to indicate the triumph of the first, enigmatic theme (A) over the lyric motive in B major (B).

Lorca's concise "Malagueña" – only sixteen brief lines long – also contains two themes, which we may denote A-B-B[1]-A[1]. Just as Albéniz's initial theme begins in the Phrygian mode, redolent of Arabic music, mystery surrounds Lorca's first theme: its protagonist is Death, "question of questions" in the poet's words (3:206), as she enters and leaves a seaside tavern in three brief, rapid verses (3, 4, and 5 syllables), setting up a dreamlike atmosphere like the one pervading the start of Albéniz's "Málaga," in no sense an elegiac piece. Lorca's first theme recurs at the end, as does Albéniz's first theme. Lorca's second theme, in two four-line strophes resembling the four-bar units of Albéniz's piece, sets before the reader two multiple metaphors with human protagonists, imagery to be integrated by that reader, though not necessarily in any given fashion. The images deepen the poem through a song being played within a song, the *malague-ña* or poetic framework itself, establishing an air of intrigue and murder: "Through deep [hondos] roads / of the guitar" go "black horses and sinister people."[21] A lyric potential emerges here as in Albéniz's second theme. Within the frame of the *malagueña*, a deeply moving song has emerged from the guitar about individuals engaged in suspicious activities. A smell of salt and female blood is perceptible on the feverish nards of the seashore. What connections exist between the sinister people and the odour? Do the nards have phallic symbolism? Is eroticism involved? The text does not require any single, univocal interpretation. Nor do we know who has died, how, or why. We only know that these contents probably belong to a song sung in the tavern, through whose doors Death enters and leaves, and that the entrance and departure are this time repeated twice in the last of the four strophes, as if to offer an emphatic coda, frequent in Albéniz. The poet eliminates rhyme and chooses irregular rhythms in the main passages about death. The *coplas* containing the secondary theme about the sinister intrigue have four lines each in alternating heptasyllables and pentasyllables. What results from the interaction of the two themes is poetry lacking plot or concrete meaning, yet approaching music, with a mood oscillating between that of a dirge and that of a ballad about a crime.

Lorca's poem on Malaga calls for reader collaboration on the theme of death, but his composition "Barrio de Córdoba" leaves little to the imagination. The word "Barrio" implies spatial limitation. The city of Cordoba recalls the contrast from the earlier poem "Sevilla": "Sevilla para herir. / Córdoba para morir" [Seville for wounding. / Cordoba for dying] (*PCJ* 195–6). If the city exists for the purpose of dying, then death becomes commonplace, a "tópico nocturno" [nocturnal topos], to employ the poet's subtitle. The piece by Albéniz best corresponding to the poem may well be the piano nocturne "Córdoba" from *Chants d'Espagne* (op. 232), a piece whose score is still to be found in Lorca's personal library.[22] According to Walter Aaron Clark (*Isaac Albéniz* 100), "the introduction begins with an open-fifth pedal between F and C in the left hand that suggests the tolling of church bells in the distance. Above this soon floats an enchanting hymn in G Dorian." Suddenly the melody shifts from F major to D minor. Two loud descending arpeggios, still in the same minor key, introduce the second theme, entering at measure 101: a highly lyrical dance in 3/4 time played in D minor and resembling guitar music. Gilbert Chase savours this "hauntingly beautiful melody, set against the acrid dissonances of the plucked accompaniment imitating the notes of the Moorish *guzlas*" (Chase, *Music of Spain* 155; cf. Albéniz himself: Clark, *Isaac Albéniz* 101, n.).

The soft bells at the beginning of the piece could convey tolling for a death. In Lorca's poem, within the house, mourners ward off the stars, symbols of transcendent reality, lying beyond immediacies. Rejection of the metaphysical, stellar world recurs in Lorca's early poem "Los encuentros de un caracol aventurero" [The encounters of an adventurous snail] (*Obras completas* 1:13), in his first play "El maleficio de la mariposa" [The butterfly's curse] (2:6), in "Suite de regreso" [Suite of Return] (1:744), and much later in his mature drama *La casa de Bernarda Alba* [The house of Bernarda Alba] (2:1049–50). Instead, Cordobans fasten on positive reality, lying at hand: here, the passing on of a young girl. Like the arpeggios in Albéniz's nocturne, "night tumbles down" [la noche se derrumba]. Solemnity reigns, like that of Albéniz's simple, hymn-like initial theme. In Lorca's poem the little girl lies with a modest red rose in her hair. The poetry ends with two mournful metaphors related to the guitar. Six nightingales lament her by the grillwork of her window. The obeisance of animals in unison to an honoured personage, already seen in "Muerte de la Petenera," adds an Eastern nuance, as Albéniz hoped to provide in his nocturne. In his lecture on deep song, Lorca remarks that when its *copla* reaches an extreme of grief and love, it affirms its kinship to the verses of Arabian and Persian poets: "en el aire de Córdoba y Granada quedan gestos y líneas de la remota Arabia" [In the air of Cordoba and Granada remain gestures and lines of faraway Arabia] (3:211). The six nightingales may also stand for the six strings of the guitar. In Lorca the guitar blends East and West (3:221), as does Albéniz's nocturne, and the "appearance of the nightingale" is a convention of classical elegy (Cannon, "Llanto" 230). The poem concludes with sighs of the guitarists, their heart-shaped instruments open like their hearts [guitarra abiertas]. They are "open" to death in their creativity towards it.

The poem on Seville differs from the ones on Malaga and Cordoba in omitting the experience of death. However, elegiac tradition in Castilian poetry enshrines the theme of the fugacity of youth and feminine beauty. The topos appears in Jorge Manrique's *Coplas*, as well as in Fray Luis de León's ode "On Mary Magdalen," to a woman whose youth has passed and whose golden tresses, now snow white, call for an attitude of repentance (Manrique, *Obra* 116, *copla* 8; León, *Obras* 2:753–5). In Spanish music, the theme easily loses didactic seriousness and acquires irony. In *El sombrero de tres picos*, the middle-aged Corregidor, with his limp and comical bassoon music, becomes a ludicrous figure when pursuing the miller's youngish wife. Since, in writing on Andalusian cities, Lorca does not wish to exclude Seville, a search for a musical model may have brought him back to Falla's *Fantasía bætica* (see ch. 2).

Just as the *malagueña* exemplifies the flamenco art of Malaga, the *sevillana* represents Seville's.[23] The *Fantasía bætica*, beginning in a serious mood, at the ninth measure breaks into the mirthful rhythm of a *sevillana*, swift and in ternary rhythm, which by contrast with the opening of the piece seems to J.B. Trend like a "mocking laugh" (*Falla* 93–4). Both hands play percussive chords in the treble with the score marked *Giocoso (molto ritmico)* [Jocose (very rhythmic)] (Falla, *Fantasía*, score, measure 9, p. 1). Lorca's attention to this ironic dance recalling Seville may not have come so much from the city itself as from its association with Bizet's opera *Carmen*, to which Falla had considered composing a sequel during his Parisian years (Pahissa, *Falla* 117–18). The novelist Juan Valera had deplored foreign stereotyping of Spanish women as smokers and wearers of daggers in their garters like Mérimée's and Bizet's heroine.[24] While Falla had never followed through on his Carmen project, Lorca may have tried his own hand at an original sequel. Bizet's Carmen, a Gypsy worker at a Sevillian cigarette factory, has a reputation as a flirt and a wayward woman. Lorca incorporates into his poem "Baile" [Dance] Carmen's attention to many swains and the disapproval she aroused in Spain. However, in writing his sequel, he half-mawkishly ages the seductive heroine and places her critics chastely behind closed curtains:

La Carmen está bailando
por las calles de Sevilla.
Tiene blancos los cabellos
Y brilliantes las pupilas

¡Niñas,
corred las cortinas!

En la cabeza se enrosca
una serpiente amarilla,
y va soñando en el baile
con galanes de otros días.

¡Niñas,
corred las cortinas!

Las calles están desiertas
y en los fondos se adivinan
corazones andaluces
buscando viejas espinas.

¡Niñas,
corred las cortinas!

[That Carmen is dancing
Through the streets of Seville.
Her tresses are white
And her pupils are bright.

Girls,
Shut the curtains!

On her head there is coiled
A yellowish serpent.
She dreams while she dances
Of bygone romances.

¡ Girls,
Shut the curtains!

The streets are deserted.
Beyond them are sensed
Old Andalusian hearts
Longing to break again.

Girls,
Shut the curtains!][25]

"Baile" displays a metric regularity characteristic of the *sevillana*, with three octosyllabic quatrains in assonance. Each strophe is divisible into two motifs, with the first two lines offering an observation about the dance and the second two, ironic remarks about the aged dancer, Carmen. Thus, the first two lines simply inform that she is dancing through the streets of Seville. In the second two, though, the poetic voice reveals a suspicious contrast between her white hair, characteristic of age, and her shining pupils, proper to youthful hopes. In the second quatrain, first half, the yellow serpent coiling on her head symbolizes choreographic adroitness, as in "Paso de la siguiriya" (cf. Karageorgou-Bastea, *Arquitectura* 83n38). To finish the quatrain, an amused poetic voice reads her heart: she goes dreaming along, as she dances, of "gallants from yesteryear" [galanes de otros días, here rhythmically translated as "bygone romances"] where the word *galán*, dated in Lorca's time (Quance, *Contradiction* 36), expresses bittersweet humour, and the expression *de otros días* makes courtship painfully impossible. Finally, the third quatrain refers, like the beginning of the poem, to the dance, now invisible as Carmen passes out of sight. This strophe ends by indicating that her nostalgia lingers, but in such a way that irony at her expense forms a finale graceful in form but awkward in content. There is an either-or about this poem, ambivalence as in "Muerte de la Petenera," reluctance to take a definite stance towards Carmen, as if otherwise something fragile would shatter.

Uneasy about gender conventions, Lorca may have assumed an ambiguous posture towards Carmen's unconventional art as a pitiful by-product of the Andalusian character. She wants to relive the sweetness of her youthful pain, but her desire transcends her reality or "ineluctable fate" (Quance, *Contradiction* 99), much as does Lorca's own gnawing desire for personal sufficiency. She moves oblivious to time, age, and traditional propriety.[26] To complicate the dynamic of this Sevillian street scene, someone in authority wishes to veil the spectacle of Carmen from innocent eyes. Hence the two-line refrain, ironic from Lorca's standpoint, "Girls, / Close the curtains!" (*PCJ* 250–1) Like *Fantasía bætica*, "Baile" depends on alternating tonalities, even shifting tempos, here between a languorous dance and sharp commands; and like Falla's piano solo, Lorca's poem, for the purpose of savouring all its irony, calls for contemplation from a distance as a rich artistic whole, all the more painful because it does not favour any single part. Of the three Andalusian cities portrayed, Seville enjoys the upper hand in subtlety and variety of perspectives, while Malaga calls for accompanying the author in a whodunnit, and Cordoba furnishes a direct experience of human mortality. All three poems, whether formally based on Albéniz or Falla, show differing varieties of openness to death in the sense of cultural creativity. Different qualities of that openness have also appeared in the poetry on the cantaores Silverio Franconetti, Juan Breva, and Dolores la Parrala.

8

"Seis caprichos" or Virtuosity
and Art at a Distance

Mocking continues without transition from the poem "Baile" to the next section of *PCJ*, "Seis caprichos" [Six caprices]. Lorca dedicates this eighth part, originally intended to be the last, to his friend, the guitar virtuoso Regino Sainz de la Maza (*PCJ* 253). Sainz's virtuosity offers a key to the "capriciousness" of this poetry. In music, the capriccio or caprice normally consists of an instrumental piece more or less free of formal rules, with a lively tempo and surprising virtuosity at the performer's whim (Kennedy, *Oxford Dictionary of Music* 115).[1] An example is Rimsky-Korsakov's *Capriccio espagnol*, mentioned by Lorca in his lecture "Cante jondo. El primitivo canto andaluz" (*Cante jondo*. Primitive Andalusian song). Lorca noted that the Russian composer, attracted to Spanish folk music, structured his works in accordance with Andalusian patterns (*Obras completas* 3:203). Falla, author of his own *Vals-capricho* for piano (1900), praised the ease of the Russians' assimilation of *cante jondo* to classical music "by mixing the elements characteristic of some songs and rhythms or another, and by forming that unmistakable style that represents one of the highest values of Russian music from the end of the last century [nineteenth]" ("*Cante jondo*" 150).

In view of Falla's appreciation of Andalusian folk instruments,[2] two of Lorca's six poetic caprices have an instrumental focus: "Adivinanza de la guitarra" [Riddle on the guitar] and "Crótalo" [Castanet]. Both show surprising and skilful metaphorical play. One poem, "Candil" [Oil lamp], refers deep song to Eastern culture, as Falla did, but with a visual metaphorical skill all Lorca's own.[3] Two, "Chumbera" [Prickly pear] and "Pita" [Agave], metamorphose flora from the arid Andalusian landscape into figures of Lorca's fantasy, because deep song, as Falla suggested, emerges

from the contours of the land.[4] Finally, "Cruz" is a poetic witticism coming last, since all human efforts, as cante jondo and Lorca himself hold, end
at the grave.

Poetic virtuosity stands out in "Adivinanza de la guitarra." The title
misleadingly reflects an aim to tell a riddle about six maidens dancing at a
round crossroad, three of flesh and three of silver. Why, then, de Paepe
wonders, does the solution appear within the poem as its last line: "¡La
guitarra!" [The guitar!]" (*PCJ* 254n1)? The three maidens of flesh symbolize the catgut strings, the three of silver those of metal (255). The riddle
unexpectedly lies not in the solution, but in the mode of riddling. Lorca
shows virtuosity by using the guitar to exhibit his unique gift for myth-
making. After creating the six damsels of one miniature myth, he ends
his narrative with another. The poetic voice fancies the instrument as a
Polyphemus of gold, as enamoured of feminine beauty as the Cyclops from
Ovid's *Metamorphoses,* and as much a captor of souls as the same one-eyed
giant in Homer's *Odyssey,* where he jailed the hero and his men inside his
cave. Lorca's mythical giant keeps the six maids captive in an embrace that
prevents them from escaping into "dreams of yesteryear" [sueños de ayer]
– as did Carmen of Seville in "Baile" (254). Guitar listeners must avoid
absorption into the nostalgic content of the music to appreciate the dexterity of the instrumentalist. Likewise, poets like Lorca who compose caprices prefer to be admired more for their skill than for their poetic themes.
The lesson of aesthetic aloofness is implicit in Don Quixote's conduct towards Master Peter's puppet show. This episode from Cervantes's novel
attracts Falla, who ends his puppet opera *El retablo de maese Pedro* (1923)
with the mad knight's attack on the puppets, rather than with his subsequent monetary compensation to the puppeteer for damages as in
Cervantes (Hess, *Modernism* 199–200). Falla, although himself disciplined,
here exalts unfettered imagination, while Lorca glorifies fantasy tamed by
artistic dexterity.

His poetic virtuosity also shines in "Crótalo," not only through metaphor, but also through onomatopoeia recalling his and Falla's favourite
poet Darío, who in *El canto errante* [The wandering song, 1907] mimicked
a Nicaraguan stratovolcano with verbal sounds: "¡Oh Momotombo ronco
y sonoro!" [Oh Momotombo, raucous and sonorous!] (*Obras completas*
5:967). At the beginning and end of Lorca's poem on the castanet, he rhythmically repeats, while also making sounds imitate the object, "Crótalo./
Crótalo./Crótalo./Escabarajo sonoro" [Castanet./Castanet./Castanet./
Sonorous little scarab]. In the middle, he amuses with zoological metaphor,

picturing the castanet as a beetle swallowed by the spider of a dancer's hand and curling the warm air before drowning (like an incompetent cantaor, too close to his art) in its own wooden trill (*PCJ* 238). We saw in the poem "Conjuro" the comparison of the dancer's hand to a mole [topo] or an indecisive butterfly [mariposa indecisa] amidst evil omens and magic rites also visible, for instance, in *El amor brujo* (Falla, *Sorcier*, score, 61–2; *PCJ* 241–2). All such comparisons stress the closeness of *cante jondo* to nature, for Falla its greatest merit.

However, even the primitive act of metaphor-making has its limits. Lorca praises the "anonymous poet of the people" for capturing in metaphor, well proportioned to the verse it occupies, the complexity of life's loftiest sentimental moments (3:205). Yet Lorca recognizes his own distance, as a learned poet, from anonymous folk ones, just as Falla, immersed in the European musical canon, distinguishes himself from folk musicians spinning out songs at an instant. Concentrating metaphorical talents on grasping the essence of Andalusia may often prove to be fruitless. Falla, we saw, discovered a peculiar music, a collective essence perceived with the ear, yet implied even in the Spanish landscape. In the 1915 version of *El amor brujo*, he hoped to capture the essence of the Andalusian Gypsies, and his libretto contains the brief notation of the Gypsy witch's cave with surrounding vegetation, typical of the region: "The cave is lonely and dark, but in the background is seen a mountain road with prickly pears and underbrush, lit by moonlight."[5] Lorca's poem "Chumbera" depicts the prickly pear. What can a cultivated writer say of this cactus? His gift for metaphor, if unchecked, could act as a Trojan horse, betraying him into oblivion. Lorca knows the sculpture of Athenodoros of Rhodes depicting the Trojan priest Laocoön and his two sons, who had warned their people in vain about the Greeks' equine gift (Bonaddio, *Poetry of Self-Consciousness* 71). The goddess Athena sent two sea serpents to crush Laocoön and the youths to death.[6] Why, then, compare an Andalusian prickly pear, for its twisted forms, to a "wild Laocoön"? Just as absurd would it be to compare the cactus to the nymph Daphne, turned to the wood of a laurel tree,[7] for the older parts of the prickly pear become wooden. Even more extravagant would be the analogy between the prickly pear and Atys, transformed by Cybele into a fir tree.[8] Yet the poetic voice stuffs both mythological figures into a single line, and for good measure makes them sympathetic to the cactus's plight: "Daphne and Atys / know of your pain."[9] This is not primitive poetry, for it sets cultural distance between itself and the nature it is portraying.

Contradicting the ungrounded mythical suppositions of the plant's grief, the speaker recognizes its harmony with its Andalusian environment: "How well off you are/under the half-moon!";[10] "how well off you are/ threatening the wind!"[11] In the fourth line of the nine-line poem, practically at its midpoint, there appears the comparison of the prickly pear to many round fruits and to an athlete with many balls in a handball court [Múltiple pelotari]. Mythopoeia serves primitives for interpreting poorly understood natural reality. For self-critical, sportive, ironic modern poets, though, the prickly pear remains "inexplicable," the final line of this poem (*PCJ* 260).

A more measured, though also ironic, attempt at metaphor-making about the land appears in the companion poem "Pita." Here the poetic voice never loses sight of dealing with a natural phenomenon, the agave, when skilfully limiting itself to comparisons with other such phenomena. The plant, with fleshy long leaves forming a rosette that curves upward from the ground, looks like a "petrified octopus" [pulpo petrificado] according to the first and sixth line of this ekphrastic six-verse poem. Seen from afar in clusters, the agave, varieties of which are greyish green, seems to the bemused poetic subject to put ash-coloured waistbands around the bellies of the hills. Its adherence to the hillsides makes it appear to bite the narrow mountain passes with "formidable molars" [muelas formidables] (261).

A poet's reflection on his own metaphorical art reappears in the poem "Candil," concerning an oil lamp at a Gypsy's wake. This poem contains a critique of pure metaphor, a metaphorical reflection upon reflection itself, parodying "Poema de la soleá," the dancer's reflection upon pain. The lyric voice likens the lamp flame to an Indian fakir contemplating his own body – his "entrail of gold" [entraña de oro]. For de Paepe, this simile recalls Falla, who traced *cante jondo* to India (256n3). However, the seriousness attributed to the flame in the first two verses does not extend to the poetic voice, continually outshining itself in metaphorical agility. In *El amor brujo*, the protagonist Candelas engages in wordplay on her own name as she leaves her lover. She identifies herself to him as "Candeliya, little candle, who burned for you alone, and who now leaves you in the dark forever and ever, amen!"[12] Analogously, though with more brilliant metaphor, after Lorca's fakir simile appears the image of a flame producing its own eclipse – light and shadow at once – while creating dreamlike atmospheres with no wind (*PCJ* 256). The flame, like a "creationist" poet, like a composer, dreams up worlds from within, seemingly oblivious to outer change. The examination of creativity continues with the metaphor of the flame as an "incandescent stork" [cigüena incandescente], a bird symbolising birth. This luminous creature opposes the dark (recalling the Asian Zoroaster's religion contrasting light and dark), and bites with its beak at shadows (256).[13] However, light and dark, life and death form part of the same Andalusian reality for Lorca. This jarring juxtaposition has appeared in the poem "La soleá," where the earthen sky swooped through the balcony to inter the dancer alive while she reflected on pain. In "Sorpresa," we have read the echo of Calderón with no one capable of looking out of a dead man's eyes. The present poem ends with the flame atremble, looking out of the eyes of a dead little Gypsy, as if reflected in them. In sum, reflection on birth and life inevitably ends as reflection on death. Therefore the final poem of this sextet, "Cruz," after two humorous fantasies of desert plants on the barren *cante jondo* landscape ("Chumbera," "Pita"), offers us the cross as the "Final point in the road."[14] The point, a term used in geometry, also means in Spanish a period, marking the end of a sentence. It becomes ironically multiplied as much as it gets reflected over and over in the irrigation channel to form ellipses [Punto suspensivos] (*PCJ* 262), indicating mystery, an endless need to keep reflecting further ... like a candle in the water (Bonaddio, *Poetics of Self-Reflection* 74).

If Lorca originally intended, as it appears, to have concluded *PCJ* here, then he has wanted to leave it open-ended (Karageorgou-Bastea, *Arquitectura* 171). A mosaic on the wall of the Alhambra allows for indefinite extension as long as there is space for a tile repeating a given design. The line described by the melody and the dance of the siguiriya, archetypal musical form of *cante jondo*, has its end point at infinity (3:218). The cultural sedimentation process originating the Andalusian musical soul as understood by Falla and Lorca never finishes. Therefore reflection upon this process also should never end. Falla's artistic reflections have justified timeless artworks in the Andalusian idiom, and have also led to Lorca's skilful and amusing artistic reflections, found in his poetry, which in turn has inspired the verse and the music of other poets and musicians.

9

Falla on Deep Song and Lorca's
Romancero gitano

In *Romancero gitano* [Gypsy ballads], the most reprinted and critiqued poetry book in Spanish literature (Gibson, *Life* 212), critics have yet to examine the author's admitted debt to Falla (Lorca, *Obras completas* 3:953). His impact largely explains Lorca's differences from other artists of his age group. The anthology, published in June 1928, drew immediate fire from his contemporaries. In a letter of September 1928, Salvador Dalí synthesized the main reservations of others: docility to traditional poetic norms, stereotyping and conformist commonplaces, excessive coherence and rationality deforming poetic objects, unnecessary detail in customs and anecdotes, and literary immorality à la Cocteau (Gibson, *Life* 220–1).[1] One of Lorca's oldest, most measured poetic coevals, poet-critic Pedro Salinas, remarked that he did not detach himself from tradition, but narrated and described (practices rejected by those poets) (*Ensayos* 332–3). A younger, more negative poet of the group of 1927, Luis Cernuda, criticized Lorca's narrative and lyric obscurity: his ballads "are and are not" narratives, his language "is and is not" Gongorine, and his finished product "is and is not" folkloric. Two main defects that Cernuda deplored were excessive theatricality and triteness in portraying customs and mores (*Estudios sobre poesía española* 214–15). Yet, the astonishingly high readership of *Romancero gitano* and the aesthetic enjoyment it affords even to sensitive readers make these reservations nugatory.

A prime factor distinguishing Lorca from less traditional, self-styled "purer" poets of his literary *pléiade* was his closeness to Manuel de Falla between 1920 and 1929. Early fascinated by folk and classical music, Lorca drew creative analogies between Falla's music and his own writings. Since Falla gained fame from his Andalusianism (Mora Guarnido, *Lorca y su mundo* 155), his elevation of Southern Spanish folk-music conventions to the classical canon, Lorca performed the same experiment with Andalusian folk poetry and achieved comparable success through his unique musicality. In *PCJ* and *Romancero gitano* he emulated Falla in *Noches* and *El amor brujo*, among other works. Both artists invited audience recognition of familiar folk art and enjoyment of the author's skill in musically modernizing that art.[2] Moreover, both encouraged listener or reader participation. Since the end of Falla's pantomime *El Corregidor y la Molinera* left the question unresolved as to whether or not this couple committed adultery, the program notes affirm, "The authors of this farce let the spectators solve the case in the direction that pleases each one most."[3] Likewise, as Cernuda suggests, Lorca's ballads seek maximum openness of meaning, requiring readers' choice between interpretive possibilities and co-authorship with the poet.

On one point, however, Falla and Lorca insist: the Andalusian Gypsy allows access to the essence of Andalusia. For Cadiz-born Falla, Andalusia forms the essential Spain, for foreigners imitate Andalusian music when seeking the essence of Spanish music ("*Cante jondo*" 149, 151–2). Their own music takes on traits of Andalusian deep song, derived, according to Falla, from the Andalusian "cultural spirit" (142). He traced this musical heritage from Mozarabic plainchant to Moorish song and dance to its purest synthetic form in song and dance of the Gypsies, fugitives in Spain from India, whose scales and rhythms they imported into Europe (140–1). The Gypsy siguiriya has Asian features: use of the enharmonic modality, varying several notes of the gamut and even dividing and subdividing them into intervals too small for the tempered scale; melodic range rarely exceeding the sixth; obsessive repetition of a single note, often accompanied by ascending or descending appoggiaturas; use of melodic adornments only as demanded by the emotion of the text; and audience participation with screams of encouragement to the performers (143–6).

Jesús Torrecilla maintains that Lorca identified the Gypsy with deep song, the art which he perfected (231). To Torrecilla's statement we add that the qualities ascribed by Falla to the siguiriya gitana, the genre typical of deep song, came to be attributed by Lorca to the Gypsy himself, its partial producer. Those qualities were (1) elevation, (2) depth, (3) aristocracy, (4) genuine Andalusianism, and (5) universality. For Falla, the siguiriya epitomized deep song, just as for Lorca the Gypsy embodied Andalusia. (1) Falla found the siguiriya the only European music that in structure and style preserved "the highest qualities" [las más altas cualidades] of primitive Asian song ("*Cante jondo*" 142). Accordingly, Lorca regarded "Gypsy" as synonymous with what is "loftiest" in Andalusia ("lo más elevado": 3:340).

(2) The loftiness of the siguiriya referred for Falla to its depth, since its scale derived from vocal range as in ancient Indian song ("*Cante jondo*" 144). Lorca inferred that the music "bears in its notes the naked, chilling emotion of the first Oriental stocks,"[4] and that the Gypsy acquired the profundity of contact with that atavistic emotion. (3) Falla revered deep song as noble for its restraint in adorning melody only in response to textual emotion, as opposed to the economic motivation of commercialized flamenco. In deep song, word and melody, wrote Falla, obeyed natural need, imitating the sounds of nature ("*Cante jondo*" 144, 146). Therefore, Lorca's Gypsy communicated everything that human beings had in common with nature, especially "the Pain that filters into the marrow of the bones and into the sap of trees."[5] (4) For Falla, the song peculiar to Andalusia assumed "so intimate, so unique, so national a character, that it makes it unmistakable."[6] Lorca revered the Gypsies as creators of that song, expression of the Andalusian cultural soul and thus tantamount to the "soul of our soul."[7] (5) Falla regarded deep song as universal in two senses: first, it afforded insight into the history of human sounds and, second, it had attained global diffusion. With its obsessive insistence on one note, it approached primitive magic charms, suggesting that in general song preceded language (Falla, "*Cante jondo*" 145).

Further, "natural Andalusian music," as Falla called deep song (147), was the only Spanish music consistently imitated in Europe, especially by French and Russian composers (150–2). When they wanted to write Spanish music, the Russian Group of Five and French Impressionists looked to Andalusia. Lorca wrote, "The sad modulations and the serious Orientalism of our song has influence everywhere, from Granada into Moscow." Even Debussy, he reminded, steeped himself in deep song performed by Spanish Gypsies at the 1900 World Fair.[8] To synthesize, by extending traits noted by Falla in Gypsy song to the characteristics of Lorca's literary Gypsies, we find in them (1) life in harmony with nature, (2) antagonism towards social, commercial, or economic constraints, (3) obedience to natural emotion, (4) primitive fear of occult forces of nature, accompanied by a sense of personal powerlessness, and (5) insecurity about the mystery of the universe, whether in natural, social, or personal contexts. The poem most studied in *Romancero gitano*, "Romance sonámbulo" [Sleepwalking ballad], seemed to its author "one of the most mysterious of the book."[9] To avoid diminishing aesthetic enjoyment, he never dispelled the mystery. Hence, while not denying one interpretation of the poem as an expression of Granada's yearning for the sea, he affirmed that the work could just as easily have meant something else (3:343). If, however, we look at its theme as the beauty of mystery, and if in the process we employ analogies from the music of Falla, we may also find a key to this poem. In defiance of critics who find its plot "brilliantly clear" [nítido] (e.g., García-Posada, in Lorca, *Primer romancero gitano* 122–3, n.), "Romance sonámbulo" retreats from all plots like an asymptote from its axis, and ends up as verbal music. "'Romance sonámbulo,'" as Federico Bonaddio skilfully puts it, "is not concerned with the process of telling but rather with the process of not telling, and so the very human desires of the poem's figures have been sacrificed in favour of the elusively poetic and transformational desire evoked by the refrain" (*Poetics of Self-Consciousness* 120). The plot usually attributed to the ballad is quite weak: a girl, despairing because of her lover's absence, one night hurls herself into a reservoir. He returns mortally wounded, pursued as a smuggler by Civil Guards. His beloved's father comes to meet him, and both climb to the father's home (123). Were this plot essential to the poem, it would attract few readers, just as Falla's operas and ballets with their flimsy arguments would garner few spectators. The ballad acquires musicality mainly from the hypnotic refrain recited by the first-person speaker:

Verde que te quiero verde.
Verde viento. Verdes ramas.
El barco sobre el mar
y el caballo en la montaña.

[Green for I want you green.
Green wind. Green branches.
The boat upon the sea
And the horse in the mountain.]   (1:400, ll. 1–4)

The syntagma "X, for I want you X" potentiates the speaker's will, giving expression to creativity (Salvador, *Glosas* 23–4). He gathers strength or dips a paintbrush anew into green pigment before continuing his creation. His artistic effort is so mysteriously haunting, that like the initial vibrato phrases of Falla's "En el Generalife," the sound vibrates beyond its temporal limits, forming what Adorno has called a "sensible infinity." This denial of limit constitutes "the poetic halo of impressionism," the procedure of Debussy among others (Adorno, *Philosophie der neuen Musik* 168–9). The *sfumato* effect, erasing differences between sounds and between images, hinders determination of the addressee in the phrase "Green for I want you green." Does the "you" refer to the ballad itself, as Salvador thinks, or even to the girl with green flesh? To grasp with at least some small certainty the meaning of each phrase as well as its music, it helps to resort to demonstrable sources. Juan Ramón Jiménez related having heard as a child the verses, "Verde que te quiero verde, / del color de la aceituna" [Green, for I want you green, / The colour of the olive].[10] The lover wishes his beloved to have as olive a complexion as possible.

The incessant repetition of green in Lorca's poem finds an explanation in Falla's pamphlet El "cante jondo" (Canto primitivo andaluz) [Deep song (Primitive Andalusian song)]. The composer attributed repeated, obsessive use of the same note as in deep song to certain formulas of enchantment (145). Lorca revealed in a lecture-recital that his poem had emerged from the "Andalusian depths" [fondo andaluz] (3:343), in other words, from the cultural spirit of the Southern region. The poet had borrowed his expression directly from Falla, who identified the "primordial Andalusian depths" [fondo primigenio andaluz] as the agent that, to form deep song, "fuses and forms a new musical modality with the contributions it has received" from the Church, the Moors, and the Gypsies.[11] "Romance sonámbulo" closely approaches deep song in that the first-person speaker serves as a medium for the Andalusian Volksgeist when conjuring up a green-skinned girl, just as Candelas conjures up the phantom of her dead lover in El amor brujo. Here as in Lorca's poem "Conjuro" (Conjuration) (PCJ 241–2), the spell affirms the conjurer's personal power over the world.

"Romance sonámbulo" is interpretable as Lorca's original verbal music with two related main themes: one about the interaction between the first-person conjurer and the green-skinned girl he calls forth in a deep-song sequence; the other, about the dialogued interaction between her lover and her father. The two themes, initially at odds, gradually merge towards the end until the interaction of narrator and girl returns as a reprise, a finale rounding off the whole with a definitive, Falla-like coda. In two quatrains the poetic voice depicts the green girl as a phantom, fearful but funny, like the ghost from Falla's newly revised ballet El amor brujo, who haunts "in an old Gypsy costume, with blackened face and an appearance that is at once comic and hideous" (Amor brujo, score, 1).[12] Lorca's female character has "green flesh, green hair, / with eyes of cold silver."[13] Guillermo Díaz-Plaja links the first line to Juan Ramón's poem "El pajarito verde" [The little green bird], with its verses "Green is the girl, she has / Green eyes, green hair."[14] Not only could the mysterious girl therefore remind Lorca of a grotesque bird – Falla's Salud compares herself to a bird awaiting her mate (*Vie brève*, I, rehearsal 27, p. 23) – but her cold silver eyes may connote folly. In Lorca's poem "Canción tonta" [Foolish song] from the anthology *Canciones* [Songs], a child tells his mother, "Mama, I want to be of silver," but she responds, "Son, you will be very cold."[15] However, green and silver also hold sinister connotations in Lorca. Green may stand for decay, silver for the moon, a lethal being in *Romancero gitano*.[16] The green girl dreams on her railing with her "shadow on her waist" [Con la sombra en la cintura] as if cast there by the moonlight, marking her for a tragic fate.

The middle section of the poem, slicing through the vague, green atmosphere like a dagger, abruptly sets direct dialogue before the reader. The juxtaposition of fragments, seen in traditional balladry, gives this verbal music a jagged edge with few transitions as in Falla. Two voices alternate, one of a gravely wounded youth, the other of a rueful mature man. Their dialogue resembles the juxtaposition of two melodies, as in the middle part of Falla's third nocturne of *Noches*, where motif 5 of the work, a loud, agitated *petenera* based on a three-note descent (see "Introduction," this volume, musical example 3), brusquely cedes to a softer, slower, nostalgic Gypsy *zorongo* (score, 3, rehearsal 39, p. 77). The young Gypsy sounds urgent notes by demanding a bed of fine linens in which to die, while his interlocutor, the girl's father, looks back to a happier time.

The young man wishes to transform his entire being in a single moment from motion to stillness: he would trade a horse for a home, a mount for a mirror, a knife for a blanket, with a final instant of decorousness coming through death in bed. To drive home his urgency, he displays his fatal wound. The girl's father acknowledges his need in folkloric metaphor, musically revealing the impossibility of a viable future, the young man's with his daughter. In a traditional Gypsy wedding song or *alboreá*, roses symbolize the blood of the bride's virginity.[17] In "Romance sonámbulo," however, roses refer instead to the luckless youth's blood: "Three hundred darksome roses/your white shirt-frill is wearing."[18] After the older man twice bars his way from a home no longer psychologically his own, the dying Gypsy, in an access of idealism, begs to be allowed to climb at least to the lofty railings of his beloved. These railings become a high point, symbol of her wait for him, like a touch of heaven from his perspective. The notion of an elevated site with ideal connotations appears in Falla's "Danza lejana," where distant elevation serves as a lofty aesthetic space (see "Introduction," this volume). Yet Lorca's Gypsy flies ever higher. Rhetorically echoing the idealist Don Quixote, the green girl's lover refers to her high railings as "balustrades of the moon/through which the water roars."[19]

The youth's idealism wins out as together the two men climb towards the "high railings," their tribulations left behind – the young man's "trail of blood" and his companion's "trail of tears" in a balance of two verses after the earlier opposition between them (1:401, ll. 55–6). Responding to their emotions, Andalusian nature, harmonizing with Lorca's (and Falla's) Gypsies, reacts in two memorable metaphors. On rooftops little tinplate lanterns tremble in the faint light, as if physically shuddering, while "a thousand crystal tambourines/[are] wounding early dawn"[20] in a brusque lighting effect transferred by synaesthesia to instrumental sound. From the musical standpoint, percussion instruments – kettledrums, tiny bells, standard drums, cymbals, or triangles – cause discontinuity. They pass from sounding to non-sounding, from being to non-being (García Bacca, *Filosofía de la música* 626). Through a loud musical call to attention, the poetic voice percussively breaks artistic continuity and signals passage to a major part of the poem, as happens at the end of part one of Falla's *El sombrero de tres picos*. The initial theme of "Romance sonámbulo" (conjuring of the green girl) will link up to the second theme (troubled dialogue between the two men).

For the first time since the end of part one, centering on the green Gypsy girl, the initial two lines of the poem recur, as if the wilful speaker were gathering new force to underscore subsequent events. He ties together the two main themes of the ballad, the one on his interaction with the green Gypsy, the other the dialogue between the two Gypsy men. As they ascend towards the railing, nature foreshadows tragedy as in "Romance de la luna, luna" [Ballad of the moon, moon]. In the mouths of both characters the wind leaves tastes associated with greenness, colour of the girl: bile, mint, and sweet basil, a bittersweet combination. Conversation between the men focuses directly on her for the first time. Nostalgia conquers agitation, as in the third movement of Falla's *Noches*. When the youth asks the girl's father for her whereabouts, he responds with doleful longing, recalling time before the start of the poem, that is, before she turned green: "How many times she waited,/how many times she had been waiting,/ fresh face, black hair,/upon this green railing!"[21]

The final part of the ballad, a return to atmospheric vagueness, abruptly transports the reader again to the anguish of the initial scene. The girl returns to centre stage with her bizarre green flesh and green hair, contrasting with her father's fresh-faced description of her. Now she rocks over the face of the reservoir, now an icicle of moon maintains her over the water (ll. 74–5, 77–8). Does she merely view her own reflection, or is she dead and lying afloat? Critics disagree, but the answer does not matter from the musical standpoint. She has always been existentially nil. The poem, drawing to a close, loses tension and repeats earlier melodies now calling for reading with a melancholy *rubato*, a slowing down, as in the final bars of the last nocturne of *Noches*. Two striking images signal the conclusion of the ballad. In the first, wherein "the night became intimate,/like a small plaza,"[22] the artist draws a small black frame around his entire composition, now complete. In the second, where "drunken Civil Guards/came knocking at the door,"[23] critics assume that they have arrived to arrest the wounded young Gypsy, a smuggler. However, the ballad says nothing explicit about smuggling. The poem mentions a horse in the mountain and a ship on the sea, as well as mountain passes of Cabra, well-known in the nineteenth century for banditry. Yet horse and ship form part of a traditional prayer seeking protection for the rider in the mountain and the sailor (a smuggler?) in the sea.[24] References to the horse and the ship here take on a ritualistic sing-song quality that habitually complements the two incantatory, repeated verses, "Green for I want you green,/Green wind. Green branches." Yet what can we say of the Civil Guards? Their drunken stupor incapacitates them for any function in the poem except an auditory one – "Romance sonámbulo" is almost music – of providing through their knocking a loud bass drum roll signalling discontinuity again, here the end of the work, repeatedly indicated with percussions as in Falla.[25] Finally, the four verses forming the beginning recur at the end to finish the ballad as it began, offering another concluding frame in a reprise, also frequent in Falla's music.

A second enigmatic ballad, "Muerto de amor" [Dead of love], displays structural similarities to "Romance sonámbulo." In a Granadan setting, terror once more joins hands with the comic as in Falla, though in poetry typical of Lorca for expressing fear of death. In Sacromonte, the old Gypsy quarter in Granada (Josephs and Caballero, eds., Lorca, *Romancero gitano* 268), a mother and a son dialogue about phantasmal lights he glimpses in the night sky. She explains them away by attributing them to copperware gleaming above in the kitchens of their riotously funny British neighbours, the Charles Temples (referred to as "la gente aquella").[26] Moon and night actively participate, like mythical characters of deep song. In a half-humorous, half-eerie gesture, the waning moon with fibrous beams affixes yellow switches of hair for mourning to the towers. A storm metaphorically materializes when the poetic voice imagines night as a trembling stranger, knocking at balcony windows to escape a thousand pursuing watchdogs in a whimsical, comically embarrassing situation even for a potentially terrifying nocturnal figure (1:421).

The final part of "Muerto de amor" forms an elegy to any youth who dies, and ends by prophesying the young poet's death. The first quatrain may well indicate that someone young has passed away:

Brisas de caña mojada
y rumor de viejas voces,
resonaban por el arco
roto de la media noche.

[Breezes of wet reed
And murmurs of old voices,
Resounded through the broken
Arch of the midnight hour.]   (421–2, ll.19–22)

Disembodied voices, representing fatality, are heard from offstage in Falla's Andalusianist works like *La vida breve* and *El sombrero de tres picos*. In "Muerto de amor" ancient voices mournfully resonate with much the same mood as that created by Falla in the repetitive main melody of his guitar *Homenaje* to the deceased Debussy. After this seven-note motif, the guitarist strums descending glissandi three times, like an obsessive downward vibration analysed into its tonal components and obliterating boundaries between discrete notes. In the above-quoted verses from "Muerto de amor," a rolling double r-sound recurs at regular intervals (b*r*isa, *r*umor, *r*esonaban, *r*oto), lending its phonemic vibration to the vibration implied in the imagery (*rumor* meaning murmur, *resonaban*). Ancient voices of death have returned to accompany a young man's soul, which the narrator envisions as the breeze of a riverside reed.[27] A gypsum arch stands for death in the poem "Muerte" [Death] from *Poeta in Nueva York* [Poet in New York] (1:503, l. 19), and here an arch lies broken at midnight, symbolizing a life brusquely ended (1:422, ll. 21–2). While all nature slumbers, represented by oxen and roses, something other-worldly, supernatural, occurs: four funereal lights cry through the lofty corridors. In "Reyerta" [Feud], mourning old women watch from the treetops like a part of the landscape. Here, in two parallel quatrains, two sets of mourning women identify with the land: some from the valley, others from the river. As in classical elegy, the mourners recognize death as universal (Cannon, "*Llanto*" 230). In Falla's antiwar "Oración de las madres" [Prayer of mothers], a mother prays to avoid her baby eventually being drafted and causing her to suffer what these mourners do now: "Me lo matarán, y era mi alegría" [They will kill him, and he was my joy] ("Oración de las madres," *Songs and Piano Music*). In the ballad at hand, women of the valley act in an even grimmer situation while lowering into the earth the blood of their son, at peace after being cut down in the flower of youth, yet bitter because of the brevity of life. Hence, as with classical elegy, this poem recognizes death for its present beauty as redemptive, conciliatory, and tranquil. At the same time, death in the elegiac tradition appears inevitable (Cannon, "*Llanto*" 229–31). Women by the river weep for a moment frozen in time, made up of their unbound hair and unforgettable names (Lorca 1:422, ll. 27–34). The clock has stopped both for the dead and for their mourners. Elegiac poets fix in human memory the instant of death to save the deceased from oblivion. In classical elegy, divinities mourn the illustrious dead with music (Cannon, "*Llanto*" 232). In "Muerto de amor," angels join Gypsies to play instruments as movingly humble as accordions (Lorca 1:422, ll. 37–8).

The last four quatrains of Lorca's ballad form the least coherent of the total verbal collage on death. The first and the fourth seem the more intimate; the second and third appear the least personal, least obscure, and more relevant to the theme of lethal love. The second develops imagery associated with deep song. The frontispiece of Falla's pamphlet *El "cante jondo" (Canto primitivo andaluz)* contains a drawing of the Virgin of Sorrows' heart, pierced with seven swords. De Paepe discovers an allusion to that Virgin in "Muerto de amor" in its anguished repetition of the number seven: "Siete gritos, siete sangres, / siete adormideras dobles / quebraron opacas lunas / en los oscuros salones" [Seven screams, seven bloods, / seven double poppy flowers / shattered opaque mirrors / in the darkened parlours] (*PCJ* 211n13). The cantaor Silverio Franconetti, admired by Falla and Lorca, opened mirrors with his screams, and for this reason, according to García-Posada (Lorca, *Primer romancero gitano* 179n43–6), the quatrain also ends with an image of shattering mirrors. The quatrain that follows offers the theme of amorous betrayal. Oaths taken require hands raised; oaths broken seem to call for hands cut off. Couple these amputated members with coronets of flowers, like those of orange blossoms at weddings, and a sarcastic combination of metaphors emerges to denote betrayal in love (Lorca 1:422, ll. 47–50).

The most personal quatrains of the ballad stem from the author's premonitions of his premature death. Without warning, in the midst of describing a Gypsy funeral, the speaker lifts a curtain and makes the reader privy to an imagined statement of the poet to his mother, whom he expects to predecease:

Madre, cuando yo me muera,
que se enteren los señores.

Pon telegramas azules
que vayan del Sur al Norte.

[Mother, when I die,
Let the gentry know.
Send from South to North
Blue telegrams of woe.]   (1:422)

Lorca could likely have foreseen his tragic end in the more conservative, more homophobic South, as well as the need of high-placed liberals in the more progressive North (where he attended classes) to announce his death to the world. "Muerto de amor" ends on a note of high tension, a clap of thunder, as percussive a break with narrative continuity as Falla's musical finales and as the drum roll of the Civil Guards in "Romance sonámbulo." Lorca's brother Francisco recounts that the final quatrain of "Muerto de amor" recalls an incident from early adolescence (*Federico y su mundo* 19). A sudden thunderstorm caught them by surprise in open country. As they bolted for shelter, young Federico felt lightning from an angry sky grazing his cheek and fatefully marking him forever:

Y el cielo daba portazos
al brusco rumor del bosque,
mientras clamaban las luces
en los altos corredores.

[And the sky was slamming doors
To the brusque sound of the woods,
As the lights kept wailing on
In the lofty corridors.]   (1:422)

Primitive fear of obscure natural forces pervades the mysterious music of "Romance sonámbulo" and "Muerto de amor." The interpretation of such forces generates myth, for which Lorca has consulted sources like Hesiod's *Theogony* (Gibson, *A Life* 69) and Ovid's *Metamorphoses* (García-Posada, in Lorca, *Primer romancero* 110). Falla employs myth between dialoguing characters in the original 1915 version of *El amor brujo* to reflect Gypsy witchcraft and naturalistic pantheism. As Lorca writes to Jorge Guillén, "In this [first] part [of *Romancero gitano*] I manage to harmonize Gypsy mythology with what is merely ordinary in present-day life, and the result is strange, but I think endowed with a new beauty."[28]

In *El amor brujo* of 1915, Falla's protagonist, the Gypsy girl Candelas, re-cites a ballad narrating how she wandered along seeking her love, asking everyone she met whether he had been spotted. By a riverbank a fisherman was singing of his own lost love. Suddenly, according to Candelas, the river water rose up and told both lovers to seek relief for their pain at the cave of a Gypsy witch, who could cure them (Falla, *Vie brève*, program 65–6). An autographed score of this mythical ballad, "Canción del pesca-dor" [The fisherman's song], appears in Lorca's personal library collection (Tinnell 414). Likewise, two mythical ballads initiate *Romancero gitano*, each with a musical theme. In both, a dancing figure moves to music with world-shaking impact: in "Preciosa y el aire" [Preciosa and the air], a Gypsy girl, whose dancing and tambourine-playing makes nature play music, arouses the wind's sexual passion; in "Romance de la luna, luna," the moon's dance of death overcomes a Gypsy child.

The lunar ballad, written by autumn 1923 (Mora Guarnido, *Lorca* 209–10; Gibson, *Life* 134), occupies a privileged place as a paradigm for many of the others. As Falla's new librettist, Lorca must have been consulting libretti not only of *El amor brujo*, but also of Falla's early opera *La vida breve*, whose success in Brussels in May 1923 had elated the poet (Lorca 3:793). From this work he could have derived the idea of setting his myth about the moon in the Granadan Gypsy district of El Albaicín, where *La vida breve* begins. Falla's friend Joaquín Turina explains in 1917 that the opera unfolds "in the yard of a house of Gypsies (...) in [which] there is a smithy that holds, within the plot, characteristics of a symbol, since from it come sad voices and desperate songs, as if they represented the pain of life reflected in continuous toil."[29] Offstage, to the metallic beat of ham-mers in forges, a male chorus sings a *martinete* with a mournful melody in a modal key, filled with presentiments. "Woe to the man, woe, / Born to a fate he'll dread! / Woe to the man born an anvil, / And not born a hammer instead!"[30] Allusions to aggressive hammers and helpless anvils recur in "Romance de la luna, luna" and in two other ballads,[31] imparting to the smithy tools the fatalistic symbolism they hold in *La vida breve*. However, in Lorca, the Gypsy child and the moon each manipulate blacksmith refer-ences at whim, giving their dialogue a kind of fascinating capriciousness. The child, startled by the strange shining figure with bare breasts and bus-tle of nards, threatens her with reification at the Gypsies' hands: they will convert her gleaming metal whiteness into rings and necklaces (1:393, ll. 10–12). She, on the other hand, reverses the image: when the Gypsies re-turn, she insists, they will instead find the luckless child lying on the anvil with eyes shut (ll. 14–16).

Falla may have contributed to Lorca's costuming of the moon. Lorca combines terror and humour in characterizing the moon, following Falla's example in *El amor brujo*, although the humour has a lascivious cast foreign to the composer's works. Her mildly obscene gesture of flaunting hard tin breasts does not terrify but amuses. Further, her bustle, in Lorca's time an antiquated garment (García-Posada, in Lorca, *Primer romancero* 105n1–8) – and for good measure a bustle made of white nards (moonbeams) – shows her as comically anachronistic as the *vihuela*-playing death figure, dressed as a bride in "Gráfico de la Petenera" (ch. 6). Yet, personifying mortality, she inspires terror. The moon's rejoinder to the child not to soil her as she dances her dance of death continues this mixture of humour and frightfulness: "Niño, déjame, no pises/mi blancor almidonado" [Child, leave me alone, don't tread/on my perfect starched whiteness] (Lorca 1:383, l. 13).

To increase Lorca's macabre humour, the poem takes on qualities of a lullaby. His last two lines reproduce two verses of a Granadan Gypsy lullaby, which he quoted in a rough copy of his public lecture "Canciones de cuna españolas" [Spanish cradle songs, 13 December 1928]:

Tengo una choza en el campo.
Tengo una choza en el campo.
El aire la vela, vela.
El aire la está velando.

[I have a hut in the country.
I have a hut in the country.
The air keeps watch, keeps watch.
The air is keeping watch.]

(García-Posada, in Lorca, *Primer romancero* 107n35–6)

Repetition lulls a child to sleep, satisfying rhythmic expectations, offering security. In his lecture on lullabies, Lorca reveals his interest in those melodies under the guidance of Falla, for whom the poet would transcribe them. Keys to the origins of folk songs, exported from one region to another, are only decipherable, in Lorca's judgment, "by technicians as deep as Falla, who, in addition, possesses an artistic intuition of the first order."[32] Falla had read in Pedrell that he could learn to absorb musical dictation by noting down songs mothers sing to babies to make them sleep. This practice of taking down the often tender and intense tunes of mothers would one day, according to Pedrell, be used by folklorists (*Cancionero*

12). The intense strains of the Andalusian "Nana" in Falla's *Siete canciones populares españolas* [Seven popular Spanish songs], hypnotically repeating the phrase "Duérmete" [Go to sleep], cannot have escaped Lorca's notice. Repetition in "Romance de la luna, luna" takes place lullaby-style. Lorca tries to show the same artistic craftsmanship in his medium as does Falla while underscoring almost with delectation as Falla never did the child's fear of death. After the approach of the strangely attired moon, "The child just stares and stares at her, / The child is staring at her" [El niño la mira, mira. / El niño la está mirando]. The rhythm reproduces that of the last two lines of "I have a hut in the country," but the reader remains unapprised until reaching the end of the lunar ballad. Quoting an artist's source within a work takes place in Falla's elegiac *Homenaje* to Debussy, whose coda quotes at the end from the French composer's *La soirée dans Grenade,* and whose melody, slightly modified, appears to have originated the main theme of Falla's guitar tribute (ch. 6). However, the final two lines of Lorca's ballad offer a surprise, an ironic shift in meaning of the original lullaby quoted. The verb *velar,* to maintain vigil, can also signify to spend the night at a wake, keeping watch over the dead. Here, the air stays vigilant over the smithy where the child lies lifeless. Readers could have predicted this tragic dénouement had they not succumbed to the lulling effect of the repetition. Indications of the child's distress abounded. He twice urges the moon, "Huye, luna, luna, luna" [Away, moon, moon, moon!] (1:103, ll. 9, 17).

The Gypsies with whom the child has threatened the moon live in harmony with Granadan nature. A Gypsy rider approaches the city from the *Vega,* the Granadan lowland, "tocando el tambor del llano" [playing the tambourine of the plain]. His companions may be singing deep song. F.M. Pabanó, writing on Gypsy history and customs in a book owned by Falla, describes the typical Gypsy singer as follows: "The cantaor, his head thrown back, lightly half-closes his eyes and with a voice of virile timbre, while embroidering the lacework of his sentiments, tosses his sung verse into the air."[33] Hence, Lorca's poetic voice describes the advancing Gypsies as possibly lost in song, "their heads held high, / and eyes half-closed."[34] Made of "bronce y sueño" [bronze and dream], of bronze for their olive skin tones, of dream for their shortsightedness, they end up mourning the child. They had seen bad omens while heading homeward. In *El amor brujo,* "screams of auguring birds seem to be suggested in the orchestra when Candelas appears at the door of the [witch's] cave."[35] In Lorca's ballad a barn owl "sings" [canta] as part of the natural concert, and the narrator twice repeats that verb while inserting the rueful exclamation "¡ay!," as if to portend evil (l. 30). From beginning to end, Lorca, affected by Falla, though reacting in his own unique way, has produced a dreamy mythical world, both hideous and lewdly comic. Repetition acquires a hypnotic, magical quality, calming the reader into lesser awareness (Loughran 255).

While "Romance de la luna, luna" imaginatively builds on the tragicomic atmosphere pervading *El amor brujo*, the second Gypsy myth, "Preciosa y el aire," seems inspired by Falla's humorous puppet opera *El retablo de maese Pedro* (1923). Falla finished *Retablo*, based on *Don Quixote*, part 2, chapter 26, around the same time that Lorca started writing *Romancero gitano* in 1923, although "Preciosa y el aire" is of later vintage. José Mora Guarnido informs that in 1923 Lorca participated in two stages of *Retablo*: the first consisted of joining a small group of friends to advise Falla about the libretto. He enquired of them which phrases he should omit without amputating Cervantes's original, and how to seek a precise fit between words and rhythm without slowing the recitative (Mora Guarnido, *Lorca* 158).[36] The second phase amounted to resolving the problem of staging. Lorca helped Falla decide to use life-sized puppets for Don Quixote and Sancho, and doll-sized puppets for the chivalric figures of Master Peter's puppet show (164–5). Likewise, "Preciosa y el aire" borrows snatches of poetry from Cervantes's exemplary novel *La gitanilla* [The little Gypsy] and adapts it to an agile, octosyllabic narrative pace. Further, as in Falla's emerging work, Lorca used characters of disparate sizes, the child Preciosa and her gigantic accoster, the wind, archetype of sexual passion.

In Falla's musical tribute to Cervantes, he imitated the author of *Don Quixote* in combining a wide variety of sources. In a play between different chivalric textual authorities in the novel, Cervantes employed a pseudo-Carolingian ballad for the scene of Melisendra's liberation from the Moors by her husband, the knight Don Gayferos, together with conventions drawn from chivalric novels. By analogy, Falla mixed ballads and learned musical sources from Cervantes's period, but also contemporary Andalusian street peddlers' sung calls or *pregones* used to hawk their wares, together with the loud sing-song of town criers (Hess, *Passions* 141–3). Likewise, García Lorca for his ballad on Preciosa blended literary sources from Cervantes's era – Cervantes himself and Góngora – along with contemporary composers – Falla and Debussy – and impressions of urban life in Granada. The parallel to Falla produces astonishment with Lorca's metaphorical skill, surprise at his striking visual effects, and laughter more raucous than the refined amusement elicited by Falla's art.

García-Posada, among other scholars, notes Lorca's debt to Cervantes's exemplary novel, *La gitanilla* (García-Posada in Lorca, *Primer romancero*

111n1–2). The poet takes material from that work either recited or sung by its characters. The title "Preciosa y el aire" stems from a sonnet by Cervantes that the Gypsy girl's suitor Andrés reads to her:

> Cuando Preciosa el panderete toca,
> y hiere el dulce son los aires vanos,
> perlas son que derrama con las manos;
> flores son que despide de la boca.

> [When Preciosa the tambourine is playing,
> And striking empty air with her sweet sound,
> Pearls are what she strews with her hands;
> Flowers, what she spews from her mouth.]   (Cervantes, *Obras* 787)

Just as Lorca helped Falla adjust Cervantes's text to the music, so in the Preciosa ballad the poet reduces Cervantes's hendecasyllables to his own denser octosyllables. Concerned with plasticity, Lorca replaces Cervantes's conceits of pearls and flowers with his contemporary Góngora's visual metaphors. In Góngora's *Fábula de Polifemo y Galatea* (Fable of Polyphemus and Galatea), the nymph Galatea, pursued by the marine god Glaucus in the sea, flees him on land: "calzada plumas, / tantas flores pisó [Galatea] como él espumas" [shod with feathers (like the god Mercury), / she trod as many blooms as he did whitecaps] (Alonso, *"Polifemo"* 1:395). Superimpose flowers and foam, and an amphibious path like the one taken by Lorca's Preciosa emerges. Crystals may refer to waves, laurels to grass,[37] and the parchment moon to her tambourine:

> Su luna de pergamino
> Preciosa tocando viene
> por un anfibio sendero
> de cristales y laureles.

> [Her moon made out of parchment
> Preciosa has come to play
> On crystals and on laurels
> Along her amphibious way.]   (Lorca 1:395, ll. 1–4)

Lorca's first borrowing from Cervantes appeals to the reader's sight, and the second to hearing. In Cervantes, Preciosa sings a ballad in honour of Queen Margarita of Austria, containing the following four lines:

La alegría universal,
huyendo de la congoja,
calles y plazas discurre,
descompuesta y casi loca.

[The joy of all the world,
escaping from its sadness,
Streets and plazas rambles,
Undone and close to madness.]   (Cervantes, *Obras* 776–7)

This time Lorca's modifications convey auditory sensations. Cervantes's antonyms of joy and anguished sadness cede to Lorca's of silence and rhythmic sounds:

El silencio sin estrellas,
huyendo del sonsonete,
cae donde el mar bate y canta
su noche llena de peces.

[The silence without stars,
escaping sounds and rhythms,
Falls where the sea strikes, singing
Its night awash with fishes.]   (1:395)

Alliteration of swishing s's in the first two lines seems to imitate the high clinking sounds of tambourine metallic discs. In the third line, a grouping of hard stops (c-, t-, c-, t-) against a resonating background of open a's mimics the splash of jumping fish striking the water. All nocturnal nature accompanies Preciosa in her music and dance. The fish raise arbours of conch shells in the general festivities of Preciosa and her natural surroundings (1:395).

In the second division of this ballad, the wind enters as an erotic giant with a lust as large as his person, outsized like Góngora's passionate Cyclops Polifemo. A reference to the wind playing "una dulce gaita ausente" [a sweet but absent bagpipe] (1:395, l. 24) may allude to the (absent) Asturian bagpipes that the English horn and oboe mimic in the fanfare to Falla's *Retablo*,[38] though in a context unrelated to sexuality. Lorca owes much of his description of the wind to Cervantes, whose character Preciosa recites a spell to prevent vertigo and cardiac disorders, a spell to keep one's head, be confident, and banish injurious thoughts while producing marvellous visions, "Dios delante / y San Cristóbal gigante" [With God in front / and giant Saint Christopher] (Cervantes, *Obras* 788). Lorca also incorporates a reference to Saint Christopher:

Al verla se ha levantado
el viento que nunca duerme.
San Cristobalón desnudo,
lleno de lenguas celestes.

[On seeing her, up rises
The wind that never sleeps.
Saint Christopher, big and naked,
With heavenly tongues replete.]   (1:395, ll. 16–20)[39]

In syntax and vocabulary, these lines echo Falla's libretto of the original 1915 version of *El amor brujo*, where in the fisherman's ballad the mythical figure of the river rises up, though not described as naked:

El agua se levantó
al oir hablar
de penas de amantes.

[The water rose up
On hearing them speak
of troubles of lovers.]   (Falla, *Amor brujo*, score, 65)

Stressing the wind's power, Lorca's reference to that giant's multiple tongues recalls Góngora's poem the "Soledad primera" [First solitude], with its northerly wind Cierzo, "expirante por cien bocas" [exhaling through a hundred mouths], a line quoted in Lorca's lecture on Góngora (3:232). Like the river in *El amor brujo*, commanding the lovers to visit the witch, Lorca's wind gives (flowery) commands to the Gypsy girl to have sex with him. Preciosa flees, followed by the impassioned wind, disconcerting all nature, just as happens in Góngora's *Polifemo* when the Cyclops blows his deafening pan pipes:

La selva se confunde, el mar se altera,
rompe Tritón su caracol torcido,
sordo huye el bajel a vela y remo:
¡tal la música es de Polifemo!

[The woods get dumbfounded, the sea disturbed,
And Triton breaks his twisted horn of shell.
With sails and oars, the deafened boat takes flight:
The music of Polyphemus gives such fright!]   (Alonso, *"Polifemo"* 1:17)

In three brief lines, each imitating Góngora by condensing its own pic-
ture of a different aspect of agitated nature, Lorca employs synaesthesia to
depict the sea frowning with its thrashing, while olive trees turn pale as the
wind, passing through them, turns the dark green side of their leaves over to
expose a lighter colour on the reverse. For Góngora's image of the boat
fleeing, deafened by the sound, Lorca substitutes a passing allusion to the
third movement of Debussy's suite *La Mer*, titled, "Dialogue du vent et de
la mer." The movement begins with the crash of a gong and yields to flute:

Frunce su rumor el mar.
Los olivos palidecen.
Cantan las flautas de umbría
y el liso gong de la nieve.

[The sea murmurs frowningly.
Olive trees their pallor show.
Flute songs emerge from shadows
To the smooth gong of the snow.]   (1:396, ll. 33–6)

All nature orchestrates Preciosa's flight as the narrator, directly addressing her, urges her to escape the "nasty old wind" [viento verde] (l. 38). The
irreverent humour increases with an apostrophe to the wind as if it were
an enormous image in a religious procession. Here sounds a brief saeta,
but in verbal, not melodic, form – a saeta speaking of Christ in a serious
tone in *PCJ* but here talking of the wind in a comic sense: "¡Míralo por
donde viene!" (1:396, l. 40; García-Posada, in Lorca, *Primer romancero*
113n40). Yet another infusion of humour appears with the intervention of
non-mythical, everyday Granadan reality in this ballad. Granadans of
Lorca's time, according to David Bary, regarded the English colony living
on the hill to the Alhambra as eccentric. One of the British vice-consul's
neighbours, Charles Temple, living at one of the highest spots, must have
struck Lorca as "quite mad and (...) wildly funny" (Bary 515). For this
reason, when the poetic voice mentions the English near the start of the
poem, Granadan readers must have smiled. Yet, when Preciosa, pursued by
the wind, seeks refuge in the English consul's home high above the pines,
the same readers must have guffawed. The kindly yet odd Englishman

offers the child, along with warm milk, a cup of gin, which she rejects, and the contrast produces additional merriment. Finally, the ballad ends with the most comical touch. While the frightened Preciosa narrates her tale to those comical Britons, outside the consulate, the wind bites the roof in sexual frustration. In conclusion, the union of multiple sources bridging many eras may mimic Falla's handling of borrowings in *Retablo*, although with an eye to achieving sexual-based humour.

Falla influences at least two other major aspects of *Romancero gitano*: Lorca's treatment of the Gypsy as a piece of nature and his vision of non-Gypsy reality as denaturing and dehumanizing. The Gypsy's unity with nature reflects Falla's notion that the scales of deep song imitate natural sounds (Falla, "*Cante jondo*" 144; Lorca 3:200). Such Gypsies form part of the natural order when they fight, make love, or worship. Identification of fighting Gypsies with natural objects takes place in "Reyerta" and "Muerte de Antoñito el Camborio" [Death of Antoñito Camborio].

In "Reyerta" Lorca endows the fight with pictorial dimensions as a bull ascending the barriers of the arena: "El toro de la reyerta / se sube por las paredes" [The bull of the feud / clambers up the walls] (1:398, ll 11–12). Murderous knives "relucen como los peces" [gleam like fish] (l. 4). Mourning old women perch on olive treetops as if part of the Andalusian vegetation (ll. 9–10). Equally vegetative, one Gypsy fighter rolls over a cliff, his body full of funereal lilies, a pomegranate on his temples, symbolizing his bleeding wound (ll. 17–18). Gypsy nature is the expression of the Andalusian landscape, which configures the collective spirit. As in "Baladilla de los tres ríos," that spirit assumes a plural form – in this ballad, that of earthy angels:

Ángeles negros traían
pañuelos y agua de nieve.
Ángeles con grandes alas
De navajas de Albacete.

[Angels of black were bringing
Kerchiefs and melted snow water.
Angels with mammoth wings
Made of Albacete daggers.]   (ll. 13–16)

Falla's music paints Andalusia as a land of artistic contrasts. Here Lorca, more graphic and violent, personifies the contradictions as angels, superhuman embodiments of a *Volksgeist* beneficent yet injurious, ministering to the wounded while bearing nightmarish wings of the blades that arm the combatants. The poem ends with the angels' flight through the sunset with long tresses, as if in mourning, and with "olive-oil hearts" [corazones de aceite], that is, with the essence of their persons derived from the vegetation typical of the land (1:399, ll. 35–8). As the judge and the Civil Guards make their enquiry through the olive groves, the poetic subject suspends all astonishment. What has happened on this characteristic patch of Andalusian soil repeats a timeless ritual: "Han muerto cuatro romanos / y cinco cartagineses" [Four Romans have fallen dead / And five Carthaginians].[40] As Lorca remarks elsewhere, he expresses in "Reyerta" the fight underlying Andalusia and all Spain between groups engaging in warfare "for mysterious causes, for a look, (…) for a love of two centuries ago."[41] The symbol of a remote erotic cause, appearing in one of the best-known images of the poem, conveys the naturalness of the conflict: "Sangre resbalada gime / muda canción de serpiente" [Scudding blood bemoans / a mute serpent's song] (1:399, ll. 25–6). The blood sliding along the ground in serpentine form silently sings of an archaic passion dating back to Original Sin.

In "Muerte de Antoñito el Camborio" [Death of Antoñito el Camborio], the hero meets his fate of a violent end reintegrating him into nature. Alienated from his family, he fights out of self-defence against his relatives, dishonoured by his antisocial conduct of letting himself be captured without resisting the arresting Civil Guards. Disembodied voices like those employed by Falla at the outset of *La vida breve* and *Sombrero* appear here in the initial quatrain, with its largely dactylic rhythm, interrupted every even line with a final accented i, as if the mass of sounds simulated a funeral march with cortège, starting and stopping at regular intervals:

Vó-ces de muér-te so-ná-ron
cér-ca del Guà-dal-qui-vír.
Vóc-es antí-guas que cér-can
vóz de cla-vél va-ro-níl.

[Voices of death were resounding
Next to the Guadalquivir.
Voices of old that lay siege to
Voice of carnation, all male.]   (1:419, ll. 1–4)

The voices of old belong to the tribe whose code Antonio has violated. Since "Baladilla de los tres ríos," Lorca links the Guadalquivir to Seville, where Antonio was headed to see the bullfights but ironically never attained his goal. He resembles the bulls he never was able to witness when his own fight for life animalizes him, the way combat did the contenders in "Reyerta." He deals his attackers "mordiscos de jabalí" [bites of a wild boar], and in the struggle takes leaps "jabonados de delfín" [lathered with dolphin] for his grace and agility. At mid-poem, the lyrical voice addresses him as a natural hero, worthy even of his family name. That voice ennobles him by accumulating epic epithets referring to his naturalness and virility: "Camborio de duro crin,/moreno de verde luna,/voz de clavel varonil" [Camborio with hard main,/swarthy as greenish moon,/voice of carnation, all male]. When the poetic voice, whom Antoñito calls by the poet's name, "Federico García," advises him to prepare his soul for death, he responds that his body has broken like a corn stalk, a chunk of the natural order. Like a Falla work (for instance, the *Homenaje* to Debussy), this epic ballad ends with an emphatic conclusion repeating many of the notes and the rhythms of the beginning. As the four avenging cousins reach their home once more, "voces de muerte cesaron/cerca del Guadalquivir" [voices of death stopped resounding/next to the Guadalquivir] (1:420, ll. 51–2).

As hostile as they are to life, Antonio's foes enable him to realize his natural potential. Yet, in *Romancero gitano*, forces that hinder natural self-realization receive descriptions as dehumanized and denatured. No example surpasses the murderous rural police in "Romance de la Guardia Civil Española" [Ballad of the Spanish Civil Guard]. The poetic voice presents that armed force as pillaging robots. Their victims, the Gypsies of the city of Jerez de la Frontera, behave as innocent children of nature, attuned to the Andalusian collective spirit. Since Falla has represented the Gypsies as heirs to the Moors in achieving artistic contact with that spirit, Lorca makes use of the late medieval convention of Morisco ballads, conceiving the ruling warrior as husband of a region (Menéndez Pidal, *Flor nueva* 201, n). Jerez will become a woman with whom the poetic voice dialogues about her as a superhuman individual, her Gypsies, and the Civil Guard aggressors. Four levels of consciousness lend structure to this ballad: the omniscience of the narrator, the collective awareness of the city (manifestation of the regional *Volksgeist*), the natural ingenuousness of the Gypsies, and the killing instinct of the Civil Guard.

At three different points in the narrative, the poetic voice addresses Jerez with the words, "Oh, city of the Gypsies!" [¡Oh, ciudad de los gitanos!], and each apostrophe signals a different stage in the action. The first serves as foreshadowing, the second as a warning to avert imminent catastrophe, and the third as an epilogue after the destructive raid. In the first, the narrator marvels in the city's company at the harmony between her earth and sky, humanity and nature under the reign of the Gypsies, all too temporary. An enumeration of merely three objects, the moon, the pumpkin, and cherry preserves, characterizes the entire city on Christmas Eve. Heaven and earth coexist in harmony, for the yellow roundness of the pumpkin matches the moon's. Moreover, the time has arrived to break out the preserves and titillate the festive palate. Yet the lyric voice sounds lugubrious notes, presentiments of approaching disaster. After addressing once again the city, the narrator employs an elegiac formula, "Who ever saw you and does not recall you?" [¿Quién te vio y no te recuerda?]. Nostalgia for a bygone, more idyllic state inheres in this rhetorical question.

The second series of verses addressing the city occurs at the midpoint of the poem, after the fanciful lyric description of Christmas Eve festivities. Lorca, steeped like Falla in folk tradition in his compositions, recalls that in a ballad from the epic cycle of the Cid, the narrator tries (in vain) to advise King Sancho that an assassin is on his way: "Watch out, watch out, King Don Sancho!/Don't say I didn't warn you/That from within Zamora/A traitor has come out."[42] Likewise, Lorca has his narrator caution the city (in vain), "Turn off your greenish lights,/for the Civil Guard is coming."[43] However, once more the narrator repeats the nostalgic form, "Who ever saw you and does not recall you?" Addressing the readers directly, this narrator commands them to leave this woman (the city) far from the sea of dying while she mourns without combs for her unbound hair.[44]

The final address to the city appears in the last eight verses of the ballad. Here the initial line of each quatrain repeats the formulaic "Oh, city of the Gypsies!" as if the last opportunity had arrived to evoke her memory. Having perpetrated its carnage, the Civil Guard departs through what the narrator calls a "tunnel of silence," an artificial passageway, with silence signalling a forced interruption to festive music, for flames surround the city. For the third time the narrator, though now in an elegiac tone, exclaims, "Who ever saw you and does not recall you?" The final couplet communicates an ambivalent message. On the one hand, it may mean that posterity should seek the destroyed city in the mind of the narrator where it can live forever. On the other hand, it may signify that such a collectivity is a mere figment of the teller's fantasy, born of moonlight playing on sand: "Que te busquen en mi frente./Juego de luna y arena" [Let them seek you on my brow./Play of moon and sand] (1:430).

The city represents the Gypsies' collective consciousness, yet within her live the Gypsies in childlike innocence, communing with nature. In Falla's ballet *El sombrero de tres picos*, the two innocent protagonists, the

Miller and his wife, also harmonize with the birds around them, and each receive leitmotiv pertaining to the natural music of the region from which each one hails. Contrariwise, the antagonist, the Corregidor, whose three-cornered hat symbolizes his tyrannical authority, disturbs nature, tumbling into the millstream or interfering with natural matrimonial bonds. Music associated with his person, anachronistically in the style of the eighteenth century, recalls the artificiality of Madrid. Lorca draws creative analogies for each term of this antithesis. Just as the Miller and his wife tame the blackbird to tell the hour, so the Gypsies of Jerez in preparing for Christmas festivities create a new nature in their art: "los gitanos en sus fraguas / forjaban soles y flechas" [the Gypsies in their smithies / were forging suns and arrows]. Underscoring the Gypsies' innocence, the poetic voice repeatedly echoes a familiar *villancico* or Christmas carol, "En el portal de Belén" [In the doorway to Bethlehem], in a version present, for instance, in Falla's 1903–4 collection, *Cantares de Nochebuena* [Songs of Christmas Eve]:

En el portal de Belén
hay estrellas, sol y luna,
la Virgen y San José
y el Niño que está en la cuna.

[In the doorway to Bethlehem,
There are stars, sun, and moon,
The Virgin and Saint Joseph
And the Child in the cradle.][45]

As the childlike Gypsies celebrate Christmas Eve with their art and processions, the Virgin and Saint Joseph consort with them and even plan on making music in their parade: "La Virgen y San José / perdieron sus castañuelas, / y buscan a los gitanos / para ver si las encuentran" [The Virgin and Saint Joseph / have lost their castanets / and go look for the Gypsies / to see if they have found them]. Nature delights in this innocent festival of the Nativity: "The crescent moon was dreaming / the ecstasy of a stork" [La media luna, soñaba / un éxtasis de cigüeña]. The stork represents birth, the half-moon a celestial smile. The Gypsies display the natural ingenuousness of babes, and the poetic voice intones nonsense verses from a fictitious lullaby ("When the night was arriving, / night that night would night" // "on the silvernocturnal night / night that night would night").[46] As in "Romance de la luna, luna," with its lullaby repetitions, readers get lulled like the Gypsies into unawareness of lurking danger.

When the Civil Guard emerges as an unnatural force of evil, Lorca admits the grotesque into lyric poetry, unlike other poets of his generation but not unlike Falla. Massine introduced the grotesque into Falla's *Sombrero*. The "unmasking of the (lascivious) Corregidor," his being tossed up as a *pelele* or rag doll in a blanket at the end, the background of grotesque, deformed peasants, and Falla's parody of the traditional *jota* made a deep impression on Lorca's friend Adolfo Salazar, music critic for Ortega's journal *El Sol* in 1921 and reviewer of the ballet after its Madrid debut.[47] Salazar found the "intensity of the grotesque" comprehensible for only a select few (Hess, *Modernism* 152–3). Lorca apparently decided to attack the misery inflicted by the authorities on the Andalusian Gypsy populace by resorting to the grotesque. He determined to unmask them for the murderous robot-like marauders they were. Like Falla's grotesque Corregidor, a hunchback with a limp and a three-cornered hat, Lorca's Civil Guards, not comically affected like Falla's villain, also wear "tricornios," three-cornered hats (1:418, l. 28). The first four quatrains describe their anti-natural quality. As often as the lyrical voice likens the hero Antoñito el Camborio to natural creatures – animals and growing plants – it compares the anti-heroic Civil Guards to manufactured, highly processed matter, corresponding to the artificiality of the Corregidor's music. Over the capes of the Civil Guards shine candle wax and ink stains. The poetic voice endows them with patent leather souls, because with three-cornered hats made out of that material, they identify with their office. Their skulls consist of lead, the metal with which they kill. They not only lack affects, but also carry in their brains uncharted projects for the use of their pistols ("a vague astronomy / of inconcrete pistols").[48] Instead of walking erect in the light of day like Antoñito, they are "hunchbacked and nocturnal" [jorobados y nocturnos] (1:426, l. 9). After they wreak their destruction, their innocent victims gather "in the doorway to Bethlehem"[49] – title of the traditional Christmas carol – to enable the infant Jesus's parents to minister to their ills. A wounded Saint Joseph helps them bury their dead, while the Virgin cures wounded Gypsies "with spittle from stars," an expression of natural healing refashioned from Góngora.[50] In sum, Lorca's most ambitious ballad in *Romancero gitano* owes much of its inspiration, with its contrasts of nature / artifice, innocence/murderousness, creativity / destructiveness, gracefulness / the grotesque – to Manuel de Falla, much less sombre and less consciously satirical than Lorca.

The synthesis of the whole anthology and Falla's contributions to it appears in "Romance de la pena negra" [Ballad of black pain]. For Lorca, black pain, or existential dissatisfaction, lies at the root of Andalusia (3:344).

Since Andalusia is the victim of her fate, the poet echoes the *martinete*, the blacksmith song, from *La vida breve*, which has also influenced "Romance de la luna, luna": "Woe to the poor female / Born to a fate she'll dread! / Woe to one born an anvil, / And not born a hammer instead!"[51] Lorca's character Soledad Montoya has copper flesh and smoky anvils for breasts, moaning doleful songs (1:408, ll. 58). Like Candelas from the 1915 version of *El amor brujo*, she comes alone seeking her person and her love. The poet attempts to prepare a sensuous atmosphere appropriate for flamenco. The striking metaphor that begins the ballad, showing roosters with pickaxes (of their beaks) digging for the dawn, starts a poem "La bulería de la muerte" [The *bulería* of death], originally planned for *Poema del cante jondo* but suppressed (*PCJ* 314). The pain of Soledad's loneliness – an emotion felt by a poet uncomfortable with fixed gender roles – originates in the land itself. Victim of the reifying male, she turns pitch-black with suffering (1:409, ll. 31–2), yet can never find contentment in a Spain of civil strife and of nature in a Heraclitean war with itself. As in a number of the Gypsy ballads – "Preciosa y el aire," "Reyerta," "Romance sonámbulo," "San Gabriel (Sevilla)," "Prendimiento de Antoñito el Camborio en el camino de Sevilla" [Capture of Antoñito el Camborio on the way to Seville], "Muerte de Antoñito el Camborio," "Romance de la Guardia Civil Española" – the poetic voice addresses the protagonist to enable her to express herself with a theatricality foreign to the art of Lorca's coevals and possibly even going beyond that seen in Falla's operas and ballets.

Here Lorca's authorial voice waggishly assumes the position of a folk moralizer to whom Soledad can take exception and display the full extent of her anguish. Her confession that she is seeking her joy and her person implies that she feels joyless and unfulfilled. When admonished by the moralizing speaker that a horse with no bridle risks running to the sea and drowning in the waves, Soledad identifies the natural origin of her black pain, not as the sea, but as the "lands of the olive."[52] Lorca could have learned this lesson of the anguishing spirit of the land from the music and theory of the Andalusianist Falla on deep song. Yet he saw Falla's art as merely the musical confirmation of his own independent, tragic inner gnawing, embellished and enriched by its ability to laugh at itself even in ballads as diverse and unique in his generation as the ones on sleepwalking, the moon, Preciosa, Antoñito el Camborio, and the Spanish Civil Guards.

10

Andalusia's "Cultural Spirit" in Two Trios of Gypsy Ballads

Poema del cante jondo and *Romancero gitano* stem from Lorca's attempt to preserve an endangered Andalusian "cultural spirit." This regional creative principle, as applied to Andalusia by Falla and as modified by Lorca, provides a basis for at least six of Lorca's Gypsy ballads. Three concern individuals: the triptych of "Martirio de Santa Olalla" [Martyrdom of Saint Olalla], "Burla de don Pedro a caballo" [Mockery of Don Pedro on Horseback], and "Thamar y Amnón" [Tamar and Amnon];[1] and three deal with cities: "San Rafael (Córdoba)" [Saint Raphael (Cordoba)], "San Miguel (Granada)" [Saint Michael (Granada)], and "San Gabriel (Sevilla)" [Saint Gabriel (Seville)]."

In these two trios of ballads, Lorca makes original changes in Falla's notion of the Andalusian creative principle. "Burla de Don Pedro a caballo," dating back to 1921 and based on old historical ballads, originates in a gay poet's crisis of self-confidence. Subsequently, he integrates the poem into *Romancero gitano* by identifying its protagonist with sentiments he later will associate with the "cultural spirit" of Andalusia: a feeling of insufficiency in the cosmos, dread of dying with the prospect of nothingness after death, and the mystery of creativity in the face of such a fate. The enigma of aesthetic creation becomes the theme of "Martirio de Santa Olalla" and "Thamar y Amnón." The three historical ballads, appealing to readers' atavism, operate over a vast geographic area affected by old literary traditions, a map introduced to Lorca by Falla. All three poems employ foreshadowing, characterizing primitivist writing and exemplified by the Phrygian modal wails of "Canción del amor dolido" [Song of painful love] from *El amor brujo* (Hess, *Modernism* 56).[2] All three of Lorca's ballads express powerlessness in the face of uncontrollable cosmic forces, as do Salud's arias and recitative in *La vida breve*. All offer aesthetic responses with problematic results: in the autobiographic centre of the triptych, the plunge of Don Pedro, a quixotic, guitar-playing knight, to the bottom of a lagoon where he suffers oblivion as a artist; on the left, the virginal martyr Olalla's aesthetic contemplation of her pain, elevating her at best merely to the threshold of heaven; and on the right, the interaction of a disparate couple – a frigid lunar maiden, Thamar, whose singing leads to her violation and who vainly resorts to a compensatory social fiction, and her Don Juan of a half-brother, Amnón, whose eloquence and artistic body language momentarily gratify him, but ultimately enrage and frustrate him.

The ballads on the three Andalusian cities emerge from Lorca's ingenious personifications of the Andalusian "cultural spirit." The pluralization of the Hispanic ethos had appeared in Falla before Lorca. More explicitly than Granados in *Doce danzas españolas* [Twelve Spanish Dances] and Albéniz in *Iberia*, Falla in his *Piezas españolas* [Spanish pieces, 1907] for piano had purported to "express the soul of each of the regions indicated in the titles of this work" ("Aragonese," "Cuban," "Rural Santanderine," "Andalusian") by imitating rhythms, modalities, melodies, adornments, and cadences of the folk airs of each.[3] What Falla had done with regional melodies, Lorca decided to do in his inimitable plastic form, using religious statuary to identify masculine beauty with essential characteristics of three cities. Already in "Reyerta" [Feud], angels had embodied the Andalusian collective spirit, creative as well as destructive. Since Michael, Raphael, and Gabriel appear together as seventeenth-century sculptures in the Granadan hermitage San Miguel el Alto (Couffon, *Granada and Lorca* 40), in Lorca each angel embodies the creative principle of a different city. "San Gabriel (Sevilla)" offers a Sevillian Gypsy perspective on the Annunciation, foretelling the birth of a perishable Christ-like Gypsy in donjuanesque dialogue, conceived by poet-playwright Lorca as appropriate for the seducer of Seville. In "San Miguel (Granada)," without a Gypsy theme, a simple pilgrimage reveals the collective character of Granada, musically creative, yet permeated with preciosity. "San Rafael (Córdoba)" transforms a riverside scene of nocturnal voyeurism into a visual artwork, produced by the culturally hybrid creative principle of Cordoba, its nature, and its civilization. Let us consider the historical ballads first.

1. The Three Historical Ballads and the Andalusian "Cultural Spirit"

Lorca conceives "Burla de don Pedro a caballo" [Mockery of Don Pedro on horseback] as a palimpsest stemming from Andalusian variations on an old Castilian historical theme.[4] As a collector of folk tunes, encouraged in this endeavour by Menéndez Pidal and Falla, he heard Granadan children singing verses from the cycle of Pedro I the "Cruel" of Castile (García-Posada, in Lorca, *Primer romancero* 207). Late in 1921, while undergoing a crisis of personal and poetic confidence, he annexed his individual problem to a long tradition of balladry (Martín, *Heterodoxo y mártir* 349). Between the lines, he presented his own conflict as the most recent step in the decay of the King Pedro legend. Agustín Durán, whose edition of *Romancero general* [General Collection of Ballads, 1916] Lorca had consulted, had traced the evolution of historical ballads from the first creative spark of the *Volksgeist* in oral composition to the death throes of balladic literature in periods of national decline (Durán XXVII–XXVIII).

Before 1928, date of the first printing of *Primer romancero gitano*, "Burla de don Pedro a caballo" bore the title "Romance de lagunas" (Ballad with lacunae). This became its subtitle when the poem passed into the anthology (de Paepe, in Lorca, *Primer romancero* 281n1). The change responded to two needs: the naming of Don Pedro, the hero mocked, would underscore the historicity of the theme, appropriate for the section "Romances históricos"; and, more significantly, the new title would contribute to Lorca's self-flagellation, produced by his flagging self-assurance. The *burla* or mockery of a hero forms a subgenre of the ballad (de Paepe, in Lorca, *Primer romancero* 281n1). The poet parodies the figure of a less heroic ballad. Hence, the cycle of Pedro the Cruel originates ballads on Don Bueso or Boyso (García-Posada, in Lorca, *Primer romancero* 207). The widely diffused "Romance de don Bueso" [Ballad of Don Bueso], gathered by Lorca,[5] on the hero who seeks a mistress only to find a lost sister, uses the hexasyllabic form or *romancillo*; and Lorca's "Romance de lagunas" employs a flexible *romancillo* pattern (García-Posada, in Lorca, *Primer romancero* 260). Traces of the Don Pedro cycle accompany the parody of "Romance de don Bueso" in Lorca's ballad, mocking numerous works. The last of these is Gerardo Diego's "Don Luis a caballo" [Don Luis on horseback] (1927), a parody, composed during the Luis de Góngora tercentenary, of Lorca's ballad "Arbolé, arbolé" [Tree-oh, tree-oh] and of various Gypsy ballads circulating among his friends before he published *Romancero gitano*. Therefore "Burla de don Pedro a caballo" parodies a parody with Lorca as its object.

He could have found a precedent in Falla, who quotes folk tunes within works submitting them to parodic variations. In his ballet *Sombrero*, the self-proud Corregidor first enters in march time to the children's tune "El serení" – a ludicrous use of the music in itself. Later, when the Miller suspects his wife's infidelity with that Corregidor, a nervously hurried version of "El serení" plays (Hess, *Modernism* 94–5; García Matos, "Folklore I"

53), parodying the original music parody. In Lorca too, mirrors within mirrors set up puns within puns as the *Volksgeist* passes from one ballad to another until becoming submerged in an anguished poet's self-critique. A mirror image simplifies reality. Without denying the living reality of a human being, the image hides it, retains it in a state of being unalive, two-dimensional (García Bacca, *Filosofía de la música* 680). Therefore, a reflection from one mirror, seen in a second mirror, a third, and a fourth, becomes ever simpler, less alive. In his "suite of mirrors," Lorca has written, "Behind each mirror / There's a dead star / And a baby rainbow / Asleep."[6] All reflecting has as its limit an absence of life and hope – death and despair. Whatever Falla contributed here to Lorca's poetry ends up expressing the poet's fear of oblivion.

His punning "Romance de lagunas" plays on the two meanings of the Spanish word *laguna*, literally, a lagoon, a body of stagnant water, and figuratively, a void, a lacuna (de Paepe, in Lorca, *Primer romancero* 280n1). The figurative meaning is a simplified mirror image of the literal meaning. In oral transmission, according to Durán, change stems from memory lapses and produces new versions of ballads with each singing. Empty spaces fill up when memory fails, adding or subtracting lines from the original (1:XXV). To Alfredo García-Casas, who heard Lorca early read and comment on "Romance de lagunas," the poet, with his acute visual sensitivity, expressed an aspiration to "give plasticity to the lacuna, that is, the place where things are submerged, the words, in this case."[7] Lorca recognized that the cycle of Pedro the Cruel contained *lagunas* in both senses. Roberta A. Quance informs that in two versions of a hunting ballad on King Pedro the Cruel, the hero sees evil omens at a lagoon, foretelling his demise ("Don Pedro" 80). When Granadan children sang multiple versions of this legend, they generated textual lacunae.

Lorca's "Romance de lagunas" contains three lacunae, each followed by free verse touching on a different problem. The reader must fill in the gaps. The first enigma concerns the cause of Don Pedro's unexplained grief; the second, the possibility of his salvation; and the third, the question of his artistic self-immortalization. After the third and final lacuna appear the two lines, "Bajo el agua / están las palabras" [Under the water / The words are found], suggesting the finality of the underwater answer to the question of immortality (Lorca, 1:437, ll. 64–6). The imagery following the first lacuna expresses the hallucinatory object of Don Pedro's grief. On the lagoon bank a child sees the moon reflected in the water, enabling him to fantasize the equality of the reflected circle to the celestial one, and he equates both to musical cymbals, which he commands the night to play (436–7, ll. 15–23). Viewing absence as presence is child's play, and the quixotic equalization may account for Don Pedro's mysterious tears. A melancholic, with his quest and awkward mount, he resembles Don Quixote, yearning for the absent Dulcinea. Don Pedro is erotically aware of his personal insufficiency – perhaps the poet's homosexuality in a disapproving universe. Incapable of achieving satisfaction, his life itself is a lacuna, a privation. Images following the second lacuna of the ballad assert that his melancholy generates guitar music: "Concrete dream with no polestar/For guitar wood."[8] His disorientation, lack of "norte" [polestar], augurs failure. Like the evil omens seen by King Pedro, which the poet submits to self-deprecating humour, birds amidst flames circle above the lagoon's "hairdo" [peinado] of water lilies. Waterside onlookers realize better than Lorca's "hero" the deficiency defining his existence (ll. 40–5). Metaphors succeeding the third and last lacuna prove his shortcoming. The words of his art remain underwater like loam derived from voices lost in the past. History differs from art. The concept "historical ballad" can potentially prove contradictory. Most ironically, Lorca's Don Pedro lies forgotten and dead atop the frigid flower of his poetry, as a sorry playmate of frogs in what was once an epic lagoon in the cycle of Pedro the Cruel (ll. 64–9).

"Burla de don Pedro a caballo" closely resembles the other two historical ballads in the provenance of all three from many folkloric and learned sources, with the multiple venue proving their proximity to the "cultural spirit." Menéndez Pidal came to Lorca for help on local Granadan folk song, but Falla widened his horizons to embrace popular tradition all over Spain.[9] Critics have perceived many influences on "Burla de don Pedro a caballo," but not on "Martirio de Santa Olalla." Yet Lorca stresses this multiplicity by enigmatically stating that Eulalia's city of Merida – situated in Extremadura! – is "just as Andalusian as is Tetouan [a former Spanish protectorate in North Africa]."[10] In other words, many areas share the same balladic themes compatible with the Andalusian ethos. Eulalia, patron saint over more than three hundred towns in Spain, has lent her name to eighty more (Camisón, "Santa Olalla de Mérida"). Thanks to Lorca's friend Dalí, in 1925 the poet first visited Barcelona (Gibson, *Life* 167), of which Saint Eulalia is co-patron along with Our Lady of Mercy. For his Andalusian Gypsy Eulalia, or Olalla, as he calls her, Lorca could have borrowed elements not only from the Roman poet Prudentius (348–413?), writing on Saint Eulalia of Merida, as critics have observed (de Paepe, in Lorca, *Primer romancero* 201), but also from the Bishop of Barcelona Quiricus (d. 680), with his hymn on Saint Eulalia of Barcelona. Dalí viewed the martyr Saint Sebastian, patron saint of the resort Cadaqués, as a symbol of detached estheticism (Gibson, *Life* 167). Lorca made his

Olalla a similar symbol. The ballads on her martyrdom concern the mystery of aesthetic creativity at the core of the Andalusian "cultural spirit" and form part of a larger triptych on the same theme. The autobiographical ballad on Don Pedro occupies the centre and the one on Tamar and Amnon stands at the other end.

Within the larger threefold framework, Lorca structures "Martirio de Santa Olalla" as a smaller triptych (Scobie, "Lorca and Eulalia" 296). The first part offers historical background, "Panorama de Mérida" [Panorama of Merida], contrasting the leering Romans and Olalla, a Gypsy saint moaning for redemption in deep song resonances. The central part, "El martirio" [The martyrdom], paints her tortures in terms compatible with Dalí's aesthetics of "Holy Objectivity" (cf. Southworth, "Religion" 134–5). The third part, "Infierno y gloria" [Hell and glory], views her judgment and apotheosis from an aesthetic distance, with crucifixion in the first half and possible resurrection in the second. She shares with Lorca's Don Pedro (and Lorca himself) the Andalusian root sentiment of personal insufficiency. Around her, anti-Christian, pagan Roman roosters crow about their personal power, the potency of their gods, and the Christian God's weakness ("From time to time were sounding / Red-crested blasphemies"),[11] like the Roman praetor challenged by Eulalia in Prudentius's hymn (Bodelón García, "Quirico y Prudencio" 36–7, ll. 64, 99–100). Yet Lorca's Olalla instead chooses to "moan" [gemir] for redemption, as in *Romans* 8:22, where Saint Paul reminds Roman Christians, "We know that the whole creation has been groaning in travail until now" (*Holy Bible* 176). The moan paraphrases in Andalusian fashion Prudentius's characterization of Eulalia as yearning for heaven, as "extending herself toward the soil of her Father above."[12] In the "Gypsy" anthology her ballad originally bore the title "Martirio de la santa gitana Olalla de Mérida" [Martyrdom of the Gypsy Saint Olalla of Merida] (García-Posada, in Lorca, *Primer romancero* 201, n.). Accordingly, her moaning breaks goblets, like the screams of the artist Silverio Franconetti, praised in Lorca's and Falla's daily *tertulia* (García-Posada 202nn15–16).

In the central panel of Olalla's poetic triptych, depicting the martyrdom, Olalla sublimates her pain into aesthetic experience. Lorca's friend Dalí had converted Saint Sebastian into an embodiment of the "Holy Objectivity to which he felt contemporary art should aspire. The saint's passivity, serenity, and detachment as his flesh is pierced by arrows (...) were the very qualities the painter aspired to express in his own life and work, as he explained to Federico" (Gibson, *Life* 167). Federico, in turn, passed Dalí's lesson of emotionless beauty on to Falla.[13] As an Andalusian variant on the Saint Sebastian theme, Olalla takes an active artistic stance towards her pain: "Naked Flora is climbing / little ladders of water."[14] Alternative versions cited by de Paepe from Lorca's manuscript allow identification of Flora, Roman goddess of flowers and spring, with twelve or thirteen-year-old Olalla in the springtime of her life when undergoing martyrdom.[15] She removes herself from her earthly situation by scaling mysterious waters. The presence of gardens ("Flora") with irrigating fountains may contain mystical symbolism borrowed from the travel book *Granada (guía emocional)* [Granada (affective guide)], by Falla's librettist María Lejárraga. In a passage that probably inspired Falla's nocturne "En el Generalife" [In the Generalife] (see Introduction this volume, n. 56), Lejárraga equates the Generalife to "a perron of gardens that leads up to a belvedere, degrees of contemplation ever more perfect, that lead to the ultimate vision of spiritual serenity."[16] This would be a vision worthy of an Andalusian saint seeking "Holy Objectivity." As water descends the irrigating railings in the Generalife gardens, plant life blooms in an upward direction.

Like Lorca's Gypsy from "Canción del gitano apaleado" [Song of the horse-whipped Gypsy], who, in a song likely inspired by Falla, transmutes a beating into art, even when calling for water ("Water with fishes and boats. / Water, water, water, water"),[17] Lorca's Olalla metamorphoses pain into beauty. She resembles Lorca's *cante jondo* artists of centuries later. Different aspects of her torture point to this artistic metamorphosis. Of Saint Sebastian, Dalí writes in painterly terms, "In certain areas of his body, veins appeared on the surface with their intense blue of Patinir's stormy skies, and described voluptuously painful curves upon the coral pink of his skin."[18] Lorca's reference to Flora colours her veins green, and the allusion to mystic waters brings those vessels to the surface. The torture the poetic subject stresses most is removal of Olalla's breasts. To embellish this hideous punishment, Lorca remakes an image of Saint Teresa of Avila. When espousing the human soul, she writes, the Lord places that soul in His dwelling, the seventh and loftiest in the soul, "because just as He holds it in heaven, so He should have a dwelling in the soul where only His Majesty lives, or we may say, *another heaven.*"[19] Olalla's maimed torso acquires Teresian heavenliness: "Through the red holes / where her breasts used to go, / Tiny heavens are seen / And streams of white milk flow."[20] The milk streams recall the moaning for redemption with birth pangs.

The final part of the triptych, " Infierno y gloria," [Hell and glory] presents her crucifixion and problematic salvation from a saint's perspective of pure art, cleansed of sentimentality. Latinate concision prevails, as in the Góngora loved by Lorca and Falla. Articles disappear ("Taut night shines"; "Departed night begins"; "Angels and seraphim").[21] Brief, one-line sentences abound, each full of symbolic substance. With restraint Lorca presents symbols of Olalla's salvation like the monstrance, as if she were seated at the Lord's table. The sacred host shines above skies scorched by martyr's flames, while nature celebrates her spiritual liberation. In the case of Olalla, mythically transfigured into the goddess Flora, spring has returned amidst winter as song emerges from the "throats" of the brook and the nightingales (Lorca 1:435, ll. 67–70). The ballad thereby becomes an original myth by Lorca on mild weather in habitually cold months.

The final two lines of the poem envelop her sainthood in folkloric formulas compatible with the Andalusian "cultural spirit": "Ángeles y serafines/ dicen: Santo, Santo, Santo" [Angels and seraphim/ "Holy, holy, holy," say] (1:435, ll. 71–4). The line "angels and seraphim," though apparently redundant, nonetheless appears in a Trisagion sung by the García Lorca family.[22] Daniel Devoto traces the final line to religious *coplas*: "The priests in mass/ Say, "Holy, holy, holy." / The angels in heaven / repeat the same song" ("El elemento tradicional en Lorca" 145). The ending of Lorca's ballad, therefore, serves as a stamp of approval of the Andalusian "cultural spirit."

Like the preceding two historical ballads, the final one, "Thamar y Amnón," displays plural venue, a sign of contact with the regional "spirit." Denizens of the Granadan hills and the interior of Cordoba province brought to their recitation of the ballad on Tamar and Amnon something of the land in which they live, or so Lorca could have gathered from Falla's notions on the Andalusian *Volksgeist*: "The poet has largely grounded himself on oral Granadan tradition, as M. Alvar (…) has shown" (García-Posada, in Lorca, *Primer romancero* 212, n.). Lorca's brother Francisco recorded a ballad on the theme in the Sacromonte. On a 1920 visit to the Albaicín in search of balladic folklore, Lorca and Menéndez Pidal heard Gypsies sing of "Altamares" (Tamar) (Guillén, *Federico en persona* 56). To justify the biblical theme within the Andalusian framework, Lorca characterized the ballad as "Judaeo-Gypsy, as (…) are the people that inhabit the hills of Granada and some town or other of the Cordoban interior."[23]

Unlike its folkloric precedents, Lorca's biblical narrative follows "Burla de Don Pedro a caballo" in poetizing the mystery of creativity while accenting the enigmatic note. The poem falls in the tradition of the *Allegretto tranquillo e misterioso*, Falla's nocturne "En el Generalife," associated by Lorca with the Andalusian creative spirit. A strange hierarchy emerges of creators and creatures, including a cruel Jehovah-like figure, the implied author; King David, who sings his praises while flouting his laws; and the children of David, Tamar and Amnón, as talented in the arts as their father, yet as susceptible to erotic passions as he. The first part introduces

the fiction of a Davidic Israel, merciless yet beautiful, with evil lunar premonitions and with an enigmatic creator, who sets tigers and flames in the
sky, mythical lightning storms. Moreover, the psalmist David governs a
pastoral kingdom, marred with wars that raise doubts about the justifica-
tion of his creativity. In the second part, the singing of melodious but frigid
Tamar arouses Amnon's lust, while in the third his erotic overtures make
use of impressive tropes on her eyes, breasts, and hands, worthy of Don
Juan, for the purpose of seducing her. In the fourth, he translates body
language into plastic art as he violates her (1:441, ll. 75–6). In the fifth, she
engages in a symbolic Gypsy wedding ceremony, the *alboreá* (Alvar,
Romancero 248), metaphorically legitimating her deflowering. In the sixth
part, while an enraged Amnon flees, King David brusquely suspends his
psalm-making and implicitly his praise of the Creator. Hence, all six parts
concern aesthetic experience while questioning the web of creation.

2. Falla, Lorca, and the Three Urban Andalusian Archangels

As of 1925, Lorca restudied the Baroque poet Góngora's cultivated style
in preparation for the tercentennial of his death (1927). This style influenced Gypsy ballads emerging in 1926, and it was then that he passed to
Falla Góngora's sonnet "A Córdoba," which Falla set to music. In Lorca's
three 1926 ballads on Andalusian cities – Granada, Cordoba, Seville – he
posed the problem of how to make prosaic themes afford refined aesthetic
enjoyment as Góngora had. Lorca's solution consisted of making archangels symbols of the "cultural spirits" of those cities, whose visible and
hidden beauties he accented.

Ideas from Lorca's 1926 public lecture on Góngora apply to "San Rafael
(Córdoba)" and to Falla's 1927 piece, "Soneto a Córdoba," shedding light
on the other two ballads. The main thrust of the lecture is that Góngora
"loved objective beauty, pure, useless beauty, exempt of communicable
anguishes."[24] He realized the ephemeral quality of human sentiment and
its expressions. Therefore, according to Lorca, he sought "metaphor
cleansed of realities that die, (…) metaphor built with a sculptor's spirit."[25]
Góngora's sonnet "A Córdoba," as set by Falla to music, recalls "early
baroque monody" and "reflects the composer's increasing attraction to
starkness, economy and 'pure music," that is, unsentimental music (Hess,
Passions 157).

Both Falla's "Soneto a Córdoba" and Lorca's "San Rafael (Córdoba)"
emerged around the same time, between summer 1926 and spring 1927,
but we cannot determine which came first.[26] Both originated in Granada,

the beautiful city at hand, yet dealt with Cordoba, the beautiful city hidden from view. This duality reproduces the circumstances of Góngora, residing in Granada when composing the sonnet to Cordoba eventually set by Falla to music. The dichotomy attracted Falla to the sonnet because it described his own situation.[27] Just as Lorca's lecture-recital of *Romancero gitano* distinguishes between the visible and the invisible Andalusias, so Lorca's Cordoban ballad, with Góngora between the lines, praises aesthetic values of both what stands revealed and what lies concealed. In his 1926 Góngora lecture, he quotes from *Fábula de Polifemo y Galatea* [Fable of Polyphemus and Galatea], lauding Sicily for both its visible and its unseen fertility. Fruit meets the eye, yet in addition stays hidden. Góngora writes, "Sicily in what she hides, in what she offers, / Is Bacchus's cup, Pomona's orchard-bed. / The goddess gifts her with as many fruits / as bunches of Bacchus's grapes adorn her head."[28] The vineyard drinks up sunshine, while pomes lay hidden in hay beneath the tree.[29] Beauty inhabits surfaces and depths, and Lorca's beautiful Cordoba offers proof. To understand the proof in all its richness, let us examine the treatment of space and time in Falla's and Lorca's perspectives on Cordoba.

Music obeys the laws of physics and can express space as well as time. Newtonian physics makes space completely independent of time. Geometrically plotted, they form a right angle, with the vertical space axis perpendicular to the horizontal time axis. Yet the theory of relativity regards no phenomenon as purely spatial or purely temporal, but rather only more-or-less spatial or more-or-less temporal, "space-like" or "time-like." A "space-like" thing or event has a dose of intrinsic time that cannot be lost. A "time-like" thing or event has some measure of intrinsic space that cannot be set aside. Geometrically, this relationship is expressible on a graph with an acute angle between the space travelled by a body and the time taken for such travel. In music, chords cannot exist with totally simultaneous tones. Their "space-like" component, dictated by the theory of relativity, impels them towards succession. Even on a single instrument, a chord is played with one note slightly after another. Conversely, the most perfect melody presents some component of a chord, of simultaneity. The amount of simultaneity (chord) and succession (melody) varies with every piece and every performance. The melodic flow or "time-like" component of a piece contrasts with its "space-like" component, represented by chords (Garcia Bacca, *Filosofía de la música* 173–4).

Falla's "Soneto a Córdoba" maximizes the "space-like" component or use of chords while minimizing the "time-like" or melodic part. The score for voice and harp reveals much empty space in the treble (a clef filled with

complex melodies and vocal adornments during Falla's Andalusianist period). In the sonnet set to music, a "declamatory vocal line" receives only
"sparse chordal accompaniment" (Hess, *Modernism* 265), frequently ar-
peggiated to provide at least a simple "time-like" ornament, relieving it of
some heaviness. "Every musical quivering turns the notes, chords, phrases, themes … into images (…) traces, shadows, echoes of notes, phrases …
themes not affected by the trill. It makes them (…) something airy, graceful, halo, floating."[30]

   The music fits the text, Góngora's panegyric of airy Cordoban space.
The octave of his sonnet contains apostrophes to different parts of the city
distributed over a vast area: the wall, majestic towers, Guadalquivir, plain,
lofty sierras, sky, and the poet's homeland as a whole. The sextet also com-
presses as much open space as possible into few lines. The first tercet mentions the Granadan setting where Góngora writes, surrounded by ruins
that the Genil River enriches and the Darro bathes. The final tercet completes the notion that if the poetic subject's conduct was not inspired by
his memories of Cordoba, may he never deserve to see her wall, towers,
river, plain, and sierra, a summing up in the two packed final lines of all the
space described in the octave.[31] Falla sets the sonnet to music because, as
Lorca has quoted him, "Cordoba (…) is Roman, Roman as Don Luis [de
Góngora] saw it, and not Arab. There is not one allusion in that sonnet
that is not Roman, Christian."[32] J.B. Trend, Falla's biographer, writes, "For
some years the Roman idea of Andalucía had been taking possession of
him, chiefly (...) for artistic reasons – for the force and economy of expression, and for the permanence of Roman types among the country people
of Southern Spain. He wishes to be Latin, to affirm his Latinity (…) in the
sense in which Latin stands among all the other languages. He would like
his music to be (…) as economical and expressive as Latin, with its grandeur, permanence, and universality."[33] These factors would explain the
starkness, structural monumentality, and conciseness of expression of this
piece (see musical example 12).

   While unable to pinpoint the exact date of Lorca's or Falla's work so as
to say which preceded which, we can affirm that both artists, in Granada
at the time, must have discussed their laboriously emerging compositions
pertinent to Góngora.[34] Lorca's poem has three parts, with the third consisting of merely three lines summing up the whole and resembling a musical coda. The ballad in its totality poetizes many contrasts between surface
and depth, between what is apparent and what lies hidden in Cordoban
time and space. All three parts contain river imagery, compatible with
Góngora's and Lorca's poetic sensitivities (Dolan, "Pictorial Space" 247;

cf. ch. 2, above).[35] The first part (ll. 1–26) contrasts manifest to recondite beauty. The second part (ll. 27–46) reconciles the opposites. The coda re-affirms the opposition but also the reconciliation of both (ll. 47–50). Lorca's lyrical voice everywhere associates Andalusian Latinity with sur-face and Andalusian Semitism with depth. He could have derived the Latin-Andalusian connection from Falla, who espoused the idea much earlier; but the Semitic-Andalusian link belongs to Lorca, probably fol-lowing the Granadan essayist Ángel Ganivet and separating Lorca from Falla as the more ecumenical of the two, the artist taking into account the outcast minorities.[36]

Like Góngora's sonnet appreciated by Falla, Lorca's ballad praises Cordoba's beauty, visible from her streets and from night reflections in her Guadalquivir – in short, from the manifest and from the hidden perspec-tives. Lorca's ekphrastic, purely descriptive poem reduces action and time flow to a minimum while maximizing spatiality. The description largely emerges from multiple metaphors, with several strata of meaning, each striking the reader almost at the same time, like plural notes of a musical chord. A summation of the poetic content appears in the final three lines: "Dos Córdobas de hermosura./Córdoba quebrada en chorros./Celeste Córdoba enjuta" [Two Cordobas of beauty./Cordoba broken into jet streams./Heavenly dry Cordoba] (1:413, ll. 48–50). In the first part, refer-ences abound to this beauty. Cordoban statuary and architecture display loveliness, and so do Cordoban nature, youths, and manufactures. In the first quatrain, river waters smooth out a surface like a canvas in anticipa-tion of a composition to follow. While closed cars with hidden passengers reach the riverbanks, waves [ondas] lend smoothness to "romano torso desnudo" [naked Roman torso]. The torso forms a multiple metaphor, re-ferring either to statuary in the water, to a sculpture on land but reflected in the river, or to a young Cordoban swimmer with Roman features, such as Falla imagines in Cordoban physiognomies. Góngora uses the Latinism "ondas" to denote waters, and Góngora teaches Lorca to omit the article as in Latin and before Lorca's word "torso."[37]

The second quatrain prioritizes Góngora's theme of *natura artifex*, na-ture the artesan, capable, for instance, of gilding pears by ripening them. The river wondrously makes an artwork of the cars reflected in its waters beneath "laminates of flowers" [láminas de flores] with storm clouds re-sounding in the background (1:412, ll. 7–8). Children, viewed by Lorca as pieces of nature (3:287), in Cordoba engage in artisanship, spinning out and singing songs about worldly disillusionment [el desengaño del mundo]. Lorca associates Góngora with the Roman Neostoic Seneca, a Cordoban

SONETO A CÓRDOBA

de

LUIS DE GÓNGORA
(1561–1627)

English version by
J. B. TREND

MANUEL DE FALLA

(*) sempre largamente arpeggiato e con forza

12   Falla, "A Córdoba."

native, who disdained worldly goods as ephemeral. However, in Lorca's ballad, such disillusionment forms merely part of a multiple metaphor with a deeper layer of meaning. He interprets Góngora's Stoicism in a Platonic fashion, detaching beauty (as did Plato in the *Symposium*) from earthly passion and contemplating it as pure form in and of itself.[38] Distant aesthetic contemplation is the lesson that the Cordoban children "weave and sing" [tejen y cantan] in the third quatrain. Yet, passengers in the cars – voyeurs, say critics – disregard that lesson, lost [perdidos] within the night song [nocturno], the art, of the boys (1:412, ll. 11–12), viewed as mere erotic objects. Cordoba herself sees more clearly, and the Latin-loving Falla would not have disagreed. She does not "tremble / beneath muddled mystery" [el misterio confuso]. The night shadow wafts away "the architecture of smoke" [la arquitectura de humo], a misty structure of vapours rising off the river surface. Against this nocturnal blurriness, the city asserts the brilliance of its statuary, represented by a sculpted marble foot [pie], chaste [casto] and demanding detached contemplation as a pure artistic form (1. 18).

In the following two quatrains, manufactured products of Cordoba also "create" beauty. Dalí conveyed to Lorca the aesthetic perfection of modern machinery (cf. Armero, *Lorca* 103). Accordingly, machines and their products become a poetic theme. In Lorca's ballad, a tin can opened in the form of flower petals on the river surface can, like a second nature in Cordoba, perform works of artisanship, doing appliqué work on the grey thunderheads reflected in the water (Lorca 1:412, ll. 19–20). The corolla of this tin flower floats unfolded over the reflection of the triumphal arches of the bridge. The poetic voice paints beauty in the most prosaic, recondite aspects of the city. Further, as Southworth ingeniously perceives ("San Rafael" 90–1), the bridge functions like a flautist. Its arches serve as finger holes through which it blows wind from the river, called "Neptuno," a metonymy found in Góngora (*Soledad Primera*, ll. 1029–30, in Alonso, *Góngora y el Polifemo* 1:416) and also affirming Cordoba's Latinity. With the evocation of the sea god, the poem reaches a moment of high intensity. In an intense instant of an opera, Debussy once advised Falla, a discreet orchestral background serves better than a group of performers onstage singing curses. Even if the orchestra played the French nursery rhyme "J'ai du bon tabac" [I have some good tobacco] and in a minor key for good measure, the audience, caught up in the action, would never notice.[39] In Lorca's ballad, during the stirring of Neptunian waters, accompanied by "flute-playing" of the bridge, tobacconists escape through a broken wall (1:413, ll. 23–6). Critics like Southworth, García-Posada, and Ramsden propose without documentation that the sneaky tobacco sellers are smugglers.[40] Why could they not be Debussy's tobacco sellers escaping the attention of readers too caught up with Neptune, the majesty of the river, to notice the intruders?

In part 2 of Lorca's ballad, displaying the poet's gift for pictorial vision, Cordoban nature shows the artistic skill needed to produce a painting in the style of synthetic cubism. At first, the speaker poses a riddle, saying that a lone fish in the water joins two Cordobas, one of bulrushes, the other of architecture, that is, one belonging to water, the other to land, in short, one concealed and the other visible. On the riverbank, children consider doing mischief, perturbing the fish by jumping into the water after it while ironically asking whether it prefers to be cooked or to escape. In Lorca's poetic terms, the fish is asked whether it wishes to be caught and baked in fine white wine [si quiere flores de vino] (l. 37) or desires freedom to take half-moon leaps [o saltos de media luna] (l. 38). However, the fish, the great mediator, has a loftier plan: to give those young Cordobans a lesson in design, for nature acts as the supreme artificer. The fish gilds the surface of the water with golden scales while blackening with its shadow the depths, where the marble torsos swim. Its beautifying action reconciles what is patent with what is hidden:

Pero el pez, que dora el agua
y los mármoles enluta,
les da lección y equilibrio
de solitaria columna.

[But the fish that gilds the water
And blackens the marbles
Teaches them a lesson of balance
As a solitary column.]   (1:413, ll. 39–42)

The word *dora* [gilds], a dynamic metaphor of colour, appears in Góngora's sonnet "A Córdoba," where day gilds [dora] the landscape (Alonso, *Góngora y el "Polifemo"* 1:367). Likewise, Góngora's word *luto* for black, colour of mourning, in another poem describes a heroine's brows: "El corvo suave luto / de unas cejas" [the curved soft black / of some eyebrows].[41] Lorca, for his point of reference, may have in mind a synthetic cubist composition, painted by Picasso between 1922 and 23. *Still Life with Fishes* shows three fishes on a table forming a cross before an open balcony, while a single fish stands on its tail like a vertical column.[42]

Moreover, the comparison of Lorca's fish to architecture, a column, shows its permanence. García-Posada suggests that the fish is actually the sculpted one on the high columned statue called "El Triunfo," an image of Saint Raphael holding the animal (Lorca, *Primer romancero* 155n39–42). A denizen of the surface, that fish also reaches depths in its reflection in the river. The entire ballad presents Cordoba's embellishment by nature and culture, depth and surface, closure and openness. Lorca's poem appropriately ends by stressing synthesis: it repeats "One lone fish in the water" [Un solo pez en el agua] (l. 47) as the reprise of a melody (like reprises often employed by Falla),[43] a melody enriched by the sounds coming before, and it notes that the fish synthesizes two beautiful Cordobas, the one in the water and the one of solid, sculpted material on land.

What role has the archangel Raphael played amidst all this beauty? In the ballad, he appears by name only in the penultimate quatrain. The poetic voice presents him as *aljamiado*, that is, Moorish or Jewish, though Castilian-speaking (l. 43). In him everything in the poem associated with Cordoba comes together. His Hispano-Roman aspect is manifest, but his Semitic aspect underlies it, and the two aspects achieve reconciliation in his person, just as the surface and the depth of Cordoba attain synthesis in a fish's form. The poetic voice dresses the archangel in "lentejuelas oscuras" (l. 44), "dark sequins" of Arab adornment (García-Posada, in Lorca, *Primer romancero* 155n36). Sequins are tiny laminas of metal, like the "láminas de flores" [laminates of flowers] of the seventh line of the ballad and the petals of thin tin of line 19. Both cases show Cordoba the artificer: Cordoban nature (the floral laminas), on the one hand, and Cordoban culture (the tin flower), on the other hand. Here, nature and culture merge in this collective spirit of Cordoba. The hybrid angel seeks "rumor y cuna" [murmur and cradle], or a soft rippling sound, along with his proper origin, in the "mitin de las ondas," the civic debate between the waves in the water (l. 45) (García-Posada, in Lorca, *Primer romancero* 155n43–6). From the depths of the Guadalquivir, denoted "ondas" [waves] with Góngora 's lexicon, has emerged the spirit of the city, along with the public discourse that has helped build its shining Latinate surface. From Falla, in conclusion, Lorca may have derived a Latinate perspective on Cordoba, but he balances this viewpoint with a Semitic one, helping him to emphasize the division established by Góngora and Falla between the visible and the invisible city.

Ideas from "San Rafael (Córdoba)" can clarify "San Miguel (Granada)." The ballad on Granada originated shortly before 9 September 1926,[44] although whether it antedated or followed the poem on Cordoba, we cannot determine. If Falla helped Lorca to reach Cordoba's essence in what typifies the city, he may also have aided him in attaining a poetic definition of Granada. Instead of focusing on unique aspects of the community – the Alhambra, Carlos V's palace, Sacromonte – Lorca excludes tourist attractions and favours what is typical: a modest pilgrimage in Granada to honour its tutelary saint, Michael. The aspects of the pilgrimage he paints generally escape notice: mules carrying sunflowers for festive kiosks, shadows of the animals on hills, reflections in the distant sea, and ordinary pilgrims. He foregrounds the obscure Granada, while concentrating the patent Granada in the statue of Saint Michael, sculpted by Bernardo Francisco de Mora in 1675 and topping an altar in the space behind the choir in the hermitage of San Miguel el Alto (de Paepe, in Lorca, *Primer romancero* 213, n.t.; García-Posada, in Lorca, *Primer romancero* 145). The ballad alternates the latent with the open, manifest city in a pattern of A-B-A-B, which turns out to be musical – rhythmic and symmetrical.

Where "San Rafael" often emphasizes Cordoba's Latinity, "San Miguel" stresses Granada's musicality. In 1933 Lorca affirmed, "Granada is made for music because it is an enclosed city, a city among sierras, where the melody is returned and filed down and retained by walls and rocks."[45] Other cities have many geographical outlets for their music, while Granada is "secluded, apt for rhythm and echo, substance of music."[46] Moreover, "Granada culminates in its orchestra of fountains full of Andalusian pain and in its *vihuela*-player Narváez and Falla and Debussy."[47] Recognizing Debussy's attraction to Granada, Falla himself adopted Granada in 1920 as his "spiritual homeland," giving to it "the best part of his life, his most fruitful, densely active and creative years" (Mora Guarnido, *Lorca* 148).

In "San Miguel (Granada)" Lorca sidesteps eye-catching elements of the pilgrimage while preferring typical vistas ordinarily escaping notice, yet lending themselves to musical expression. His criteria for these panoramas appear in his 17 October 1926 lecture honouring Granadan poet Soto de Rojas, imitator of Góngora. The Soto de Rojas lecture depends on the Góngora one given eight months earlier. The contrast between cultural display and inconspicuousness passes from one to the other lecture and into the ballad being examined.[48] Lorca finds that Soto de Rojas's poem "Paraíso cerrado para muchos" [Paradise closed for many], metrically imitating Góngora's *Soledades* [Solitudes], does not describe the manifest Granada, but the concealed one, as it expresses few touches of local interest. Its Granadan quality lies in its technique and in the poet's posture towards its development. What makes it Granadan is not its use of data, but its "spirit," its "theme," and in its way of attacking it, as well as description for its own sake and appreciation of tiny objects (Lorca, *Obras completas* 3:249). Lorca's distinction between factual data and spirit stems from Falla's 1917 article "Nuestra música" [Our music], stating that to nationalize Spanish music it is unnecessary to incorporate documented folk song into the melody. While in specific cases he thinks this procedure indispensible, he maintains that in folk song "the *spirit* matters more than the *letter*. The rhythm, the modality, and the melodic intervals that determine their undulations and cadences, constitute what is essential to those songs."[49]

Musicality marks the four parts of "San Miguel (Granada)," treating Granada's pilgrimage the last Sunday of September from the Albaicín to the highest point of Sacromonte, where the Hermitage of San Miguel el Alto stands (García-Posada, in Lorca, *Primer romancero* 145). The first and third parts describe minutiae tangential to the pilgrims, while the second and the fourth depict the archangel's image. Everything stays on a small scale within visual limits. To capture the Granadan *Volksgeist*, the poet imitates its rhythms through repetition in the first quatrain:

Se ven desde las barandas,
por el monte, monte, monte,
mulos y sombras de mulos
cargados de girasoles.

[From the railings can be seen,
On the mount, the mount, the mount,
Mules and shadows of mules
With sunflowers loading them down.]   (Lorca, *Ombras completas*
                                                              1:410, ll. 1–4)

The "spirit" supersedes the text or "letter" in Falla's terms, with auditory predominating over visual effects and the same steady rhythm perceptible in both. In "San Rafael (Córdoba)" Lorca strove to capture spatiality, but in "San Miguel (Granada)" he limits space and accumulates time-like elements: repetition of the same or similar sounds (monte, monte, monte,/ mulos, mulos), references to changing weather conditions, and allusions to hours of the day and to bygone eras. The second quatrain unites an echo of Góngora to a sensation of Granadan air at dawn. In a ballad, Góngora describes the wounded warrior Medoro, "his veins devoid of blood,/ his eyes replete with night."[50] In Lorca's ballad, night blackness becomes a visual impression as the eyes of the mules, blackening in shadows, "grow dim with immense night" [se empañan de inmensa noche] (l. 6). Just as shadows on the mountains have copied the forms of the mules, so do the clouds, forming "a sky of white mules" [un cielo de mulos blancos] with quicksilver eyes (ll. 9–10), seeming to shut as the clouds move past the sun. Even water from a sudden storm, rushing down the hillside, gathers in its descent the visual and auditory rhythm of the mules: "Crazy water in the open/through the mount, the mount, the mount" [Agua loca y descubierta/por el monte, monte, monte] (1:410, ll. 15–16).

The Mediterranean south of Granada echoes visual rhythms of nature reflected in the faraway view of the mules, the perception of their shadows, and repetitive cloud formations: "The sea dances on the beach,/A poem of balconies" [El mar baila por la playa,/un poema de balcones]. The surf, regularly ebbing, flowing, and swishing, dances ashore, while a series of balconies, reflected in the water, appears in the regularity of its forms to make a wordless poem with repetitive rhythms (1:411, ll. 29–30). In the third part of the ballad, pilgrims move at the rhythms strewn about the land. The arrival of the human element receives notice through the trampling of bulrushes and the sound of voices. A concise contrast emerges, added to the reflection of the moon seen by day in the water. Gongorine terseness generates an odd moonscape: "The riverbanks of the moon/lose bulrushes, gain voices" [Las orillas de la luna/pierden juncos, ganas voces] (ll. 31–2).

A procession of typical Granadan pilgrims follows, depicted with sensuous humour and abundant temporal elements. The approach of the *manolas*, women of easy virtue who also figure in local folk song, enables Lorca to link up to his initial visual and auditory sensations of the mules with their sunflower burdens:

Vienen manolas comiendo
semillas de girasoles,
los culos grandes y ocultos
como planetas de cobre.

[Along come *manolas*
Eating sunflower seeds,
With big, covered rumps
Like planets of copper.]   (1:411, ll. 33–6)

The reference to female derrières establishes a humorous phonetic echo [*ulos* (…) *ultos*] of the sounds, rhythms, and visions found in "*mulos* y sombras de m*ulos*" [mules and shadows of mules] (l. 3). The hyperbole of the copper planets increases the hilarity.

In this ballad of heightened *temporality,* other aristocratic pilgrims focus on the past: tall gentlemen and ladies of sad demeanour display nostalgia for the nightingales of yesteryear (1:411, ll. 37–40), a more melodious
time. Heading the parade, the Bishop of Manila is a figure anchored in
time, in history, since his title is an alternate one for the Bishop of Granada,
here pictured as he offers communion.[51]

The ballad alternates its four parts between the outdoors and the interior of the hermitage housing the archangel's image. For Lorca, Soto de
Rojas's art exemplifies typical "Granadan preciosity" [preciosismo grana-
dino] (3:251), and Lorca's Saint Michael has the same quality. Affectation
requires self-ostentation, like the lace-clad Corregidor's in Falla's ballet
Sombrero. In a hidebound Granadan community with rigid norms for the
conduct of each sex, a mischievous Lorca takes pleasure in depicting the
city's sexually fluid archangel. Lorca's Saint Michael shows his "beautiful
thighs" [bellos muslos] (l. 19) much as the boys by the Cordoban riverside displayed their waists.[52] With lacy sleeves and "petticoats encrust-
ed / with small mirrors and lace strips" (ll. 47–8),[53] he smells of cologne
inside the tower of the hermitage, far from the natural fragrance of the
flowers outside (ll. 27–8). A creature of limitless temporality because of
his mythical stature, he is an "efebo de tres mil noches" [ephebe of three
thousand nights], three times as fabled as Scheherazade with her mere
thousand and one nights (l. 26). Described in terms of time, he holds his
right arm on high at a position of twelve o'clock, brandishing a sword
while lightly treading on a devil in the shape of a defeated Moor. His
boyish face affects a stern expression (1:411, ll. 21–4). Of Granada, Lorca
writes, "Everything has on the outside a sweet domestic air, but, actually,
who can delve into the interior?"[54] Granada's intimacy has multiple layers.
How else can we explain the sweetness of Saint Michael's wrath towards
the Devil, anger as soft as the white plumes on his head and as lyrical
as nightingales?

Finally, Lorca offers his own reading of the last two lines of the ballad,
referring to Granada's "Berber beauty / of screams and belvederes" [primor
berberisco / de gritos y miradores] (ll. 51–2). He provides a musical interpretation like the one preferred here of the poem as a whole: by situating the
worship of the archangel in the elevated Hermitage of San Miguel el Alto
in the Albaicín district, Granadans can savour from there the delicious,
African-derived song that is the entire city spread out below. "It is a muddled melody that is heard. It is the whole song of Granada heard at the
same time: rivers, voices, strings, flora, parades, a host of fruit, and triumphal music of swings."[55]

The third and final ballad on an Andalusian city, "San Gabriel (Sevilla)," lacks the intimacy of "San Miguel (Granada)" and the depth of "San Rafael (Córdoba)" while showing greater dramatic qualities, perhaps influenced by Falla. Lorca here returns to the Gypsy theme of the anthology. This poem, like "San Rafael (Córdoba)," composed slightly before or at the same time in 1926 (de Paepe, in Lorca, *Primer romancero* 43), has two parts and a coda. The first part offers a physical description of the image of Gabriel at the Hermitage of San Miguel el Alto; the second shows Gabriel's interaction with the Gypsy Anunciación de los Reyes, to whom he announces the birth of her child and foretells its violent life history; and the coda narrates the conception of the singing child while the angel rises heavenward. The Annunciation, religious point of departure of the ballad, serves merely as a poetic pretext for subtly exploring the treatment of an oppressed minority by a beautiful but cruel heavenly order.

Falla has honoured a Christian Cordoba through Góngora, and Lorca Christianizes Góngora's imagery to represent Gabriel's male beauty. The description visualizes him as a boy made of bulrush for his slimness and straightness, a metaphor present in "San Rafael (Córdoba)," with its Góngora-style riverside imagery. Gabriel's broad shoulders and slim body precede the word painting of his skin with an echo of Góngora. In the *Polifemo*, the poetic voice calls the apple deceitful, not for its pallor, but for its feigned rouge, its red exterior masking its inner whiteness.[56] In Lorca's ballad, the archangel's skin has the colour of an apple seen at night [piel de nocturna manzana: l. 3]. The darker, Gypsy skin tone masks its redness, and the nuanced word painting could hardly be more precise.

Lorca's praise of Gabriel's height, majesty, and brilliance echoes the Latinist Góngora, revered by Falla, and author of a learned reinterpretation of the Polyphemus myth from Ovid's *Metamorphoses*, Bk. 13. Lorca transforms Góngora's Polifemo by eliminating his self-touted, grotesque enormity. Polifemo boasts of his stature in these terms: "Sentado, a la alta palma no perdona / su dulce fruto mi robusta mano" [When I am seated by the lofty palm, / My robust hand its sweet fruit does not spare] (Alonso 2:30, ll. 409–10). Lorca's speaker, more measured, affirms that the archangel outdoes the palm tree in height and straightness: "No hay palma que se le iguale" [There is no palm to equal him] (1:414, l. 12). Polifemo praises himself as son of Neptune, the "Jupiter of the waves" (Alonso 2:30, l. 401), and Lorca's archangel surpasses in kingliness any "crowned emperor" (1:414, l. 13). Polifemo calls himself a "human heaven" with an eye like a sun in his face (Alonso 2:30, ll. 423–4); and Saint Gabriel outshines any "walking morning star" (Lorca 1:414, l. 14).[57]

A magical atmosphere of Gypsy miracles envelops Saint Gabriel. Guitars, the preferred instrument of Gypsy deep song applauded by Falla ("*Cante jondo*" 153–5), here make music by themselves in honour of the archangel (Lorca, 1:414, ll. 19–20). With joy he opposes weeping willows, while giving them a lesson in erect posture (ll. 21–2). In view of Gabriel's powers, the speaker, identifying with the Gypsies as Falla did in *El amor brujo*, asks the angel to succour the Gypsy woman Anunciación in a plea couched in humorous, homespun, quid pro quo terms: the Gypsies dressed his image, and now he should aid one of their tribeswomen (1:415, ll. 23–6.)

The second part of the ballad, dramatizing the archangel's annunciation, portrays the pregnant Gypsy with echoes of Góngora, for whom a young bull is a "novillo tierno,/de bien nacido cuerno/mal lunada la frente" [Tender yearling/With well-born horns/But badly lunared brow], that is, unable to defend itself with moon-shaped horns that have not sprouted as yet (Alonso, *Soledad Segunda* in *Góngora y el "Polifemo"* 1:422, ll. 17–19). A verbal antithesis contrasting "well" and "badly" ("bien ... mal") passes from Góngora to Lorca, but Góngora's neologism "lunada" changes meaning in Lorca. Here it means "born under a favorable lunar sign." Applied twice to the Gypsy Anunciación, "lunada" gathers the force of an epithet, defining her as "bien lunada y mal vestida" (well-lunared but badly dressed). Within the Gypsies' syncretic world view, observed as well in Falla's *El amor brujo*,[58] Anunciación has the moon in her favour. She belongs to invisible, latent Seville, in the shadows of visible, manifest, goal-oriented Seville, embodied by Saint Gabriel.

The dialogue between the angel and the Gypsy prophesies new life, but with a cruel promise of imminent death. In reality, Lorca, a skilful playwright, subtly makes what seems like a dialogue two monologues. The earthbound Mary figure reacts to obscure sensible experiences at hand, while the angel deals in predictions of events too remote for her to fathom. In an early manuscript of the ballad, faced with Saint Gabriel's dire forewarnings, the Gypsy pleaded in vain for help,[59] but the poet subsequently painted her as obedient, resigned, or silent. In Lorca's ballad she tells the angel that he now strikes her "with three nails of joy" [con tres clavos de alegría], as if she instinctively sensed the crucifixion to follow (1:415, l. 40). The angel's heavenly brightness appears to this creature of nature to open the beauty of jasmine flowers over her face (l. 41). He greets her with a biblical salutation from Luke 1:28, followed by an earthy flirtation, worthy of Don Juan Tenorio: "God save you, Anunciación./Wondrous dark-skinned girl."[60] The aesthetically sensitive Saint Gabriel foretells that Anunciación will have a child more beautiful than stems waving in the breeze (ll. 45–6), a comparison related to the image of the male body as straight and slim as the bulrush. Her response, born out of her naturalness, also draws upon a humorous concrete image from the vegetable kingdom: she would love to seat Gabriel on an easy chair made out of pinks (ll. 49–50). When he foretells the crucifixion, symbolized by a scar and three wounds on her son's breast (ll. 53–4), Anunciación offers no verbal reaction, but merely focuses on her own breasts, where she feels the milk entering (ll. 57–8). Finally, his prophecy of her future fertility contrasts with the sterility of the landscapes he predicts her many future sons will traverse on horseback. She does not respond. Something about the dialogue rings hollow, with the two participants not fully communicating, despite endearments Anunciación lavishes on the celestial Don Juan in response to his compliments (1:415, 416, ll. 47, 48, 56).

The coda of the ballad contains two quatrains, one on the ill-fated child, the other on Gabriel, exiting as dramatically as he entered. Lorca encloses his ballad in a musical framework whose finale emphatically recoups the beginning as often happens in Falla. In the first quatrain, the child sings in his mother's breast, three bullets of bitter, unripe almond in his voice, hence, a taste of premature death in his infant mouth, with stars above metamorphosing into funereal houseleeks (1:416, ll. 65–6; de Paepe, in Lorca, *Primer romancero* 229n36). Gabriel's final action consists of ascending to heaven on Jacob's ladder (Lorca 1:67–8; de Paepe, in Lorca, *Primer romancero* 162n68), another reality not immediately present to the unfortunate Gypsies. Visibility keeps its distance from invisibility, earth from heaven, introducing painful irony into what could have been a joyous ballad.

In conclusion, the ballads on the "cultural spirits" of three Andalusian cities derive from embellishment of down-to-earth urban sensations. Lorca attracts Falla to Góngora between 1926 and 27 for his Christian Latinity. The sonnet "A Córdoba," Falla's musical version, and Lorca's "San Rafael (Córdoba)" all contrast unperceived with obvious reality. Falla's musical work exalts the manifest Roman culture of absent Cordoba while composing in present Granada. Lorca's "San Rafael (Córdoba)" more closely imitates Góngora in extolling the beauty of what is concealed as well as that of what is plain to view, and among recondite realities includes Cordoba's Semitic characteristics. Lorca develops Góngora's theme of *natura artifex*, and in addition introduces Dalí's notion of the machine and its products as artisans of beautiful (Cordoban) objects. Where Cordoba partakes of Latinity, Granada for Falla and Lorca participates in musicality. This characteristic accounts for Falla's attraction to the city in the first place as well as for Lorca's treatment of Granada in "San Miguel (Granada)." Granada enjoys a patent and a hidden rhythm, perceptible in multiple aspects of the annual pilgrimage in honour of the archangel. Falla's attention prior to 1923 to the meaning over the specific content of Andalusian folk music enables the acutely visual Lorca to seek Granadan rhythms in usually unnoticed quarters: mules' movement towards the city, their shadows against the hills, balconies reflected on the sea, bodily motions of pilgrims towards the hermitage. These unnoticed rhythms alternate with the manifest music made by Saint Michael, effeminate and affected in his tower, presiding over a stunning auditory experience of the song of all Granada rising from below. Finally, elements from the ballads on Cordoba and Granada make their way into "San Gabriel (Sevilla)." Góngora influences the physical depiction of Saint Gabriel as well as of Anunciación de los Reyes. Like the singing Saint Michael, Saint Gabriel makes music, descending from heaven rhythmically to harps and Gypsy guitars, and eventually conveying his musicality to the hapless child singing in the Gypsy woman's womb. In a disjointed dialogue between the archangel and Anunciación, he focuses on prophecies in the air, she on immediacies on the ground, thereby reproducing between them the dialectic between concealment and manifestation present in the other two ballads. Embodiments of three urban "cultural spirits" in the poetry on Andalusian cities compete in vividness with the incarnations of the Andalusian ethos in the four individuals of Lorca's historical ballads.

11
Lorca's Artistic Tributes to Falla

If I had to identify the two creators that left the deepest imprint on [Lorca's] creation, I would not hesitate to respond, Manuel de Falla and Salvador Dalí.

Maurer, "Lorca y las formas" 238.[1]

Between 1920 and 1929, Lorca habitually paid tribute to his friend Falla. His postcard to Falla of 8 May 1923 contains a gratuitous expression of admiration, provoked by the Belgian triumph of *La vida breve*: "I already know the great success that you had in Brussels and that gladdens me as if it had been my own, since you already know the affection and great, enthusiastic admiration that I hold for your work and your person."[2] At three points in their lives, Lorca's admiration assumed artistic form. On 31 December 1920, he engineered a musical prank, but one showing high regard for Falla's art. In February 1927 he wrote a sonnet in honour of Falla's fiftieth birthday, a poem signed by the author's family and friends. Finally, in December 1927, he published the first half of an ode to the Sacred Host and dedicated it as a "tribute to Manuel de Falla" [homenaje a Manuel de Falla]. The present chapter studies the three tributes and plots the trajectory of the friendship between Falla and Lorca.

On New Year's Eve 1920, Federico and Francisco García Lorca played an elaborate joke on Falla and his sister María del Carmen. Outside the composer's home, the brothers had stationed musicians from the municipal band to render Federico's comical arrangement for trombone, clarinet, tuba, and cornet of the sublimely mysterious "Canción del fuego fatuo" [Song of the will-o'-the-wisp] from *El amor brujo*, normally sung by a contralto with orchestral accompaniment. When Falla and his sister heard

the music, they laughed so hard that, by Lorca's account, they could barely arise to admit the group. Praising the instrumental arrangement as "genial," Don Manuel pushed the band members into his music room and
made them play encores, accompanied by him on piano (Lorca, *Epistolario*
1:50). Thanks to Lorca, Falla discovered the comic possibilities of the
"Canción del fuego fatuo." In a musical afterthought of January 1923, he
humorously inserted a brass and xylophone arrangement of that piece into
his *Retablo* (see musical example 13) (Torres "Cisne" XVII). The song,
about fleeing from the pursuing will-o'-the wisp, sounds while the knight
Don Gaiferos flees with his wife Melisendra from the pursuing Moors. At
the bottom of the page of the score of this rehearsal number 75, Falla has
scrawled, "Rectify the correction" [Rectificar la corrección], showing his
last-minute insertion.

With an exuberant spirit, this time foregrounding admiration, Lorca
wrote the following "Soneto de homenaje a Manuel de Falla ofreciéndole
unas flores" [Sonnet in tribute to Manuel de Falla while offering him some
flowers] in 1927 in honour of Falla's fiftieth birthday:

> Lira cordial de plata refulgente
> de duro acento y nervio desatado,
> voces y frondas de una España ardiente
> con tus manos de amor has dibujado.
> En nuestra propia sangre está la fuente
> que tu razón y sueños ha brotado.
> Álgebra limpia de serena frente.
> Disciplina y pasión de lo soñado.
> Ocho provincias de la Andalucía,
> olivo al aire y a la mar los remos,
> cantan, Manuel de Falla, tu alegría.
> Con el laurel y flores que ponemos
> amigos de tu casa en este día,
> pura amistad sencilla te ofrecemos.

> [Oh heartfelt lyre made of refulgent silver,
> With daring beat and energy impassioned,
> Voices and verdure of an ardent Spain,
> With skillful hands of deepest love, you've fashioned.
> In our own blood is to be found the fount
> From which your reason and your dreams have streamed.
> Pure algebra that rose in tranquil brow.

13 Manuel de Falla, *El retablo de maese Pedro*, Manuscript, rehearsal 75. Staffs "2c," "xil,"
and third from the bottom contain "Canción del fuego fatuo." The staffs in descending order
belong to the flute (Fl.), the oboe (Ob.), the English horn (C. i.), the bassoon (F.), 2 horns
(2c), trumpet (Tr., crossed out), drums (Timp.) kettledrum (Tamb.), xylophone (xil.) harpsichord (cemb.), harp-lute (A.L.), puppet-interpreter's voice (tr.), first violin (Vl. 1), second
violin (Vl. 2), 2 violas, violoncello (vc.), bass horn (c.b.), then three staffs with the "Canción
del fuego fatuo" rewritten and accompanied. Reproduced with gracious permission of the
Archivo Manuel de Falla (Granada).

Passion and discipline of all you've dreamed.
Eight provinces that make up Andalusia,
Olive trees in air and oars dipped in the sea,
Sing loud, Manuel de Falla, of your glee.
With laurels and flowers that we offer,
We friends of your household on this day
In simple friendship tribute to you pay.]   (Lorca 1:930)

The sonnet begins by echoing Falla's favourite poet Darío, regarding French Symbolist Paul Verlaine as an archetypal poet-musician, an Orpheus or "heavenly lyre-bearer" [liróforo celeste] (Darío 5: 820). In Greek mythology, after the Thracian Bacchants slew Orpheus, Zeus ordered his lyre placed in the sky as the constellation Lyra (Bulfinch, *Mythology* 187). The new Orpheus is Falla. The refulgent silver of his lyre shines with heavenly light, yet also pulsates in tune with his heart. "Hands of deepest love" wield Falla's pen and play piano with consummate skill. The "love" receives clarification in memoirs of Lorca's sister Isabel, for whom Falla's "sentiment with regard to musical creation [was] the work made with love. Love was the great moving force of his life. His genius and deep love of God impelled him to make a perfect work, since he was convinced he had to labour and strive to do the best possible with something that had been given to him."[3] Though a skilled musician, Falla saw himself as a humble craftsman with divine inspiration. His lyre played stressed rhythms [acento duro], because in his Andalusianist period, "his music requires (…) as a rule, a definite accent on the first beat of the bar" (Trend, *Falla* 85). In Lorca's sonnet, he musically sketched the fertile space and voices defining this impassioned area of Spain, viewed by Falla as its prototype: foreign composers characterized all Spanish music with Andalusian melodies (Falla, *"Cante jondo"* 147). From the blood of all Andalusians sprang the Andalusianist composer's creative dream, which consisted of musically capturing the essence of his region.

His music has a serene Muse, almost mathematical in precision and having an Andalusian nuance, visible in the Hispano-Arabic origin and name of algebra (Lapesa, *Historia de la lengua* 101). In modulating melodies, he made algebraic substitutions when passing from one key to the next to preserve the needed intervals (Collins, "Falla and Resonance" 79). He composed with mathematical awareness of harmonic modes, and also governed melodic tensions and distensions with particular intervals and chords. Such was the disciplined emotion, often affected by Louis Lucas's philosophy of music (Falla, *"Cante jondo"* 144), pervading his artistic dream. In the first tercet, the speaker marvels at the vastness of Andalusian geography honouring Falla on land, sea, and air. The "glee" here mentioned characterized Falla: "Don Manuel smiled a great deal at what he liked, and would always adapt to the situation."[4] Finally, in the second tercet, by contrast, the lyric voice modestly narrows its focus to the friends and neighbours paying tribute to Falla out of simple friendship. Therefore, while the first-person plural of the first line included all Andalusians, in the twelfth verse the pronoun "we" embraces a concrete, intimate group of Andalusians.

From 1920 until 1929, therefore, Falla had maintained a friendly, good-humoured relationship with Lorca, whose family treated the composer and his sister like family members.[5] However, early in 1929 Falla learned with surprise that the previous December, in Ortega's *Revista de Occidente* (121), Lorca had published the first two parts of his "Oda al santísimo sacramento del altar" [Ode to the Holiest Sacrament of the Altar], subtitled, "Homenaje a Manuel de Falla" [Tribute to Manuel de Falla]. In a courteous letter of 9 February 1929, written in two columns (Falla liked to conserve paper), in an uncommonly legible handwriting for Don Manuel, showing careful reflection, he expressed gratitude to Lorca for the unexpected tribute, yet also disapproval of the style of devotion to the Eucharist reflected in the ode:

Granada, 9 February 1929

Dear Federico:

You had said nothing to me about the work that you were preparing, nor this time, consequently, did you tell me that you had intended to dedicate it to me.

Now, with Pepe Segura back from Madrid, I find it out from him, and when I wanted to acquire an issue of the journal, I received the one that Adolfo Salazar sent me for me to read his article.

Do not find it odd, therefore, that I have not written you before to express my gratitude for the honour that your dedication does me.

To you, who know me so well, I need not tell you what the differences are that separate us on the theme of your Ode. If I treated it, I would do so with my spirit *on its knees*, while aspiring for all mankind to be deified by virtue of the Sacrament.

And with it the offering: gold, incense, and myrrh. Pure; without mixtures …

You understand me, Federico, and forgive me if I annoy you in any way. How sorry I would be! …

It is clear that as always happens in your works, in this one there are indisputable beauties and expressions that hit the mark; but because this concerns you, I could not hide from you – as I might in another case – my exact impression.

That would run counter to the friendship and loyalty I owe you. Furthermore, I place my hope in the definitive version and in the rest of the poem.

To Don Federico [the poet's father] and to Paco [the poet's brother] I send my affectionate regards. All your family is well. Today I had the great pleasure of seeing them.

A very grateful embrace from Manuel de Falla.

(Translated with gracious permission of the Archivo Manuel de Falla)[6]

Falla employed the metaphor of kneeling before the Eucharist in thanksgiving. Proof of thanks to God with works comes in the form of singing the hymn *Pange lingua* attributed to Saint Thomas Aquinas (García Bacca, *Filosofía de la música* 80) and quoted at the very start of Lorca's ode. Since Falla did not find Lorca's poetic subject consistently genuflecting in the ode, but mixing reverence with secularity, he took it upon himself as a loyal friend, concerned with the poet's spiritual wellbeing, to convey his disagreement. The discrepancy led at first to repentance on Lorca's part, but later to affective leave-taking from Falla, a reaction not visible on the warm surface of their relationship, yet a reaction which may have proved ultimately fatal for the poet in his final days.[7]

Others besides Falla reacted with discomfiture to the ode. In 1930, after Lorca's completion of parts 3 and 4, a Havana audience heard some of it recited, and many came away shocked.[8] Perhaps to avoid further criticism, among other reasons, Lorca left the work as a whole unpublished. Before examining its text, we must first recognize that while writing it Lorca was oscillating in 1928 between faith and eroticism; that he had first conceived the ode as a paean to Falla as composer in 1927 of incidental music for Calderón's *auto sacramental El gran teatro del mundo* [The great world theatre]; that Lorca mistakenly viewed Falla's religious devotion as closer to his own than it was; that since Falla's religious music mixed traditional faith and modernity, Lorca had hoped to devise an analogous mix for his own ode; and that the "modern" component of the ode consisted of Salvador Dalí's influence, which clashed (in Falla's sensitivity) with components congenial to Falla.

In 1928, like Darío before him,[9] Lorca vacillated between traditional piety and eroticism. While composing the "Oda al santísimo sacramento del altar" with religious elements, he was also writing his erotic "Oda a Sesostris" [Ode to Sesostris] (Lorca, *Epistolario* 2:120). The oscillation showed up even within the religious ode, begun in January of 1928 and finished as late as 17 September 1929 (Martín, *Heterodoxo y mártir* 264, n.). Possibly he conceived this ode as a fitting accompaniment for Calderón's *El gran teatro del mundo*, the *auto sacramental* musically arranged by Falla and presented in Granada on 27 May 1927 and thereafter for the feast of Corpus Christi. Steeped in Golden Age letters, Lorca knew the old custom of supplementing these one-act allegorical *autos* or plays with other music and poetry exalting the Eucharist. Both Falla and Lorca intended to glorify the Sacred Host with words and music in their own ways. Lorca wrote Zalamea that the ode was "perhaps the greatest poem that I have made."[10]

Ultimately affected by his mother's association of Catholic worship with beauty,[11] Lorca probably wished to participate with Falla in Corpus Christi activities in Granada centred on the Eucharist. In 1927 Falla was absorbed in composing incidental music to *Gran teatro* fully half a year before Lorca began elaborating his ode. "I have neglected almost everything else because of the Auto," wrote Falla in May to his friend Ángel Barrios, director of the planned Granadan performance of Calderón's *auto*.[12] Falla's Corpus Christi project took him from May to June of 1927 to complete, the very month the *auto sacramental* was to be staged. According to Theodore Beardsley, "the multiple indications of the manuscript reveal a noteworthy effort on Falla's part to create an original score which at the same time is based on sources either appropriate or contemporary with *Gran teatro* thus attempting to re-create the flavor of the lost original music. Falla's procedure," Beardsley concludes, "seems to combine the roles of composer and musicologist" (Beardsley, "Falla's Score for *Gran teatro*" 72). His composing consisted of arranging and scoring baroque and earlier Spanish music for a modern audience's ears. Tradition and modernity went hand in hand. The final product, debuting 27 June 1927, employed a mezzo-soprano, a chorus, two guitars, an oboe, four clarinets, a bassoon, two trombones, a tuba, and timpani. Lasting eight minutes, the work contained seven individual pieces (Harper, *Falla. Life* 394–5), most sung by female voices. Beardsley shows that Falla had carefully studied Valbuena Prat's 1926 edition of *El gran teatro del mundo*. Where the text calls for music, Falla intercalated it in sixteen places, using seven difference pieces, some repeated verbatim as in a sacred rite (Beardsley, "Falla's Score for *Gran teatro*" 67).

Calderón grounds his *auto* on the metaphor of the world as a stage. God the Author sets the moment for the play within a play to start. Two globes open, the sphere of life eternal and the sphere of earthly life. Music sounds here at the beginning (*Teatro* 1:139 before l. 628) and also at the end of the play within a play (1:174, before line 1437), when the heavenly globe appears once more and in it a table with chalice and Sacred Host. Near the start, the nun Discreción [Discretion] sings a hymn of praise to God based on Daniel 3:62–3, 76, 66–72 (Beardsley, "Falla's Score for *Gran teatro*" 67). Five times throughout the work, the Ley de la Gracia [Law of Grace] sings the greatest lesson of the *auto*, a lesson titling the play within a play: "Do good works since God is God."[13] A mezzo-soprano identified by Beardsley as the voice of Death periodically announces to the main characters – the King, Beauty, the Peasant, the Rich Man, the Poor Man – the respective ends of their acting roles. Falla set all the lines of the voice to music, including Death's response to Beauty about the limits to her "eternity" (ll. 1073–4; Beardsley, "Falla's Score for *Gran teatro*" 67). Finally, for the end of Calderón's work, Falla like Calderón (1:178 after l. 1568) required the singing of *Tantum ergo*, the two final strophes of the *Pange lingua*. The *Tantum ergo* is sacred music venerating the Eucharist and calling for devotion to Father, Son, and the Holy Ghost proceeding from each. In this way, Falla recognized the Church custom of introducing that music into the Mass during veneration and benediction of the Most Blessed Sacrament (Henry, "Pange Lingua"; Beardsley, "Falla's Score for *Gran teatro*" 67).[14]

While Falla's musical arrangement of *Gran teatro* debuted in Granada, Lorca followed the debut from Catalonia, where he was accompanying Dalí (Lorca, *Obras completas* 3:1095). In May 1927 he wrote to the director Antonio Gallego Burín, "I am very happy that the *autos sacramentales* are being put on. Write and tell me things about this matter. In Granada the most beautiful things in the world can be put on."[15] Calderón's *auto*, presented May 27, with scenery in an open space on the grounds of the Alhambra, enjoyed such success that it was repeatedly staged until 1935 in various sites of the city (Mariano de Paco, "Auto sacramental en el siglo XX" 367). In July 1927 Lorca wrote Falla from Barcelona, "That business of the *autos sacramentales* has at last been a great success in all Spain and a success of our friend [Hermenegildo] Lanz [stage designer], who day after day modestly manages to earn our greatest admiration. This makes me exceedingly happy and shows me how very much can be done and what we should do in Granada."[16] Since Falla had previously lent Lorca his notes on *Cante jondo* in 1922 (Persia, *I Concurso* 89–93), surely he would have shared with him the score of the music he had set to Calderón's *auto*.

Just as Calderón indicated passages to be set to music, so Lorca built instructions into his ode. Religious epigraphs relating to the Eucharist head each of its four parts. In this poetic tribute to Falla, Lorca aspired to win his approval at least for parts 1 and 2, both published in 1928. The last piece of music mentioned on Falla's score to be played at the Granada production of *Gran teatro* is the *Tantum ergo*, which accompanied the display of the Sacred Host at the end. Lorca's first epigraph borrows the first two lines from *Pange lingua*, the same hymn from which the *Tantum ergo* derives: "Pange lingua gloriosi / corporis mysterium" (Sing, my tongue, the Saviour's glory, / Of His flesh the mystery sing).[17] Lorca honoured Falla by implying that his own ode began where the composer left off.[18] Perhaps the poet designed his work to be read after the performance of Falla's composition at some future Corpus Christi celebration in Granada. In the Golden Age, the *loa*, or short rhymed prologue, contained a brief panegyric of the dedicatee of the play, or else described the plot (Anonymous, "Loa" 954). Lorca's ode, however, reads like an epilogue. Mostly written in the past tense from a spectator's vantage point,[19] it seems to presuppose Falla's musical arrangement of *El gran teatro del mundo* and to contain implicit praise of him as an artist for making Christ visible in the Eucharist. As we shall shortly point out, Lorca's ode resembles sixteenth-century poet-theologian Fray Luis de León's ode "A Francisco Salinas" [To Francisco Salinas], except that Lorca seemed to have in mind the performance of Falla's musical arrangement already mentioned, whereas Fray Luis lauded all performances of religious music by his friend Salinas, an organist and music theorist in Salamanca.

The first two lines of *Pange lingua* form the epigraph of part 1, the "Exposición" (Exposition) of the Sacred Host. The remaining three parts take as their epigraphs brief sacred statements capable of being sung and pertinent to the three enemies of the soul – the world, the devil, and the flesh – combated by the Sacred Host. The treatment of a different enemy in each of parts 2, 3, and 4 shows Lorca's would-be collaboration with Falla as musical arranger of Calderón's *autos*. Always concerned with spiritual self-purification, Falla studied Calderón's handling of the doctrine of the three enemies of the soul, as Lorca surely knew. In the edition of Calderón annotated by Falla, Valbuena Prat distinguishes ten *autos sacramentales* on biblical parables and narratives, and singles out for beauty and feeling *A tu prójimo como a tí* [Thy neighbour as thyself], based on the good Samaritan parable (Luke 10:30–5). Here Original Sin, accompanied by the World, Lust, and the Devil, waylay the Human Being, traveller on the road of life, and rob his jewels, symbols of his senses and spiritual potencies. The Levite and the priest go by without aiding him. They symbolize respectively Natural Law and Written Law. The Samaritan succouring him is Christ; the inn where he takes him, the Church; the innkeeper, Saint Peter, who administers the remedies of the sacraments (Valbuena Prat, 1916 ed., LXXIV). Falla bracketed a stage direction in which Lust comes onstage on one side, and Original Sin, the World, and the Devil on the other; and these three dialogue in unison with Lust (192).[20]

World, devil, and flesh each receive in Lorca's ode an epigraph relevant to the Eucharist. For the epigraph against worldliness, he chose the invocation to the Lamb of God intoned during the fraction of the Host: *Agnus Dei qui tollis peccata mundi. – Miserere nobis* [Lamb of God that takes away the sins of the world, have mercy on us]. This doctrine has generated much outstanding music either as part of a Mass or played alone. Inspired examples include Bach's Mass in B-minor, Mozart's *Requiem*, and Beethoven's Mass in D (Henry, "Agnus Dei"). Lorca must have hoped to please Falla with the *Agnus Dei* quotation, because, as Francisco García Lorca reminds (*Federico y su mundo* 154–5), the pious composer wished to compose a Mass someday.[21] The possible presence of Beethoven's *Agnus Dei* in Lorca's ode will later be shown.

All Falla's objections would have concerned Lorca's controversial personalization of an ode to the holiest sacrament. Instead of reverently kneeling before the gift of the Eucharist, Lorca viewed divinity face to face.[22] He mixed secular with religious sentiments. Since 1918, probably without Falla's knowledge, he had experimented with projecting personal problems onto biblical figures. In his immature "religious tragedy" *Cristo* (1919?), young Jesus becomes his alter ego, torn between earthly love and his mission to serve humanity.

Lorca misunderstood Falla's piety. To his friend Sebastián Gasch, he characterized Falla's religious devotion in a letter written between December 1927 and early 1928. He tried to recall what Falla once had said to him: "'Don't talk to me about supernatural things. How disagreeable Saint Catherine [of Siena] is!,' says Falla."[23] Yet Falla would never have contradicted the dogma of Christ's supernatural power to transform bread and wine into his flesh and blood. In a 1933 interview, Lorca once more mentioned Saint Catherine as interpreted by Falla, but this time his version of Falla's words differed, showing memory lapses on religious affairs: "His faith is of such magnitude, of such a pure quality, that he rejects miracles and protests against them. His faith does not need proofs for belief. One day I read *Saint Catherine of Siena* by Johannes Jørgensen, and I took him the book all excited, thinking I could bring him some pleasure. After a few days he said to me, 'I don't like that book. Saint Catherine is not a true saint … she's an intellectual …'"[24] Still, Falla would not have rejected the miracle of transubstantiation, essential to the dogma of the Eucharist, wherein the substance of the bread and wine change into the substance of Jesus's body and blood.

Lorca misinterpreted the tenor of Falla's religious devotion. Federico's younger brother Francisco, who knew him intimately, contrasts his religious attitude with Falla's: "Falla's orthodox Catholicism and the scrupulous performance of his religious duties did not sully the heartfelt, friendly relationship that united him to our group of young men, *very indifferent in religious matters*."[25] Focusing on the *Oda*, Francisco reflects in hindsight that Federico believed foolishly [ilusoriamente] in the appeal of its theme to Falla, when the composer's idea of religious art differed from Federico's. Francisco contrasts Falla's hope of achieving the concentration and devoutness needed to write a Mass with Federico's relaxed attitude [desenfado] even in expressing Eucharistic symbols in his ode with dehumanizing metaphors (the Sacred Host as a manometer, a little tambourine of flour, or a shot at the target of insomnia) (Francisco García Lorca, *Federico y su mundo* 154–5). Yet we will observe that Federico's metaphors are not as outlandish as Francisco believes.

The first part of the ode, "Exposición," is divisible into two segments, a nostalgic remembrance of having perceived the Holy Eucharist transubstantiated into Christ's body (strophes 1–4) and an ardent desire to renew this spectacle (strophes 5–9). Nostalgia in an ode for the return of a past mystic experience appears in Fray Luis de León's ode "A Francisco Salinas" (León, *Obras* 2:748, ll. 38–40) and in Saint John of the Cross's *Cántico espiritual* (Spiritual canticle) (Cuevas, in Saint John of the Cross, *Poesías* 44, ll. 1–5). Lorca viewed Falla as an appreciative reader of Fray Luis and John of the Cross. A lay brother of the Order of Carmen,[26] the composer heavily annotated the works of the Carmelites John of the Cross and Teresa of Avila.[27] Falla owned an anthology of the poetry of John of the Cross and Fray Luis de León[28] and major theological writings by León.[29] Further, Lorca recognized Falla's appreciation of León to such a degree, that on 29 May 1932 he sent him from Salamanca a postcard depicting nothing touristic, but Fray Luis's university chair still preserved there.[30] The music of the blind composer and organist Salinas (1513–90), so praised by Fray Luis, had also entered Falla's art in the form of a *tonada* or song incorporated into *Retablo* (Hess, *Passions* 211). Hearing Salinas play his pious music on the organ in the Salamancan Cathedral, Fray Luis's soul rose to a perception of the harmony of the spheres and to a beatific vision of God playing the universal instrument. In a Horatian anticlimax, his poetic voice laments having to return to the world of the senses instead of remaining suspended in its heavenly experience (Alonso, *Poesía* 198). Lorca's ode refers not to a musician's playing in general, as did Fray Luis, but to a specific performance of sacred music, the singing of the *Tantum ergo* while the Host was being elevated at the end of Calderón's *auto sacramental* arranged by Falla. The exposition of the Host formed the high spot of the entire program. The first part of Lorca's ode also has a kind of Horatian climax, rising into exclamations at the wonder of Falla's musical arrangement.

Lorca's use of the *Pange lingua* as an epigraph links his ode to that arrangement. The female singers in Lorca's first verse may refer to the mostly female voices there employed by Falla.[31] The nailed wall through which the voices carry may allude to the scenery constructed for that performance

by Hermenegildo Lanz. A tribute to the efficacy of Falla's arrangement
lies in the ability of the singers to make the poetic subject *see* Christ's body.
Lorca's ode stresses the instantaneousness of the revelation through the
use of the preterite [*te vi, Dios* (I saw you, God): l. 2] amidst the continuous singing in the imperfect tense [*cantaban* (they were singing), l. 1]. The
divine presentation is a consequence of the singing, and this causal relationship forms Lorca's tribute to Falla:

> Cantaban las mujeres por el muro clavado
> cuando te vi, Dios fuerte, vivo en el Sacramento.
> Palpitante y desnudo, como un niño que corre
> perseguido por siete novillos capitales.

> [The women were singing through the wall of nails
> When I saw you, strong God, alive in the Sacrament.
> Throbbing you were and naked, like a child who flees
> While being chased by seven deadly yearling bulls.]

(Martín, *Heterodoxo y mártir* 267, ll. 1–4)

Popular Catholic piety stresses the epic battle between good and evil
(Harnack, *Dogmengeschichte* 439–45), a theme of mystery plays and eventually *of autos sacramentales*. Lorca, however, in the attempt to recapture
his childhood faith, humorously presents Christ as the child-God who
thrusts himself, like a brave Spanish village child, into a ring with yearling
bulls. In the poem, seven cardinal sins pursue the innocent. The child
Jesus does not emerge unscathed. At the end of Calderón's *auto sacramental*, the monstrance was elevated while the sun showed through it, as if
piercing the wafer. Lorca's lyric voice imagines God the Father applying to
His Son a needle of light (Martín, *Heterodoxo y mártir* 267, l. 6). To elicit
compassion for the man-God, singled out for suffering, the speaker compares him to an experimental frog's heart, beating rapidly in a physician's
test-tube – an image calculated to startle the philistines, *épater les bour-
geois*.[32] However, the complexity of the image, multilayered like many of
Lorca's, points to the deep nuance of the healing love for mankind of a
God serving as a heavenly physician.[33]

The mix of old and new, such as Lorca perceives in Falla, continues into
the third strophe, where images drawn from the Bible meld with others
taken from Freudian eroticism, favoured by the surrealist Dalí. The biblical Christ, the lone rock [Piedra de soledad],[34] has earth moaning for redemption [la hierba gime],[35] and revives stagnant water [agua negra] or
human spirit with new spirit.[36] Spiritual impurities, the three enemies of

the soul, are as alien to spirituality as hostile intonations in a language spoken with purity. These contaminants besmirch the spirit like three "accents" [acentos] in the water (Martín, *Heterodoxo y mártir* 267, l. 10). Priests raise the portable monstrance, the column, like a flower stem sustaining the snowy whiteness of the Host. This elevated position symbolizes Christ's superiority to the corruption of the world, with the wheels [ruedas] of its machinery and the phalli [falos] of its unbridled sexuality. Dalí's influence is manifest, since he not only praised to Lorca the beauty of machines (Ades, *Dali* 42–3; Martín, *Heterodoxo y mártir* 268, ll. 11–12), but also began populating his canvases with phalli as of 1928 (Ades, *Dali* 56–7).[37]

Purified by contemplating the Eucharist, the speaker recalls having experienced its healing powers. The expression of such a cure uses hunting metaphors, offensive to Francisco García Lorca, yet traceable to Spanish mystic poetry. In Luis de León's "Oda a Salinas" [Ode to Salinas], the soul, upon hearing Salinas's music, "again acquires its aim" in the universe [torna a cobrar el tino] (Leon, *Obras* 2:747, l. 8). Likewise, Lorca's lyric subject remembers how the Eucharist guided him to needed serenity on a sleepless night. Like an expert marksman, narrowing his eyes, he accurately shot at the target of his insomnia. No longer would he suffer the threat of the nothingness, symbolized by Poe's raven of the Nevermore, the black bird of the poem: "y entornaba mis ojos para dar en el dulce / blanco de insomnio sin un pájaro negro" [And I half-closed my eyes so as to hit the sweet / Target of sleeplessness without a bird of black] (Martín, *Heterodoxo y mártir* 268, ll. 15–16). With Falla's Corpus Christi music now only a memory, the poetic voice in quatrains 5 and 6 repeats its desire to possess God anew. The God to be reacquired is an "anchored God" [Dios anclado], one giving hope, a "sure and steadfast anchor of the soul" seeking salvation (Hebrews 6:19; Martín, *Heterodoxo y mártir* 268, l. 17).

Another image follows in praise of the Eucharist, an image reprehensible for Francisco García Lorca, yet drawn from mystic tradition. In "Ode to Salinas," music raises the soul to the vision of God the great Maestro, playing the music of the spheres on His vast instrument (León, "A Francisco Salinas," *Obras* 2:747, ll. 21–30). Could not God also make music within the Eucharist? Federico's ode, to his brother Francisco's dismay, deems the wafer a celebratory little tambourine of flour for the newborn soul (Martín, *Heterodoxo y mártir* 268, l. 18), a metaphor in which the poetic subject tries to recapture the innocence of childhood faith. In the Sacred Host, body and soul unite, "breeze and matter" [brisa y materia], into a precise sign, the Logos, promise of salvation, out of love of sinning flesh ignorant of that name (l. 19). The newborn soul imitates Christ in his innocence, a baby Jesus in the wafer, "God in swaddling clothes, minute and eternal Christ" [Dios en mantillas, Cristo diminuto y eterno] (l. 22). Distributing the Sacred Host reproduces Christ a thousand times over, imitating the miracle of the loaves, while reiterating His affliction produced by human sinning.[38]

Yearning for Christ to reappear in the Host, the speaker tries again to reconstruct his memory of the singing and to exalt the Eucharist. The poem climaxes with the recollection of God transcending His sacrament. Now the women were singing no longer before the nailed setting, but in the wilderness of the world at large, lacking guidance or purpose (*sin norte*). Here Hermenegildo Lanz's nailed wall has given way to the wastelands as in the biblical phrase, "voice crying in the wilderness" (Isaiah 40:3–5). Then the poetic subject did not see Christ *in* the Holy Sacrament but *above* it. Now he calls to mind the neutral-coloured dome [cúpula neutra] – if not of a chapel, then of grey sky or an indifferent heaven – against which cavorted five hundred bright seraphim rendered in pen and ink to enjoy the vine that is Christ. The exhilaration of these verses, unequalled in the ode, nonetheless underscores the fictitiousness of the angels:

> Cantaban las mujeres en la arena sin norte,
> cuando te vi presente sobre tu Sacramento.
> Quinientos serafines de resplandor y tinta
> en la cúpula neutra gustaban tu racimo.
>
> [The women were singing in the uncharted sand
> When I saw you present above your Sacrament.
> Five hundred seraphim of brilliance and of ink
> Within the neutral dome were savouring your vine.]
>
> (Martín , *Heterodoxo y mártir* 268, ll. 25–9)

Wherever possible, the poet has accented the skill of the artistic artifice as a fiction: the women's singing as a vivid memory, the nailed wall built by Gil, the ink-sketched angels, and especially Falla's music, a dexterous blend of tradition and modernity capable of generating sacred visions. Part 1 of Lorca's poem closes with two quatrains containing exclamations of praise for the sacred Form, with four verses out of the eight beginning with the exclamation "¡Oh!," like Fray Luis's exclamations of rapture in the antepenultimate strophe of the "Oda a Salinas." In Fray Luis the exclamations signal a climax followed by a Horatian anticlimax; in Lorca, the series climaxes the remembered experience of the Sacred Host produced by Falla's music. The music has offered the sensation of the sacred Form drawing together the cosmos as its centre:

¡Oh Forma sacratísima, vértice de las flores,
donde todos los ángulos toman sus luces fijas,
donde número y boca construyen un presente
cuerpo de luz humana con músculos de harina!

[Oh very sacred Form, oh vertex of the flowers,
Where all angles receive its stationary lights,
Where voice and interval construct bodily presence
Of human luminosity with muscles made of flour!]

(Martín, Heterodoxo y mártir 268, ll. 29–32)

This quatrain bears the imprint of Fray Luis de León's "Oda a Salinas."
Lorca's learned adjective *sacratísima* (extremely sacred) recalls Fray Luis's
Latinism *sacro* (sacred), applied to the choir of his friends whose voices,
accompanying Salinas's organ in the Salamancan Cathedral, blend into a
glory worthy of the musician Apollo [gloria del apolíneo sacro coro]
(Luis, *Obras* 2:748, l. 42). Lorca's speaker exalts the holy Form as sacred
centre, vertex, of the offertory flowers on the altar. In the geometry formed
by the bouquets, often composed of lilies, all angles reflect the stable light
emanating from the Eucharist.[39]

The unwavering luminosity, referring to sunlight on the monstrance,
may symbolize the eternity of redemption, removing spiritual darkness;
or else, it may allude to the mythology of the Empyreum, "this eternal
celestial sphere" [aquesta celestial eterna esfera], the highest sphere of the
fixed stars in Fray Luis's ode "Noche serena," [Serene night]. Lorca may
thereby hope to convey the lofty heavenliness of the Sacred Host within
the cosmos (cf. León, "Noche serena," in *Obras* 2:759, l. 32). Lorca's poly-
valent metaphors correspond to the polyphony of Victoria and Falla, with
their vocal simultaneity. In the holy vertex sketched by Lorca, Falla's music has a sacral effect. Harmonious musical intervals [número] and singing
mouth [boca] construct the presence of a body of light, the body of Christ,
with strength derived from his corporality, his participation in humanity.
In Fray Luis's "Oda a Salinas," harmonious proportions [números con-
cordes] apply to the balance between faculties of the soul, as harmonious
as earthly music and as the music of the cosmic spheres (747, l. 27). In the
case of Falla's music, we remember that Lorca's birthday sonnet lauded his
"algebra," his attention to mathematical proportions or musical intervals
in his Andalusianist pieces.

However, Lorca recognizes a difference of musical "temperature" between Falla's composing styles. The Andalusianist works convey heat,
recognized in the birthday sonnet of 1927: Falla's most often played work,

the "Fire Dance" from *El amor brujo*, has agitated rhythms and impassioned discords. The neoclassical compositions, however, display crystalline coolness. They surround the host like "musical icebergs" in the quatrain concluding Part 1 of his ode:

¡Oh forma limitada para expresar concreta
muchedumbre de luces y clamor escuchado!
¡Oh nieve circundada por témpanos de música!
¡Oh llama crepitante sobre todas las venas!

[Oh form severely limited to convey a concrete
Multitude of lights, a cry for aid that's heeded!
Oh snow that's circumscribed by icebergs full of music!
Oh crackling flame that burns surmounting all the veins!]

(Martín, *Heterodoxo y mártir* 268, ll. 336)

The concreteness of Christ's body, the limitedness of his form, communicates for all to see the "multitude" [muchedumbre] of lights,[40] of votive candles, lit by souls in need, and succours those needing aid. In its purity, the Sacred Host resembles snow [nieve] surrounded by "icebergs" [témpanos] of music, pure but deep in artistic beauty. The final verse contains yet another mystic echo. The living flame of divine love eloquently poetized by Saint John comes across in the last line, where it presides over all humans, symbolised by the "veins" from all human hearts.

Part 2 of Lorca's ode, titled "Mundo" (World) and beginning with its epigraph from the *Agnus Dei*, itself contains two parts: description of the sins of the world (strophes 1–6) and praise of the Sacred Host for assuaging the anguish they cause (strophes 7–10). This verse expresses the poet's struggle between existential nothingness and orientation by the Eucharist: "Mundo, ya tienes meta para tu desamparo,/Para tu horror perenne de agujero sin fondo" [World, now you have a goal for your sense of great neediness,/ And for your endless horror of the bottomless hole] (Martín, *Heterodoxo y mártir* 271, ll. 73–4).

Since Falla evolved towards deeper devoutness after the crisis of his Parisian years, by 1928 he could not have identified with Lorca. Yet the poet might have been trying, albeit in vain, to win Falla over with musical metaphors known to both, first from Debussy, next from Beethoven. Falla, in correspondence to Lorca, would write snatches of melody to convey opinions and sentiments.[41] Lorca may also have resorted to musical symbolism. Debussy's "Les Parfums de la nuit" [Perfumes of the night], second movement of the suite *Ibéria*, was well known to Falla, who had annotated its score.[42] Lorca may have referred to it between the lines to envision worldliness as a sensuous night. His first six strophes depict the "sad night of the world" [triste noche del mundo], a world sunken into a night of nihilism. In Granada, Lorca, while penning part 2 of his ode, wrote to Zalamea, "You can't imagine what is it to spend whole nights on the balcony, seeing a nocturnal Granada, empty for me without holding the least consolation for anything."[43] "Les Parfums de la nuit," a slow, dreamy habanera, glides through sensuous chromatic passages into cadences conveying intense emotion.[44] Early on, oboes, English horns, and clarinets blow pianissimo in alternately rising and falling glissandi (*Ibéria*, rehearsal 38, measures 1–4, 56), as if imitating night winds. Near the end of the movement, soft bells chime (rehearsal 52, measures 1–2, 80), like distant morning church bells.

"Mundo" moves from dark, desolate night, with audible winds, to morning light and faith. Lorca's first four strophes convey an ambiance of urban lifelessness with distance set between reader and text through use again of the imperfect. A night wind blows from rooftops and walkways, spreading residue. Whistling by expressionless eyes of pigeons, it tosses algae and crystal against buildings, the "hombros de cemento" [shoulders of cement] (Martín, *Heterodoxo y mártir* 269, ll. 37–40). Hope has vanished where the razor blade rests on bureaus with impatience to sever necks, while in dead men's houses children chase a "sierpe de arena" [sand serpent], temptation to sin in a sterile wilderness (ll. 41–4). Scribes, defeated by their concupiscence, doze on the fourteenth floor. A prostitute appears with sullied, scratched crystal breasts. Telephone wires against the moon tremble like insects, increasing the panoramic bleakness. Dehumanized bars lack customers. Disembodied screams sound in the night. Heads float in the water, the bodies invisible (Martín, *Heterodoxo y mártir* 268, ll. 45–8). To murder the nightingale – symbol perhaps of a poet feeling threatened by the community – three thousand men approach, knives glistening (270, ll. 49–50). Old women and priests fend off a "rain of tongues" – possibly injurious speech – as well as "ants in flight," the atmosphere of impurity (ll. 51–2). Night wears a "white face," revealing blankness, nihilism, and a lack of humanness, the facelessness of that negativity (l. 53). A child founders beneath the wing of the dragon, the monster of sin threatening to devour his innocence (l. 57).

The final four stanzas of "Mundo" characterize the Holy Sacrament as a force moderating uncontained worldly desires. The speaker describes the Host as "light in balance" [luz en equilibrio], stable illumination, assuaging the anguish of boundless passion. Of all composers able to express passion and purify it musically, Beethoven stood out in Lorca's mind. He

and Segura Mesa had revered him. Further, Falla wrote a tribute to that
composer on the centennial of his death (26 March 1827), and he consulted
Vicenta Lorca for her opinion on the text.[45] This woman, sensitive to classical music, had raised a family in peace, and Falla's personal notes reflect
his aspiration to free himself of "contrary forces" [fuerzas contrarias] in
his spirit. He felt antagonism between himself as a Latin and the Germans
(the enemy in the First World War). Yet, as he scrawled on scratch paper
titled "Beethoven," "Every stock [raza] should express what may be beautiful and great in the opposed ones."[46] Beethoven praised love for all and
among all, and to say as much is to render the greatest tribute to that "genial" composer, in Falla's judgment. To sum up Beethoven's message in
three words, Falla wrote in Latin and underscored "Pax in terra."[47] To determine whether he had managed to convey this message, Falla showed his
tribute to Lorca's mother. Further, in the *Enciclopedia abreviada de música* [Abbreviated encyclopedia of music], prefaced by Falla and written by
his friend and fellow Andalusian composer Joaquín Turina, Lorca could
have read Turina's panegyric of the *Agnus Dei* (with its message of peace)
as the best part of Beethoven's *Missa Solemnis* during a period of complete
technical mastery (2:250–1). This *Agnus Dei* could have been playing on
Lorca's gramophone when he was penning the conclusion to his December
1917 poem "Elogio. Beethoven" ("Paean. Beethoven"):

> Que unos sones gloriosos cieguen tus ojos,
> Que una orquesta dulce toque en tono menor,
> Que te pierdas en la noche lentamente,
> Que se esfume tu silueta suavemente
> Y que se oculte en el reinado del sopor ...

> [May some glorious sounds blind your eyes,
> May a sweet orchestra play in a minor key,
> May you get lost in the night unhurriedly,
> May your silhouette fade out very gently,
> And may it hide in the kingdom of sleep ...][48]

The *Agnus Dei* begins with the orchestra playing *adagio* in B minor and
sustaining the minor almost everywhere throughout the movement. A soft
but powerful bass voice sings, "Agnus, Agnus Dei," then the remainder of
the brief prayer, shortly followed by a mezzo-soprano singing the same. In
Mass, it is customary to sing twice "Agnus Dei, qui tollis peccata mundi,
miserere nobis" [Lamb of God, who removes the sins of the world, have
mercy upon us] followed by "Agnus Dei, qui tollis peccata mundi, dona

nobis pacem" [Lamb of God, who removes the sins of the world, give us peace], but Beethoven omits from the third line everything except the final three words. His aim, as he has indicated on his score, is to provide "Prayer for inner and outer peace" [Bitte um innern und äussern Frieden]. During the singing of the "Dona nobis pacem," trumpets and drums initiate a march in a major key that critics call the (Napoleonic) "war interruption." However, soloists overcome this martial "disturbance" by repeating "Dona nobis pacem," starting loud but softening in volume before the final coda.[49]

Yearning for peace permeates the final four strophes of Lorca's "Mundo." Like Beethoven's text, Lorca's uses double repetition to placate anguish. The text begins with the anaphora of "Sólo tu Sacramento" [Only your Sacrament] to express symmetrically that the Eucharist alone, with its balanced light, can calm the "anguish of unbridled love" [angustia del amor desligado]; that the Eucharist alone serves as a saving pressure gauge [manómetro] to preserve hearts from beating at breakneck speed (Martín, *Heterodoxo y mártir* 271, ll. 61–4). Lorca's brother Francisco finds this mechanical image inappropriate for the sacred theme. Yet Beethoven's revered *Agnus Dei*, with its unorthodox repetitions, revolutionizes traditional sacred ritual (García Bacca, *Filosofía de la música* 635–42), just as Dalí with his aesthetic contemplation of machinery tries to revolutionize poetry and the plastic arts. Soothing anaphora returns at the start of the second and third of the four strophes. Why does the Sacrament alone bring peace? the lyric voice implicitly asks. A twofold response lies in the Logos, sign of salvation promised by the Eucharist. The second strophe of the four is reducible to the phrase "Because your sign [Porque tu signo] is a key to the riddle of heaven"; and the third strophe, to the phrase "Because your sign [Porque tu signo] reconciles worldly contraries." Lorca writes in the same conciliatory spirit as Falla, author of the 1927 tribute to Beethoven.

Unlocking the mystery of heaven has long concerned Lorca. The concern appears as early as "Elogio. Beethoven" and recurs, as we saw, in the first part of the ode. "If you are resting in grey eternity," the poetic voice of the early Lorca says to Beethoven, "Silence is no reward for your anxiety, maestro."[50] Likewise, in the segment of the mature Lorca's ode titled "Exposición," we sensed the delight of the seraphim in the vineyard of the Lord mitigated by the neutrality [cúpula neutra] of the heaven they inhabited, as well as by the fictitiousness of those ink-sketched angels (Martín, *Heterodoxo y mártir* 268, ll. 27–8). The key to the celestial plain [llanura celeste] of equanimity lies in music. In this heaven of balance, with no ups and downs, the playing card [naipe] of evil fortune and the wound [herida] of defeat join through song [cantando]. Misfortune and its pains undergo artistic purging, as Falla and Lorca learned from deep song. Singing about the Eucharist can afford even deeper purification. If the Sacred Host sheds a holy light of love, then it shuns violent excesses of luminosity – fanaticism – symbolized by a shining bull whose bellow is curbed [la luz desboca su toro relumbrante]. This moderation of passion, even for divinity, constitutes true catharsis. Hence, the fragrance of the "tempered rose" [rosa templada] receives affirmation (Martín, *Heterodoxo y mártir* 271, ll. 65–8). Beethoven gently breaks rules to produce sacred beauty.

In Lorca's text, cathartic tempering of extremes supposes a synthesis of opposites. The Sacred Host implies for the poetic voice the Logos of a God who dies to save others, and who communicates both the living soul or breeze [brisa], and decay or the worm [gusano]. Since divinity presupposes limitless temporality – continuity – the Logos unites the century with the minute (or finiteness of the flesh), eternity with the instant. The Logos welcomes into its clear world generations of the dead as well as an anthill [hormiguero] of the living, all awaiting salvation. In this buzzing heap of life are to be found the virtuous and the immoral alike, the man made of snows and the individual blackened with the flames of sin, all subject to the same saving principle (Martín, *Heterodoxo y mártir* 271, ll. 69–72). In the final strophe of "Mundo," Lorca imitates Beethoven in turning to the embattled world outside him, if only for an instant. The lyric voice no longer addresses Christ, but his ambiance (called "Mundo": l. 73), helplessly immersed in sin, mired in fear of the nothingness. The Logos offers the world a saving norm of conduct. In closing, just as Beethoven's soloists imposed a norm of peace at the end, so Lorca's poetic subject closes with a direct address, once again, to Christ and his sacrament. Like Beethoven's soloists, the lyric "I" begins loud but finishes in a calm tone. First it compassionately exclaims that the Lamb of God lives captive to three equal voices [tres voces iguales] (l. 75) – world, flesh, and the devil. Next, it affirms in a final, more soothing exclamation that the sacrament of the Sacred Host stabilizes through its immutability, comforts through love, and gives orientation through discipline [¡Sacramento inmutable de amor y disciplina!] (l. 76).

In conclusion, Lorca wrote the first half of his ode while attentive to Falla in hopes that he would decipher the musical code underlying the structure of the poem. However, Falla, probably distracted by unsettling borrowings from Dalí, missed the music beneath the surface, the subtle transition from Debussy to Beethoven in the part devoted to "Mundo," and the allusions to Falla's own arrangements of *Tantum ergo* as well as to related Golden Age mystics in the part titled "Exposición."

Before composing parts 3 and 4 of the ode, Lorca received Falla's critique of parts 1 and 2, published and here examined. Therefore parts 3 and

4 do not entirely belong to the "Homenaje a Manuel de Falla" [Tribute to Manuel de Falla] as do 1 and 2.[51] Still, considerations of symmetry and continuity make the final two parts a tacit tribute insofar as they are influenced by 1 and 2. As to content, a change has taken place, a franker concentration on carnal sin, since in mid-1928 Lorca broke with his lover, the sculptor Emilio Aladrén, and suffered an inner crisis that caused the poet to flee to New York City (Nandorfy, *Poetics of Apocalypse* 20). Part 3, "Demonio," therefore, presents a seductive devil, foreign to any orthodox Catholic source except an immature Calderón.[52] Part 4 is largely a surrealist-style diatribe against unbridled sexuality (Lorca, *Epistolario* 2:120). In its final five strophes, the only ones of any possible relevance to Falla, the poet inverted his devil's traits to describe Christ in the Eucharist.[53] The characterization of the devil relies on Beauty's self-description in Calderón's *Gran teatro*: "Prodigal I am with colours" [Pródiga estoy de colores] (*Autos sacramentales*, 1940 ed., 57, l. 516). Making use of Calderón's play title, *El mágico prodigioso* [The prodigious magician], with its magician devil, Lorca's poetic voice presents the evil angel as the "prodigious magician of fires and colours" [mágico prodigioso de fuegos y colores] (Martín, *Heterodoxo y mártir* 274, l. 110). To combat this illusionist, Lorca's Christ undergoes transubstantiation. The *Pange lingua* sings of the "Corporis mysterium/Sanguinisque pretiosi" [Mystery of precious body and blood] that Christ sheds to redeem the world. Hence Lorca writes, "You give your heavenly body with your divine blood/in this Sacrament of concreteness that I sing."[54]

Since part 3 of Lorca's ode equates the devil to lust in a heterodox view of his attractiveness, little remains unsaid in part 4 on the flesh. By now, settled at Columbia University in New York City, Lorca probably lost sight of Falla. In the dehumanized metropolis, Original Sin acquired new meaning. In "Carne" [Flesh], Eve, banished from Eden, requires redemption by the Sacred Host. In Calderón's *auto sacramental Tu prójimo como a ti* [Your neighbour as yourself] the devil is a servant of Original Sin, and in the final division of his ode Lorca transferred Original Sin to "Carne." The poem ends with a reminiscence of the *Tantum ergo*, like Falla's arrangement of *Gran teatro*. However, here there appears little more than a ceremonial echo of the Sacred Trinity without mentioning that faith replaces sensory evidence in the veneration of the Sacrament. The first two lines of the final stanza of the *Tantum ergo* symmetrically laud the first two members of the Trinity: "Genitori, genitoque/laus et iubilatio" [To the Father and the Son,/Praise and jubilation]. In parallel syntactical structure follows the call to praise the Holy Spirit, proceeding from both Father and Son: "procedenti ab utroque/compar sit laudatio."[55] Lorca's transformation of the *Tantum ergo* responded to his need to deal with the flesh according to the overall scheme of his ode. Hence the lyric subject fantasizes Eve taking communion and burning in the fire of the Holy Spirit after honouring the names of the Father and the Son. Such fire is visible in iconography found in El Greco paintings like *Pentecost* and also in the mystic poetry of Saint John of the Cross, as previously noted:

> Por el nombre del Padre, roca, luz y fermento.
> Por el nombre del Hijo, flor y sangre vertida,
> en el fuego visible del Espíritu Santo
> Eva quema sus dedos teñidos de manzana.

> [In the name of the Father, rock, light, and ferment.
> In the name of the Son, flower and shed blood,
> In the visible fire of the Holy Spirit
> Eve burns her fingers all tinted with apple.]
>
> (Martín, *Heterodoxo y mártir* 275, ll. 129–32)

For Original Sin, Eve undergoes purification, burning her nails lacquered with the red of the apple from the tree of knowledge. In the last three quatrains of the poem, the speaker refers to the line of Lope's *auto sacramental* quoted in the epigraph. The reference to the "gallant's body," that is, Christ's, here shows it martyred, only to conquer and shine over human flesh in the Host. Adam becomes light as he awaits the resurrection of the flesh in this rotting world (l. 167; see Martín, *Heterodoxo y mártir* 318). The final quatrain of the ode, comprising three exclamations starting with "¡Oh!," parallels the final strophe of part 1. However, there the object of the wonder expressed by the exclamations was the Host. Here the object is its *impact* on the sinner.

In the final two quatrains of Part 1, we remember, four exclamations beginning with "¡Oh!" successively embellish the sacred Form. These lines contrast with the finale of the entire ode. Eutimio Martín gathers from rhythmic irregularities that Lorca has left the poem unfinished (Martín, *Heterodoxo y mártir* 318). Nevertheless, his poetry, like Michelangelo's, sometimes cultivates a rough-hewn texture.[56] Parallels between the final quatrain of the poem and the last quatrain of "Exposición" (part 1) may merely give the impression of inconclusiveness. Lorca could have decided not to publish his manuscript not only from fear of offending believers like Falla, but also from the frustration of having reached an affective impasse. In a verse with one syllable too many for an alexandrine, the speaker stresses the silence of the Sacred Host, whereas previously, as seen, he had emphasized the music it generated, specifically, Falla's: "¡Oh Corpus Christi! ¡Oh Corpus de absoluto silencio" [Oh, body of Christ! Oh body of absolute silence!] (Martín, *Heterodoxo y mártir* 276, l. 169). In this body the swan burns [se quema el cisne] (l. 170), in other words, art for art's sake vanishes in favour of didacticism. Moreover, in the body of Christ the leper shines [fulgura el leproso] (l. 170), one of the sick and needy he miraculously healed.

Next follows the other irregularity concerning Martín, the use of a single hemistich in a line instead of the usual two, thereby producing an unexpected silence: "Oh white and sleepless Form!" [¡Oh blanca Forma insomne] (l. 171). The last line of the poem shows the Host prohibiting any creaturely sound in order to keep watch over earthly needs: "Angels and barking against the sound of veins!" [¡ángeles y ladridos contra el rumor de venas!] (l. 172). This verse presents a strange contrast to line 36, the last verse of part 1, "Exposición": "Oh crackling flame that burns, surmounting all the veins!" [¡Oh llama crepitante sobre todas las venas!] (Martín, *Heterodoxo y mártir* 268, l. 36). Once exultation, music, and joy prevailed; now, silence, sleeplessness, and solemnity.

In conclusion, the ode's fourfold macrostructure obeys musical and literary suggestions from Falla and Calderón. Examined part by part, however, the work shows growing distance from Falla. Part 4, with oneiric sexual visions, stylistically approaches surrealism even if Lorca did not practise surrealistic automatic writing, and part 3 in a heterodox fashion accents the devil's comeliness. Part 2 seeks Falla's sympathy through musical settings of nihilism and temptation, echoing Debussy's "Les Parfums de la nuit," and through praise of the Eucharist, following vocal patterns of Beethoven's *Agnus Dei*. Part 1 implicitly addresses Falla by reconstructing the impact of his musical arrangement of *Tantum ergo* and by making use of reminiscences of Luis de León. Yet even here, touches from Dalí probably repelled Falla. The ode welds tradition with modernity in imitation of Falla as Lorca perceives him. Falla's inability to share this perception explains that Lorca's ode never formed part of Granada's Corpus Christi celebrations after 1929. Unhappily, Lorca had travelled far in his relationship with Falla from the jocose tribute of 1921 and the admiring birthday sonnet of early 1927.

After Falla's complaint that parts 1 and 2 of the ode mix spiritual purities with impurities, Lorca did penance. Falla's letter bore the date 9 February 1929. In March, Lorca secretly joined the newly founded Religious Brotherhood of Saint Mary of the Alhambra (Granada). On Holy

Thursday, 27 March 1929, in a procession, he accompanied the Virgin of Anguishes while dressed as a penitent, his face covered, feet bare. He carried a heavy insignia at the head of the procession, never letting it touch the ground for four hours. Afterwards, he thanked the other members of the religious brotherhood for allowing his participation. Then he quickly departed Granada (Campos, "Lorca, cofrade" 45). This penance took place after Lorca had completed the first half of his ode and before starting the second. Subsequently, his religious fervour cooled, showing the oscillation between faith and eroticism marking his adult life.

Postlude with Coda

1. General Conclusions on the Lorca-Falla Artistic Relationship

The most salient conclusion that a book on the Falla-Lorca relationship can reach is its own inconclusiveness. The mutual impact of both artists has so many aspects and subtleties that exploration can proceed endlessly. To review our finds, a mantle of saintliness, religious hero-worship linked to music, passed from the shoulders of the teenaged Lorca's piano teacher Segura Mesa to those of the renowned Falla in the poet's youth and maturity. Trained by his mother to look for beauty in religion, he made a religion of beauty. Vicenta Lorca Romero also loved classical piano music, just as her husband Federico García Rodríguez enjoyed guitar folk song. A sexual crisis of puberty caused their son Federico to take music as an exercise of self-purgation, cleansing him of sin (E. Martín). The crisis aroused in him a desire for the impossible, a longing he would one day label "black pain" (C. Maurer, "Introducción," *Prosa inédita* 34–5), perhaps a sublimation of his uneasiness about conventional gender roles (R. Quance). At the start of his literary career in 1917, he found modernism in vogue, with its religion of music and its aspiration to fuse all arts into a universal expression of reality.

The drive for artistic synthesis, also perceptible in Falla, remains in Lorca's works all his life. In early poetry and prose, he experimented with analogizing music and letters. The analogies grew ever more refined and caused him to transfer forms of music to literary forms and to fill them with his own emotional content in his poetry and theatre. As he matured, he increasingly discerned the distinction between writing *about* music and literature, and writing verbal music (see García Bacca). His early poetry and essays deal *with* music or letters, while the mature writings, aided by

Falla and the avant-garde, approach musical performance. Falla taught Lorca to listen with his intimate ear, bringing him national fame in 1928. Though merely a tourist under Domínguez Berrueta's direction when hearing Gregorian chant in 1917, he changed, by imitating Falla, into a writer capable of identifying with folk musicians, so as to capture their art and atavistic experience. Later he imitated in his works the styles of Debussy, Falla, and Albéniz; while always keeping an eye on Falla, he eventually absorbed even the religious styles of Beethoven and Bach.

When Lorca came to Falla's door in Granada to befriend him in 1920, he already seemed receptive to Falla's Andalusianism thanks to Rubén Darío, influencing Falla's music as well; to modernists like Juan Ramón Jiménez; and to vanguard writers of his own age, interested in integrating all the arts. The early essay "Digression. Rules in Music" may have its origin either in Falla's 1916 stress on imagination (Persia) or else simply in Darío's Symbolist-inspired aesthetics. In Darío, moreover, Lorca found Neo-Pythagorean aestheticism, which dictates living and writing in accordance with cosmic rhythms. This stage quickly passed with Lorca's absorption of Futurist-style writing, learned from the *ultraístas* and the *creacionistas*. Accordingly, he wrote *Suites* – some sentimental, others anti-*ultraísta* (Quance), and most anti-subjective (Bonaddio) – together with *PCJ* and later *Canciones*, largely derived from *Suites* but also conceivable as a dialogue with the *creacionistas*. Exposure to Falla's impressionism from about 1920 helped teach Lorca a distant, muted art – "ghostly" [espectral] as he called it (3:204) – which persisted through Falla's Andalusianism and neo-classicism. Both stages, consciously setting the aesthetic object at a distance, coincided in this sense with Dalí's early cubist objectivism. In the Góngora years (1926–7), Lorca transmitted Dalí's aesthetic influence to Falla without the composer's knowledge. Dalí's evolution towards surrealism, however, while captivating Lorca as early as 1928, did not influence Falla, who was instead turning increasingly to religious music, to which he exposed Lorca.

Descending to concrete works, we note that Lorca confessed Falla's presence in the Andalusianist poetry of *PCJ* (1921–31) and *Romancero gitano* (1923–6). Further, critics find both the Andalusianist and the neoclassical Fallas in Lorca's mature farces, while omitting specifics of this influence. To synthesize Falla's formal contributions to *PCJ*, he gave Lorca a musical conception influencing the work as a whole, its individual divisions, and poetic pieces within each. That musical conception is the arabesque. Often Debussy and Falla made a motif or melodic line seem to determine its own progressions, and these thereby acquired melodic qualities in themselves.

Falla's personal library holds two copies of Debussy's early pieces, *Deux arabesques* for piano, both bearing Falla's annotations. In arabesques in general, autonomous but melodically related structures interlock, variously repeating and suggestively integrating themselves into different bodies of sound through the work,[1] like plazas along a well-travelled avenue. The arabesque is an inductive structure, starting with particulars and ending with a universal design, reiterating with variations time and again. Examples in Falla's music are *Noches* and the *Homenaje* to Debussy. To justify the "purity" of his deep-song-based Andalusianism, with "purity" understood as closeness to nature, to the land, and to the Andalusian "cultural spirit," he rationalized his compositional practice using ideas of Louis Lucas. In a notebook compiled in the early 1920s while composing *Retablo*, Falla wrote, "Just as we order sounds at will to form those series we call scales in a successive way, we can also produce at will simultaneously a series of intervals above or below a given sound. The latter and nothing else is the chord that [for Lucas] has an immutable form: we call it a perfect major."[2]

Analogously, in Lorca's poetry one finds many series of discrete elements, afterwards gathered up to form an all-encompassing poetic concept. Visual metaphorical examples like the following abound: "Cirio, candil,/ farol y luciérnaga, // La constelación de la saeta" [Easter taper, oil lamp/ lantern and firefly, // The constellation of the saeta] (*PCJ* 94). Auditory metaphorical concepts also belong to his repertoire: "Crótalo./ Crótalo./ Crótalo./ Escarabajo sonoro" [Castanet./ Castanet./ Castanet./ Sonorous little scarab] (285). However, the most ambitious series consists of the eight discrete, seemingly autonomous poetic segments of *PCJ* with thematic resonances between them. Presentiments of subsequent relationships early appear in the initial "Baladilla de los tres ríos," yet a reading of the ballad by itself allows nothing more than a vague prescience of the verse to follow. An obscure perception of parallels and other links between the parts gradually dawns upon the reader. The gathering of the total impact, however, awaits the end in "Caprichos," which signifies musical caprices, where Lorca sharply distinguishes (with Falla) between the practice of virtuosic art, its objects, and the need for keeping aloof from both. The essence of *PCJ* lies in artful self-distancing from folk music and folk poetry.[3]

Lorca owed more than poetic form to Falla. The composer lent substance and depth to his content. In Falla he found conceptions of the Andalusian "cultural spirit" translated into music, a notion received from Pedrell and modified by Falla in Paris; musical atmospheres or moods dependent on that creative cultural principle; folkloric and learned musical

genres through which the principle supposedly finds expression; instrumental techniques analogized to poetic ones; data on ballet, folk dance,
and folk song, which received ingenious literary analogues; and ways to
incorporate all this material into the European cultural canon. Falla's vision of the Andalusian musical character was ultimately based on the precariousness of existence, stemming from the uncertainty of life in the
Spanish South, which led to concern with the mystery of death.[4] This insecurity largely stemmed from perception of the contradictoriness in material reality and sentimental affairs. Therefore, arabesques in Arabic
architecture like those of the Alhambra may reflect in their symmetry
Muslim philosophical and theological solutions, as the poet Paul Drouot
has seen;[5] but the arabesques in Falla's music and Lorca's poetry only form
systems of problems. Lorca's originality lies in transferring by analogy
Falla's musical language into poetic musicality and in stamping the analogies with his acute visual powers and unique affective seal. These affects
encompass frustrated and impossible love, fear and fascination with death,
anxiety about fixed social gender roles, and existential insufficiency. Falla
transmitted to Lorca musical vessels. Lorca transmuted the vessels into
words and filled them with his own lyric wine. Lorca's Andalusia itself
took on his unique personal characteristics of "black pain," love and fear
of mystery, and a will to engage in creativity in the face of such fear.

    With methodical rigour, Christian de Paepe shows Falla's impact on the
structure of the first four parts of *PCJ*. Yet his presence appears in all
the others. We have revisited de Paepe's analysis of the first four to point
out their organization as part of the ritualistic purgation of pain in *cante
jondo*. Lorca creatively revises Falla's stylization of deep song to purify
Andalusian music. In configuring this purgation, Lorca followed indications from Falla's music that Falla never precisely conceived, though implied in *La vida breve* and *El amor brujo*: presentation of pain ("Poema de
la siguiriya"); consciousness raising of the pain ("Poema de la soleá"); oblation of the pain ("Poema de la saeta"); and death, a humbling aftermath
("Gráfico de la petenera"). Parallelisms between the four parts show guitaristic counterpoint appreciated by Falla, integrating a maze-like design
similar to those that adorn ceilings and inner walls of the Alhambra. The
four-part pattern shows up slightly modified form in the theme groups of
"Baladilla de los tres ríos": presentation of the rivers, reflection on their
substance and historical uses, appreciation of their values, and annihilation
of these values. That pattern persists throughout the anthology.

    The first four parts of *PCJ* begin with the varied Andalusian landscape,
seat of the regional "cultural spirit" mentioned in Lorca's public lectures on
deep song. From *Fantasía bætica*, a synthetic musical return to Andalusian

sources, Lorca may have derived the late idea (1931) of prologuing *PCJ* with "Baladilla de los tres ríos." The ballad unfolds a painterly Andalusian panorama, characteristic of the poet and permeated by the contrast between the Guadalquivir and the two Granadan rivers. Falla's piano piece, though more complex, may have influenced Lorca's thematic organization, with five theme-groups composed of two motifs each, all forming a fabric of themes that in Lorca unravels at the end. Lorca's rivers, taken together, symbolize the Andalusian creative principle, originator of deep song.

Falla may have given Lorca ideas for settings of other parts of *PCJ*. With Granada envisioned as birthplace of deep song, "Poema de la siguiriya gitana" has a Granadan ambiance near the Alhambra. From the caves of Sacromonte like those sketched in *El amor brujo* may have come the setting for "Cueva" [Cave] in the "Poema de la soleá." There Gypsies dream of remote places, perhaps their mysterious Asian origins, hypothesized in Falla's music and essays. However, the cave itself is *psychologically* situated in no particular region of Spain, but all over, wherever singers lament loneliness as Lorca himself often did. In the poem "Danza. En el huerto de la Petenera," a poetic "night in a garden of Spain" unfolds, distant verbal music within verbal music, inner auditory and visual rhythms, and a sense of foreboding also heard in Falla's *Noches*. To all this Lorca added the notion of a guitarist's fingers as anguished poets, creatively mourning the loss of the artist Petenera.

Falla leaves his mark not only on Lorca's landscapes and cityscapes, but also on melodic and non-melodic elements of deep song celebrated in his poem. Four poems concern the guitar, exalted by Falla for its permanent contributions to European music. In Lorca's "La guitarra," onomatopoeia imitates the instrument as Falla did with piano and strings of the traditional orchestra, following the examples of his contemporaries in Paris and earlier composers of nineteenth-century Russia. Lorca's guitar, however, is a projection of his own unfulfilled desires and atavistic longings (Bonaddio, *Poetics of Self-Consciousness*). In "Seis cuerdas" a verbal guitar, more distantly communicating such emotions, accompanies souls in pain doing the Dance of the Tarantula like Candelas in *El amor brujo*. We have already considered the lyrical meaning of "Danza. En el huerto de la Petenera." "Riddle of the Guitar" offers a brain-teaser about the instrument, framed in two myths, whose solution is the poet's own metaphorical virtuosity, comparable to Regino Sainz de la Maza's guitar skill and Falla's pianistic dexterity. Other poetic references to musical instruments bear Falla's stamp. The onomatopoeia of "Crótalo" gives way to a dancer's imitation of multiple, varied natural forms, proof of the closeness of *cante jondo* to nature, as Falla maintains in various essays. Finally, in "Clamor," Death's *vihuela* parodies the guitar of *cante jondo*, although Falla's disdain for the rich Spanish *vihuela* tradition eventually disappears.[6]

Among non-melodic elements of deep song, the scream occupies a sacred place in Falla's essays and music. Musical screams become audible in the soleá singer of *La vida breve*, in Murcian and Andalusian folk song of *Siete canciones populares españolas*, in two songs performed by Candelas in *El amor brujo*, and in pianistic imitation of the screaming voice in *Fantasía bætica*. Lorca dedicates two poems, the strongly visual "El grito" [The scream] and the funereal "¡Ay!," to the scream as such.

After the scream comes silence, an essential part of the rite of deep song. Silences are as real in music as sounds (García Bacca). Falla carefully notated silences as musical rests of varying lengths – longer in the singer's soleá of *La vida breve*, and more moderate after the "Ay"'s of Candelas's two main songs in *El amor brujo*.[7] "El silencio" [Silence] in "Poema de la siguiriya gitana" contains a father's suggestion to his son to be reverent, bowing towards the earth, when the hush takes place.

Following parallel considerations of sounds and silences in cante jondo, Lorca's artistic mazes introduce onstage different performers symbolizing given genres – the siguiriya gitana, the soleá, the petenera. A fourth poetic division substitutes for the artists the adored images of the Virgin Mary and Christ crucified, addressed by the unaccompanied saeta singer. Falla has composed Gypsy siguiriyas, soleares, and peteneras, all familiar to Lorca. His treatment of the saeta follows the example he himself sets in translating Falla's musical conceptions into poetry by performing a like operation with Albéniz's "Fête-Dieu à Seville" [Corpus Christi in Seville].

Lorca's arabesque extends beyond his first four parts. Falla influences the remainder of the poetry as well. His Andalusian music oscillates between agitation and nostalgia; Lorca's *Poema*, between dread of dying and unfulfilled love. The "conflicting rhythms" of Falla's Andalusian musical idiom, to use Trend's language (*Falla and Spanish Music* 46), pass to Lorca, who makes his unique modifications. In *El amor brujo*, where Falla attempts to express the "soul of the [Gypsy] stock" (Gallego, *Conciertos de inauguración* 132, cit. in Hess, *Sacred Passions* 81n41), contrasting tempos without transition everywhere occur, and antithetical emotions show up in the heroine Candelas's first solo as she edges towards madness[10] (Hess, *Sacred Passions* 82). Likewise, from beginning to end, Lorca emphasizes Andalusian contradictoriness. "Baladilla de los tres ríos," with many traces of Falla and fluvial antitheses, establishes a pattern that persists to "Seis caprichos." "Viñetas flamencas" counterpoises nostalgic portraits of two singers and a dancer with an ever-present fear of mortality.

The dark sounds of *Noches* and *El amor brujo* bear witness to the constant questioning of the mystery of death in deep song. Lorca's elegiac poetry touches multiple registers and seeks many contrasts, as does Falla's music. Hence his verse can range between the two poles of the fatalism of "Lamentación de la muerte" (Lament of death), echoing Juan Breva's disillusionment, and the forceful "Memento," self-affirmation of an artist seeking burial with his guitar. The first reference to death in Lorca's poem, the will-o'-the-wisp of screams carried away by waters, contains a tribute to the composer of the "Canción del fuego fatuo" as early as the "Baladilla de los tres ríos" (M. Hernández). Afterwards, allusions to death multiply, referred to various stages of purging pain through *cante jondo*. In the "Poema de la siguiriya," the dusky dancer shows the dagger that will eventually strike at the heart, in the same way that Salud in *La vida breve* early soliloquizes about dying out of abandonment by her lover. In the "Poema de la soleá," the landscape is reduced to a gas lamp, the knife in the heart, and the East Wind, recalling the Asian origins of deep song (Falla). In "Poema de la saeta," underscoring with Falla the closeness of deep song to nature, the agonizing Christ receives the saeta as an oblation. "Gráfico de la petenera," originally dedicated to Falla, greets the final hour of a cantaora with ambivalence, ironizing about her erotic excesses while stereotyping her mourners. A falsetto vocal also masks astonished admiration behind the irony of mourners shedding false tears. Falla too mocks female fickleness, though much more lightly, less grimly, in the folk song "Seguidilla murciana" [Seguidilla from Murcia] in *Siete canciones populares españolas*. In male-female symmetry visible in *El amor brujo*, yet assuming a fateful form never found in Falla, Death strikes down the Petenera and her hundred suitors, dresses as a bride, takes her place at the church, and sings and plays to the clangour of funeral bells.

Just as antitheses appear between the rivers in "Baladilla de los tres ríos," so they show up in the treatments of death in the cities of "Tres ciudades." "Malagueña," the poem on Malaga, structurally influenced by "Málaga" (Albéniz), shows dying as a seaside mystery with erotic components. "Barrio de Córdoba," whose structure resembles that of Albéniz's "Córdoba," envisions death as immediate anguish, lamented on passionate guitars with Oriental inflections ("Barrio de Córdoba"). "Baile" offers an elegiac but ironic *sevillana* on old Carmen, too enthralled with her art to recognize the passage of time, yet mocked and pitied by the lyric subject. "Seis caprichos" proposes avoiding Carmen's quixotism and encouraging aesthetic distance from art. To the degree that Lorca was Falla's student, this lesson has proved the most significant in refining his poetic musicality.

From start to finish *PCJ* exalts artistic reflection as such on life's primitive immediacies.

Primordial experience, to which Asian song and *cante jondo* allow access, as Falla has learned from Lucas, leads Lorca to his own all-encompassing treatment of nature in *PCJ*. The Andalusian "musical soul" as envisioned by Lorca has rivers that help define it, fans itself in olive groves, impels folk singers to dialogue with air, land, and sea, attires the Virgin like a tulip and likens Christ's blood to carnations, honours the Petenera at death with horses trotting in unison, imitates beetles with castanets and spiders in the hand movements of *bailaoras*, and mixes lemon with honey in the voices of cantaores who express its being.

By conversing with Falla, by reading his unpublished notes, by digesting his published articles, and especially by absorbing his music in scores, librettos, rehearsals, concerts, and in his own mind, Lorca has conceived a way to reach atavistic experience, guided, he believes, by the Andalusian musical ethos. This must be the new orientation for his writings to which he refers in his letter of 1921 to Salazar on his *PCJ*. His effort in this direction continues into the better-known *Romancero gitano*.

Falla's presence in the work helps account for Lorca's discrepancies from other members of his poetic Generation of 1927. Narration, description, attention to custom, moments of satire, and the grotesque, alien to Lorca's coevals but not to Falla, endow those ballads with a new metaphorical and rhythmic beauty as well as humour. Gypsy myth-making, seen in Falla's "Romance del pescador" [Ballad of the Fisherman] (*El amor brujo*), encourages Lorca to indulge his own gift for mythopoeia especially in "Romance de la luna, luna," "Preciosa y el aire," "Martirio de Santa Olalla," and "Thamar y Amnón." Falla's main contributions to *Romancero gitano* are reducible to two: first, his praise of the Gypsy siguiriya becomes applied by Lorca to the character of the Gypsies themselves (Torrecilla); second, his conception of the Andalusian "cultural spirit," when added to Durán's vision of historical ballad, generates Lorca's original "historical ballads"; and, when given plastic form as archangels symbolizing urban traits, originates a unique vision of Cordoba, Granada, and Seville.

Of the three ballads on Andalusian cities, the one on Cordoba transforms prosaic reality into Góngora-style beauty. Like Falla's arrangement of "Soneto a Cordoba," Lorca's poem accents space-like elements in the largely temporal genre that is poetry. He enriches Falla's Cordoba by balancing Roman surface with Semitic depth. Prompted by Falla's musical Andalusianism, he embellishes "San Miguel (Granada)" with time-like musical elements and temporal poetic references. Yet he also mischievously mocks Granadan preciosity in the sexual ambivalence he attributes to the archangel's image. He combines delicacy and pomp as Falla does in *Retablo* in his portrait of Saint Gabriel, a theatrical archangel whom Lorca sets cruelly above earthbound creatures like the Gypsy Mary figure Anunciación de los Reyes and her unfortunate child, destined to suffer.

From Falla, Lorca learns to marry mystery and humour, modified to express his own erotic sensuality and dread of dying. The phantom in *El amor brujo* wears a costume both hideous and humorous. The ballerina moon of "Romance de la luna, luna" is even more seductive and terrifying in her flowering bustle. The oversexed wind pursuing Preciosa resembles the giant figure of a Holy Week procession. The most elaborate mix of horror and humour appears in the "Romance de la guardia civil española." Falla's innovative use of the grotesque in El *sombrero de tres picos* kindled Lorca's fantasy. He carefully noted Falla's grotesque authority figure, the Corregidor with his three-cornered hat, while portraying his own civil guards in the ballad. Killing machines in humanoid form grimmer than their model in Falla, they pillage the Gypsy community of Jerez de la Frontera, whose denizens have all the innocence of the Virgin and Saint Joseph from the Lorca family's favourite Christmas carol, earlier set to music by Falla, "En el portal de Belén" (In the Doorway to Bethlehem). Humorous suggestions of lullabies and unreal cinnamon towers spice the violent ballad with whimsy.

Just as Falla reused musical material – Lorca himself had inspired the incorporation of "Canción del fuego fatuo" into *Retablo* – so Lorca recycled the theme of the May-September marriage in his theatre. Possibly inspired by Falla's immensely successful *Sombrero,* which he much admired, Lorca put into play his own gifts for theatre by recognizing and exploiting the dramatic potential of the age difference between the overripe Corregidor and the young Miller's Wife. The comic disparity forms a theme of the traditional Andalusian hand-puppet theatre in which Lorca interests Falla to the degree that they resolve (in vain) to take their folkloric puppet show on a European tour. Influenced by Falla's evolving art, Lorca devised original variations on the theme of the mismatched beauty. He dramatized feminine fantasy, seen in Alarcón's novella *El sombrero de tres picos,* which is based on the salacious ballad, "El Molinero de Arcos" [The miller of Arcos]. Falla, rejecting the ballad, preferred Alarcón's nostalgic irony for his ballet *Sombrero.* Lorca at first imitated the ballet too closely in his unfinished libretto, *Lola la comedianta* [Lola the actress]. Yet after his and Falla's interest waned in that project, Lorca returned for inspiration to "The Miller of Arcos" in "La casada infiel" [The faithless wife], a spicy tour de force with gender-role switches, written in Falla's company.

Falla's greatest contributions to Lorca's theatre appear in *La zapatera prodigiosa* [The shoemaker's prodigious wife], finished in 1928 (Gibson, *Life* 205), and *Amor de don Perlimplín con Belisa en su jardín* [Love of Don Perlimplín with Belisa in his garden], possibly completed by 1926 (156). Folk song in *Sombrero* and *Lola* characterizes individuals by their regional origins, but in Lorca's *La zapatera prodigiosa*, traditional song helps define unique personalities. In Falla's *Retablo*, aesthetic distance between the fictional spectator and the play-within-the-play diminishes gradually, while in *Zapatera* that distance at every moment threatens to disappear.

Lorca's most ambitious farce, *Don Perlimplín*, shows the structural influence of Falla's other neoclassical masterpiece, the *Concerto per Clavicembalo (o Pianoforte), Flauto, Oboe, Clarinetto, Violino e Violoncello*. Its third movement, the jocose *Vivace*, as well as the dialogue in Lorca's play, proceed with Scarlatti-style motivic pairing arranged in sonata form. The difference lies in the tragic element introduced by Lorca to metamorphose impotence into heroism, aided by the protagonist's imagination, which he uses to dominate his wife's. Ultimately, the problem of impotence insinuated in Lorca's self-ridiculing "Burla de don Pedro a caballo" [Mockery of Don Pedro on horseback] receives an imaginative, if fatal, solution in *Don Perlimplín* – a Wagnerian love-death thematically present in *Noches*, but treated as a dramatic reality here.

Lorca's relationship to Falla proceeds smoothly and productively until February 1929. The poet's three artistic tributes to the composer help map out an ascent of Lorca's friendship up to the point of crisis, when Falla adversely reacts to "Oda al santísimo sacramento del altar." Lorca's New Year's Eve musical prank of 1920 arouses good-humoured laughter. The birthday celebration of February 1927 envelops the fifty-year-old Falla in warmth and fellowship. However, the ode conveys Lorca's admiration through a musical and poetic code that Falla overlooks, distracted by unconventional metaphors.

Part 1, "Exposición," exalts the performance of Falla's musical arrangement of *El gran teatro del mundo* with its finale of the *Tantum ergo*. The verse celebrates the capacity of such music and its source the *Pange lingua* hymn to make the body of Christ visible through the Sacred Host. Accordingly, Lorca imitates the nostalgia for mystic experience in Fray Luis de León's "A Francisco Salinas" [Ode to Francisco Salinas]. Part 2, "Mundo," shows the ability of Christ's body, once musically contemplated, to give life direction. At the start, aimlessness, the sense of nothingness in daily living, comes across through the projection of Lorca's demoralization over Debussy's sensuous "Les Parfums de la nuit," admired both by Falla and

Lorca. Afterwards, new purposefulness becomes evident through allu-
sions to the *Agnus Dei*, Beethoven's call for peace on earth in his *Missa
Solemnis*. In a journalistic tribute to Beethoven, shown to Lorca's mother,
Falla had implied the German composer's desire for world peace.
Apparently Falla missed Lorca's call for spiritual peace. Although no written answer from Lorca to Falla's disapproving letter has ever been located,
Lorca's immediate reaction was one of contrition. Therefore he participated in ritualistic penance of the Brotherhood of Mary of the Alhambra
less than a month after receiving Falla's letter of February 1929.

Lorca's brother Francisco informs that the friendship between the two
artists never diminished, as evinced by testimonies of "mutual admiration
and affection" after 1929 (*Federico y su mundo* 156 n). Still, Federico's
visits to Falla's home decreased in frequency (Gibson, *A Life* 225). Even a
late autographed dedication by the composer of a score of his "Soneto a
Córdoba" to the poet reflects nostalgia: "To Federico García Lorca in
proof of good remembrance, with an embrace from Manuel de Falla."[8]

2. Other Works by Lorca Influenced by Falla.
His Presence in *Llanto por Ignacio Sánchez Mejías*

In the final seven years of his tragically short life, Lorca kept experiment-
ing with atavistic art, to which Falla had led him. Lorca's other good friend
and mentor Fernando de los Ríos had pointed out the "affinity" between
the music of the American blacks and Andalusian deep song (Gibson, *Life*
255). Lorca sought to pursue primitive emotion through identification
with the American black ethos in 1929 in *Poeta en Nueva York* [Poet in
New York], as he had through empathy with the Gypsy spirit in *Romancero
gitano*. Talented at analogizing, Lorca likened the New York blacks to the
Andalusian Gypsies. Reasoning from Falla's description of the Gypsy
siguiriya, Lorca had attained a characterology of the Gypsies, embodying
the most elevated and essential aspects of Andalusia. Likewise, the blacks,
amidst representatives of all races in New York, epitomized for Lorca
"what is most spiritual and most delicate" in North America.[9] Just as Lorca
had wanted to compose the poem of Andalusia, so he wished to write "the
poem of the black race in North America and underscore the pain that the
blacks have about being black in a contrary world."[10] This grief is obviously "black pain" [pena negra], dissatisfaction with life in general, transposed to the New World.

In Lorca's theatre of the 1930s, Falla's experiments in puppet opera could
have helped generate the poet's most radical experiment in avant-garde

drama, *El público* [The public, 1929–30]. Its puppet-like characters undergo destruction at the hands of a marauding audience, like Don Quixote
with Maese Pedro's puppets (Newberry). Falla for his puppet opera
Retablo became interested in Pirandello from 1923 onward (Christoforidis,
"Hacia nuevos conceptos de 'opera'" 366). The composer probably conveyed this interest to Lorca. His play *El público* has one act with multiple
tableaux (*cuadros*), a structure resembling that of *Tragicomedia de Don
Cristóbal y la señá Rosita* [The tragicomedy of Don Cristóbal and Missy
Rosita], which is a Grand Guignolesque farce modelled after traditional
Andalusian puppet theatre. As in Pirandello's *Six Characters in Search of
an Author*, however, *El público* centres on metatheatre, reflections on theatre as part of the spectacle, with the characters as projections of the
Director's mind (Martínez Nadal 63). Early in the first tableau, these characters rebel against him and manipulate him. Similarly, in Cervantes's *Don
Quixote* and later in Falla's music, the Knight of La Mancha, unwittingly
duped by the *trujamán*, identifies with the fleeing puppets and tries to aid
their escape from the Moors.

To Pirandello and Cervantes the author of *El público* adds more than a
dash of Jean Cocteau's racy *Orphée* for his play-within-a-play of *Romeo
and Juliet*: "human horses" stand in for Romeo, and an adolescent male
actor plays Juliet as in Shakespeare's time (Gibson, *Caballo azul* 235).
Lorca's metatheatre theme implies two other interlocking themes, the relationship between life and literature (a theme of *Don Quixote* and of Falla's
Retablo) and homoerotic love, a daring theatrical concern for a poet raised
in a homophobic milieu.[11] On the theme of life and letters, Lorca, who
contributed to the final revision of the *Retablo*, knew that Falla had eliminated from his adaptation of Cervantes certain trivialities of plot that he
regarded as aesthetically unfit.[12] The contrast between off-colour veracity
and traditional theatrical beauty looms large in *El público*. The drama
turns on the distinction between open-air, traditional theatre and theatre-
under-the-sand, seeking radical, if unseemly, truths.

Besides Lorca's boldest play, Falla might have influenced one of his
most admired long poems, the elegy to his friend the Sevillian bullfighter-
writer Ignacio Sánchez Mejías, fatally gored in the arena of Manzanares in
1934. The *Llanto por Ignacio Sánchez Mejías* [Lament for the death of
Ignacio Sánchez Mejías] (1935) synthesizes Lorca's Andalusianist borrowings from Falla. The guitar *Homenaje* to Debussy, present in the conception of "Muerte de la Petenera," may also have left its mark on the structure
of part 1 of the four-part elegy "La cogida y la muerte" [The goring and
the death]. Falla had quoted Debussy's music in his own guitar elegy to

Debussy, with an initial repetitive seven-note motif remade from the first two notes of *La soirée dans Grenade*, only a half-step apart, and frequently reiterated in treble and bass. Perhaps following Falla's lead, Lorca incorporated notions from his own honoured figure's writings – Sánchez Mejías's autobiographical drama *Zaya* on the paralysis of a bullfighter's time. Hence Lorca's famous refrain, "At five in the afternoon" [A las cinco de la tarde],[13] repeated thirty times. Temporal implosion takes place in a figurative sense in *Zaya*, where the existential clock stands still, while life seemingly continues on the external level for the bullfighter-protagonist. Likewise, in the first part of the *Llanto*, being gored, receiving medical treatment, and dying become synchronized. The poetic voice invents a fantastic instant in time, encapsulating all the details of the bullfighter's demise into a single terrifying instant – past, present, and future – and all tantamount to the lethal moment (Ochoa Penroz, "Lorca o la palabra que gime" 60–1). Just as Falla and Lorca had hoped to adopt the Gypsies' perspective in *El amor brujo* and *Romancero gitano*, so Lorca aspired to provide direct touch with the bullfighter's. His verses lyrically chronicle what Ignacio would have perceived from within upon dying, using the irrational immediacy of nightmarish vision, often associated with surrealist writing. Falla employs emphatically repetitive, percussive finales in the two *Danzas* of the opera *La vida breve*, act 2; the "Ritual Fire Dance" of *El amor brujo*; "The Miller's Dance" of *Sombrero*; and the piano solo *Fantasía bætica*, among other Andalusianist works; and part 1 of the *Llanto* ends with the loud repetition of "five in the afternoon" in five successive lines (1:552, ll. 48–52).

In part 2, "La sangre derramada" [The spilt blood], Lorca's myth-making glorifies Ignacio as an Andalusian bullfighter sacrificed in a cosmic ritual involving Iberian mythical bovine figures. Falla at the time was employing heroic pan-Hispanic myth in *Atlàntida*, the scenic cantata which he had played for Lorca.[14] In the *Llanto*, the ancient Tartesian cow goddess of pre-Roman, pre-biblical times, "queen of Andalusian cattle ranches" [reina de las ganaderías andaluzas] asks for the sacrifice each year of the world's best toreros (Lorca, *Obras completas* 3:470). Accordingly, in the presence of the prehistoric bull statues of Guisando, she licks up Ignacio's blood, shed on the ground, and thereby reintegrates him into the cosmos (1:553, ll. 67–74).

Lorca idealizes him as the archetypal Andalusian in terms compatible with Falla's Andalusianism. The composer musically juxtaposes opposites, nostalgic airs and relentless rhythms. By analogy, Lorca represents Ignacio as a figure of contradictions, with peaceful sentiments struggling against warlike impulses, the dove against the leopard (1:551, l. 13):

¡Qué gran torero en la plaza!
¡Qué gran serrano en la sierra!
¡Qué blando con las espigas!
¡Qué duro con las espuelas!
¡Qué tierno con el rocío!
¡Qué deslumbrante en la feria!

[What a great torero in the ring!
What a great mountaineer in the sierra!
How gentle with the wheat stalks!
How severe with his spurs!
How tender with the dewdrops!
How dazzling at the fair!]   (1:555, ll. 114–19)

The exclamations, without finite verbs, avoid temporal flow and situate nouns and adjectives in the realm of archetypes. Ignacio epitomizes Andalusia. The ascendant enumeration of attributes, in a climb prefigured in Manrique's *Coplas* (in *Obra* str. 26, 128), proceeds from one pair of opposites to the next, each more striking than the preceding ("gran torero"/"gran serrano," "blando ... espigas"/"duro ... espuelas"/"tierno ... rocío"/"deslumbrante ... feria"). The reversal of order between arena and mountainside in the third and fourth verses avoids any mechanical feel in the series, humanizing the enumeration. Lorca's Ignacio, whatever his contradictions, becomes engagingly human.

In *Fantasía bætica* and Falla's arrangement of "A Córdoba," he exalts Roman Andalusia. Lorca too lauds Ignacio's Roman aura: "Aire de Roma andaluza/le doraba la cabeza" [An air of Andalusian Rome/Was gilding his head]. With this majesty goes a pointed humour, laughter spiked with wit and wisdom, making Ignacio more human. The poet saw his humour as a nard ("nardo": 1:555), a costly pungent fragrance used in Roman times and mentioned by Pliny (*Natural History* Bk. 12, ch. 26, p. 42).

Lorca's poetic voice compares Ignacio's "wondrous strength" [maravillosa fuerza] to a "river of lions" [río de leones] and his "pictorial prudence" [dibujada prudencia] to a "marble torso" [torso de mármol] (1:354, ll. 108–9). The "river of lions" ostensibly expresses boundless fortitude, as opposed to the self-containment implied by prudence. Yet the leonine river has unsuspected metaphorical depth like Falla's Andalusianist works, with many interrelated passages. In his *Coplas,* Jorge Manrique's lyric subject equates the poet's father to a lion for his fierceness towards harmful enemies (*Obra* str. 26, 123; García-Posada, in Lorca, *Primer romancero*

231nn114–21). However, in Lorca's "Baladilla de los tres ríos" there appears Manrique's metaphor of human life as a river, conveying its transience. Therefore Ignacio's personal power may seem limitless, but his mortality limits him.

Lorca's Ignacio dies as a victim of his fate. Gibson (*Life* 389) emphasizes Sánchez Mejías's foolhardiness in his last moment. He sat on the ledge of the ring at the base of the barrier to let the bull charge by him, but instead the animal unexpectedly gored him. Lorca transfers the incident to a mythical sphere: Ignacio's eyes stayed unflinchingly open when the horns approached, yet the terrible "mothers," the three Fates, reared their heads (Martínez Nadal, *Lorca and* The Public 186). In different works by Falla, voices coming from backstage or the orchestra pit foretell or accompany calamities, and such voices have made their way into Lorca's poetry ("Muerte de Antoñito el Camborio," "Muerto de amor"). In the *Llanto*,

A través de las ganaderías
hubo un aire de voces secretas,
que gritaban a toros celestes
mayorales de pálida niebla.

[All throughout cattle-ranches was present
An air filled with profound, secret voices,
And with foremen of pale mist all howling
To the bulls that were roaming the sky.]   (1:354, ll. 98–101)

Lorca's anapaestic decasyllables are worthy of his and Falla's preferred poet Darío,[15] for like Darío (5:794–803), Lorca combines ancient myths for his own ends – here, Sánchez Mejías's cosmic aggrandizement. The heavenly bulls refer to the constellation Taurus, and the head herdsmen, to Boötes, the ox-driver (García-Posada, in Lorca, *Primer romancero* 230nn98–101). Ignacio's tragic fate propels him to the stars.

Four woeful exclamations beginning with "¡Oh!" contrast with the exultant ones from Góngora's sonnet "A Córdoba," respected by Lorca and Falla for its nobility:

¡Oh excelso muro! ¡Oh torres coronadas
de honor, de majestad, de gallardía!
¡Oh gran río, gran rey de Andalucía,
de arenas nobles, ya que no doradas!

[Oh lofty wall! Oh towers crowned with honour
With majesty, with gallantry untold!
Oh great river, great King of Andalusia,
Whose sands are noble, even if not gold!]

(Alonso, *Góngora y el "Polifemo"* 2, 367)

Lorca writes,

¡Oh blanco muro de España!
¡Oh negro toro de pena!
¡Oh sangre dura de Ignacio!
¡Oh ruiseñor de sus venas!

[Oh white wall of Spain!
Oh black bull of pain!
Oh sturdy blood of Ignacio!
Oh nightingale of his veins!]   (*Obras completas* 1:555, ll. 134–7)

The first exclamation in the elegy reduces all Spain to a whitewashed
bullring, with all the narrowness and combativeness implied for artists as
peace-loving as Lorca and Falla. The second exclamation equates life in
Spain to a bullfight with black pain, dissatisfaction with existence in general, like the symbolic Soledad Montoya's in *Romancero gitano*. The third
exclamation makes the spectacle of the valiant Ignacio's blood proof positive of that dissatisfaction. He returned to the bullring in 1934 when dis-
contentment with himself at age forty-two dictated his return (Gibson,
Life 387). The metaphor of his blood as a nightingale presents him as the
poet of his own existence, trying (like Lorca himself) to give living the most
aesthetically satisfying configuration possible.

Just as *PCJ* envisions Seville as a deep-song singer, so here the Sevillian
bullfighter's blood sings like a *cantaora* of its pain while following its noble but hapless course:

Y su sangre ya viene cantando:
cantando por marismas y praderas,
resbalando por cuernos ateridos,
vacilando sin alma por la niebla.
tropezando con miles de pezuñas
como una larga, oscura, triste lengua,
para formar un charco de agonía
junto al Guadalquivir de las estrellas.

[And his blood goes singing along,
Singing through marshes and meadows,
Sliding through freezing horns,
Wavering, listless, through mist.
Stumbling on thousands of hooves
Like a long, dark, grieving tongue,
Forming a pool of agony
Near the starry Guadalquivir.]   (Lorca, *Obras completas* 1:555, ll. 126–33)

Falla finds deep song dependent on obsessive use of the same note, often accompanied by upper or lower appoggiatura. While rich in adornments, the melody uses them only at the suggestion of the text (*Escritos*
145). The lines quoted employ internal rhyme and assonance, as if to express the use of the same note through the ending in the assonant rhyme
of –é-a, with the appoggiatura conveyed by repetition of the word *cantando*, followed by three more gerunds ending in *–ando*. The text calls for
such adornment through its meaning and cumulative stress from one line
to the next. Each gerund conveys ever-diminishing freedom, from unbound singing to sliding through frigid horns, to hesitating through the
mist, to colliding with taurine hooves. The simile of the blood as a tongue,
sad like its melody, parallels the cow-goddess's tongue, licking up the
blood. The singing blood also favours Ignacio's integration into the cosmos. The "starry Guadalquivir" may refer to stellar reflection in the river
of Seville, although we may also equate the river to the Milky Way, the
galaxy affected by Ignacio's self-sacrifice. Falla's *Atlàntida*, following
Verdaguer, harmonizes pagan with Christian mythical symbolism; but
Lorca's "La sangre derramada" shows that the blood of Sánchez Mejías,
crying out for recognition, makes him loftier even than a Christ-like martyr: the deep song of his blood is so moving, that no chalice can contain it,
no frosty dawn cool it, no saeta nor flood of offertory lilies render tribute
to it, no reliquary of crystal can cover it with silver.[16] Pagan, and even
Christian-style, mythopoeia persists until the end of "La sangre derramada," the most lyrical segment of the *Llanto*, and the one most influenced by Falla.

In part 3, titled "Cuerpo presente" [Body lying in state], Ignacio's precise
physical form, once a nightingale in its poetry of movements, disintegrates.
The absence of exact contours had previously obscured Lorca's "Romance
sonámbulo." Like Falla's mysterious nocturne "En el Generalife," with its
phantasmal initial *sfumato*, Lorca's first motif of "Romance sonámbulo"
enveloped all realities in an atmosphere of mystery, blurred outlines. Here,
however, unyielding alexandrines offer a disheartening vision of a body *in*

the process of losing its outlines, the poetic musicality of its rhythms, and its solidity as it fills with bottomless pits, black holes.

Aggressiveness, once attributed in *PCJ* to the guitar, now becomes ascribed to death, symbolized by the mortuary slab [la piedra] (l. 147). In the earlier anthology, the poem "Las seis cuerdas" [The six strings], influenced by *El amor brujo*, pictures the instrument as it "makes dreams cry" (1:191, l. 2) swallowing up sobs of lost souls through its round mouth (1:191). "Cuerpo presente," however, attributes human features to the slab. It acquires a "brow where dreams moan" [frente donde los sueños gimen], misshapen night visions lacking the gentle forms of nature, like meandering streams [agua curva], or even the last vestiges of life, like cypresses of a cemetery frozen in winter [cipreses helados] (1:356, ll. 148). The slab becomes a human back weighted down with time, the lifetimes of bullfighters lying upon it (1:556, l. 3).The final line of "Cuerpo presente" addresses three commands to Ignacio to vanish into nature, imitating the sea as it dissolves its waves on the surf or crashes into rocks ashore: "Duerme, vuela, reposa: ¡También se muere el mar!" [Sleep, fly off, and rest: The sea is dying too!] (1:557, l. 195). The Sevillian poet Gustavo Adolfo Bécquer's *Rima* LI, "Olas gigantes que os rompéis bramando" [Gigantic waves that break apart while roaring], set to piano and voice by Falla (ca. 1900), also calls for waves to wash away the speaker in order to impede him from facing his pain alone.

The last part of Lorca's poem, "Alma ausente" [Missing soul], stresses Ignacio's loss of identity at death: however outstanding his life, he expired like every earthly being, forgotten on a heap of snuffed-out dogs (1:558, ll. 208–11). For Juan Breva, respected by Falla and Lorca, everyone, no matter how successful, dies miserably, "with an oil lamp and a blanket on the ground" (Francisco García Lorca, *Federico y su mundo* 41; Federico 1:206).

Nonetheless, neither Falla nor Lorca gives pessimism the final word. Guitarist Miguel Llobet's student Rey de la Torre, we have seen (ch. 6, n. 3), found Falla's *Homenaje* to Debussy unusual as an elegy for its sensuous habanera rhythm. To play it as a dirge is a mistake due to its subtle lilt, its slight bounce (Dimmock). Likewise, the laments in Lorca's elegy always have the counterweight of praise for a hero who loved living ... and loving (Gibson, *A Life* 198). After accenting the universal impossibility of recognizing his corpse, and after comparing his death to a dog's, the lyric voice purports to celebrate him "para luego tu perfil y tu gracia" [for your silhouette and grace afterwards] (*Lorca* 1:558, l. 213). The *Llanto* completes Ignacio's person. His "grace" has consisted of the maturity of his knowledge in the bullring and out; and the key to his contradictory character lies in the line, "Your hunger for death and the taste of its mouth" [Tu apetencia de muerte y el gusto de su boca"] (1:554, l. 215). Falla once contemplated composing incidental music for Martínez Sierra's 1921 tragicomedy *Don Juan de España* (Hess, *Modernism* 182); and Ortega y Gasset in 1921 called the adventure-loving Don Juan Tenorio "the genuine, maximum Sevillian" [el sevillano auténtico y máximo], with death the "essential background of [his] life, counterpoint and resonance of his apparent merriness."[17] This would explain the donjuanesque Sánchez Mejías's root sentiment, "the sadness to be found in all your valiant joy" [la tristeza que tuvo tu valiente alegría] (1:558, l. 215).

Ignacio had failed to secure his person or "sure silhouette" [perfil seguro] because of disorientation in his final bullfight (354, ll. 81–2). The hero needed to rely for self-completion on a poet whose own root sentiment consisted of insufficiency in the universe. Lorca found consolation in the knowledge that in youthful daydreams Ignacio had envisioned olive trees (the archetypal Andalusian vegetation) doing obeisance to him as a bullfighter when the breeze moved through them (García-Posada, in Lorca, *Primer romancero gitano* 240n220). Hence the poetic voice at the end recalls a "brisa triste" [sad breeze], perhaps symbolizing Ignacio's spirit,[18] passing through the olive trees to receive its tribute (1:558, l. 220). Falla, modified by Lorca's own feelings on living, left his mark on the great elegy, a reaffirmation of Andalusianism five years after the forceful lyric of New York.

3. Coda: Falla in Lorca's Final Hours

In Lorca's last hours, Falla felt impelled to show love of God and charity towards his talented friend and student. On 16 August 1936, shortly after the outbreak of civil war, the poet no longer felt safe in Granada even in hiding from death squads of the Right at the home of his fellow poet Luis Rosales. His hosts proposed flight to Falla's home as his only remaining option (Gibson, *Federico García Lorca* 2:468). But the suggestion came too late. The fascists arrested Lorca at the Rosales's that afternoon (469). Falla wasted no time in acting consistently with his ever-growing piety and changing attitudes towards deep song. Some months before, reports Mora Guarnido,[19] Falangist youths had visited him to ask the most famous Spanish composer to write them a hymn. Falla politely declined because of religious scruples. He could not artistically celebrate violence and internecine strife. His tribute to Beethoven nine years earlier had reflected love of peace on earth.

Falla's religious scruples had increased over the years. In his will of February 1932, he had demanded the observation of the "purest Christian morals" in the performance and staging of his works. In 1935, reports Carol Hess, he prohibited his music from being performed unless his heirs needed the earnings for their own material support. Would pleasure from works like *El amor brujo* (based on witchcraft to solve an amorous problem) lead to sin? Was there not something pagan about Salud's suicidal character in *La vida breve* (Hess, *Passions* 201)? Yet Falla's piety transcended the negativity of prohibitions. Hess also notes that "Falla gave to charity even when in straitened circumstances himself; that he repudiated worldly goods such as property; ... and that his tone was customarily gentle, with references to spiritual matters often surfacing in his everyday conversation" (300). Generosity, therefore, coupled with heartfelt friendship, explains his attempt to save Lorca when all else had failed. He had always been generous towards Lorca and his friends. When they visited him at his home, he had spoken of music as a mere trade and not as an exalted profession. He had generously shared his talents as a pianist with his youthful audience, playing abundant works of the most varied composers for their enjoyment (Mora Guarnido, *Lorca* 157).

On 16 August 1936, while closed up in his home from dismay at the fascist triumph in Granada, Falla felt distress at the news of Lorca's arrest. Mora Guarnido reports Falla's sense of urgency, his need to do everything possible to rescue Lorca quickly (199). Yet no one could. Lorca's friends were falling to the assassin's bullet or else scattering and hiding. Only Falla himself, though ailing, risked acting (203). He nearly lost his own life in the attempt. He went to ask the Falangist youths who had visited him previously to intervene on Lorca's behalf, but the composer had unknowingly arrived too late (200). When he tried to appeal to the new authorities for Lorca's life, the fascists, according to one account, marched him into a patio and prepared to execute him as well, with only the intervention of a sympathetic officer saving him (Gibson, *Asesinato* 249–50). Lorca's ignominious shooting confirmed the cantaor Juan Breva's opinion: no matter how lofty the individual's achievements, he always ends up "with an oil lamp and a blanket on the ground."[20]

Notes

Prefatory Pages

1 *Concise Oxford English Dictionary*, 11th ed. rev. s.v. "appoggiatura."
2 Anonymous (Antonio Quevedo), *El poeta en La Habana, Federico García Lorca*, 17–18.

Introduction: The Intersection of Two Artists' Lives

1 Of himself Lorca wrote, "Como sus padres no permitieron que se trasladase a París para continuar sus estudios iniciales, y su maestro de música murió, García Lorca dirigió su (dramático) patético afán creativo a la poesía" [As his parents did not allow him to move to Paris to continue his original [music] studies, and as his music teacher died, García Lorca addressed his (dramatic) pathetic creative enthusiasm toward poetry]: Lorca, *Obras completas* 3:397. Walters ("Parallel Trajectories" 92) finds Lorca's study trip with his art history professor Martín Domínguez Berrueta of decisive importance for the change of vocation.
2 We can document only one difference of opinion, Falla's criticism of Lorca's "Oda al Santísimo Sacramento del altar" [Ode to the holiest sacrament of the altar], which distressed Lorca in February 1929: see our ch. 12.
3 Hess, *Sacred Passions*, 129. For an ample list of musical works based on writings of Lorca and encompassing about nineteen composers: "Federico García Lorca," *Wikipedia*, http://en.wikipedia.org/wiki/Federico_Garc%C3%ADa_Lorca, 21 February 2011.
4 "nuestros motivos puros y bellos en su lejana forma espectral": Lorca, *Obras completas* 3:204.
5 "la fuente pura y renovadora": Lorca, *Obras completas* 3:204.

6 For Falla's definition: Falla, "*Cante jondo*," 142; for Lorca's definition: Lorca, *Obras completas* 3:196. The gypsy *siguiriya*, whose forms vary by region and singer, in theory contains quatrains with even lines in assonance. This genre, unaccompanied at first, eventually received guitar accompaniment. The guitar furnishes the pattern for the main rhythm, competing with another pattern given by the handclapping of the performers. The guitar introduction precedes the *cantaor*'s scream, afterwards a silence (though not always), and finally two strophes: Miller, *Lorca's PCJ* 27–8. The *soleares*, less intense than the *siguiriyas gitanas*, hold a slightly lower rank in deep song. The melody of the *soleá*, generally in the Doric mode, stylizes a long lament in ternary tempo, normally accompanied by guitar: 21–2. *Polos*, merrier than the sombre *martinetes* (prisoners' or workmen's songs), also consist of quatrains of octosyllables, but unlike *martinetes* take guitar accompaniment: 22.

7 *Malagueñas* are songs originating in Malaga; *granadinas*, songs derived from Granada; *sevillanas*, songs from Seville (but with Castilian origins in the *seguidilla*); and *peteneras*, songs perhaps coming from the town of Paterna de la Rivera, near Cadiz, or else from a *cantaora* of that town: Miller, *Lorca's PCJ* 35–7. When Lorca alludes to all these songs in his *Poema del cante jondo*, the reader should bear in mind models or paradigms present in the works of Falla.

8 1:153–241. In the present book I rely on Christian de Paepe's critical edition of *Poema del cante jondo*, henceforth abbreviated *PCJ* with page number.

9 "un *puzzle americano*, ¿comprendes? El poema empieza con un crepúsculo inmóvil y por él desfilan la siguiriya, la soleá, la saeta y la petenera. El poema está lleno de gitanos, de velones, de fraguas; tiene hasta alusiones a Zoroastro. Es la primera cosa de otra orientación mía y no sé todavía qué decirte de él ..., ¡pero novedad sí tiene! El único que lo conoce es Falla y está entusiasmado": Lorca *Epistolario*, 1:49.

10 "La afición de ambos por lo popular y la idea de que allí es posible encontrar las esencias que les permitan construir su propio lenguaje (…) les lleva a trabajar en trabajos comunes": Persia, "Lorca, Falla" 75.

11 "Algunas canciones populares andaluzas (…) suscitan reminiscencias atávicas en mí": Igor Stravinsky, "Los españoles en los Ballets Russes," *Comoedia* (15 March 1921), cit. in Christophoridis, *Acercamiento* 13.

12 "el primer llanto y el primer beso": Lorca, *Obras completas* 3:204.

13 Hess, *Passions* 131. Walters bluntly says that "the festival was not a success" since Falla became embroiled in the contention about reinvesting the profits (for future deep song contests) and since the organizers had largely over-looked established professionals in favour of amateurs in the art of deep song: "Parallel Trajectories" 94. Yet does money measure success? For García

Montero,"lo verdaderamente importante es la significación cultural del
proyecto, muy vinculada a la lectura espiritual, poco costumbrista, de las
tradiciones naturales y primitivas" [what is really important is the cultural
meaning of the project, heavily linked to the spiritual reading – virtually free
of prevailing customs – of natural and primitive traditions]: "Introducción,"
in Lorca, *Poema del cante jondo* 30.

14 "el alma de Don Quijote, ingrávida como un vilano, como una hoja seca":
Ortega y Gasset, *Meditaciones* 380. Hess, *Modernism*, 222–3, hints at Ortega's
influence on Falla's orchestration. If Don Quixote housed a "weightless"
soul, an overfed actor could not play him. Contrariwise, Falla's music
expresses "weight" in the heavy percussion passages of the fandango
of the plump Miller's Wife from the ballet *El sombrero de tres picos.*

15 In a performance of Lorca's *Tragicomedia de don Cristóbal y la señá Rosita*
[Tragicomedy of Don Cristóbal and Missy Rosita] in Buenos Aires of 1934,
the puppet Don Cristóbal announced to the audience that in the poet's house
some time ago, with Falla at the piano, *L'histoire d'un soldat* first debuted
in Spain: Gibson, *Life* 118–19.

16 Lorca, 3:547: "Pues estoy preparándome para el concierto de su teatro."

17 "resultó ser un prolegómeno de lo que en el mismo año (…) había de estrenarse
en París con el nombre de 'El retablo de maese Pedro.'": Nommick,
"Día de Reyes" 62.

18 In addition, Christoforidis ("Hacia nuevos conceptos" 364) finds the influence
of Stravinsky's *Renard* and *Les noces* on the syllabic and monotonal style
of the *trujamán* or puppet-show interpreter in *Retablo.*

19 In operas and ballets Falla once aspired to regenerate Spanish musical theatre.
In 1914 he hoped to write an opera based on Calderón's religious drama,
La devoción de la Cruz [Devotion to the Cross]: Christoforidis, "Ópera" 364.
In 1926 he wished to write an opera based on Calderón's *auto sacramental*
Los encantos de la culpa [The charms of sin]. He wrote incidental music not
only for *El gran teatro del mundo*, but also in 1935 for Lope de Vega's *auto*
sacramental La vuelta de Egipto [The return from Egypt]: Weber ("Misterio"
908).

20 According to Weber ("Misterio" 914), as in Calderón's *autos sacramentales*,
in *Atlàntida* the entrances of the protagonists are unrelated to the other
characters, the roles are all monologues, some characters seem allegorical and
symbolic without psychological characterization, and the work provides a
Christian interpretation of Greek mythology onstage with music, dance,
pantomime, and lighting effects.

21 The translation was to appear in the program notes. The Archivo Manuel de
Falla holds Falla's unpublished letter of 11 September 1924 to Jean-Aubry

about Federico's translation, and Francisco García Lorca (156) mentions his own inability to make the translation. He also remarks that Falla tended to link his friends (like the two Lorca brothers) to his own musical profession. Falla's *Psyché* contained "chantlike lines" recalling Falla's experiment with declamation in R*etablo* of the previous year: Hess, *Modernism* 178.

22 "La amistad con Falla, bebiendo aire cálido de los cármenes granadinos, le dicta los versos del *Romancero gitano*": Lorca 3:537.

23 "Ese poema de Andalucía, que lo tiene que hacer usted, que tiene que ser algo hermoso y grande ... Trabaje usted ... Trabaje ... Cuando se haya muerto, se arrepentirá usted de no haber trabajado": Lorca 3:546.

24 Notable exceptions are Falla music historians Carol A. Hess and Michael Christoforidis, on whose rigorous, wide-sweeping studies I heavily rely. Among Hispanists, Christopher Maurer shows deepest penetration into Lorca vis-à-vis Falla. I disagree with Roberta Quance ("Trouble" 406), otherwise extremely perspicacious, that Lorca identified Falla with his (transitory) impressionist aesthetic. Falla educated Lorca on his entire artistic evolution from *La vida breve* to *Atlàntida*.

25 In August 1923, between the compositions of *PCJ* and *Romancero gitano*, Lorca wrote Falla that he was attempting to pick out on his own guitar Falla's *Homenaje: Pièce de guitar écrite pour le tombeau de Claude Debussy*: Lorca *Epistolario*: 1:83.

26 Ellipses that appear within parentheses originate with the present author.

27 The note mentioned appeared in *García Lorca Review* 4 (1976): 115–19. This summation of the note appears in Klein, "*La vida breve*" 92.

28 Falla saved numerous paper birds fashioned by Miguel de Unamuno and given to him as a gift. These flocks survive in the Archivo Manuel de Falla. Falla obviously knew the comical "Tratado de cocotología" [Treatise on bird-making] appended to Unamuno's novel *Amor y pedagogía.* Oddly, no works by Unamuno appear in Falla's library collection.

29 "La unión y compenetración de don Manuel [de Falla] con Federico fue muy profunda, y juntos recorrieron muchos pueblos para recoger canciones populares." Isabel García Lorca, *Recuerdos* 125.

30 "En Granada nace y se desarrolla una amistad, un profundo cariño y respeto mutuo entre dos personalidades tan distantes pero a la vez tan próximas en su modo de ver y entender el arte, en su forma de crear": María Isabel de Falla, "Presentación" 9. Falla's niece is almost certainly relying on uncited second- ary sources, as she spent but a few months with him in 1939 when she was ten years old. Authors like Jaime Pahissa and Francisco García Lorca confirm her opinions.

31 Klein, "Influence of Falla" 115. In Spain there is gossip about a physical relationship between Falla and Lorca. Yet no concrete written evidence exists

nor any traces of such a relationship in their works. A presumption of eroticism between them would clarify the art of neither, whereas Lorca's presence in Dalí's art illumines the painter's canvases (Gibson, *Caballo*, inset III–V). Finally, Ian Gibson's exhaustive study of Lorca's homosexuality mentions Falla without ever ascribing homoeroticism to him (*Caballo* 56, 82, 127, 128, 161, 194). The present book therefore omits any such assumption.

32 Walters ("Parallel trajectories" 94) mentions the *Retablo* offhandedly as having been "begun" when Lorca and Falla planned the Three Kings Day entertainment. Nothing more is said.

33 Walters (93) makes Falla's "misgivings"of the 1930s about his Andalusianist works of the 1910s an argument for discontinuing work on *Lola* as of 1923. In my article "Married Temptresses," I try to show that Falla lost interest in *Lola, la comedianta* because much of it mimics Falla's ballet *El sombrero de tres picos*.

34 Walters (95) finds *Noches* "the most sensuous composition of this ascetic man." Yet his languorous Cadiz tango in 7/8 time titled *Pantomima* from *El amor brujo* is probably even more sensuous.

35 "la protoforma musical de cada obra musical (...) es oída *en bloque* en cuanto al número y calidades de sus notas. Por esto se la percibe como real; y es por tal realidad blocal por la que se nota que se está oyendo realmente música real": *Filosofía de la música* 208. *Protoforma* translates Schenker's term *Ursatz* from *Der Meisterwerk in der Musik*, wherein the prefix *proto-* or *Ur-* means "original, originating, [and] primitive": 201.

36 On the gypsy theme in general, see Christian Wentzlaff-Eggebert, "Zigeunerinnen als Vertreter des romantischen Spanien" [Female gypsies as representatives of Romantic Spain]; on nineteenth-century European music and Spanish poetry: Zapke, *Falla y Lorca* 13–21; and on Lorca's *Romancero gitano* in particular, see Javier Gómez Montero, "Lorcas *Romancero gitano* und die Subjektivierung des Mythos" [Lorca's *Romancero gitano* and the subjectivizing of myth], Zapke, *Falla y Lorca* 89–111. Nothing appears here on Falla's impact upon myth-making in Lorca. On historical background concerning nationalism in nineteenth-century European music, an indispens- able study is Klaus Wolfgang Niemöller, "Der Gedanke einer nationalen Musik im europäischen Raum und der musikalische Hispanismus" [The idea of a national music in European space and musical Hispanism], 25–36. On Falla's background in old Spanish music, both folk and learned, see Zapke's well-documented study "Presencia de la música antigua en la obra de Falla: La búsqueda de los orígenes" [Presence of old (Spanish) music in the works of Falla], 39–64. Only two essays in this rich volume explore the artistic link between Falla and Lorca: Jorge de Persia's excellent "Lorca, Falla y la música. Una coincidencia intergeneracional," 67–85, and the splendid, more specific piece by Eckhard Weber, "Los *Títeres de Cachiporra* und *El retablo de maese*

Pedro: Manuel de Fallas Beschäftigung mit dem Puppentheater und die neuen
Tendenzen im Musiktheater seiner Zeit" [*The Andalusian Punch-and-Judy
Puppets* and *The Puppet-Theatre of Master Peter*: Manuel de Falla's concern
with puppet theatre and the new tendencies in the musical theater of his
times], 117–53. If we accept Ortega y Gasset's generation theory, whereby
historical change takes place by generations – and I personally find the theory
problematic as applied to Spain, where intellectuals are so few and far
between and know each other intimately despite age differences (e.g., Falla
and Lorca) – then we can understand the closing study by José Luis Abellán,
"Manuel de Falla, hombre intergeneracional" [Manuel de Falla, intergenerational man], 155–60. Very little is said of the Falla-Lorca relationship: 156,
159. Abellán seems not to know that Lorca took the initiative in asking Falla
to arrange Góngora's "Soneto a Córdoba" (Sonnet to Cordoba): 156.

37 According to guitarist and music historian Christoforidis, the guitar revival
is in fact traceable to the late nineteenth century with Francisco Tárrega
(1852–1909), whose student Miguel Llobet (1878–1938) Falla heard time and
again in Madrid before 1907. On Llobet's role in the composing of Falla's
famous guitar *Homenaje* to Debussy, see ch. 6, n. 3.

38 See Lorca's remarks on Picasso in the lecture "Sketch de la nueva pintura"
(28 October 1928): 3:273–4; Gibson, *Life* 84.

39 Handwritten notes of Lejárraga and Falla in the 1914 edition they employed
of Alarcón's novella show how closely composer and librettist worked.

40 All information in this paragraph comes from my article on "Married
Temptresses." A major variation on the married temptress theme appears in
Lorca's mature farce *El amor de Don Perlimplín con Belisa en su jardín*, also
influenced by Falla's music. In structure, the work resembles the *Vivace*
movement of Falla's *Harpsichord Concerto* (1923–6). The *Vivace* illustrates
borrowings from folk *zapateados*, or dances with rhythmic foot-tappings
alternating 3/4 and 6/8 rhythms, and sonatas of Domenico Scarlatti (1685–
1757), greatly admired by Falla and Lorca alike, both of whom played them
on the piano (Francisco García Lorca, *Federico y su mundo* 429). Pahissa
describes Falla's concerto as a "work of chamber music in which the six
performers are all soloists" (*Falla* 174). Analogously, taking the theme of
troubled marriage between youth and maturity, Lorca subtitles *Perlimplín* a
"versión de cámara" [chamber version], as if he had written it for a small
audience (Lorca 2:459). The play has only six characters, each compared by
Francisco García Lorca to a particular musical instrument (315). In *Perlimplín*
as in *Zapatera*, the male character avails himself of his spouse's active
imagination, but in *Perlimplín* he uses it as a springboard from his own
docility to grandeur. Taking impotence as his point of departure, playwright

Lorca parlays this deficiency into heroism in a play employing sonata form as
its structure (cf. L.T. González-del-Valle, "Conceptión musical de *Perlimplín*"),
just as does Falla's *Vivace*. Both Falla and Lorca imitate the binary form of
Scarlatti's sonatas, though each in his own way. Given the flexibility and
jocularity of the *Vivace*, the first member of each paired theme forms an ironic
question arousing the expectation of an equally ironic answer in the second.
Pairing likewise recurs in *Perlimplín*. Francisco García Lorca finds all its
dialogue distributed between pairs of characters, speaking in pairs of lines
(*Federico y su mundo* 317). A clipped, lively tempo prevails – a *vivace* – marked
by irony at every step.

   The play's Prologue forms a sonata-form *introduction*, foreshadowing the
unveiling of the central motifs. The sonata-form *exposition* appears in scene 1,
playing the two motifs A (the failed-marriage motif) and A^1 (the love motif,
inexorable response to matrimonial failure). In scene 2, the more the marriage
wanes, the more Perlimplín loves Belisa. In scene 3, a sonata *development*
takes place, complicating the relationship of motifs A and A.^{1} Perlimplín
announces to Belisa he will help her win his own rival in love! Scene 4 brings
the sonata *recapitulation*, replaying situations from scene 1 while setting the
spouses in a new relationship with theme C (structural by-product of the love
motif), emerging as Perlimplín's love-death, and responding to C^1, consisting
of Belisa's newfound love for the self-sacrificing Perlimplín (as revealed in the
coda, or final scene).

41 Newberry, "Aesthetic Distance" 284, cit. in Weber, "Títeres" 146–7n60.

42 "síntesis de todas las artes": Maurer, "Lorca y las formas" 238.

43 For *Blood Weddings*, his most widely performed play, Lorca confessed
    indebtedness to Bach: "*Bodas de sangre* está sacada de Bach (...), ese tercer
    acto, eso de la luna, eso del bosque, eso de la muerte rondando, todo eso
    estaba en la cantata de Bach que yo tenía. Donde trabajo, tiene que haber
    música" [*Blood Weddings* is taken from Bach (…). That third act – the part
    about the moon, the woods, Death on patrol – all that was in the Bach cantata
    that I had. Wherever I work, there has to be music]: cit. Christopher Maurer,
    "Lorca y las formas" 247–8. On the family gramophone, Lorca played Bach's
    choral Cantata BWV 140 incessantly in the summer of 1931 when writing
    Blood Weddings (Isabel García Lorca, *Recuerdos* 268). Bach's cantata was to
    influence the musical structure of act 2, sc. 1, the disposition of the setting,
    and the dialogue (Maurer, "Lorca y las formas" 245). Further, following
    Falla's rigorous example in rehearsing his *Harpsichord Concerto*, Lorca
    learned to rehearse his players over and over until achieving mathematical
    precision in *Blood Weddings* in the intervals between the vocal pitches of the
    actors (Francisco García Lorca, *Federico y su mundo* 335). The main theme of

Blood Weddings, seen in the plural of its title, is the eternal return of weddings ending in tragedy in a society which sets up barriers against the natural
flow of sexual instincts (cf. Gibson, *Life* 336, 341). Therefore Lorca resorted
to a Bach-like counterpoint in the play dialogue, in other words, to a
recurrence of speeches.

44 "pensada en realismo integral": García Bacca, *Filosofía de la música* 267.

45 García Bacca, *Filosofía de la música* 16. García Bacca, born in Pamplona,
studied mathematics and physics in Munich, was long associated with the
University of Barcelona, and went into exile in Spanish America during the
Spanish Civil War: Díaz Díaz, *Hombres y documentos* 3:380–1.

46 Pahissa, *Falla* 102. For other theories on the origin of the first nocturne, see
Nommick, *Jardines de España* 13–16. Nommick discounts other theories and
concludes that the motif of "En el Generalife" has a folkloric origin: 15.

47 Since the Alhambra inspired this movement, and since the melody expresses a
ghostly sensation, Falla may well be alluding in music to Washington Irving's
Tales of the Alhambra with its Moorish ghosts.

48 Christoforidis, "The Moor's Last Sigh" 8; see Falla, *Noches*, I, score, nn. 3–4,
pp. 5–7.

49 "En 'En el Generalife', sobre el nostálgico fondo orquestal, el piano evoca a
las cuerdas del instrumento andaluz, perfilando líneas de un abstractismo
matemático, que nacen y se generan en sí mismas, que cuando semejan iniciar
un segundo tema musical, vuelven enlazadas al primero o a una de sus
variantes": Molina Fajardo, *Falla y el "Cante Jondo"* 19.

50 Lorca not only noted Falla's fascination with that second *zorongo*, but he too
loved it, arranged it for piano and dance, recorded it for His Master's Voice
with the flamenco singer/dancer Encarnación López Júlvez (La Argentinita),
and incorporated it into his farce *La zapatera prodigiosa*: Gibson, *Life* 90, 91;
Lorca, 2:439, 1174–6.

51 "el hombre de mayor cultura en la sangre que he conocido, dijo, escuchando
al propio Falla su *Nocturno del Generalife*, esta espléndida frase: 'Todo lo que
tiene sonidos negros tiene duende.'": Lorca, 3:307.

52 "el misterio, las raíces que se clavan en el limo que todos conocemos, que
todos ignoramos, pero de donde nos llega lo que es sustancial en el arte": 307.

53 "Nuestro pueblo pone los brazos en cruz mirando las estrellas y esperará
inútilmente la señal salvadora. (…) la Muerte (…) es la pregunta de las
preguntas": 206.

54 See the poem "Campana," with its Latinism "prora" (prow) also seen in Darío:
PCJ 209.

55 "don gratuito, una gracia": Francisco García Lorca, *Federico y su mundo* 149;
cf. Federico García Lorca, 3:612: "Yo estoy con Falla. La poesía es un don" [I
am with Falla. Poetry is a gift].

56 María Martínez Sierra, *Gregorio y yo* 123–4. Nommick, *Jardines de España*
    12. María's travel book, *Granada* (135–6), equates the arrangement of the
    Generalife Palace gardens to rising degrees of mystic contemplation that
    obviously spoke to Falla's religious nature. He surely found this mystic
    beauty a great consolation in his hour of turmoil.

57 To borrow a valuable concept from Christopher Maurer, "Lorca y las
    formas" 245, this poem is composed "a la manera de" Falla, in his style,
    applied to literature. No concrete textual source or influence is involved,
    merely an unmistakable likeness in theme and mood.

58 Navarro Tomás terms **o** and **u** "vocales oscuras" [dark vowels], whose
    elocutionary depth in the buccal openings seems more efficacious in lyric
    poetry when supported by "vocablos sombríos" [sombre words] **sombra** and
    noche: *Fonología española* 197. On medium **a** as a "sonido abierto y claro"
    [open, clear sound]: Tomás Navarro Tomás, *Pronunciación española*, §201,
    240. The **n**, "alveolar nasal sonora" [clear nasal alveolar], is pronounced in
    noche, gitanas, coronadas, biznagas, **n**ácar with the velum of the palate open,
    while "el aire espirado sale por la nariz" [the exhaled air comes out through
    the nose]: §110, 111. The sonority of **a** is enhanced through contact with the
    n. Lorca probably has a consciousness of this sonority in view of the musical
    theme of his poem.

59 "La misma obra musical puede estar siendo ejecutada, realizada, en lugares
    distantes": García Bacca, *Filosofía de la música* 335.

60 From the poem "Dernier adieu" [Last goodbye], *La Grappe de raisin*, 137.
    Falla copied by hand some of Drouot's verses from this collection: Archivo
    Manuel de Falla.

61 Here I agree with Ángel del Río (and the majority of Lorca critics) that in
    PCJ the poet "va a buscar el alma oculta de su tierra" [goes in search of the
    hidden soul of his land]: *Vida y obras* 70. Many explicit statements in Lorca's
    lectures on deep song and *Romancero gitano* support this interpretation. I
    present proof that Lorca derives *Volksgeist* theory from Falla, whose notions
    on the Latin and the German cultural spirits guide much of his thinking:
    Hess, *Modernism* (2001) and *Passions* (2005). In working with Falla's carefully
    crafted handwritten notes of 1927 on Beethoven, I have discovered the same
    contrast (see ch. 11, n. 45). Roberta Ann Quance, in an otherwise excellent
    book, makes the erroneous assumption that accepting del Río's reading of
    Lorca is tantamount to "endorsing a nineteenth-century belief about the
    essential links between folksong, land, and a people's character": *Contradic-*
    tion 138. No. I do not endorse *Volksgeist* theory any more than I endorse the
    theory of the four humours in Hippocratic medicine when I teach Cervantes.
    I simply use *Volksgeist* as a conceptual tool to clarify Falla and Lorca. Moreover,
    I deplore its abhorrent offshoot, fascist racism, while bracketing my abhorrence

and accepting textual evidence. There exists much more direct proof
of *Volksgeist* theory in Lorca than of Nietzsche's theory of tragedy, which
Quance (141) unconvincingly attributes to him. Breathing Nietzsche
in the air of the time differs from espousing his ideas.

62 Cit. in Hess, *Modernism* 69 from Falla's interview, "To the Young Composer:
Señor Manuel de Falla and German Formalism," *Daily Mail* (London),
19 July 1919.

63 "El canto grave, hierático de ayer, ha degenerado en el ridículo flamenquismo de
hoy. En éste se adulteran y modernizan (¡qué horror!) sus elementos esenciales
… La sobria modulación vocal – las inflexiones naturales del canto que provo-
can la división y subdivisión de los sonidos de la gama – se ha convertido en
artificioso giro ornamental más propio del decadentismo de la mala época
italiana, que de los cantos primitivos de Oriente, con los que sólo, cuando son
puros, pueden ser comparados los nuestros": Falla, *"Cante jondo"* 146–7n1.

64 "¡Señores, el alma música del pueblo está en gravísimo peligro! ¡El tesoro
artístico de toda una raza va camino del olvido!": Lorca, 3:195.

65 "el Primer Concurso de Cante Jondo fue en realidad una especie de cruzada
artística para la salvación, si era posible todavía, de un rico venero de música
natural y popular": Mora Guarnido, *Lorca* 160.

66 Due to spatial limitations, we omit analysis of "Dos muchachas" [Two girls],
whose two innocent women, the Virgin-like laundress Lola and the spinster
Amparo, contrast with the malevolent Petenera in Andalusia, land of contrasts:
PCJ 226–9. Lola "washes diapers" like the Virgin from the famous *villancico*
or Christmas carol "La Virgin lava pañales": Morris, *Son of Andalusia* 221.
Falla, who endows his fictional heroines with innocence, also has compiled
carols in *Cantares de Nochebuena* (Songs of Christmas Eve), though not "La
Virgen lava pañales." Amparo, in a *soleá*-form poem, borrows features from a
real-life figure (Mora Guarnido, *Lorca* 168–9), and, like an upper-class Salud
from *La vida breve*, awaits her lover in vain like a caged bird.

67 Instead, his editor wished him to prolong it for publication. Hence, he
concluded it with two allegorical dialogues, both influenced by Falla's vision
of gypsy music. On Falla in the dialogues, see our monograph, *El diálogo
entre Falla y Lorca sobre la creación folklórica* 25n56.

1 Music in the Letters of Lorca before Meeting Falla

1 "sufría sus antiguas pasiones al conjuro de una sonata beethoveniana. ¡Era un
santo!": Lorca, *Obras completas* 3:4.

2 "Falla es un santo … Un místico … Yo no venero a nadie como a Falla … (…)
Con el único afán de ser cada día más bueno y de dejar una obra": 3:546.

3 "Porque yo soy ante todo músico": 3:545.

4 "Canto con la lira, con la flauta, con la guitarra, con el laúd, con el crótalo, con la siringa verleniana, con el raro fagot de Baudelaire, con la espléndida trompa de Rubén. No las tañeré bien, esto lo sé, pero espero que estas estrofas malas serán letanías que me salvarán de la tentación del mal": Lorca, "Pierrot. Poema íntimo," in *Prosa inédita* 419, cit. in Martín, *Heterodoxo y màrtir* 218.

5 "un bisexualismo descompensado por el peso determinante de la homosexualidad": 216. As to the young girl to whom Lorca dedicated his early amorous verse, Gibson identifies her as María Luisa Natera Ladrón de Guevara (*Caballo* 65). Writer-historian Román Gubern has said of Lorca that he feared confrontation with the feminine sex because he identified with his mother (Gibson, *Life* 291).

6 "Introducción," *Prosa inédita*, 34–5. Maurer thinks that the sexual crisis formed merely a small part of Lorca's unsatisfied desire or "black pain."

7 "Como cada palabra tiene un alma hay en cada verso además de la armonía verbal una melodía ideal. La música es sólo de la idea, muchas veces": Darío, *Obras completas* 5:764.

8 "Para penetrar en las delicias musicales que hace sonar nuestra alma hay, sobre todo, que tener fe en el concepto de música sin sonidos, o sea, sonidos de ideas (...) las melodías de las ideas nacientes que se arrollan como olas del mar": Federico García Lorca, *Prosa inédita* 139. The final strophe of Darío's "Era un aire suave" universalizes Eulalia, removing her from spatio-temporal concreteness and idealizing her: "'¿Fue acaso en el Norte o en el Mediodía? / Yo el tiempo y el día y el país ignoro; / pero sé que Eulalia ríe todavía, / ¡y es cruel y eterna su risa de oro!" [Did it take place perchance in the North or the South? / I know not time, nor day, nor country; / but I know that Eulalia is still laughing, / and her golden laugh is cruel and eternal!]: Darío, *Obras completas* 5:768. She embodies the musical ideal, that of the archetypes.

9 An early prose poem, "Un vals de Chopin" [A Chopin waltz], can be read in 3/4 rhythm, although such a reading is not required: Lorca, *Prosa inédita* 265–7. On the other hand, according to Maurer, "dos poemas publicados en *Poeta en Nueva York*, 'Vals en las ramas' y 'Pequeño vals vienés,' recuerdan el ritmo del vals y en 1933 comentará Lorca (...) que piensa publicar 'un libro (...) que se titula *Porque te quiero a ti solamente (tanda de valses)*'" [Two poems published in *Poet in New York*, "Waltz in the Branches" and "Small Viennese Waltz," recall waltz rhythm, and in 1933 Lorca will remark (...) that he plans to publish "a book (...) which is titled, "Why I Love Only You (Set of Waltzes)"': "Introducción" to Lorca, *Prosa inédita* 21].

10 "galantes pavanas, fugaces gavotas / (que) cantaban los dulces violines de Hungría": Darío, *Obras completas* 5:766. See Lorca, *Poesía inédita* 230, for

the word "aria," 42 for "romanza," 221 and 422 for "sonatas"; 288 for "rigodón," 368 for "pavana," and 407 for "gavota."

11 "La vieja cigarra / ensaya su ronca guitarra senil, / y el grillo preludia un solo monótono / en la única cuerda que está en su violín": Darío, *Obras completas* 5:818.

12 "violín, pandero, clarín y sistro / que claro anuncia el padre sol": Lorca, *Poesía inédita* 244.

13 "Locos violines dormidos / En una nota inconsciente / Que acaba con un quejido": 396.

14 "Sol potente, quietudes inquietantes de fuego. / Remolinos de luces y cantar de cigarras. / Raros tonos de fa en trompetas enormes": Lorca, *Poesía inédita* 356. García Bacca (*Filosofía de la música* 381) explains that some historical periods have judged sounds to be produced not only acoustically but also sentimentally, so that C indicates strong, D exciting, E constant, F desolate, etc. However, in the natural physiological state, C, D, E, and F form a real, audible, sensible unity fusing and confusing them all. Hearing them separately with "sentimental indifference" ("indiferencia sentimental") is a prerequisite for hearing them perceptibly at all as sounds: 383.

15 "Hacia un ocaso radiante / caminaba el sol de estío, / y era, entre nubes de fuego, una trompeta gigante": Antonio Machado, *Soledades* 102.

16 On Mozart, "alma de clavicordio," *Poesía inédita* 43; on Berlioz, 26; on Schumann, 262.

17 "herida de Chopin y piano": 88.

18 "Nacía, gris, la luna, y Beethoven lloraba, / bajo la mano blanca, en el piano de ella": Jiménez, *Segunda antolojía poética* 84.

19 "Toda el alma de Chopin / Late en el negro piano. / Chopin de niebla y cristal, / Confuso, carnal y vago": *Poesía inédita* 331.

20 "Las eras solas. La vega inquieta, / Llena de hondura y de un *compás*, / *Tempo rubato* de plata y niebla / con *fortes* plenos de luz solar." Tempo rubato signifies suspension of strict time: Kennedy, *Oxford Dictionary of Music* 548; forte signifies a loud passage: 234.

21 "La música es el arte por naturaleza": Lorca 3:369.

22 3:370. This esoteric lexicon, added to the anti-philistine petulance, probably indicates the influence of Darío over all others, including Falla, on young Lorca's article. Even the word "Divagación" (digression) in Lorca's title (369) is a word loved by Darío: *Obras completas* 5:768.

23 "Llegó Rubén Darío 'el Magnìfico' y, a su vista, huyeron los sempiternos sonetistas de oficio que son académicos": Lorca, 3:369.

24 "comienza a cantar canciones de fuego": 3:77.

25 "templan sus violines para emborracharse al mediodía": 3:77.

26 "La melodía, como enorme columna de mármol negro que se perdiera entre las nubes, no tiene solución. Es accidentada y lisa, profunda y de un vago sentimiento interior. Van las voces recorriendo todas las melancolías tonales a través del mundo fantástico de las claves": 3:50.

27 "por encima de todas las cosas existentes": 3:50.

28 "tragedia del corazón": 3:50.

29 "huyen de los puntos emocionales. Hay jadeares enormes en los cuales una sílaba va recorriendo notas y notas, que no tienen la resolución que se espera": 3:50.

30 "melodía rarísima y arcaica": 3:50.

31 "apellido inmortal": 3:51. Lorca's religious devotion to Eastern European classical music is consistent.

32 "el hipo angustioso de su ritmo constante y de pesadilla": 3:52. The author uses the word "hipo" [hiccup] because he is playing a pipe organ. The *Allegretto* accompanies the climactic scene in the 2011 Oscar-winning film *The King's Speech* (2010), in which Colin Firth, playing King George VI, heroically labours through a broadcasted discourse calling his subjects to war.

33 Maynard Solomon writes that, according to scholars, many parts of Beethoven's Seventh Symphony "could be readily scanned according to principles of stresses and syllabication codified in classical Greek prosody" (*Beethoven*; on the *Allegretto*, 109–13). Could Lorca have been attracted to the archaic sound of the rhythm?

34 "grito doloroso": Lorca 3:70.

35 "el acento de un canto wagneriano": 3:71.

36 "una nota quejumbrosa, cantada, que vibraba como una campana en tono mayor brillantísimo, se repetía en un *andante maestoso* y hacía una pausa. Después volvía a decirse el mismo tema, ya más quedo, y, por último, para resolución, la voz tomaba timbre gutural, modulaba al tono menor y, dando una nota elevadísima, caía lánguidamente en la nota inicial. Sonaba el pregón desfallecido y fuerte como una frase de trompa del gran Wagner": 3:71.

37 On Wagner in *La vida breve*: Hess, *Passions* 35, and in *Noches*, Hess, *Passions*, 92.

38 García Matos explains that Andalusian sellers in the street use old *saetas* and flamenco songs as the most efficacious means to hawk their wares: "Folklore en Falla, II" 38–9. Maese Pedro's cry appears in Manuel de Falla, *Retablo*, score, rehearsal 9, p.16.

39 The impressionism of verbal landscape painter José Martínez Ruiz ("Azorín") – long-range vision, use of nuances, pointillism – is well known. See, for example, E. Inman Fox, "Introducción biográfica y crítica" to J. Martínez Ruiz, *La voluntad*, 11.

40 See Albéniz's piano solo "El Puerto" from the suite *Iberia* 1:8–15. In Debussy, see "Reflets dans l'eau," from *Images*, bk. 1; "La cathédrale engloutie," from *Preludes*, Bk. 1; "Jardins dans la pluie," from *Estampes*, n°. 3. Cf. *La mer* of Debussy, work for orchestra, and also the melodies for piano in Falla's "En el Generalife," from *Noches.*

41 A. Machado, "Ensueño" in *Soledades* 99–100. Poems on dreams abound in *Galerías*: 179–214.

42 *Reverie* forms part of Debussy's *Suite bergamasque.*

43 "barcas cabecean somnolientas": Lorca, *Obras completas* 3:119.

44 "A lo lejos se ven las torres de la ciudad y las pendientes rocosas del monte": 3:119.

45 "Es la hora crepuscular y empiezan a encenderse las luces de los barcos y de las casas": 3:119.

46 "El caserío invertido en las aguas en medio de los zigzás dorados y temblorosos de los reflejos": 3:119.

47 "hombrotes vestidos de azul que hablan acaloradamente": 3:119.

48 "De un piano lejano llegó la romanza sin palabras": 3:119.

49 "Empezó lentamente con aire rubato delicioso y entró después con un canto rebosante de apasionamientos. A veces la melodía se callaba mientras los graves daban unos acordes suaves y solemnes": 3:119–20.

50 Mendelssohn, *Liede ohne Worte* 118–19. The measures with crescendo are in the score, rehearsals 8, 18, 20, 29, 32, 33–34–35.

51 "llegaba sobre el puerto la música envolviéndolo todo en un fascinación de sonido sentimental": Lorca, *Obras completas* 3:120.

52 "caían lamiendo voluptuosamente las gradas del embarcadero": 3:120.

53 "muecines de la sombra, / se han quedado mudas": 1:104.

54 "ha puesto la sordina a su aristón": 1:104.

55 "Quiere dar con su mano centenaria / un cachete a la luna": 1:104.

56 *Libro de poemas* does not break with this doctrine completely, but offers a medley of styles. "Invocación al laurel" [Invocation to the laurel, 1919], for instance, still shows Darío's inspiration. The poetic voice is a prophet, a sage poet, like Darío's lyrical subject in poems of *Prosas profanas*, and he communicates with flowers and trees: 1:135–37.

57 A *suite* consists of a single theme embracing from three to fourteen brief individual poems. Lorca himself wrote to Salazar that *PCJ* "is something different from the *Suites* and full of Andalusian suggestions" [es una cosa distinta de las suites y llena de sugestiones andaluzas: *Epistolario* 1:141]. I agree that *PCJ* differs from *Suites* and, given its narrative continuity both within and among its first four parts, must respectfully disagree with Quance

about similarity of structure. The musical conceptions or structures of those two works differ the way a suite differs from an arabesque. Lorca had two musical models in mind when writing *Suites*: "An eighteenth-century composition, with a variety of moods, whose movements are only loosely linked together; and an earlier version, 'the theme and variation', or 'diferencias' to use the Spanish term employed by Lorca, which possesses a greater sense of continuity and development." Bonaddio thinks it possible to find examples of both types among the *Suites* (*Poetics of Self-Consciousness* 59). An arabesque gives the illusion of determining its own progression (see "Postlude" 1, below), whereas the composer remains perceptibly in control in a suite. Otherwise, I would agree with Quance about the community of (most) themes and style between *Suites* and *PCJ*. See, for example, my analysis of "Seis cohetes" [Six rockets] from *Suites* in ch. 3. n. 16, below.

58 "uno de los más formidables esfuerzos para construir la lírica sobre una sustancia puramente estética": Lorca, *Obras completas* 3:257.

59 "Juan Larrea y su discípulo Gerardo Diego construyen poemas a base de hechos poéticos encadenados, cada vez más limpios de imagen y de vuelo cristalino": 3:269.

60 Diego's relationship with Lorca was not as cordial as his friendship with Falla. As Lorca wrote on 30 July 1923 to his intimate friend Melchor Fernández Almagro, "To Gerardo Diego I have not written to thank him for having sent me his precious book *Soria* [a poetic anthology] ... but you know, dear Melchor, that when I am not close to the person I write to, I don't know what to say to him!, and although Diego's book is good and he is a great poet, I had trouble thanking him, praising him, and nothing else! [A Gerardo Diego no le escribí dándole las gracias por haberme enviado su precioso libro *Soria* ... pero tú sabes, Melchorito, que cuando yo no tengo confianza con la persona a quien escribo, ¡no sé qué decirle!, y aunque el libro de Diego es bueno y él es un gran poeta, a mí me costaba trabajo darle las gracias, elogiarlo, ¡y nada más!]": Lorca and Fernández Almagro, *Epistolario* 82–3. I have found little influence of Diego's writings on Lorca's. I detect no trace of Diego in *PCJ*. In *Romancero gitano*, Diego influences "Burla de Don Pedro a caballo" and "San Gabriel (Sevilla)," but only to a minimal degree. See ch. 10, n. 56, below.

61 On *creacionismo* in Lorca's *Canciones*, see my article, "El impacto del creacionismo en 'Canciones' de García Lorca," 357–74. *Canciones,* as in *Suites,* display clashes between traditional conventions from the old *Cancionero* [Songbooks] with avant-garde imagery to intensify and deepen Lorca's poetic expression. The anthology shows the deep, illuminating impact of Vicente Huidobro, a diffuse influence of Gerardo Diego, and traces of Juan Larrea.

2 *Fantasía Bætica* and "Baladilla de los tres ríos": Two Searches for Andalusian Wellsprings

1 Christoforidis, "Moor's Last Sigh" 1. "Alhambrism" is a neologism formed on the name of the Alhambra palace in Granada, inhabited by the last Moorish king Boabdil and subsequently taken over by the Catholic Monarchs Isabella and Ferdinand. Christoforidis identifies Adolfo Salazar, Lorca's friend, as source of the musical conception.

2 The quote from the prelude to *Tristan und Isolde* appears two measures before *Noches* I, rehearsal 24: Hess, *Passions* 92. For everything said here on Alhambrism in music and nineteenth-century literature, I am deeply indebted to Christoforidis, "Moor's Last Sigh" 8–9.

3 Theater producers found the work too imitative of Chopin for their tastes: Mario Hernández, "Introducción" to Federico García Lorca, *PCJ* 35; Hess, *Passions* 124–5.

4 "En el canto popular, el espíritu importa más que la letra. El ritmo, la modalidad y los intervalos melódicos que determinan sus ondulaciones y cadencias, constituyen lo esencial de esos cantos ... Me opongo a esa música que toma como base los documentos folklóricos auténticos; por el contrario, creo que es necesario partir de las fuentes naturales, vivas y utilizar las sonoridades y ritmos en su sustancia, pero no en su aspecto exterior": *Escritos* 60.

5 Manuel de Falla, *Tempo* no. 14, cit. in M. García Matos, "El folklore en *La vida breve* de Manuel de Falla" 196.

6 "¡Qué diferencia tan notable entre los versos de estos poetas y los que el pueblo crea! ¡La diferencia que hay entre una rosa de papel y otra natural!": Lorca, *Obras completas* 3:208.

7 "Los poetas que hacen cantares populares enturbian las claras linfas del verdadero corazón; y ¡cómo se nota en las coplas el ritmo seguro y feo del hombre que sabe gramáticas! Se debe tomar del pueblo nada más que sus últimas esencias y algún que otro trino colorista, pero nunca querer imitar fielmente sus modulaciones inefables": 3:208.

8 Actually, the title came to Falla late. Nancy Lee Harper, *Interpretation of Fantasía bætica*, writes, "The adjective *bætica* was added when, in 1922, Chester publishers wanted a more descriptive title. Falla was adamant about the spelling with the diphthong in order to show the ancient Roman name of Andalusia that included the areas of southern Iberian Estremadura and some parts of Portugal."

9 "traduciendo y sintetizando en un lenguaje moderno los rasgos musicales de los cantaores y bailaores, los giros ornamentales y rítmicos de la guitarra, y la simulación de las modulaciones microtonales y gamas del *cante jondo*": *Acercamiento a Falla* 13.

10 "Occidente y Oriente en pugna, que hacen de Bética una isla de cultura": 3:221.

11 Nancy Lee Harper, *Interpretation of Fantasía bætica*, identifies Debussy's *Jardins dans la pluie* (opening) in *Fantasía bætica*, measures 54–7; *L'Isle joyeuse* (ending) in measures 157–66; the *String Quartet* in measures 97–8; and *La Sérenade interrompue* (B–C–B harmonic pattern) in measures 34–46. The influence of Debussy was present in *Fantasía* before it received its final title (see n. 8, above).

12 The Sriraga scale, according to Lucas (17), consists of G–A–B–C–D–E–F, with G, B, C, and F able to vary a quarter tone at the artist's will. I employ Falla's personal copy of Lucas.

13 By 1919, however, the "savagery" reflects Falla's study of Stravinsky's and Bartók's pianistic stylization of folklore. The "running notes" mentioned by Harper may refer to the widespread impact of the Ballets Russes on this piece (as well as previously on the ballet *Sombrero*). *Fantasía bætica* is all Falla's Andalusianism in synthesis.

14 "El cante jondo se ha venido cultivando desde tiempo inmemorial, y a todos los viajeros ilustres que se han aventurado a recorrer nuestros variados y extraños paisajes les han emocionado esas profundas salmodias que, desde los picos de Sierra Nevada hasta los olivares sedientos de Córdoba y desde la Sierra de Cazorla hasta la alegrísima desembocadura del Guadalquivir, cruzan y definen nuestra única y complicadísima Andalucía": 3:201–2.

15 "torrecillas/ muertas sobre los estanques": *PCJ* 152, ll. 19–22.

16 "Granada es como la narración de lo que ya pasó en Sevilla. Hay un vacío de cosa definitivamente acabada": 3:253.

17 Lorca remarks, "En Granada se pasean los fantasmas por sus dos palacios vacíos" [In Granada ghosts go walking through its two empty palaces]: 3:322. Cf. Ganivet, *El escultor de su alma*, act II, 72: "Un sueño de largos siglos/ por vuestros muros resbala" [A dream of many centuries/ slips through your walls].

18 "Lo mismo que er fuego fatuo,/ lo mismito es er queré./ Le juyes, y te persigue,/ le yamas y echa a corré": Manuel de Falla, "Chanson du Feu Follet," en *El amor brujo*, score, 65–9. Since Lorca helped stage *El amor brujo* at his Residencia de Estudiantes, he would most likely have employed the more mature, 1916 version.

19 "¡Quién dirá que el agua lleva/ un fuego fatuo de gritos!": *PCJ* 152, ll. 25–6.

20 "Nuestras vidas son los ríos/ que van a dar en el mar/ que es el morir./ Allí van los señoríos/ para derechos a se acabar/ y consumir": Jorge Manrique, *Obra* 116. The transit of the rivers to the sea, symbol of dying, already appears in the passage quoted from the early poem "El Dauro y el Genil." See p. 51, above. Roberta Ann Quance (*Contradiction* 116–17) finds the considerable influence of Manrique's fluvial strophe upon Lorca's *suite* "El regreso" [The return].

3 "Poema de la siguiriya gitana": Return to the Sources of Deep Song

1 "Los efectos armónicos que *inconscientemente* producen nuestros guitarristas, representan una de las maravillas del arte natural": Falla, *"Cante jondo"* 154.

2 Christoforidis informs me of Falla's opinion on the basis of the composer's analysis of guitar scores.

3 "un poder mágico para saber dibujar o medir una siguiriya con acento absolutamente milenario": 3:221.

4 "prosa cantada, destruyendo toda la sensación de ritmo métrico, aunque en realidad son tercetos o cuartetos asonantados sus textos literarios": *PCJ*, 156–7. In Falla's personal notes borrowed by Lorca there appears the following statement: "consigue producir el cante jondo (la siguiriya, especialmente) la impresión de una prosa cantada, destruyendo toda sensación de ritmo métrico, aunque en realidad son versos los que forman su texto literario" [deep song (especially the siguiriya) succeeds in producing the impression of a sung prose, while destroying every sensation of metric rhythm, although in reality it is verses that form its literary text]: cit. in Persia, *I Concurso*, 92.

5 "prosa cantada, de monotonía que se va desarrollando dolorosamente": García Montero, in Lorca, *Poema* (1993) 36.

6 Musicologists identify the following pieces of Falla as imitative of the guitar: the piano solo "Andaluza" of *Cuatro piezas españolas* [Four Spanish pieces]: Demarquez, *Falla* 54–5; "El polo" of *Siete canciones populares españolas* [Seven Spanish folk songs]: Christoforidis, "Folksong models" 19; *El amor brujo* [Love the magician]: Pahissa, *Falla* 96; *Noches en los jardines de España* [Nights in the gardens of Spain]: Demarquez, *Falla* 99; *El sombrero de tres picos*: Molina Fajardo, *Falla y "Conte Jondo"* 23; and *Fantasía bætica*: Trend, *Falla and Spanish Music* 94–5.

7 "Llora por cosas lejanas": *PCJ* 158.

8 "Arena del sur caliente / que busca camelias blancas": *PCJ* 158.

9 "Llora flecha sin blanco": *PCJ* 158.

10 "La tarde sin mañana": *PCJ* 158.

11 "Y el primer pájaro muerto / sobre la rama": *PCJ* 158.

12 "¡Oh guitarra! / Corazón malherido por cinco espadas": *PCJ* 158.

13 "hace llorar a los sueños": *PCJ* 212.

14 "El sollozo de las almas / perdidas": *PCJ* 212.

15 "el enloquecimiento de un ser perdido, que no sabe dónde refugiarse": Demarquez, *Falla* 87. See Combarieu, *La Musique et la magie*, 67.

16 In "Seis cohetes" [Six rockets], dated 8 August 1922 and included in *Suites,* Lorca makes myth with the guitar, seen as a metaphor for fireworks. The six rockets of the title correspond to the six guitar strings: Seis lanzas de

fuego/suben./(La noche es una guitarra.)/Seis sierpes enfurecidas./(Por el
cielo vendrá San Jorge.)/Seis sopletes de oro y viento./(¿Se agrandará la
ampolla/de la noche?) [Six lances of fire/Climb./(The night is a guitar.)/Six
infuriated serpents./(Through the sky will come Saint George.)/Six blowtorches of gold and wind./(Will the blíster of the night/Grow large?)] (1:803).

One metaphor succeeds another in brilliant succession. The sibilant
s- abounds (*Seis*, *suben*, *seis*, *sierpes*, *seis*, *sopletes*) in imitation of rocket hisses.
The six fiery lances, representing the six rockets going off at the same time,
become six strings of a nocturnal guitar in colour and in shape, adorning the
sky with visual music in its harmony of forms. As the rockets rise, their gigantic shapes become snaky. Lorca's gift for myth-making appears in the anticipa-
tion of Saint George's slaying of the heavenly dragon of light. When the ascending sparks start following a horizontal path, they resemble blowtorches of
gold fire blown by the wind. The final metaphor brings the sky down to earth
as if it possessed vulnerable flesh, a humbling also seen in *PCJ*, with its refrain,
"Land of light,/Sky of earth" [Tierra de luz/cielo de tierra] (*PCJ* 164, 166).

17 "Las voces y gritos con que nuestro pueblo anima y excita a los 'cantaores'
    y 'tocaores' tienen también origen en la costumbre que aún se observa para
    casos análogos en las razas de origen oriental": Manuel de Falla, *"Cante
    jondo"* 146.
18 Falla, *Vie brève*, act 2, tableau 2, sc. 3, rehearsal 139, p. 36; act 2, tableau 2,
    sc. 1, rehearsal 159, p. 31.
19 To the end of the Murcian folk tune "El paño moruno" [The Moorish cloth],
    the first of the *Siete canciones populares españolas*, Falla has added an eight-bar
    "¡Ay!" not present in the source he consulted (Hess, *Passions*, 66). A like
    musical outburst appears in *La vida breve*, act 2, at the beginning of the soleá
    sung by the cantaor at Paco and Carmela's wedding (Manuel de Falla, *Vie
    brève*, act 2, tableau 1, sc. 1, rehearsal 101, p. 30), and in *El amor brujo*, at the
    start (and later at different expressive points) of Candelas's "Canción del
    amor dolido" [Song of aching love]. In the *Fantasía bætica*, in a measure
    marked *fortissimo ma dolce*, J.B. Trend hears the piano imitate a cantaor's
    prolonged "¡Ay!" before he launches into his *copla*. Trend, *Falla and Spanish
    Music* 95; Manuel de Falla, *Fantasía*, score, m. 126, 10.
20 "La elipse de un grito/va de monte/a monte": *PCJ* 161.
21 "gama oral": Falla, *"Cante jondo"* 144; Lorca, *Obras completas* 3:199.
22 "Las más infinitas gradaciones del Dolor y de la Pena, puestas al servicio de la
    expresión más pura y exacta, laten en los tercertos y cuartetos de la siguiriya y
    sus derivados": 3:205.
23 "Desde los olivos/será un arco negro/sobre la noche azul": *PCJ* 161. Cf. the
    suite "Arco de lunas" [Arch of moons]: "Un arco de lunas negras/sobre el

mar sin movimiento. // Mis hijos que no han nacido / me persiguen" [An arch of black moons/over the motionless sea. // My unborn sons / Pursue me." 1, 915. These arches may stand for arches of a grave or mausoleum in a poem lamenting the lyric subject's sterility.

24 "En la página 35, número 1, la flauta grave dibuja ... el balanceo de una malagueña, punteado por la *vocalización* de las violas": Demarquez, *Falla* 96.

25 "Como un arco de viola / el grito ha hecho vibrar / largas cuerdas del viento": *PCJ* 162.

26 "El grito deja en el viento / una sombra de ciprés": *PCJ* 179. The cypress shadow metaphor also appears in "Canción de reflejo" [Reflection song], *Suites* (Lorca, *Obras completas* 1:689), where it seems to have the same fatalistic meaning.

27 "El horizonte sin luz / está mordido de hogueras": *PCJ* 179.

28 "Todo se ha roto en el mundo. / No queda más que el silencio": *PCJ* 179.

29 In *Siete canciones populares españolas*, a measure comprised of a whole-note rest follows the final "¡Ay!" of "El paño moruno": Falla, *Seven Spanish Folk-Songs*, score, 4. Three whole-note rests follow the initial "¡Ay" of *Polo* and a measure of a whole-note rest goes after the final "¡Ay!," with rests of different length after the middle "!Ay!"'s except one, without any rest: 28–32. Falla's care in orchestrating the screams shows their symbolic importance, while his meticulousness in measuring rests displays his regard for them. Even in his early opera *La vida breve* he carefully indicated lack of sound in the score. At the start of the soleá in act 2, in honour of the bride and groom at their wedding, a precisely measured series of rests follows the singer's initial sung "¡Ay!": Falla, *Vie brève*, act 2, tableau 1, sc. 1.

30 "Oye, hijo mío, el silencio. / Es un silencio ondulado, / un silencio, / donde resbalan valles y ecos / y que inclina las frentes hacia el suelo": *PCJ* 163.

31 María Moliner, *Diccionario de uso* 2:656, *Diccionario de la Real Academia Española* 1093.

32 "mariposas negras": *PCJ* 164.

33 "blanca serpiente / de niebla": *PCJ* 164.

34 "la niebla invisible que la rodea": 3:478.

35 "Va encadenada al temblor / de un ritmo que nunca llega": *PCJ* 165n9–10.

36 "¿Adónde vas, siguiriya, / con un ritmo sin cabeza?": *PCJ* 165.

37 "¿Qué luna recogerá / tu dolor de cal y adelfa?": *PCJ* 166; cf. *Bodas de sangre* [Blood weddings], in Lorca, *Obras completas* 2:777, where the moon yearns to fill its cheeks with the "sweet blood" of a victim. In *Diván del Tamarit* [Divan of the Tamarit], 1:585, the poetic voice asks, "¿Qué luna gris de las nueve / te desangró la mejilla?" [What grey, nine o'clock moon / drained your cheek of blood?].

38 In "El grito" [The scream], the refrain is simply "¡Ay!": *PCJ* 161, 162; in "El paso de la siguiriya" [Passage of the siguiriya], it is "Tierra de luz,/cielo de tierra" [Land of light,/sky of land]: 164, 166; in "Y después" [And after that], it is "(Sólo queda/el desierto)" [(Only the desert/is left)]: 168, 169.

39 "Pero la melodía de la siguiriya se pierde en el sentido horizontal, se nos escapa de las manos y la vemos alejarse hacia un punto de aspiración común y pasión perfecta donde el alma no logra desembarcar": 3:218.

4 "Poema de la soleá": Consciousness-Raising of Pain in Lorca and Falla

1 "La tradición del arabesco de la Alhambra, complicado y de pequeño ámbito, pesa en todos los grandes artistas de aquella tierra": *Obras completas* 3:133.

2 Falla, *Sombrero,* score, rehearsal 15, pp. 45–6. García Matos, "Folklore en Falla, I," 61, identifies this music as a soleá.

3 Falla composed a soleá, today lost, which was to have been sung in Gregorio Martínez Sierra's two-act-play *La pasión* [Passion, 1914] by a character who is a Gypsy actress from and in Madrid: Hess, *Passions* 304; another soleá, as we saw in *Sombrero,* belongs to the Miller's Wife, a Navarrese woman living in the Andalusian city of Guádix; and a third receives a nasal rendering at the Granadan wedding scene in *La vida breve,* act 2, 1st tableau, sc. 1, rehearsals 103, 109, p. 31.

4 "Tierra/de la muerte sin ojos/y las flechas": *PCJ* 172–3.

5 "operarios y agentes activos de que lo musical, de que lo audible esté siendo oído en acto: sea música en acto": García Bacca, *Filosofía* 478.

6 "una veleta ideal que cambia de dirección con el aire del tiempo": 3:208.

7 "¡Oh pueblo perdido,/en la Andalucía del llanto!": *PCJ* 174–5.

8 Falla, *Sombrero,* score, rehearsal 35, pp. xiv, 57 *PCJ* 8; Budwig, "Evolution of Three-Cornered Hat" 196.

9 Hess, *Passions* 114; Budwig, "Evolution of Three-Cornered Hat" 194; Demarquez, *Falla* 110; Manuel de Falla, *Sombrero,* score, rehearsal 3, pp. 38–41.

10 In my article "Married Temptresses," I try to show Lorca's imitation of plot and dramatic structure of Falla's *Sombrero* in his libretto *Lola.* Moreover, in 1921 Lorca and Adolfo Salazar planned to interest Diaghilev and Massine in Andalusian puppet theatre so as to produce a ballet on the Andalusian Punch Don Cristóbal for the Ballets Russes: Weber, "*Los Títeres de Cachiporra,*" in Zapke, *Tradición y vanguardia* 120.

11 "Ni tú ni yo estamos/en disposición/de encontrarnos": *PCJ* 187. According to Morris, *Son of Andalusia* 210–11, the two adversaries are a masculine speaker and his female interlocutor. Still, in Lorca's neighbouring poem "Pueblo," hostile

male characters pass disguised among one another (*PCJ* 174). Also, the playwright Lorca sympathizes with cuckolded husbands: *Amor de Don Perlimplín*
(1924) and *La zapatera prodigiosa* (1930). Hence, my reading seems as plausible
as Morris's, *Son of Andalusia*. The poem admits either interpretation.

12 "Tú … por lo que ya sabes./¡Yo la he querido tanto!": *PCJ* 187.

13 "En las manos,/tengo los agujeros/de los clavos./¿No ves cómo me estoy/
desangrando?": *PCJ* 187.

14 "Sigue esa veredita": *PCJ* 187.

15 "No mires nunca atrás": *PCJ* 187.

16 "vete despacio": *PCJ* 187.

17 *PCJ* 187. This command could conceal a veiled threat to exercise prudence
lest a disaster take place between the two men.

18 Why would Lorca have referred to *La vida breve* if Falla himself was not
completely well disposed towards his early opera? Whenever the controversial composer appeared written up in the Spanish press, his entire (limited)
production underwent judgment anew. Lorca's friend the music critic Adolfo
Salazar, who loved Falla's music, did not distinguish that opera from the rest
of his works in quality (Hess, *Modernism* 253–4). His favourable reputation
in Paris also included the pre-First World War triumph of *La vida breve*
(245), and Belgium applauded the opera as late as 1923 (Salazar, "Vida breve"
69), whatever Falla's opinion of himself. Lorca's correspondence shows that
he joyfully kept abreast of Falla's acclaim abroad.

19 Falla, *Vie brève*, act 2, tableau 1, sc. 2, program, rehearsal 111, pp. 33–4. In act
2, tableau 2, sc. 2, p. 191, Salud, using final stressed ó of third person preterit,
sings about her faithless lover Paco, "¡Me perdió! ¡Me engañó! ¡Me dejó!"
[He ruined me! He deceived me! He left me!"]. The young Falla, with his
librettist and collaborator Carlos Fernández Shaw, musically exploits the
dramatic power of the stressed o.

20 "Sorprenderse, extrañarse, es comenzar a entender": *La rebelión de las masas*
144.

21 *PCJ* 182. On the hardness of the stops **k** and **p** in Spanish, see Navarro
Tomás, *Fonología española* 195.

22 Cf. Collins, "Falla and Natural Resonance" 77: "The prevalence of major
triads at final cadences in Falla's music (both of entire works and of individual
movements within them) is extraordinary."

23 "Piensa que el mundo es chiquito/y el corazón es inmenso": *PCJ* 183.

24 "Se dejó el balcón abierto/y al alba por el balcón/desembocó todo el cielo":
PCJ 184.

25 "tierra de cielo": *PCJ* 164, 166.

26 "¡Ayayayayay,/que vestida con mantos negros!": *PCJ* 184.

27 "En la voz entrecortada / van sus ojos": *PCJ* 185.
28 "Torres altas y hombres / misteriosos": *PCJ* 185.
29 Falla, *L'amour sorcier*, "Final: Las campanas del amanecer," program, rehearsal 40, 74.
30 *PCJ* 190.
31 "Las niñas de España, / de pie menudo / y temblorosas faldas, / que han llenado de luces / las encrucijadas": *PCJ* 189–90.
32 "los remotos / países de la pena": *PCJ* 192.
33 "un laberinto. / Amor, cristal y piedra": *PCJ* 193.

5 "Poema de la saeta" : The Oblation of Pain in Seville

1 Manuel and Antonio Machado, *Obras completas* 295. Machado exercises poetic licence in omitting from consideration Mary's son Christ crucified, the other dedicatee of saetas.
2 "Sólo en la bacanal místico-profana de la Semana Santa en Sevilla se oía apenas la saeta, patético lamento musical de la muerte de Cristo, pero aún la misma saeta había sufrido las influencias de la degeneración flamenca": *Federico García Lorca* 160.
3 "Al Poeta de las Andalucías Federico García Lorca, su amigo de verdad Manuel de Falla. Granada 28-11-21": Falla, *El amor brujo. Love the Magician* (London: J. & W. Chester, 1921), n. p., present in the Fundación Federico García Lorca (Madrid). See musical example 10.
4 "el último papa del cante jondo": *Obras completas* 3:222.
5 Although Lorca mentions her along with Franconetti among the masters of the *siguiriya gitana* (ibid.), when Falla heard her sing saetas during Holy Week in Seville in 1922, he found her corrupted by flamenco commercialism (Armero, *Falla* 156).
6 "imitación del canto de las aves, del grito de los animales y de los infinitos ruidos de la materia": Falla, "*Cante jondo*" 144; the same quotation of Lucas appears in Federico García Lorca, "El canto jondo. Primitivo canto andaluz," in 3:200.
7 "El universo natural no ha sido hecho tal ni *por* el hombre ni *para* el hombre, mientras que el mundo (...) de sones ha sido hecho, inventado, *por* el hombre y *para* el hombre": García Bacca 465.
8 "la constelación de la saeta": *PCJ* 194, n. 1–2.
9 Falla once wished to set to music José Zorrilla's famous drama *Don Juan Tenorio*. In 1917 he wrote to his librettist María Lejárraga about garden scenery from Seville to be used in the production: Gallego, *Manuel de Falla y El amor brujo* 69. However, he gave up the project and in the 1930s wrote

"Reservado" on the front of the book (reserved reading only with permission of his confessor) because of religious scruples: Christoforidis, "A Composer's Annotations" 38; José Zorrilla, *La leyenda de Don Juan Tenorio*.

10 Lorca experiences the child as "the first spectacle of Nature" ("el primer espectáculo de la Naturaleza": 3:287). On the agility of the child's fantasy, see "Canción tonta" [Nonsense song] from *Canciones* [Songs], 1:304.

11 On the keen interest in Albéniz of the *Rinconcillo*, Lorca's daily conversation group, see ch. 7, n. 19.

12 Isaac Albéniz, "Fête-Dieu à Seville," en *Iberia*, vol. I, no. 3, pp. 16–34.

13 Christian de Paepe, in *PCJ* 198nn9–10, relates Lorca's Durandante and Orlando the Furious (Ariosto, canto 23) to Don Quixote. The interpretation of Durandarte and the suffering Christ as alter egos of Don Quixote is mine.

14 "Nuestro Señor Don Quixote": Miguel de Unamuno, *Del sentimiento trágico* 503. In a 1934 interview Lorca exclaims, "¡Qué grande es Unamuno! ¡Cuánto sabe y cuánto crea! El primer Español" [How great Unamuno is! How much he knows and how much he creates! The first and foremost Spaniard]: 3:607.

15 In Don Quixote's dreamlike vision of Durandarte, the magician Merlin (mentioned in Lorca's poem) has enchanted Durandarte, his beloved Belerma, and Don Quixote's lady Dulcinea. Neither Durandarte can unhex Belerma, nor Don Quixote Dulcinea: Cervantes, *Don Quijote* 734–6.

16 In Don Quixote's dreamlike vision of Durandarte, the magician Merlin (mentioned in Lorca's poem) has enchanted Durandarte, his beloved Belerma, and Don Quixote's lady Dulcinea. Neither Durandarte can unhex Belerma, nor Don Quixote Dulcinea: Cervantes, *Don Quijote* 734–6. *Don Quixote*, part 2, may be serving as Lorca's poetic exhortation to Falla to complete his puppet opera *Retablo*, based on *Don Quixote*, part 2, ch. 26. His patron the Princess de Polignac's deadline for completion, July 1919, had come and gone: Hess, *Modernism* 199–200. Falla, an indefatigable literary researcher for his own music, surely understood Lorca's aim.

17 On the image of the lily of Judea: *PCJ* 201n3; on the image of the carnation of Spain: 201n4.

18 *PCJ* 203. During a Holy Week visit to Seville in 1921, Stravinsky, encouraged by Diaghilev, after seeing local songs and rhythms, mentioned his plan to write a flamenco opera based on Rossini's *Barber of Seville*, yet never did: Christoforidis, "Acercamiento" 15; Stephen Walsh, *Stravinsky* 328. When in Paris, Falla himself had told Debussy that he wanted to write a new *Barbiere di Siviglia*, which Debussy thought a "magnificent idea" but which Falla's friend Dukas discouraged: Pahissa, *Falla* 118; Christoforidis "Ópera" 363n5.

19 "Pero como el amor / los saeteros / están ciegos": *PCJ* 205.

20 In *Noches*, for example, no transition exists between the end of the second nocturne and the beginning of the third, since both, despite their different

tempos, share the same rehearsal number 22, stressing their continuity in the composer's mind (Falla, *Noches*, 2, score, rehearsal 22, 56–7).

21 "lanza sus flechas de oro, que se clavan en nuestro corazón. En medio de la sombra es como un formidable arquero azul cuya aljaba no se agota jamás": 3:208.

6 "Gráfico de la Petenera" and Fallas' Guitar Elegy to Debussy

1 My deepest thanks to Dr Michael J. McGrath, Editor of Juan de la Cuesta Monographs, for granting me permission to reproduce, with changes, in this chapter my article "Lorca's Dialogue with Falla in 'Gráfico de la Petenera,'" which appeared in *A Confluence of Words. Studies in Honor of Robert Lima*, edited by Wayne H. Finke and Barry J. Luby (Hispanic Monographs, Newark, Delaware, 2011), 357–70.

2 Lorca, "Petenera," *Intentions* 3, nos. 23–4 (1924): 31–4. The dedication "A Manuel de Falla" appears on p. 31, and there is missing a translation of the poem "Falsete."

3 José Rey de la Torre provides information given to him by Francisco García Lorca on the creative process of Falla's *Homenaje* in 1920, when Falla consulted guitarist Miguel Llobet in the García Lorca household. In a master lesson structured like a 1976 interview with Walter Spalding, Rey de la Torre remarked, "The piece, as you know, is strange … there is a dichotomy, a strange combination of factors, because it's a dirge, an elegy (…) Supposedly a sad thing, dedicated to the 'Tombeau,' his [Debussy's] grave; but on the other hand, there is the *habanera* rhythm which is not sad – it was considered almost lascivious at the time. So the combination of this funereal feeling and the Habanera together, is very strange. It's not a chordal thing – the traditional funeral march where the whole feeling is very heavy and almost arrhythmic. There is the contradiction of the rhythm itself, the Habanera, combined with the feeling of grief." John Dimmick, *Guitar.com Blog*: http://www.guitarist.com/blog/2008/07/rey-de-la-torre-discusses-manuel-de.html. A similar combination of feelings, elegiac but sensuous, appears in "Muerte de la Petenera."

4 "No se puede usted imaginar cómo le recuerdo cuando toco la guitarra y quiero *sacar* ¡a la fuerza! su maravilloso Homenaje a Debussy, del que no consigo más que las primeras notas: ¡es verdaderamente gracioso! Mi madre se desespera y esconde la guitarra en el sitio más raro de la casa": Lorca *Epistolario* 1:107–8.

5 "la esencia misma de la música española": *Escritos* 71.

6 "la evocación del embrujo de Andalucía": 71.

7 "nos hace el efecto de imágenes reflejadas al claro de luna sobre el agua limpia de las albercas que llenan la Alhambra": 71.

8 Cf. 3:203–4, with even more vivid description than Falla: "en la vaga y tierna *Soirée dans Grenade*, (…) están acusados, a mi juicio, todos los temas emocionales de la noche granadina, la lejanía azul de la vega, la Sierra saludando el tembloroso Mediterráneo, el rubato admirable de la ciudad y los alucinantes juegos del agua subterránea [in the vague, tender *Soirée en Granade* (…), in my judgment, are acknowledged all the emotional themes of the Granadan night, the blue remoteness of the lowland, the Sierra greeting the trembling Mediterranean, the admirable *rubato* of the city and the dazzling play of underground water]."

9 Miller, *Lorca's Poema del cante jondo* 37, quoting the *petenera* in Antonio Machado y Álvarez, *Cantes flamencos*; cf. *PCJ* 217n6.

10 From the sonnet "Epitalamio ancestral," *Las clepsidras*, cit. in Max Henríquez Ureña 265. My English translation.

11 Manuel de Falla, *L'amour sorcier*, program, rehearsal 11, Example 14, p. 68. In program notes of 1915, Falla refers to the "coloration and (…) evocation of primitive Arab instruments" ("colorido y […] evocación de los primitivos instrumentos árabes") in *El amor brujo: Homenaje que el Ateneo de Madrid dedica a los compositores D. Manuel de Falla y D. Joaquín Turina*, 15 Jan. 1915, p. 10.

12 Stravinsky begins this phase with the ballet *Pulcinella* (composed 1919–20), on a *commedia dell'arte* theme, associated with hand puppetry (Punch and Judy): Kennedy, *Concise Oxford Dictionary of Music* 446. Stravinsky's Pulcinella is "resurrected." With metaphor, Lorca attempts a "resurrection" of his puppet-like character Petenera: She and all her lovers lack life, and the most alive character of this poetic section is Death!

13 With Maurer, "Two Critical Editions": 223–7, and Christina Karageorgou-Bastea, *Arquitectura* 163n44, I agree that the title of this poem is "Falsete" (= the voice unnaturally forced higher), and not "Falseta," as de Paepe reads: *PCJ* 219n1.

14 "a ciertos hombres, contra anatomía y fisiología, el oficio instrumental de soprano, alto, tenor, bajo": García Bacca, *Filosofía de la música* 520.

15 For musical example 10: Falla, *El amor brujo*, score, 3–6 ("Introducción y Escena"); for musical example 11: 9 ("En la Cueva. La Noche").

16 "Pantomima" 75. The four ascending notes turn out to be the first four notes of the *tanguillo* (or *guajira*) danced by Candelas and her new lover Carmelo. By dancing with him, she triumphs over the ghost of her former lover.

17 García Bacca compares a melody to a curve: *Filosofía de la música* 736. Declarative sentences (predominating in "Gráfico de la Petenera") may be diagrammed as arches with almost flat curves: Tomás Navarro Tomás, *Manual de pronunciación española*, §234, p. 257. Such arches may be plotted on graphs of three pitches, the high, middle, and low: T. Navarro Tomás,

Manual de entonación española, 291, with middle and low pitches prevailing
for declarative sentences: 293.

18 Since the beginning of his poetic production Lorca has associated orange
blossoms with brides. See "El encanto del azahar de las novias" [The charm of
the orange-blossoms of brides], dated 30 April 1918: Lorca, *Poesía inédita* 226.

19 On stops *k* and *t* as "consonantes fuertes y sordas" [strong, mute consonants]:
Tomás Navarro, *Estudios de fonología españo*la 197. The repetition of "canta"
enables the tip of the tongue to touch the back of the lower teeth with a
regularity imitating the clapper of a bell. This impression is helped by the
openness and brillance of the *a* in contact with the reonant nasal *n*. On the
sonoridad of *a* +*n* see our "Introduction," n. 59.

20 Lorca's father loved to play guitar and sing flamenco, and his older son the
poet would imitate him. Many evenings at the end of the workday, Don
Federico García Rodriguez sang siguiriyas, soleares, and *peteneras*, among
other genres (Molina Fajardo, *Falla y "cante jondo"* 62–3). Falla's *peteneras*
include Danza 2 of *La vida breve* (Demarquez, *Falla* 67) and the fifth motif
of *Noches*. See introduction, musical example 2, and Demarquez 99.

7 Openness to Death in Flamenco Artists and in Southern Cities

1 In the stage direction in the prologue to this play, Lorca writes, "Telón
representando el desaparecido arco árabe de las Cucharas y perspectiva de la
plaza Bibarrambla, en Granada, encuadrado en un margen amarillento, como
una vieja estampa iluminada" [Curtain representing the long-gone Arab Arch
of the Knives and perspective of the Bibarrambla Plaza in Granada, framed in
a yellowish border, like an old illuminated lithograph]: *Obras completas*
2:165.

2 "Por lo demás, nuestros mayores seguían viviendo a la antigua usanza
española, sumamente despacio, apegados a sus rancias costumbres ... con su
Inquisición y sus frailes" [Nonetheless our forebears went on living in the old
Spanish style, extremely slowly, attached to their stale customs, with their
Inquisition and their friars]: Alarcón, *Sombrero de tres picos* 67. In the young
Alarcón, a liberal who later became conservative, and Falla, a liberal with
pious leanings, the irony is never total.

3 "intérpretes del alma popular que destrozaron su propia alma entre las
tempestades del sentimiento": Lorca, *Obras completas* 3:216.

4 "En el cante jondo (...) lo que hay que buscar siempre, hasta encontrarlo,
es el tronco negro de Faraón": *PCJ* 231; Alberti, *Federico García Lorca* 58–9.

5 "un profundo sentido religioso": 3:222.

6 "un solemne rito, saca las viejas esencias dormidas y las lanza al viento
envueltas en su voz": 3:222.

7 "La densa miel de Italia/con el limón nuestro,/iba en el hondo llanto/del siguiriyero": PCJ 233.

8 "Su grito fue terrible./Los viejos/dicen que se erizaban/los cabellos./y se abría el azogue/de los espejos": *PCJ* 233.

9 "Pasaba por los tonos/sin romperlos": *PCJ* 233.

10 "Era la misma/pena cantando/detrás de una sonrisa": *PCJ* 235.

11 "Evoca los limonares/de Malaga la dormida,/y hay en su llanto dejos/de sal marina": *PCJ* 236.

12 Quise llegar adonde/llegaron los buenos./¡Y he llegado, Dios mío! .../Pero luego.../un velón y una manta/en el suelo": *PCJ* 240.

13 "Limoncito amarillo/limonero./Echad los limoncitos/al viento": *PCJ* 240.

14 The Spanish word for jellyfish is "medusa." Since Lorca's initial m- resembles a capital in script, most critics, guided by other poems, here interpret "medusa" as the mythical Gorgon Medusa, whose snaky locks may suggest a deep-song dancer's serpentine motion. Yet I am inclined to interpret "medusa" as the marine animal, since the poem also refers to other animals – the mole and the butterfly – to depict the dancer's graceful hand movements. *PCJ* 241. Let the readers decide, collaborating with an ambiguous poet as they would wish.

15 "As de bastos./Tijeras en cruz": *PCJ* 241.

16 "Cuando yo me muera,/mira que te encargo:/que con la jebra de tu pelo negro/me amarres las manos": cit. from Pemartín in Miller 28–9. Lorca quotes a variant of this siguiriya in 3:213. For soleá form, cf. Falla, *Vie brève*, act 2, tableau 1, sc. 1, rehearsal 103, 31.

17 Manuel de Falla, *L'amour sorcier* (1915), score, rehearsal 7, p. 63.

18 Of Granada's twelve pieces, the second ("Orientale"), third ("Fandango"), fifth ("Andaluza"), eleventh ("Zambra"), and twelfth ("Arabesca") have an Andalusian orientation. In Albéniz, the "Evocación" and "Almería" are the only pieces with a non-Andalusian theme. Falla's *Piezas españolas* (1907) also present the essences of different Hispanic locales through folk motifs. We reserve discussion of these pieces for ch. 10 (see n. 1), since they explicitly involve *Volksgeist* theory, and so does that entire chapter.

19 "pero el acierto genial lo tuvo Isaac Albéniz empleando en su obra los fondos líricos del canto andaluz": 3:204. Albéniz enjoyed a following among cultivated Granadan youth in the 1920s . To commemorate Albéniz's stay in the Alhambra in 1882, Lorca's discussion group the *Rinconcillo* in 1923 laid a tile designed by one of their members, Hermenegildo Lanz, and saying, "A Isaac Albéniz, que vivió en la Alhambra. Primavera de 1882" [To Isaac Albéniz, who lived in the Alhambra. Spring 1882] (Viñes Millet, *Alhambra* 135).

20 From de Paepe's reconstruction of the publishing process, it appears that the poems on Malaga and Seville were published in the same collection of poems

in 1927 coupled together, and that the one on Cordoba joins them finally to form the section "Tres ciudades" of the complete *Poema del cante jondo*, published by Ulises (Madrid, 1931); *PCJ* 30, 66, 68.

21 "Pasan caballos negros / y gente siniestra / por los hondos caminos / de la guitarra": *PCJ* 246.

22 Albéniz, "Córdoba," op. 232, no. 4, in *Chants d'Espagne*, Madrid Unión Musical Ediciones, cit. in Tinnell, *Lorca y la música* 405.

23 Falla, "*Cante jondo*" 142. Lorca, in "*El cante jondo. Primitivo canto anda-luz*," 3:196, does not explicitly mention the *sevillana* as a flamenco form. Perhaps he knew that the *sevillana* was a daughter of the Castilian *seguidilla*: Kennedy, *Concise Oxford Dictionary of Music* 588.

24 "Del concepto que hoy se forma de España," in Juan Valera, *Obras completas* 3:743, cit in. Hess, *Modernism* 137–8.

25 *PCJ* 251. On the sevillana as a dance: Tony Bryant, "Sevillana," http://www .andalucia.com/flamenco/sevillana.htm.

26 Carmen's situation resembles the speaker's in the poem "Claro de reloj" [A clearing for the clock], originally written for *Suites*, later published in *Primeras canciones* [First songs, 1922] (cf. Quance, *Contradiction* 116). Having sat down in a clearing of white silence, the lyric subject finds himself caught inside an awesome ring or circle where stars collide with twelve black numbers (the face of a clock): thinking to escape time, we find ourselves fatally imprisoned within it: 1:265. Lorca dramatizes the problem in *Así que pasen cinco años* [If five years pass, 1931] and *Doña Rosita la soltera* [Doña Rosita, the spinster, 1935].

8 "Seis caprichos" or Virtuosity and Art at a Distance

1 Lorca's poem "Capricho" from "Castillo de fuegos artificiales quemado con motivo del cumpleaños del poeta" [Castle of fireworks set off to celebrate the poet's birthday] *Suites* (1:807), fits this definition: it is short, quick, and skilfully made, alternating the sounds of fireworks ("¡Tris!," "¡Tras!") with an individual's unsuccessful attempt to dazzle a female with his maleness, a comic treatment of rigid gender roles. Neither "fireworks" show succeeds because she keeps her eyes shut. Cf. Debussy's piano *Prelude* No. 12, Bk. 2, "Feu d'artifice," with regularly recurring single percussive notes to represent fireworks bursting. Also cf. Lorca's suite "Caprichos": 1:683–5. The "caprices" in the present chapter all have to do with music, although not all Lorca's caprices do.

2 "Yo me permito aconsejar a cuantos quieran hacer música estrictamente nacional, que oigan las que podríamos llamar orquestas populares (en mi tierra, las guitarras, los palillos y los panderos), y sólo en ellas encontrarán esa

anhelada tradición" [I take the liberty of advising whoever may wish to compose strictly national music to hear what we could call folk orchestras (in my native land, guitarras, musical sticks, and tambourines), and only in them will they find the tradition for which they yearn]: Falla, *Escritos* 60.

3　"Y estas tribus [gitanas] venidas (…) de Oriente son las que, a nuestro juicio, dan al cante andaluz la nueva modalidad en que consiste el cante jondo [and these (Gypsy) tribes come (…) from the Orient are those that, in our judgment, give Andalusian song the new modality of which deep song consists]": Falla, "*Cante jondo*" 141.

4　In the *Daily Mail* (London), 19 July 1919, Falla speaks of the "special music implicit in our Spanish scene, in the gait and speech of our folk, in the outline of our hills": Hess, *Falla and Modernism* 69.

5　"La cueva está sola y oscura, pero en el fondo se ve un camino de montaña con chumberas y malezas, iluminado por la luz de la luna": Falla, *Sorcier*, tableau 2, program, rehearsal 8, "Introducción (El fuego fatuo)," 67.

6　Manuel Fernández Galiano, "Los dioses de Federico," *Cuadernos Hispano-americanos*, no. 217 (1968): 35, cit. in Miller, *Lorca's Poema del cante jondo* 114n202; *PCJ* 259n1.

7　Daphne fled Apollo, who loved her and changed her into the laurel: *PCJ* 260n7.

8　To prevent him from committing suicide: *PCJ* 260.

9　"Dafne y Atis / saben de tu dolor": *PCJ* 260.

10　"¡Qué bien estás / bajo la media luna!": *PCJ* 260.

11　"¡Qué bien estás / amenazando el viento!": *PCJ* 260.

12　"Candeliya, que ardía na más que pa tí, y que te deja a oscuras pa in secula seculorum!": Falla, *Sorcier*, program, rehearsal 16 (Final. Las campanas del amanecer), 74.

13　Zoroastrianism teaches that Ahura Mazda presides over the Kingdom of Light or the good and that Angra Mainyu personifies evil or the forces of darkness. Zoroaster's hymns to Ahura Mazda seek the guarantee of divine protection and the triumph of goodness: Oxtoby, "Zoroastrianism" 988.

14　"Punto final del camino": *PCJ* 257.

9　Falla on Deep Song and Lorca's *Romancero gitano*

1　For Luis Buñuel's impassioned negative opinions on *Romancero gitano*, opinions influenced by Dalí, see Ian Gibson, *Federico García Lorca. A Life* 220, *Caballo azul* 190.

2　Lorca was not alone in modernizing folk song for verse, since other members of his generation, among them Rafael Alberti, Manuel Altolaguirre, and Emilio Prados, did the same. However, in the early 1920s they did not engage in the so-called impure poetic practices for which the author of *Romancero gitano* was excoriated by his contemporaries.

3 "Los autores de esta farsa dejan que cada uno de los espectadores resuelva el caso en el sentido que mejor le agrade": cit. in Hess, *Passions* 105.

4 "lleva en sus notas la desnuda y escalofriante emoción de las primeras razas orientales": *Obras completas* 3:197. I use the word "chilling" to translate *escalofriante*, but it is a mere approximation. Lorca refers to the deep shuddering we feel when we directly perceive something ancient, which seems to transport us to the beginning of time. The feeling is so deep that it seems to reach the marrow of our bones. Seeing the Egyptian pyramids or drawings in prehistoric cave dwellings can produce that sensation.

5 "la Pena que se filtra en el tuétano de los huesos y en la savia de los árboles": 3:340.

6 "un carácter tan íntimo, tan propio, tan nacional, que lo hace inconfundible": Falla, "*Cante jondo*" 146; to the same effect, Lorca 3:198.

7 "alma de nuestra alma": 3:201.

8 "las modulaciones tristes y el grave orientalismo de nuestro cante influye desde Granada en Moscú": 3:203.

9 "uno de los más misteriosos del libro": 3:343.

10 Juan Ramón Jiménez, "El romance, río de la lengua española," cit. in García-Posada in Lorca, *Primer romancero* 123n1–4.

11 "Funde y forma una nueva modalidad musical con las aportaciones que ha recibido": 142.

12 This score dates from 1921. Falla autographed it for Lorca with the date November 1921. See musical example 10 in the present volume.

13 "verde carne, pelo verde, / con ojos de fría plata": 1:400, ll. 7–8.

14 "Verde es la niña, tiene / verdes ojos, pelo verde": Juan Ramón Jiménez, cit. Díaz-Plaja, *Federico García Lorca* 119–20.

15 "Mamá. / Yo quiero ser de plata.// Hijo, / tendrás mucho frío": 1:304, ll. 1–4.

16 Association of silver with the moon appears in the poem "La luna asoma" ["The moon comes out"]: "When the moon comes out / with a hundred equal faces, / the silver coin / sobs in the pocket" [Cuando sale la luna / de cien rostros iguales, / la moneda de plata / solloza en el bolsillo]: 1:339, ll. 13–16.

17 "En un prado verde / tendí mi pañuelo / salieron tres rosas / como tres luceros" (In a green meadow / I stretched out my kerchief; / three roses came out / like three morning stars)": Alvar, *Romancero* 244–5.

18 "Trescientas rosas morenas / lleva tu pechera blanca": 1:401, ll. 41–2.

19 "Barandales de la luna / por donde retumba el agua": 1:401. Cf. Cervantes, *Don Quijote*, pt. 1, ch. 20, 180, the adventure of the fulling hammers at night, wherein the hero hears plunging water, which, in his words, "seems to fall

over a cliff and topple from the high hills of the Moon" [parece que se despeña
y derrumba desde los altos montes de la Luna]. In Lorca, "retumba"
phonetically resembles Cervantes's word "derrumba."

20 "Mil panderos de cristal / herían a la madrugada": 1:402, ll. 59–60.

21 "¡Cuantas veces te esperó! / ¡Cuántas veces te esperara, / Cara fresca, negro
pelo, / en esta verde baranda!": 1:402, ll. 69–70.

22 "La noche se puso íntima / como una pequeña plaza": ll. 79–80.

23 "Guardias civiles borrachos / en la puerta golpeaban": ll. 81–2.

24 "Bendita sea por siempre / la Santísima Trinidad, / y guarde al hombre en la
sierra / y el marinero en el mar" [Blessed be forever / The Holy Trinity, / And
may it guard the man in the sierra / And the sailor in the sea], from Lorca's
play *Mariana Pineda*, cit. García-Posada, in Lorca, *Primer romancero*
124nn1–4.

25 For examples of repetitive percussive finales in Falla's Andalusian-style
music, see our discussion of the finale of "La cogida y la muerte" [The goring
and the death] in *Llanto por Ignacio Sánchez Mejías*, analysed in our
"Postlude and Coda," II. Other Works Influenced by Falla.

26 The locution "*those* people" [*la gente aquella*], used by the mother in this
poem (Lorca 1:421, l. 8), repeats virtually the same ironic expression (*aquella
gente*) found in "Preciosa y el aire," where, as we will soon note, it designates
the eccentric Charles Temple's household, situated in a high place of Sacromonte and forming a source of merriment for native Granadans.

27 In *Romancero gitano* youths are often compared to straight reeds: the
Archangel Gabriel is a "beautiful child of rushes" [Un bello niño de junco]:
1:414, l. 1. He prophesies that the Virgin figure, Anunciación de los Reyes,
will have "a child more beautiful / than the stalks in the breeze" [un niño más
bello / que los tallos de la brisa]: 1:415, ll. 45–6. The breeze stands for the soul,
in the following verse: "Brisa y materia juntas en expresión exacta" [Breeze
and matter joined in exact expression]: 1:961, l. 19. Breeze and matter stand
for soul and body, of which the Sacred Host is the exact expression.

28 "En esta parte procuro armonizar lo mitológico gitano con lo puramente
vulgar de los días presentes, y el resultado es extraño, pero creo de una belleza
nueva": 884.

29 "En el corral de una casa de gitanos (…) hay una fragua que tiene, dentro del
asunto, caracteres de símbolo, pues de ella salen voces tristes y canciones
desesperadas, cual si representaran el dolor de la vida reflejado en el continuo
trabajo": Turina, *Enciclopedia* 2:221. According to Pabanó, *Historia de los
gitanos* 27, annotated by Falla and probably consulted as well by Lorca, when
the Gypsies arrived in Europe at the start of the fifteenth century, they at
once devoted themselves to raising horses and donkeys, to the smelting of
ironwork, nails, and other manufactures of iron, to basket making, to the

manufacture of wooden shoes and tubs, and to prospecting for gold in streams. References to all these pursuits appear in *Romancero gitano*.

30   "¡Malhaya el hombre, malhaya, / quien nace con negro sino! / ¡Malhaya quien nace yunque / en vez de nacer martillo!": Falla, *Vie brève* (program) act 1, sc. 1, rehearsal 4, 19.

31   These ballads are "Romance de la pena negra" [Ballad of black pain] (1:408, l. 7) and "Romance del emplazado" [Ballad of the foredoomed man] (423, ll. 18–19).

32   "por técnicos tan profundos como Falla, quien, además, posee una intuición artística de primer orden": 3:296.

33   "El cantaor, echado la cabeza atrás, entorna levemente los ojos y con voz de timbre varonil, bordando el encaje de sus sentimientos, lanza al aire sus trovas": Pabanó, *Historia de los gitanos* 76, from a book found in Falla's personal library collection.

34   "Las cabezas levantadas / y los ojos entornados": 1:394.

35   "Gritos de pájaros agoreros parecen sugerirse en la orquesta cuando aparece Candelas a la puerta de la cueva": Manuel de Falla[?], "El amor brujo." *Homenaje a Falla* (program notes, probably by the composer), part 3, 12.

36   Mora Guarnido, *Lorca* 158. Michael Christoforidis has clarified to me that Lorca and his friends probably helped Falla with the scansion and prosody of the young *trujamán* or puppet-show narrator's discourse.

37   García-Posada, in Lorca, *Primer romancero* 111n3–4. García-Posada mentions Góngora as possible source of the comparison of Preciosa's skin to crystal (a topos also present, however, in Cervantes). The laurel is the plant into which Apollo turned the nymph Daphne, who shunned his amorous advances. Preciosa likewise rejects the godlike wind's overtures. Hence Lorca offers a myth within a myth, giving new depth to Gypsy myth-making.

38   Falla, *Retablo* (score) 98. Elena Torres, "Del cisne al buho" XIV notes that Falla also consulted Galician bagpipe folk sources like the *muñeira* with chorus, "Margaritiña relouca," which may have influenced the "Symphony of Maese Pedro." Michael Christoforidis informs me that the opening fanfare of *Retablo* also evokes Castilian or Arab *dulzainas* (flageolets).

39   Lorca associates Polifemo and Saint Christopher in the *suite* "Estampas del mar" [Sea lithographs]. In the poem "Guardas" [Guards], the poetic voice attributes to the kingdom of the sea two guards, "San Cristóbal / y Polifemo. // ¡Tres ojos / sobre el viajero errante!" [Saint Christopher / and Polyphemus // Three eyes / Upon the wandering traveller!]: 1:608. Christopher is patron saint of travellers, and Polyphemus lives by the sea.

40   ll. 29–30. García-Posada discovers an ironic reference to childhood, when in Spanish religious elementary schools rival groups divided into Romans and Carthaginians: Lorca, *Primer romancero* 118n29–30. The implication is that war is at base a childish pursuit.

41 "por causas misteriosas, por una mirada, (…) por un amor de hace dos
   siglos": Lorca, *Obras completas* 3:343.

42 "¡Guarte, guarte, rey don Sancho,/No digas que no te aviso,/Que de dentro
   de Zamora/un alevoso ha salido": Durán, *Romancero general* 1:505.

43 "Apaga tus verdes luces/que viene la benemérita": Lorca, *Obras completas*
   1:428.

44 Here I more or less agree with García-Posada's interpretation (Lorca, *Primer
   romancero* 195n63–4), except I view the unbound hair as a sign of mourning.
   In a child's poem "Al estanque se le ha muerto" [The pond is now bereaved],
   the narrator sees a pond as a mother whose child (=a puddle) has died, and
   the pond in mourning "tiene suelta/su cabellera de algas" [has unbound/her
   switch of hair made of algae]: 1:294.

45 Falla, *Cantares de Nochebuena* 6. Isabel García Lorca identifies this carol as
   her favourite as a child, and her father and their servant Dolores "La Colorina"
   used to contribute parodies of that *villancico* on Christmas Eve: *Recuerdos*
   131. Falla and his sister would come to dine at Lorca's home on that holiday:
   133. All these recollections may be in Federico's mind as he writes "Romance
   de la Guardia Civil Española."

46 "Cuando llegaba la noche,/noche que noche nochera" and "en la noche
   platinoche/noche, que noche nochera": Lorca, *Obras completas* 1:427.

47 See Salazar, "Estreno de El sombrero de tres picos. Un gran éxito en el Real,"
   El Sol, 6 April 1921, in Salazar, *Textos de crítica musical* 199. The use of the
   pelele evoked Goya (author of the cartoon *El pelele* for royal tapestries).
   However, during the *jota*, the presence of crowds with hideous deformations
   and green-bearded peasants called to mind the Goya of the satirical *Caprichos*
   and the black paintings. Falla's ballet became unwittingly satirical of Spanish
   life because Russian choreographer Massine had intended merely to show the
   upsetting of social hierarchy in the tossing of the Corregidor (Hess, *Modernism*
   152–3). Lorca, however, creates conscious satire. As to what Falla's *jota* is
   parodying, Christoforidis in private correspondence has mentioned to me
   melodies resembling *jotas* in the line of showy, Spanish-style themes extending
   from Glinka (e.g., *Jota aragonesa*) down to Chabrier (e.g., *España*), Rimsky-
   Korsakov (e.g., *Capriccio espagnol*) and Ravel (e.g., *Rapsodie espagnole*).

48 "una vaga astronomía/de pistolas inconcretas": 1:426, ll. 15–16.

49 "En el portal de Belén": 1:429, l. 93.

50 "con salivilla de estrella": l. 100. Cf. Luis de Góngora, *Soledades*, 2, pt. 2,
   where, speaking of the bee, he writes that either it drinks the juice of the pure
   air, or the sweat of heaven when it sips "de las mudas estrellas la saliva" [of
   the mute stars the saliva], cit. in Lorca 3:234.

51 "Malhaya la jembra pobre/que nace con negro sino./Malhaya el que nace
   yunque/en vez de nacer martillo": Falla, *Vie brève,* act 1, sc. 2, rehearsals 90,

92, p. 29. Note that the words "la jembra" [the female] substitutes here for "el hombre" [the man or the human being].

52 "tierras de la aceituna": l. 21.

10 Andalusia's "Cultural Spirit" in Two Trios of Gypsy Ballads

1 For the first section of this chapter, I am grateful to the editors of *Decimonónica* for allowing me to reprint (with many modifications) my article "Andalusia's 'Cultural Spirit' and the Historical Ballads of *Romancero gitano*," which appeared in DXIX 9, no. 1 (Winter 2012).

2 "Cuando el río suena, / ¿qué querrá decir? / ¡Por querer a otra / se *orvía* de mí" (When the river rustles, / What does it mean? / He loves someone else / And forgets about me!"): Falla, *La vie brève* 50.

3 "Se propuso el autor expresar el alma de cada una de las regiones indicadas en los títulos de esta obra, imitando los ritmos y modalidades, la línea melódica, la ornamentación y las cadencias de sus aires": Falla, *Piezas españolas* 5. In Spanish the names of the pieces are "La Aragonesa," La Cubana," La Montañesa," and "La Andaluza." While not subscribing to *Volksgeist* theory, I find such a notion useful for clarifying Lorca's art as Falla critics do for explicating the composer's. Often it has been said that the *Volksgeist* is an intellectual construct. Simplistic as it is, defining Andalusia as a contradictory creative principle of agitation and nostalgia, arising from the people and the land, the idea enables (without deforming) understanding of music and literature of artists who profess that theory.

4 For an excellent treatment of the conception of palimpsest in the poetry of Lorca, particularly in *Suites*, see Quance, *Contradiction* 111–36.

5 *Obras completas* 1:1131–2. The version gathered by Lorca is in D minor and 4/4 time with no tempo indicated. As sung to unvarying hexasyllables, the ballad is monotonous, divided into quatrains. If Lorca has the Don Bueso melody in mind when composing "Burla de don Pedro a caballo," he relieves the monotony through multiple variations in poetic meter.

6 "Detrás de cada espejo / hay una estrella muerta / y un arco iris niño / que duerme": "Capricho," in "Suite de los espejos," 1:673.

7 "hacer plástica la laguna, es decir, el lugar donde se sumergen las cosas, en este caso las palabras": García-Posada, in Lorca, *Primer romancero* 207, n.

8 "Sueno concreto y sin norte / de madera de guitarra": Lorca, *Obras completas* 1:437, ll. 44–5.

9 Lorca admits Falla's influence in his 1928 lecture "Canciones de cuna españolas" (Spanish cradle songs), on lullabies of all Spain. There he mentions Falla's insistence on the Asturian origin of a song for swinging sung in the towns of the Sierra Nevada Mountains. Further study convinced the

composer he had erred. Granada seemed to have a treasury of songs of
Galician and Asturian tonalities, but many other influences were also in
operation. Only technicians as deep and artistic as Falla, Lorca felt (3:295–6),
could sort them out.

10 "Mérida es andaluza como por otra parte lo es Tetuán": 346.

11 "De cuando en cuando sonaban/blasfemias de cresta roja": Lorca, *Obras completas* 1:433, ll. 13–14.

12 "tendere se patris ad solium": Bodelón García, "Quirico y Prudencio" ll. 17–18.

13 On objective, passionless contemplation of beauty in Falla's "A Córdoba,"
see part 2 of the present chapter. Lorca showed the influence of Dalí's vision
of Saint Sebastian's martyrdom as a symbol of "Holy Objectivity." In
September 1926 Lorca asked fellow poet Jorge Guillén for a photograph of
Berruguete's image of that saint for lectures he was preparing on Sebastian:
Southworth, "Religion" 134–5. De Paepe, in Federico García Lorca, *Primer
romancero gitano* (37–8), situates the composition of "Martirio de Santa
Olalla" around early November 1926. Hence she could have been an
Andalusian saint of "Holy Objectivity."

14 "Flora desnuda se sube/por escalerillas de agua": 1:434, ll. 23–4.

15 De Paepe, in Lorca, *Primer romancero* 275nn23–6: "Flora desnuda sonrie
sonrie desnuda[] desnuda se aleja/evade sube/en por escalerillas de agua."
[Naked Flora smiles smiles naked naked she goes far away/escapes climbs/in
through little ladders of water]. Lorca rejects the idea of her smiling, probably
because her aloofness more easily would link her to Dalí's Saint Sebastian.
Her identification with a pagan Roman goddess shows that for Lorca Roman
paganism and early Christianity in Spain were not far apart, and that Roman
persecutions made little sense. Like Falla, Lorca hates warfare.

16 "una escalinata de jardines que leva [*sic*] á un mirador, – grados de la contem-
plación cada vez más perfecta, que llevan á la visión última de la serenidad
espiritual.": Lejárraga, *Granada* 135–6. Our Introduction showed Falla
during his Parisian crisis, unable to create until discovering Lejárraga's book.
He then wrote "En el Generalife." He was also contemplating Santiago
Rusiñol's paintings of the Generalife gardens. Falla could have lent Lejárraga's
book to Lorca, or Lorca could have read it on his own. On the impact of
Rusiñol's book of paintings *Jardins d'Espanya* on Falla, see Nommick,
Jardines de España 10.

17 "Agua con peces y barcos./Agua, agua, agua, agua": PCJ 273. Three years
before Lorca, Falla made punishment a work of art. See *El retablo de maese
Pedro* (1923), sc. 6, where music accompanies the flogging of the Moor who
dared kiss Melisendra. The hangmen flog the perpetrator with lashes that

coincide with the rhythmic accents of the music, with the whole orchestra striking vertical blows.

18 "En certes regions del cos, les venes aparexien a la superficie amb llur blau intens de tempesta del Patinir, i descrivien corbes d'una dolorosa voluptuositat damunt el rosa coral de la pell": Dalí, "Sant Sebastià" 53.

19 "Porque ansí como la tiene en el cielo, deve tener en el alma una estancia donde sólo Su Majestad mora, y digamos, *otro cielo*" (with my emphasis): Saint Teresa of Avila, *Moradas del castillo interior*, in *Obras completas* 1:439.

20 "Por los rojos agujeros / donde sus pechos estaban / se ven cielos diminutos / y arroyos de leche blanca": 1:434, ll. 35–8.

21 "Noche tirante reluce": 1:434, l. 55; "Nieve partida comienza": l. 63; "Ángeles y serafines": l. 73.

22 Mario Hernández, in Lorca, *Primer romancero* 26. According to Isabel García Lorca, *Recuerdos* 34, the family would pray with the Trisagion during a storm. The poet's mother would recite, "The Trisagion that Isaiah / wrote with great care / he heard sung in heaven / by angelical hierarchies" (El trisagio que Isaías / escribió con grande celo / lo oyó cantar en el cielo / a angelicas jerarquías). The rest of the family would afterwards repeat, "Angels and seraphim, / Archangels and cherubim / Say, Holy, holy, holy" (Ángeles y serafines, / arcángeles y querubines / dicen: Santo, santo, santo).

23 "gitano-judío, como (…) son las gentes que pueblan los montes de Granada y algún pueblo del interior cordobés": 3:346; cf. 3:317.

24 "amaba la belleza objetiva, la belleza pura e inútil, exenta de congojas comunicables": 3:229.

25 "metáfora limpia de realidades que mueren, (…) construida con espíritu escultórico y situada en un ambiente extraatmosférico": 3:228–9.

26 Falla completed his "Soneto a Córdoba" for soprano and harp at some time between June 1926 and May 1927 Hess, *Modernism* 266. Christian de Paepe dates Lorca's ballad "San Rafael (Córdoba)" to sometime between August and September 1926: Lorca, *Primer romancero* 43. Lorca's Góngora lecture (February 1926) preceded both works.

27 Pahissa, *Falla* 156. The Archivo Manuel de Falla conserves a copy of the "Soneto a Córdoba" handwritten by Falla in the baroque orthography that will pass to his score, and the words "Granada, donde fué escrito el Soneto" [Granada, where the Sonnet was written] appear handwritten at the bottom of the page with an asterisk to explain the tenth line of the sonnet, with its references to the Granadan rivers Genil and Darro (here written Dauro).

28 "Sicilia, en cuanto oculta, en cuanto ofrece, / copa es de Baco, huerto de Pomona: / tanto de frutas ésta la enriquece, / cuanto aquél de racimos la corona": Alonso 1:19, ll. 137–40.

29 Alonso, *Gongora y el "Polifemo"* 1:16, ll. 78–80. Southworth finds the aesthetic positions from Lorca's lecture on Góngora present in the poetic images in "San Rafael (Córdoba)." Yet, we disagree with Southworth that this ballad is a philosophical treatise in miniature, a "meditation on cultural continuity and change as these have affected Córdoba down through the centuries" ("On 'San Rafael (Córdoba)'" 87). Nor do we concur with Marcilly, "Il faut passer les ponts" (29–50) and Beltrán Fernández de los Ríos, *Arquitectura de humo* (113–26) that the ballad merely depicts a riparian site of male prostitution, with young Cordoban exhibitionists and hidden voyeurs. Raw sexuality is undeniably present, yet need not exclude non-sensual idealism. Integrating these two perspectives, we aim for an interpretation midway between, understanding the ballad as a lyric apology of Lorca's 1926 aestheticism combining poetic obscurity with transparency.

30 "Toda temblequera trueca las notas, acordes, frases, temas … en imágenes (…) huellas, sombras, ecos de las notas, frases… temas no afectados de trino. Las hace (…) algo aéreo, airoso, aureola, flotante": *Filosofía de la música* 626. My translation cannot achieve the musicality of García Bacca's philosophical prose. While the harp lightens the sound, Michael Christoforidis informs me that the instrument also serves as a substitute for the guitar or the *vihuela*.

31 "Ô excelso muro, ô torres coronadas / De honor, de magestad, de gallardía! / Ô gran Río, gran Rei de Andalucia. / De arenas nobles, ia que no doradas! / Ô fertil llano, ô sierras levantadas, / Que privilegia el cielo i dora el dia! / Ô siempre gloriòsa patria mia, / Tanto por plumas quanto por espadas! / Si entre aquellas rûinas y despojos / Que enriquece Genil y Dauro baña, / Tu memoria no fue alimento mio, / Nunca merezcan mis ausentes ojos / Ver tu muro, tus torres i tu Rio, / Tu llano i sierra, ô patria, ô flor de España!": Manuel de Falla's handwritten versión of "A Córdova" [*sic*] in the Archivo Manuel de Falla.

32 "Córdoba (…) es romana, romana, como la veía don Luis, y no árabe. No hay en ese soneto una alusión que no sea romana, cristiana": cit. by Lorca from Falla and printed in G(erardo). D(iego)., "La conversión de Falla" 3.

33 Trend, *Falla and Spanish Music* 99–100. Falla's piano solo *Fantasía Bætica* (1919) honours the "Latin-Andalusian race" (raza latino-andaluza): Falla's 1926 letter to José María Gálvez: Hess, *Passions* 122n51. Hence Falla's Latinism dates back to his Andalusianist period (ca. 1905–ca. 1922). Still, Christoforidis reminds me in private correspondence that in the 1920s Falla approaches Hispanic identity in richly multiple ways, first as Andalusian (cante jondo), next as Castilian (*Retablo*), and finally as classical / monumental Greek (*Atlàntida*).

34 In Granada in January 1926, "Lorca and his friends (…) inaugurated the Scientific and Artistic Athenaeum as a slap in the face to the Arts Club [which had not allowed for the continuity of the Deep Song Competition]," and

Lorca gave the inaugural address on 13 February titled "La imagen poética en don Luis de Góngora" [The poetic image in Don Luis de Góngora]: Gibson, *Life* 158. Since Falla deplored the Arts Club's conduct, he must have been present for the inauguration of the Athenaeum. Hess maintains the impact of that lecture on Falla's musical arrangement of Góngora's "Soneto a Córdoba" (*Modernism* 157).

35 On riparian imagery in Góngora, see Dolan, "Figures of Disclosure" 247. On rivers in Lorca, see my ch. 2, above.

36 In *"Cante jondo"* Falla criticized Pedrell for overlooking the Moorish contribution to deep song (140). Here, though, Lorca faults Falla for the same omission in considering the reality of Cordoba. Likewise, the Granadan Ángel Ganivet in *Idearium español* lauds the creativity of the contact between Indo-European and Semitic (=Arabic) cultures in the Iberian Peninsula (Orringer, *Ganivet*, 45–6). In his Andalusianist pieces, Falla habitually inserted Arab-sounding, Phrygian passages. Subsequently, he stressed Christianity and experimented less with modal music. In Falla's personal notes on *Retablo*, 15 he calls the three Greek modes, the Doric, Phrygian, and Lydian, "incomplete scales" (escalas incompletas). In *Retablo* he strove for greater tonality, yet his personal notes also indicate experimentation with Arab musical elements (in passages set in Sansueña, realm of the Arabs). On Falla's changing attitudes in the 1920s towards Arabic components in Spanish music, see Elena Torres Clemente, *Manuel de Falla y las Cantigas de Alfonso X el Sabio*. I owe this bibliographical reference to M. Christoforidis.

37 On "onda": *Fábula de Polifemo,* l. 210: see Alonso, *Góngora y el "Polifemo"* 2:22; l. 369: Alonso 2:28; *Soledad Primera,* l. 41: Alonso, 1:405, cf. Lorca, 3:231, and *Soledad Segunda,* l. 815: Alonso 1:431. The final line of Góngora's "Inscripción para el sepulcro de Domínico Greco" omits the article after the fashion of Latin: "corteza funeral de árbol sabeo" [funereal bark of the Sheban tree]: Alonso 1:375.

38 Lorca may be overlooking Góngora's view of physical beauty as a worldly good, ephemeral as any other. See the sonnet "Mientras por competir con tu cabello" [While trying to compete against your hair]: Alonso, *Góngora y el "Polifemo"* 1:361. However, Lorca loved Plato, his brother reports (Francisco García Lorca, *Federico y su mundo* 99), and must have known Diotima's speech in the *Symposium* 211c, teaching that the right method of boy-loving consists of ascending from perception of particular beauty to the contemplation of the universal, Beauty itself.

39 "En una escena de gran intensidad dramática lo que hay que buscar en la orquesta es formar un fondo discreto, pero nada más. Dice Debussy que, en unos casos, aunque la orquesta tocara la *Bon à Tabac* (en modo menor (!!!) el efecto era seguro, puesto que la atención del público está fijo solamente

en la acción" [In a scene of great dramatic intensity what must be sought in the orchestra is to form a discreet background, but nothing else. Debussy says that in some cases, although the orchestra played the Good Tobacco song (in a minor key (!!!) the effect was safe, since the attention of the public is fastened only on the action]: Falla, unpubl. handwritten notes on Debussy's suggestions to improve *La vida breve*,§5, from the Archivo Manuel de Falla.

40 Southworth, "San Rafael" 91; García-Posada, in Lorca, *Primer romancero* 154n25–6; Ramsden, in Lorca, *Primer romancero* 150.

41 Alonso, *Fábula de Píramo y Tisbea* [Fable of Pyramus and Thisbe] 1: 312–13.

42 Fischer 40. To see a reproduction of Picasso, *Still Life with Fishes* (1922–3), consult http://www.bridgemanart.com/image.aspx?key=213405&lang=en-gb. Salvador Dalí imitates this work in his own cubist painting *Fish and Balcony. Still Life by Moonlight* (Peix i balcon, 1926), with two fish crossed beneath a broken bust joining the faces of Dalí and Lorca (Ades, *Dali* 36). Given Lorca's intimacy with Dalí at the time, the poet may well know the Picasso work.

43 See, for instance, the endings of Falla, *Sombrero* (score), pt. I, rehearsal 54, final mm., p. 98, and of Falla, *Concerto per Clavicembalo* (score), movement 3, rehearsal 29, p. 42, and cf. Falla's call for a reprise in Lorca, *Lola* (Menarini 123n1): "De todos modos hay que volver (...) a la música del comienzo, haciendo cadencia final" [Anyhow, it is necessary to return (...) to the music of the beginning, making a final cadence].

44 Date of a letter into which Lorca copied it for his friend the poet-professor Jorge Guillén: Lorca, *Epistolario* 1:164–5.

45 "Granada está hecha para la música porque es una ciudad encerrada, una ciudad entre sierras donde la melodía es devuelta y limada y retenida por paredes y rocas": 3:321.

46 "recogida, apta para el ritmo y el eco, médula de la música": 3:322.

47 "Granada culmina en su orquesta de surtidores llenos de pena andaluza y en el vihuelista Narváez y en Falla y Debussy": 3:322.

48 Lorca's Góngora lecture was delivered 13 February 1926, and the Soto de Rojas one, 17 October 1926: 3:1094.

49 "Importa más el *espíritu* que la *letra*. El ritmo, la modalidad y los intervalos melódicos, que determinan sus ondulaciones y sus cadencias, constituyen lo esencial de esos cantos": Falla, *Escritos* 60.

50 "las venas con poca sangre,/los ojos con mucha noche": Alonso, *Góngora y el "Polifemo"* 1:287. Lorca partially (mis)quotes the lines in 3:244.

51 Ramsden, in Lorca, *Romancero gitano* 27–9. Or perhaps as Beltrán Fernández de los Ríos finds, the Bishop of Manila refers to Bernardino Nozaleda y Villa, Dominican prelate, victim of the humiliating loss of the Philippines by Spain to the United States in the Spanish-American War of 1898. Hence his description as "ciego de azafrán y pobre" [blind with saffron and poor]; in other words, he

is yellow-faced for his humiliation: *Arquitectura de humo* 111. This interpretation would support the notion of the heightening of *temporality* (here, *history*) in the present ballad. Also see Ian Gibson, *Caballo azul* 188–9, for an interesting interpretation of sexual innuendoes possibly present in these lines.

52 Ian Gibson, *Caballo azul* 190, informs that these lines repelled the homophobic Luis Buñuel and even the more moderate poet Jorge Guillén, with whom Lorca corresponded.

53 "enaguas cuajadas / de espejitos y entredoses": 1:411, ll. 47–8.

54 "Todo tiene por fuera un dulce aire doméstico; pero, verdaderamente, ¿quién penetra esta intimidad?": 3:253.

55 "Es un canto confuso lo que se oye. Es todo el canto de Granada a la vez: ríos, voces, cuerdas, frondas, procesiones, mar de frutas y tatachín de columpios": 3:331.

56 "a lo pálido no, a lo arrebolado": Alonso, *Góngora y el "Polifemo"* 2:16, ll. 83-84.

57 One of the rare instances of the *creacionista* Gerardo Diego's influence appears in the poem "Rosa mística" from *Imagen*: "Era ella / y nadie lo sabía / Pero cuando pasaba / Los árboles se arrodillaban" [It was she / and nobody knew it / But when she passed by / The trees would genuflect]. This "mystic rose" symbolizes either a virginally innocent beloved or the Virgin Mary herself: Diego, *Primera antología* 50. Of the comely Archangel Gabriel, Lorca's poetic voice informs, "Cuando la cabeza inclina / sobre su pecho de jaspe, / la noche busca llanuras / porque quiere arrodillarse" [When he bows his head / On his jasper chest, / the night seeks plains / because it wants to genuflect]: 1:414.

58 Falla, *La vie brève* 61. The Gypsy Candelas superstitiously believes in omens of nature (marine sounds, dogs barking), yet also in God: 64.

59 "¡Ay San Gabriel de mis ojos, / Gabrielillo de mi vida / Donde has dejado tus alas / para ahuyentar mis desdicha [*sic*]" [Oh Saint Gabriel, dear to my eyes, / Dear little Gabriel, my saving grace / Where have you left your wings / to chase away my misfortunes?]: ms. cit. in de Paepe, in Lorca, *Primer romancero* 230n54.

60 "Dios te salve, Anunciación. / Morena de maravilla": 1:415, ll. 43–4.

11 Lorca's Artistic Tributes to Falla

1 "Si tuviera que identificar a los dos creadores que dejaron más profunda huella en su creación, no dudaría en responder: Manuel de Falla y Salvador Dalí."

2 "Ya sé el gran éxito que tuvo V. en Bruselas, que me alegra como propio, pues ya sabe V. el cariño y la admiración tan grande y entusiasta que tengo por su obra y su persona": Lorca, *Epistolario*, 1:68.

3 "su propio sentimiento ante la creación musical: la obra hecha con amor. El
   amor fue el gran motor de su vida. Su genio y su profundo amor a Dios le
   dieron el impulso para hacer una obra perfecta, ya que él estaba convencido
   de que tenía que trabajar y esforzarse para hacer lo mejor posible algo que le
   había sido dado": Isabel García Lorca, *Recuerdos* 127.
4 "Don Manuel sonreía muchísimo ante lo que le gustaba, y sabía ponerse
   siempre en situación": Isabel García Lorca, *Recuerdos* 124; the author adds
   about Falla, "Era un niño grande, que podía dar alegría y disfrutar con la
   alegría de los demás, y gozar de lo más común y corriente" [He was a big kid,
   who could give joy and enjoy the joy of others, and take pleasure in the most
   common and current situations]: 125.
5 Pahissa, *Falla* 126–7. Falla praised Lorca's works to his father, Federico
   García Rodríguez, sustaining his hope in his son's future. Falla also enjoyed a
   deep friendship with the poet's mother. She supplied Falla with a domestic
   servant, who kept the Lorca family abreast of Falla's personal idiosyncrasies,
   his asceticism and fastidious personal hygiene. Isabel García Lorca writes that
   Falla understood her mother, who would consult him with her problems like
   a confessor. Falla admired Vicenta Lorca's character, her conduct, intelligence,
   morality, and concern with raising her children to demand the most of
   themselves. Sometimes she acted as Falla's messenger to Federico during his
   absences from Granada as in her March 1923 letter to finish the text of *Lola*:
   Isabel García Lorca, *Recuerdos* 125–6.
6 For the original Spanish, see Francisco García Lorca, *Federico y su mundo*
   155–6.
7 When the fascists came looking for Lorca in August, 1936, he had to choose
   between flight to the Republican war zone, to the home of the poet Luis
   Rosales, or to the world-renowned Falla. He did not choose Falla because of
   embarrassment about the 1929 disagreement on the *Oda*. Possibly he might
   have prolonged his life had he relied on the courageously pious Falla: Gibson.
   Asesinato 176.
8 On 9 March 1930, after Lorca's lecture in Havana about contemporary
   poetry, part of his ode was read. Traditional listeners found it "no sólo
   herética en la fe, sino falsa en la filosofía" [not only heretical as concerns faith,
   but false with respect to philosophy]: Anonymous (Antonio Quevedo), ch. 2,
   "El poeta en La Habana," subdivision titled "Las conferencias." The allusion
   to the ode is found on the fifth page of this chapter. This book lacks page
   numbers. Yet Eutimio Martín offers an orthodox Catholic reading: "Does
   Lorca commit himself (…) to remain in the fold of the Church? That is what
   the presence in his poem of the institutional hymn *Pange lingua* seems to
   indicate, and the dedication to the exemplary Catholic Manuel de Falla

corroborates as much " ["¿Se compromete Lorca (…) a permanecer (o entrar) en el redil de la Iglesia? Es lo que parece indicar la presencia en su poema del (himno) institucional *Pange lingua* y corroborarlo la dedicatoria al católico ejemplar Manuel de Falla"], *Heterodoxo y mártir* 277. In his detailed analysis of the ode, however, Martín does not take into account Lorca's mistaken perception of Falla's faith with respect to his art.

9 See Lorca's co-generationist and friend Pedro Salinas, *Poesía de Rubén Darío* 143–3.

10 "quizás el poema más grande que yo haya hecho": Lorca, *Epistolario* 2:120.

11 Isabel García Lorca: "en nosotros religión y belleza eran siempre unidas, y esto fue influencia de mi madre. Más de una vez la oi decir: 'A esa iglesia no vamos porque es muy fea'" [In us religion and beauty always went together, and this was the influence of my mother. More than once I heard her say, "Let's not go to that church because it is very ugly"]: *Recuerdos* 32.

12 "Casi todo lo tengo abandonado por causa del Auto": Beardsley, "Falla's Score for *Gran teatro*" 65. Let us recall that around spring 1913 Falla had first shown interest in adapting Calderón's theatre (specifically, the religious drama *La devoción de la Cruz* [Devotion to the Cross]): Christoforidis, "Hacia nuevos conceptos de ópera" 364. Another religious work that Falla began in (winter) 1927 was his symphonic poem *Atlàntida,* which obsessed him until the end of his life: Demarquez, *Falla* 190. Isabel García Lorca attributes Falla's inability to complete his chief work to his pain caused by the Spanish Right, which murdered his friends and collaborators, among them, her older brother: *Recuerdos* 129.

13 Calderón, *Teatro* 95, l. 736; 96, l. 790; 97, l. 808; 98, l. 832; 101, l. 942.

14 The version of *Tantum ergo* used by Falla in Calderón's *Gran teatro* is actually a "free adaptation" of the hymn by "the great polyphonist Tomás Luis de Victoria": Antonio Gallego, in Falla, *Siete canciones populares españolas.*

15 "Estoy muy contento de que se hagan los Autos Sacramentales. Escríbeme diciendo cosas sobre este asunto. En Granada se puede hacer lo más bonito del mundo": Lorca, *Epistolario* 2:61.

16 "Lo de los 'autos sacramentales' ha sido por fin un gran éxito en *toda España* y un éxito de nuestro amigo [Hermenegildo] Lanz [stage designer], que día tras día y modestamente consigue ganar nuestra máxima admiración. Esto me produce una extraordinaria alegría y me demuestra las muchas cosas que se pueden hacer y que debemos hacer en Granada": Lorca, *Epistolario* 2.71–2.

17 Lorca, "Oda al santísimo Sacramento del altar," in Martín, *Heterodoxo y mártir* 267. The English translation of the *Pange lingua* is by Edward Caswall.

18 In addition, Falla based the second movement of his renowned *Harpsichord Concerto*, written between 1923 and 1926, on the Mozarabe *Pange lingua* of the sixteenth century: Nommick, "Ambigüedad formal" 18. Lorca attended a strenuous rehearsal of the *Concerto*: Francisco García Lorca, *Federico y su mundo* 154. Therefore he could have known of Falla's reverence for that old music.

19 The spectator would have had to witness the performance of Falla's musical arrangement (for example, of May 27, 1927, when Lorca was away in Catalonia). Therefore, contrary to Martín, *Heterodoxo y mártir* 277, who naively equates Lorca and the poetic voice of the Ode (Parts I and II), we presume their difference, although both share the hope of salvation by the Sacred Host from the nothingness.

20 In 1926 Falla hoped to combine lines from Calderón's *auto sacramental Los encantos de la culpa* [The charms of sin] with some from Calderón's drama *El mayor encanto amor* [The greatest charm, love] for a new opera libretto: Christoforidis, "Hacia nuevos conceptos de 'ópera'" 369. For Falla's other Calderonian projects, see Introduction, n. 19.

21 Falla never read the other two epigraphs, but given Lorca's high esteem for his ode, he presumably chose the third and fourth to harmonize with the earlier two. For the epigraph concerning the devil, Lorca quotes from Psalm 42:2: "Quia tu es Deus meus, et fortitudo mea. Quare me reppulisti, et quare tristis incedo dum adfligit me inimicus?" [Since You are my God and my refuge, why do You forsake me? Why must I go in mourning while my enemy afflicts me?]. Falla had set a biblical text in *Gran teatro*: passages from Daniel had formed an aria for *Discreción*. Note, though, that Falla's biblical quotation praises God, while Lorca's laments being divinely shunned. For the epigraph corresponding to the flesh, Lorca departs from the liturgy and chooses lines from a winsome song ending Lope de Vega's *auto sacramental De los cantares*, catholicizing the *Song of Solomon* and praising the Eucharist: "Que bien os quedasteis/galán del cielo/que es muy de galanes/quedarse en cuerpo" [How well you came out,/Swain of heaven,/Since it is fitting for swains/to stay in their bodies]. The heavenly swain was Christ, viewed in the host.

22 Even in Lorca's posthumous "Soledad (homenaje a Fray Luis de León)" [Solitude (Tribute to Fray Luis de León)] – another poetic tribute to a revered artist – he assiduously echoes Fray Luis's odes and uses his preferred strophic form, the *lira*; yet he does this as a mere pretext for lyrically complaining about a beloved's absence (1:958–9). In fact, there are echoes from the same odes in the present ode to the Holiest Sacrament.

23 "'No me hable Vd. de cosas sobrenaturales. ¡Qué antipática es Santa Catalina!', dice Falla": Lorca, *Epistolario* 2:92.

24 "Su fe es de tal magnitud, de tan pura calidad, que rechaza el milagro y protesta contra él. Su fe no necesita pruebas para creer. Un día leí la *Santa Catalina de Siena*, de Johannes Jorgesen [Jørgensen], y le llevé el libro alborozado, creyendo que le daría un gusto. A los pocos días me dijo: – No me gusta ese libro. Santa Catalina no es una verdadera santa … es una intelectual …": Lorca, *Obras completas* 3:546.

25 "La ortodoxia católica de Falla y el escrupuloso cumplimento de sus deberes religiosos no empañaba la cordial y amistosa relación que lo unía a nuestro grupo juvenil, *muy indiferente en materia religiosa*": Francisco García Lorca, *Federico y su mundo* 153, with my emphasis.

26 In a letter written by Falla's sister María del Carmen to their brother Germán long after the composer's death, she revealed he was an "hermano del Carmen" (lay brother of a mendicant religious order): Nommick, *Jardines* 16.

27 See Falla's personal editions of Saint John of the Cross, *Obras de San Juan de la Cruz* (Madrid: Apostolado de la Prensa, 1926) and Saint Teresa of Avila, *Las Moradas* (Madrid: La Lectura, 1922).

28 Fray Luis de León and Saint John of the Cross, *Poesías* (Madrid: Hernando, 1923).

29 Fray Luis de León, *Exposición del Libro de Job* (Madrid: Pedro Marín, 1779), *La perfecta casada* (Madrid: Compañía Ibero-Americana de Publicación, n.d.), and *Traducción literal and declaración del Libro de los Cantares de Salomón* (Salamanca: Oficina de Francisco de Toxar, 1798).

30 The postcard, present in the Archivo Manuel de Falla, bears on one side a photograph of the austere classroom where Fray Luis de León taught theology at the University of Salamanca. The photograph has the inscription, "Salamanca, Cátedra de Fray Luis de León" [Salamanca, Fray Luis de León´s Chair]. On the other side, addressed to "Señor don Manuel de Falla, Antequeruela 11, Granada," Lorca has handwritten, "Un cariñoso recuerdo desde Salamanca. Federico" [An affectionate remembrance from Salamanca. Federico].

31 Martín, *Heterodoxo y mártir* 279, 281, interprets the "women" of Lorca's ode as cloistered nuns with a frustrated desire for motherhood. Hence the several references to babyhood in the ode. Such an interpretation, applicable elsewhere in Lorca, would be irrelevant in a tribute to Falla.

32 Martín, *Heterodoxo y mártir* 267, ll. 7–8. Lorca's use of the experimental frog's heart to symbolize Christ's suffering probably offended Falla: 282.

33 Lorca views Christ as an object of God the Father's experiment to show the world His love. Hence Lorca's simile, scratched out on his manuscript, of God like a physician who out of love for all life amputates hearts (Martín, *Heterodoxo y mártir* 282).

34　Martín, *Heterodoxo y mártir* 267, l. 9. Cf. 1 Peter 2:8, commanding adherence to Christ for salvation as to a "stone" rejected by builders but chosen as a cornerstone and "precious."

35　Martín, *Heterodoxo y mártir* 267 l. 9, Cf. Romans 8:22–3.

36　Martín, *Heterodoxo y mártir* 267 l. 10. According to John 7:37–8, Jesus promises the Holy Spirit in these terms: "If anyone thirst, let him come to me and drink. He who believes in me (…) 'out of his heart shall flow rivers of living water.'"

37　E. Martín thinks this image offended Falla: *Heterodoxo y mártir* 284. Actually the phallus appears in Lorca's 1917 poem "Elogio. Beethoven" (*Poesía inédita* 71, l. 39), long before Lorca met Dalí. Only after meeting him does Lorca dare publish such imagery.

38　"repetido mil veces, muerto, crucificado / por la impura palabra del hombre sudoroso" [Repeated a thousand times, dead, and crucified / by the impure word of the sweaty man]: Martin, *Heterodoxo y mártir* 268, ll. 23–4.

39　If the stability of the Host symbolizes the hope for salvation, the anchor, then the flowers, as in Saint John of the Cross, may stand for the soul's virtues (Cuevas, in Saint John of the Cross, *Poesía* 170), here reflecting the light of the Eucharist. Lorca has a gift for multilayered metaphor, and commentary must extract main layers while allowing the reader to choose among them for the most convincing elucidation.

40　The multitudinous lights echo Fray Luis de León's "innumerables luces" [countless lights] or heavenly bodies in the ode "Noche serena" [Serene night]: León, *Obras* 2:758, l. 2. The same ode refers to "la muchedumbre / del reluciente coro" [the multitude / of the shining chorus], 760, ll. 58–9, or celestial bodies, each emitting a note, with the totality of notes in harmony.

41　See, e.g., Falla's ironic 18 August 1923 letter, stating that he was being driven mad, first, by the Senegalese-like summer heat in Granada, second, by the well-known musical passage composed of E-G-C repeated three times (and written on a musical staff by Falla), and third, by his own insistence on finding an exact definition of the fourth dimension. Archivists Martínez and Chinchilla of the Archivo Manuel de Falla identify the annoying musical passage as one drawn from the popular tango milonga "Hay que ver mi abuelita" [You should see my granny] in the wildly successful zarzuela *La montería*, debuting 24 November 1922 in Saragossa with music by Jacinto Guerrero and lyrics by José Ramos Martín. The trivial words and repetitive melody explain Falla's irritation with this tune he hears incessantly: "¡Hay que ver, hay que ver, hay que ver / las ropas que hace un siglo / llevaba la mujer! ... / ¡Creo yo, creo yo, creo yo / que de una de estas faldas / salen lo menos dos!.." [You should see, you should see, you should see / The clothes that women wore / In the last century! / It seems true, it seems true, it seems true / that from one of those skirts / you can make at least two!]: "Zarzuela.net *La montería*" with my translation of the lyrics.

42 Debussy, *Estampes pour le piano*. Annotations on the inner flap of the score cover a whole page devoted to orchestral features.

43 "Tú no te puedes imaginar lo que es pasarse noches enteras en el balcón viendo una Granada nocturna, vacía para mí y sin tener el menor consuelo de nada": Lorca, *Epistolario* 2:119.

44 Falla (*Escritos* 74) and Lorca (3:203) praised Debussy's *Ibéria*. Brown finds that *Parfums de la nuit* "evokes what Falla called 'the intoxicating spell of Andalusian nights'": 114. Lorca may have projected over the seductive music his nihilism of the moment in Granada. *Parfums de la nuit*, marked *Lent et reveur* [slow and dreamy], has an introduction, central episode, and coda in sensual *habanera* time (Debussy, *Ibéria* [score] 54). Phrases expressing almost intense emotion through discords appear at rehearsal 48, measures 7–9 and rehearsal 49, measures 1–3, marked, "En animant avec une grande intensité dans l'expression" [heating up with great intensity in the expression] and "tres appuyé dans l'expression" [very emphasized in the expression]: 73–5.

45 Isabel García Lorca, *Recuerdos* 126–7. Early in 1927 the newspaper *El Heraldo* (Madrid) quoted one of Falla's offhand remarks to the effect that Beethoven was the "worst of musicians": Christoforidis, "Falla on Romanticism" 31n12. Whatever his true feelings towards Beethoven, Falla took exception. As a result he drafted a carefully worded, handwritten note on Beethoven, here quoted in its finished version, shown to García Lorca's music-loving mother Vicenta Lorca Romero, and afterwards published in German translation on 26 March 1927 in the *Vossische Zeitung* of Berlin and in Spanish in *La Noche* of Barcelona (Christoforidis, "Falla on Romanticism" 28): "Independientemente de la admiración debida a Beethoven y de la mayor o menor coincidencia de sentimientos y aspiraciones con su obra, ésta nos ofrece tres poderosos ejemplos que siempre me esforzaré por seguir: (1.) La nobleza y el desinterés con que sirvió a la Música, convencido de su altísima misión social. (2.) Su anhelo de pureza rítmico-tonal-melódica. (3.) El decisivo empeño de Beethoven en germanizar su música; empeño que debe servirnos de luminoso ejemplo para procurar que el genio latino, en sus diversas modalidades, se refleje con la mayor intensidad posible en la producción artística de nuestra raza" [Independently of the admiration owed to Beethoven and of the greater or lesser unanimity of sentiments and aspirations with his work, the latter offers us three powerful examples that I have always strived to follow: (1) The nobleness and disinterestedness with which he served music, convinced of his very lofty social mission. (2) His yearning

for rhythmic, tonal, melodic purity. (3) The decisive insistence of Beethoven on Germanizing his music – an insistence that should serve us as a shining example to enable the Latin genius, in its diverse modalities, to be reflected with the greatest possible intensity in the artistic production of our stock] (quoted with the gracious permission of the Archivo Manuel de Falla). Note the disguised negativity of Falla's initial phrase, his insistence on *Volksgeist* theory, the "we-they" mentality (Latins versus Germans), learned from association with *Les Apaches* in Paris, and the pious resolve to surmount cultural differences.

46 "Cada raza debe expresar lo que haya de bello y grande en los opuestos": on a handwritten sheet titled Beethoven and containing Falla's primitive version of his 1927 Beethoven article. In Christoforidis's words, Falla was practising "something akin to self-censorship" in masking his true "antipathy" towards most Romantic composers for their "excess": "Falla on Romanticism" 26–7. Lorca may not have known Falla's true attitude towards Beethoven, particularly since Falla received enthusiastic applause at a concert on 6 April 1927 in the Granada Ateneo in which "he played Beethoven's *Pathetique* sonata and conducted the Septet op. 20": Christoforidis 28. Falla always posed ascetic challenges for himself.

47 Falla scrawled this phrase on a page numbered 2 and underscored the Latin phrase.

48 *Poèsia inédita* 71, ll. 56–60. Isabel García Lorca recalls her brother Federico's overuse of the gramophone in the family home, the Garden of Saint Vincent (Huerta de San Vicente), as of 1925 (*Recuerdos* 268). Lorca overplayed Bach, Mozart, and deep-song records.

49 This analysis of Beethoven's "Agnus Dei" comes from my listening, from García Bacca, *Filosofía* 420–1, plus the excellent part-by-part description made online by Professor Tom Neenan.

50 "Si estás reposando en la gris eternidad, / No es premio a tu ansia el silencio, maestro": Federico García Lorca, *Poesía inédita* 70, ll. 31–2.

51 Before Lorca published *PCJ* in 1931, he removed the dedication to Falla of the section on the Petenera. He acted not from mean-spirited spite, but from fear of offending Falla, who was gradually growing more pious.

52 According to Parker, the Devil, appearing in forty-seven of Calderón's *autos sacramentales*, in the early *El veneno y la triaca* (1634?), seems "too striking and too sympathetic": "Devil in Calderón" 5–6.

53 The devil was matter from the outset, but Christ takes on material form at will. The devil wielded swords from the beginning, and Christ wins without one. The devil brandished plural weapons and qualities, while Christ

possesses a simple unity in the Sacred Host. The last three strophes stress the joy emanating from God and the sacred Form, as opposed to the sorrow coming from the devil. Martín, *Heterodoxo y mártir* 274, ll. 113–15.

54 "Das tu cuerpo celeste con tu sangre divina / en este Sacramento definido que canto": Federico García Lorca, *Oda al santísimo sacramento del altar*, Martín, *Heterodoxo y mártir* 274, ll. 111–12.

55 "Tantum ergo / Down in Adoration Falling," http://www.seadoration.org/ Hymns/tantum_ergo.htm, accessed 26 February 2010.

56 Cf. the first line of "La casada infiel" [The faithless wife] from *Romancero gitano;* "Y que yo me la llevé al río" [And I took her to the river], a rustic enneasyllable in an otherwise octosyllabic work: 1:406, l. What Roberta Quance has said of Lorca's *Suites* applies equally well to this ode: "We readers are called upon to (re)create a text that the author himself has left partially unwritten – while recognizing that the ambiguity arising therein, from its being partially unwritten – is all of a piece with the lyric as Lorca conceived it": "Trouble" 399.

Postlude with Coda

1 Françoise Gervais, "Notion d'arabesque chez Debussy" 3–23. The arabesque refers to the "harmonic" character of the melodic line, as opposed to its "monodic" quality, relating to the independence of the melody with respect to the accompanying harmony. While both types of melodic lines appear in Debussy and Falla, during Falla's Andalusianist period, the "harmonic" type predominates. An example of monody, however, is the sonnet "A Córdoba" of 1927.

2 "Del mismo modo que ordenamos a voluntad los sonidos para formar, de un modo sucesivo, esas series que llamamos escalas, podemos, también a voluntad, producir simultáneamente una serie de intervalos sobre o bajo un sonido dado. Éste y no otro es el acorde que sólo tiene una forma inmutable: la del llamado perfecto mayor": Manuel de Falla, "Cuaderno del *Retablo*," folio 20, cit. in Chris Collins, "Falla and L'Acoustique nouvelle" 77. We hypothesize that Falla preferred to end his pieces in perfect chords because of his teacher Felipe Pedrell's statement that Christ's divine mission, given to man to share in the common work of redemption and salvation, received its symbol and expressive means in music. The harmonic principle of good, the consequence of fulfilling moral law, was expressed by the perfect major chord, while the discordant principle of evil was conveyed by dissonances (Pedrell, *Por nuestra música*, 123, with Falla's marginal annotation x). Little wonder, then, that

Lorca too, perhaps imitating Falla, enjoyed tying his poetry together by ending with a reference to the beginning, as if to express perfect concord with what had come before.

3 Moreover, because the arabesque is a linking of seemingly autonomous units, Lorca has felt free to attach a new unit, the two dialogues, to the end at the last minute to lengthen *Poema del cante jondo* at the behest of his editor.

4 Examples appear in Falla's song, setting Bécquer's *Rima* 73 to music, "¡Dios mío, qué solos se quedan los muertos!" [My God, how lonely are the dead!], and the longer works *La vida breve*, *Noches*, and *El amor brujo*.

5 Drouot refers to the architect of the Alhambra as "the adorner of the Sacred Book / written at the margins of the old fortress" [L'ornemaniste du Saint Livre / Ecrit aux marges du vieux fort]: *Grappe de raisin* 120. Ornamented passages from the Koran are carved onto the walls.

6 Chase, *Music of Spain* 195–6 finds that in 1927, when arranging Góngora's *Soneto a Córdoba* for voice and harp, Falla uses a tradition of declaiming from old *vihuela* composers like Luis Milán, Alonso de Mudarra, and Miguel de Fuenllana.

7 Michael Christoforidis reminds me that beyond the Andalusianist works, silences formed a significant element in Falla's neoclassical compositions, particularly in the *Lento* and the *Vivace* movements of his *Harpsichord Concerto*.

8 "A Federico García Lorca, en prueba de buena memoria, con un abrazo de Manuel de Falla, Granada, Abril 1932": Manuel de Falla, "Soneto a Córdoba," visible in the Fundación Federico García Lorca, Madrid.

9 "lo más espiritual y más delicado": Federico García Lorca 3:515.

10 "el poema de la raza negra en Norteamérica y subrayar el dolor que tienen los negros de ser negros en un mundo contrario": 515. In the sprawling anthology *Poeta en Nueva York*, only three poems broach the African-American theme, "Norma y Paraíso de los negros" [Norm and paradise of the blacks] (1:457–8), "El rey de Harlem" [The king of Harlem] (1:459–63), and "Danza de la muerte" [Dance of death] (1:469–72), while the majority movingly deal with Lorca's loveless loneliness and sense of personal inadequacy. See Gibson, *Caballo azul* 202–26. Jazz syncopation perhaps is to be found in the metre and repetitions of "El rey de Harlem." Lorca also heard black spirituals, songs, and dances, which he compared to "our Andalusian *cante jondo*" (Gibson, *Life* 255).

11 Gibson views homoeroticism as a main theme with characters modelled after the real-life love triangle of the poet, his lover Emilio Aladrén, and Aladrén's fiancée Helen Dove (*Caballo* azul 235). The evidence is sketchy about a Lope

de Vega–like fusion of theatre and life because unhappily we know all too little about Aladrén and Dove. Equating Aladrén to the Director leaves unexplained the tension this character feels between traditional and avant-garde art, and the Helen figure's destructive traditionalism.

12 The fair lady Melisendra spits and wipes her sleeve after a Moor forcibly kisses her, and her dress gets snagged on the balcony rail during her escape from the Moors, suspending her in mid-air. Falla omits these incidents as "slapstick" (Hess, *Modernism* 207).

13 According to Ignacio's 1925 article "La hora de Belmonte y Gallito," the journalist Gregorio Corrochano had discovered that Belmonte's finest bullfights always occurred at his special hour, twilight, when light was vanishing from the arena (*Escritos periodísticos* 17; cf Lorca, 3:392). However, Sánchez Mejías's *Zaya* refers to the nullification of time, which might have influenced Lorca's fatalistic tolling of "las cinco de la tarde." Ex-bullfighter Zaya's manservant Espeleto recalls Zaya's participation in a bullfight with the well-known matador Bocanegra. After Espeleto's vivid recollections in Andalusian dialect, Zaya's indifferent son José Antonio asks him for the time. He receives a poetic response, referring to Zaya's departure from bullfighting: "It's the time for bullfights, which comes very seldom in this house" [La hora de lo toro, que en esta casa suena poca vece]. The boy insists on knowing the correct time on Espeleto's watch, but he only responds, "On my watch none at all. When I speak of your father, my Time has stopped" [En mi reló ninguna. Cuando hablo de tu padre se quea parao mi Tiempo]: Sánchez Mejías, *Teatro* 85 . Five o'clock is institutional bullfighting time, when the fights usually begin. It is almost as if the institution had foredoomed Ignacio to death at the moment he entered the arena (although Lorca knew his friend died much later at a Madrid clinic, away from the Manzanares bullring, at 9:45 a.m. on 11 August 1934: Gibson, *Life* 390). Ignacio's final bullfight started late (388). He felt that his bull "Granadino" had a hostile look (389). After the goring, the newspapers stressed "elements of fatality," evil omens, marking Ignacio's final moments (388).

14 *Atlàntida* sets to music the Catalan poet-priest Jacint Verdaguer's epic on Hercules's campaigns against the monster Geryon in the Iberian Peninsula; Hercules's separation of Spain from Africa, destroying Atlantis and producing the Mediterranean; and a religious premonition, in Queen Isabella's dream, of discovery of the New World (Macdonald, Program Note 34–5). In 1932, we recall, Falla played for Lorca segments of this work (Orozco 186).

15 See Darío's "Blasón" [Coat of arms]: Darió, *Obras completas* 5:776; Christoforidis, "A Composer's Annotations" 37.

16 1:555, ll. 140–4; Lázaro, "Lectura del 'Llanto'" 9, cit. García-Posada in Lorca, *Primer romancero gitano* 232nn140–4. In Falla's *Atlàntida*, Christian symbols prevail; in Lorca, pagan symbols.

17 "el fondo esencial de la vida de Don Juan, contrapunto y resonancia de su aparente jovialidad": Ortegas, *Obras completas* 6:129, 136.

18 The breeze symbolizes spirit in "Muerto de amor" (1:421, l. 19) and "Oda al santísimo sacramento del altar" (1:961, l. 19).

19 Mora Guarnido, *Lorca* 199. On the military hymn that Falla reluctantly promised General Luis Orgaz, see Hess, *Passions* 224–5.

20 "con un velón y una manta en el suelo": *PCJ* 239. Antonio Quevedo notes that the morning of August 1936, when the fascists shot Lorca in an open field, he did not even have the comfort of a lamp and a blanket: ch. 3. *Poeta en La Habana* "Hacia la muerte," third page of this chapter without page numbers.

Works Consulted

Abellán, José Luis. "Manuel de Falla, hombre intergeneracional." In *Falla y Lorca*, ed. Susana Zapke, 155–60. Kassel: Edition Reichenberger, 1999.

Acereda, Alberto. "La modernidad existencial en la poesía de Rubén Darío." *Bulletin of Spanish Studies* 79, nos. 2–3 (March–May 2002): 149–69. http://dx .doi.org/10.1080/147538202317344961.

Acereda, Alberto and Rigoberto Guevara. *Modernism, Rubén Darío, and the Poetics of Despair*. Lanham, MD: University Press of America, 2004.

Ades, Dawn. *Dali*. Rev. ed. London: Thames & Hudson, 1995.

Adorno, Theodor. *Philòsophie der neuen Musik*. Tübingen: J.C.B. Mohr, 1949.

Alarcón, Pedro Antonio de. *El sombrero de tres picos*, 18th. ed. Madrid: Rivadaneyra, 1914. (Annotated ed. used by Falla and María Lejárraga.)

Albéniz, Isaac. *Iberia. Complete suite. I. Evocation, El Puerto, Fête-Dieu à Seville. For Piano Solo*. New York: Edward B. Marks Corp., 1936. Score.

– *Iberia for piano solo, 3. Málaga. Jerez. Eritaña*. Nueva York: Edwin F. Kalmus, 1909. Score.

Alberti, Rafael. *Federico García Lorca. Poeta y amigo*. Granada: Andaluzas Unidas, 1984.

Alonso, Dámaso. *Góngora y el "Polifemo."* 2 vols. Madrid: Gredos, 1961.

– *Poesía española. Ensayo de métodos y límites estilísticos*. 4th ed. Madrid: Gredos, 1962.

Alvar, Manuel. *El Romancero. Tradición y pervivencia*. Barcelona: Planeta, 1970.

Anonymous. (Antonio Quevedo). *El poeta en La Habana: Federico García Lorca*. La Habana: Consejo Nacional de Cultura, Ministerio de Educación, 1961.

Anonymous. *Cantar del mio Cid*. Ed. Menéndez Pidal Ramón Madrid. 3 vols. 4th ed. Espasa-Calpe, 1964.

Anonymous. "Loa." In *Dictionary of the Literature of the Iberian Peninsula, L–Z*. Ed. Germán Bleiberg, Maureen Ihrie, and Janet Pérez. Westport, CT/ London: Greenwood Press, 1993. 954.

Anonymous. "El molinero de Arcos." In Agustín Durán, *Romancero general o colección de romances castellanos*. 2 vols. Madrid: Atlas, 1945. 2:409–11.

Arbós, Maestro. *Cuarto concierto de abono*. *Orquesta sinfónica de Madrid*, año XIV, 3rd Pt, Teatro Real, 29 April1917. Program notes.

Armero, Gonzalo, ed. *Manuel de Falla. His Life & Works. Poesía. Revista ilustrada de información*. Intro. Jorge de Persia. Trans. Tom Skipp. Madrid: Ministerio de Cultura, Ediciones Opponax, 1996.

– *Federico García Lorca. Vida. Poesía*. In *Poesía. Revista ilustrada de información poética*, No. 43. Huerta de San Vicente (Granada); Casa-Museo Federico García Lorca, 1998.

Asensio García, Jesús. "La tradición calahorrana (II). Canciones, oraciones, dictados y fórmulas." *Kalakorikos* 10 (2005): 279–318.

Bary, David. "Preciosa and the English." *Hispanic Review* 37, no. 4 (1969): 510–17. http://dx.doi.org/10.2307/471518.

Barzun, Jacques. *Darwin, Marx, Wagner*. 2nd ed. rev. Garden City, NY: 1958.

Baudelaire, Charles. *Les Fleurs du mal*. 7th ed. Ed. Enid Starkie. Oxford: Basil Blackwell, 1962.

Beardsley, Theodore, Jr. "Manuel de Falla's Score for Calderón's *Gran teatro del mundo*: The Autograph Manuscript." *Kentucky Romance Quarterly* 16, no. 1 (1969): 63–74. http://dx.doi.org/10.1080/03648664.1969.9932977.

Beer, Rudolf. "Wolf, Ferdinand." *Allgemeine Deutsche Biographie*. Munich, Leipzig: Bayerische Kommission der Wissenschaften. Munich, Leipzig: 1875–1900. Vol. 43 (1898): 729–37.

Beethoven, Ludwig von. *Sixth and Seventh Symphonies in Full Orchestral Score*. Nueva York: Dover Publications, 1976. Score.

Bell, Robert E. *Women of Classical Mythology*. Oxford: Oxford University Press, 1991.

Beltrán Fernández de los Ríos, Luis. *La arquitectura del humo: una reconstrucción del "Romancero gitano" de Federico García Lorca*. London: Tamesis, 1986.

Bodelón García, Serafín. "Quirico y Prudencio: Himnos a las dos Eulalias." *Revista de Estudios Extremeños* 51, no. 5 (1995): 25–48.

Bonaddio, Federico. *Federico García Lorca. The Poetics of Self-Consciousness*. Woodbridge, Suffolk, UK ; Rochester, NY: Tamesis, 2010.

Brown, Matthew. *Debussy's Ibéria*. Oxford, New York: Oxford University Press, 2003.

Bryant, Tony. "Sevillana," Andalucia.comSL, 1996. http://www.andalucia.com/flamenco/sevillana.htm.

Budwig, Andrew. "The Evolution of Manuel de Falla's *The Three-Cornered Hat, 1916–1920*." *Journal of Musicological Research* 5 (1984): 191–212.

Bulfinch, Thomas. *Bulfinch's Mythology*. New York: Avenel Books, 1979.

Calderón de la Barca, Pedro. *El gran teatro del mundo*. In *Autos sacramentales*, 2 vols. Ed. Ángel Valbuena Prat. Madrid: La Lectura, 1926. 1:111–78.

– *La vida es sueño*. 29th ed. Ed. Ciriaco Morón Arroyo. Madrid: Cátedra, 2005.

Camisón, Juan José. "Santa Olalla de Mérida en una cantilena francesa del siglo IX." Merida, 10 Dec. 2003. http://www.telefonica.net/web2/juanjosecamison/eulalia.htm#_ftnref39, consulted 29 August 2010.

Campos, José María. "Federico García Lorca, cofrade activo de Santa María de la Alhambra, de Granada" (1966). *Real Cofradía de Santa María de la Alhambra: LX Aniversario*, 1988. 45.

Cannon, Calvin. "Lorca's *Llanto por Ignacio Sánchez Mejías* and the Elegiac Tradition." *Hispanic Review* 31, no. 3 (July 1963): 229–38. http://dx.doi.org/10.2307/471631.

"capriccio." *Merriam-Webster Online Dictionary*. 2009. Merriam-Webster Online. http://www.merriam-webster.com/dictionary/capriccio, consulted 29 April 2009.

Caswall, Edward. *Thesaurus Precum Latinarum. Treasury of Latin Prayers*, Copyright Michael W. Martin, 1998–2009. http://www.preces-latinae.org/thesaurus/Hymni/Pange.html, consulted 22 February 2010.

Cernuda, Luis. *Estudios sobre poesía española contemporánea*. Madrid: Guadarrama, 1957.

Cervantes, Miguel de. *Don Quijote de la Mancha*. Ed. Martín de Riquer. 3rd. rev. ed. Barcelona: Juventud, 1955.

– *Obras completas*. Ed. Ángel Valbuena Prat. Madrid: Aguilar, 1960.

Chang, Chin-Chuang. "Nationalism in the Piano Works of Manuel de Falla." Unpublished PhD thesis. Cincinnati, Ohio: University of Cincinnati, 2000.

Chase, Gilbert. *The Music of Spain*. 2nd rev. ed. New York: Dover, 1959.

Christoforidis, Michael. "A Composer's Annotations to his Personal Library: An Introduction to the Manuel de Falla Collection." *Context* 17 (1999): 33–68.

– "Aspects of the Creative Process in Manuel de Falla's *El Retablo de Maese Pedro and Concerto*." 2 vols. PhD diss., University of Melbourne, 1997.

– "Folksong Models and Their Sources: Manuel de Falla's *Siete canciones populares españolas*." *Context* 9 (1995): 13–21.

– "Hacia nuevos conceptos de 'ópera' en los Proyectos de Manuel de Falla (1911–1923)." In *La ópera en España e Hispanoamérica*. Ed. Emilio Casares Rodicio and Álvaro Torrente, 363–71. Madrid: Instituto Complutense de Ciencias Musicales, 2001.

– "Manuel de Falla, Flamenco and Spanish identity." *Western Music and Race*. Ed. Julie Brown. Cambridge: Cambridge University Press, 2007. 230–43.

– "Manuel de Falla on Romanticism: Insights into an Uncited Text." *Context* 6 (1993–4): 26–31.

– "The Moor's Last Sigh: Paris, Symbolism and the Alhambra". Unpubl. lecture. 9-page typescript.

– *Un acercamiento a la postura de Manuel de Falla en el "Cante jondo (canto primitivo andaluz)."* Granada: Archivo Manuel de Falla, 1997.

Clark, Walter Aaron. *Isaac Albéniz. Portrait of a Romantic.* Oxford: Oxford University Press, 1999.

Collins, Chris. "Manuel de Falla and L'Acoustique Nouvelle: A Myth Exposed." *Journal of the Royal Music Association* 128, no. 1 (2003): 71–97.

Combarieu, Jules. *La Musique et la magie. Étude sur les origines populaires de l'art musical, son influence et sa fonction dans les sociétés.* 2nd. ed. Ginebra: Minkoff Reprints, 1972. Reprint of the 1909 ed. consulted by Falla.

Comellas, José Luis. *Historia de España moderna y contemporánea (1475–1965).* Madrid: Ediciones Rialp, 1967.

Concert VI, Associació de música "Da cámara" de Barcelona, 9 February 1925. Program.

Concert XIII of the Sociedad Nacional de Música (Madrid), Teatro de Eslava, 17 June 1919. Program.

Couffon, Claude. *Granada y García Lorca.* Trans. Bernardo Kordon. Buenos Aires: Losada, 1967.

Crosbie, James. "Structure and Counter-Structure in Lorca's 'Romancero gitano'." *Modern Language Review* 77, no. 1 (Jan. 1982): 74–88. http://dx.doi .org/10.2307/3727495.

Dalí, Salvador. "Sant Sebastià," *L'Amic de les arts*, year 2, no. 16 (31 July 1927): 52–4.

Darío, Rubén. *Azul…* Prologue Juan Valera. 12th ed. Buenos Aires: Espasa-Calpe, 1957.

– *Obras completas.* Vol. 5. Madrid: Afrodisio Aguado, 1953.

Debicki, Andrew. *"Federico García Lorca: estilización y visión de la poesía",* en Estudios sobre poesía española contemporánea. Madrid: Gredos, 1968. 202–23.

Debussy, Claude. *Deux Arabesques.* Paris: Durand, 1904. Score.

– *Estampes. Pour le Piano.* I. *Pagodes.* II. *La Soirée dans Grenade.* III. *Jardins sous la Pluie.* Bryn Mawr, Pennsylvania: Durand & Cie, Éditeurs, París, and Elkan-Vogel, 1903. Score.

– *Ibéria. "Images" pour orchestre,* no. 3. Paris: Éditions Durand & Cie., 1910. Score.

– *Monsieur Croche et autres écrits.* Paris: Gallimard, 1971.

Demarquez, Suzanne. *Manuel de Falla.* Barcelona: Labor, 1968.

Devoto, Daniel. "Notas sobre el elemento tradicional en la obra de García Lorca." *Federico García Lorca*, ed. Gil Ildefonso-Manuel. Madrid: Taurus, 1973. 115–64.

Díaz Díaz, Gonzalo, "García Bacca, Juan David." *Hombres y documentos de la filosofía española*. III (E-G). Madrid: Consejo Superior de Investigaciones Científicas, 1987. 380–92.

Díaz-Plaja, Guillermo. *Federico García Lorca*. Buenos Aires: Espasa-Calpe, 1954.

Diego, Gerardo (pseud. Federico García Lorca). "Don Luis a caballo." *Lola* 2 (Jan. 1928): 2.

Diego, Gerardo. *Primera antología de sus versos*. 5th ed. Madrid: Espasa-Calpe, 1958.

Dimmock, John. "Rey de la Torre discusses Manuel de Falla's Homage to Debussy," 7 July 2008. John Dimmick, *Guitar.com Blog*. http://www.guitarist .com/blog/?s=Falla, consulted 13 June 2011.

Dinverno, Melissa, "García Lorca´s *Suites* and the Editorial Construction of Literature." *Modern Language Notes* 119, no. 2 (March 2004): 302–28.

Dolan, Kathleen Hunt. "Figures of Disclosure: Pictorial Space in Marvell and Góngora." *Comparative Literature* 40, no. 3 (1988): 245–58. http://dx.doi .org/10.2307/1771016.

Doménech, Ricardo. *García Lorca y la tragedia española*. Madrid: Fundamentos, 2008.

"Dos conciertos de música contemporánea." Grupo de cámara y solista, Orquesta Filarmónica de Madrid, 12 and 19 June 1934. Program.

Drouot, Paul. *La Grappe de raisin*. París: Éditions de la Phalange, 1908.

Dupin, Marc-Olivier. "Édito," *L´Île joyeuse. Journal de l´Orchestre Nationale d´Île de France* (2007): C.

Durán, Agustín, ed. and prologue. *Romancero general o colección de romances castellanos*. 2 vols. Madrid: Sucesores de Hernando, 1916.

Durán, Manuel. "Lorca y las vanguardias." *Hispania* 69, no. 4 (1986): 764–70.

Emerson, Ralph Waldo. "Goethe or the Writer." In *Representative Men* (1850). Ralph Waldo Emerson Texts. © 1996–2001 09/03/2009 17:36:09. http://www .emersoncentral.com/goethe.htm.

Falla, Manuel de. *El amor brujo (L'Amour sorcier)*. London: J. & W. Chester, 1924. Score.

– *Canciones populares españolas*. Teresa Berganza y Narciso Yepes. CD Recording. París: Editions M. Eschig. Deutsche Grammophon, 1977. LP.

– *Cantares de Nochebuena para voz y guitarra*. Madrid: Manuel de Falla, Ediciones, 1992. Score.

– *El "Cante jondo" (Canto primitivo andaluz)*. In *Escritos sobre música y músicos*, 140–7.

- *Concerto per Clavicembalo (o Pianoforte) Flauto, Oboe, Clarinetto, Violino e Violoncello.* Paris: Éditions Max Eschig, 1928. Score.
- *Escritos sobre música y músicos.* 4th. ed. Ed. Federico Sopeña. Madrid: Espasa-Calpe, 1988.
- *Fantasía Bætica for Piano.* Londres: J & W Chester/Edition Wilhelm Hansen, 1922. Score.
- *Homenaje. La Tombeau de Claude Debussy for Guitar Solo.* 2nd. rev. ed. Ed. John Duarte. London: J & W Chester / Edition Wilhelm Hansen, 1984. Score.
- *Noches en los jardines de España. Nuits dans les jardín d'Espagne. Impressions symphoniques pour piano et orchestee en trois parties.* Paris: Max Eschig et Cie. Editeurs, 1922. Score.
- *Piezas españolas,* in *Homenaje que el Ateneo de Madrid dedica a los compositores D. Manuel de Falla y D. Joaquín Turina* (Madrid, 15 Jan. 1915). Program, 5–8.
- *El retablo de maese Pedro. Adaptación musical y escénica de un episodio de "El ingenioso caballero D. Quixote de la Mancha" de Miguel de Cervantes.* Edición facsímil de los manuscritos fundamentales. Granada. Junta de Andalucía. Centro de documentación musical de Andalucía. Ayuntamiento de Granada. Manuel de Falla Ediciones, 2011.
- *El retablo de maese Pedro.* London: J. & W. Chester, 1924. Score.
- *Seven Spanish Folk-Songs.* New York: Associated Music Publishers, 1949. Score.
- *El sombrero de tres picos.* Londres: Chester Music, 1921. Score.
- *Soneto a Córdoba de Luis de Góngora. Canto y arpa (o piano).* London: Oxford University Press, 1932. Score.
- *Songs and Piano Music. Selections.* Merlin Quaife, Soprano. Len Forster, Piano. Hong Kong: 8.54498 Naxos Music Library. 2004. Audio CD.
- *La vida breve. El amor brujo. El sombrero de tres picos.* Victoria de los Ángeles, Rafael Frühbeck de Burgos, Carlo Maria Giulini. Orquesta Nacional de España, Philarmonia Orchestra. Instituto Ramiro de Maeztu, 1965. London: EMI Recordings, 2001. Audio CD.
- *La vie brève. L'amour sourcier. Les Tréteaux de Maître Pierre.* Paris: L'Avant-Scène Opéra, Éditions Premières Loges (May–June), 1997.
Falla, María Isabel de. "Presentación. Falla y Lorca. Entre la tradición y la vanguardia," ed. Susana Zapke, 9. In *Falla y Lorca.*
Fernández Galiano, Manuel. "Los dioses de Federico." *Cuadernos Hispanoamericanos* 217 (January 1968): 31–43.
Fernández Montesinos-García, Manuel. "Descripción de la biblioteca de Federico García Lorca. Catálogo y estudio." MA diss., Universidad Complutense, 1985.
Fischer, Robert. *Picasso.* New York: Tudor, 1966.
Forster, J.C. "Posibles puntos de partida para dos poemas de Lorca." *Romance Notes* 11 (1969–70): 498–500.

Fox, E. Inman. *La invención de España. Nacionalismo liberal e identidad nacional*. Madrid: Cátedra, 1997.

G.D. (pseud. Gerardo Diego). "La conversión de Falla," *Lola amiga y suplemento de Carmen, 1. Crónica del centenario de Góngora (1627–1927)*, in *Carmen. Revista chica de poesía española*, 1 (Dec. 1927), 3.

Gallego, Antonio. *Conciertos de inauguración del Archivo Manuel de Falla.* Granada: Archivo Manuel de Falla, 1991.

– In Manuel de Falla, *Siete canciones populares españolas,* Victoria de los Ángeles, Orquestra de Cambra teatre Liure, Josep Pons. Arles: Harmonia Mundi, 2008. 17. CD HMG 501432. Audio CD.

– *Manuel de Falla y* El amor brujo. Madrid: Alianza, 1990.

Ganivet, Ángel. *El escultor de su alma.* Ed. María Carmen Díaz de Alda Heikkilä. Granada: Archivum, 1999.

García Bacca, Juan David. *Filosofía de la música.* Barcelona: Anthropos, 1990.

García Lorca, Federico. *Conferencias.* 2 vols. Ed. Christopher Maurer. Madrid: Alianza, 1984.

– *Cristo. Tragedia religiosa.* In *Teatro inédito de juventud.* Ed. Andrés Soria Olmedo. Madrid: Cátedra, 1994. 233–96.

– *Epistolario.* 2 vols. Ed. Christopher Maurer. Madrid: Alianza, 1983.

– *Lola la comedianta.* Ed. Piero Menarini. Madrid: Alianza, 1981.

– *Obras completas.* Ed. Arturo del Hoyo. Prol. Jorge Guillen. 23rd ed. 3 vols. Madrid: Aguilar, 1989.

– "Oda al Santísimo Sacramento del altar." In Eutimio Martín, *Federico García Lorca, heterodoxo y mártir. Análisis y proyección de la obra juvenil inédita.* Madrid: Siglo Veintiuno de España Editores, 1986. 267–76.

– "Petenera," tr. Jean Cassou. *Intentions* 3 (1924): 31–4.

– *Poema del cante jondo.* Ed. Christian de Paepe. Madrid: Espasa-Calpe, 1986.

– *Poema del cante jondo,* 9th. ed. Ed. Luis García Montero. Madrid: Espasa-Calpe, 1993.

– *Poema del cante jondo: 1921. Seguido de tres textos teóricos de Federico García Lorca y Manuel de Falla.* Ed. Mario Hernández. Madrid: Alianza, 1982.

– *Poesía inédita de juventud.* Ed. Christian de Paepe. Madrid: Cátedra, 1994.

– *Primer romancero gitano.* Ed. Christian de Paepe. Madrid: Espasa-Calpe, 1991.

– *Primer romancero gitano. Llanto por Ignacio Sánchez Mejías.* Ed. Manuel García-Posada. Madrid: Castalia, 1988.

– *Primer romancero gitano (1924–1927). Otros romances del teatro (1924–1935).* 3rd ed. Ed. Mario Hernández. Madrid: Alianza, 1983.

– *Prosa inédita de juventud.* Ed. Christopher Maurer. Madrid. Cátedra, 1994.

– *Romancero gitano.* Ed. Allans Josephs and Juan Caballero. Madrid: Cátedra, 1978.

- *Romancero gitano*. Ed. Herbert Ramsden. Manchester: Manchester University Press, 1988.
- *Suites*. Ed André Belamich. Barcelona: Ariel, 1983.
- García Lorca, Federico, and Melchor Fernández Almagro. *Crónica de una amistad. Epistolario (1919–1934)*. Granada: Fundación Federico García Lorca, Caja de Ahorros de Granada, 2006.

García Lorca, Francisco. *Federico y su mundo*. 2nd ed. Ed. Mario Hernández. Madrid: Alianza, 1981.

García Lorca, Isabel. *Recuerdos míos*. Ed. Ana Gurruchaga, prologue Claudio Guillén. Barcelona: Tusquets Editores, 2002.

García Matos, Manuel. "El folklore en *La vida breve* de Manuel de Falla." *Anuario Musical* 26 (1971): 173–97.
- "Folklore en Falla, I." *Música* 2, nos. 3–4 (1953): 47–67.
- "Folklore en Falla, II." *Música* 2, no. 6 (1953): 33–52.

García-Posada, Miguel. "La vida de los muertos: un tema común a Baudelaire y Lorca," *Anuario de la Sociedad Española de Literatura General y Comparada*, Año 1978: 109–18.

Gervais, Françoise. "La Notion d'arabesque chez Debussy." *Revue Musicale* (Paris) 241 (1958): 3–23.

Gibson, Ian. *El asesinato de García Lorca*. Barcelona: Plaza y Janés, 1997.
- *Caballo azul de mi locura: Lorca y el mundo gay*. Madrid: Planeta, 2009.
- *Federico García Lorca*. 2 vols. Barcelona: Grijalba, 1985.
- *Federico García Lorca. A Life*. New York: Pantheon Books, 1989.

Gómez Montero, Javier. "Lorcas *Romancero gitano* und die Subjektivierung des Mythos," ed. Susana Zapke, 89–111. In *Falla y Lorca*.

González-del-Valle, Luis T. "La concepción musical de *Amor de Don Perlimplín con Belisa en su jardín*." *El teatro de Federico García Lorca y otros ensayos sobre literatura española e hispanoamericana*. Lincoln, NE: Society of Spanish and Spanish American Studies, 1980. 61–79.

Góngora, Luis de. See under Alonso, Dámaso.

Guillén, Jorge. *Federico in persona*. Milan: All'insegna del pesce d'oro, 1959.

Haboucha, Reginetta. "Pérez de Hita, Ginés." In *Dictionary of the Literature of the Iberian Peninsula*, L-Z. Ed. Germán Bleiberg, Maureen Ihrie, and Janet Pérez. Westport, CT, London: Greenwood Press, 1993. 1259–61.

Harnack, Adolf von. *Lehrbuch der Dogmengeschichte*, I. 3d. rev. ed. Freiburg i. B.: Mohr, 1894.

Harper, Nancy Lee. "The Interpretation of Manuel de Falla's *Fantasía Baetica*," European Piano Teacher Association. Piano Teacher Associates of New York. Dr Salvatore Moltisanti, pianist, Chairman, Partial Transcripts from the VIII Annual World Piano Teachers Associates Conference, New York University

Casa Italiana, 27–9 April 2008. http://www.ibla.org/events/2005_wpta_ publication.php4#nancy_l.

– *Manuel de Falla. His Life and Music*. Lanham, MD, and Oxford: Scarecrow Press, 2005.

Henríquez Ureña, Max. *Breve historia del modernismo*. 2nd ed. Mexico: Fondo de Cultura Económica, 1962.

Henry, Hugh. "Agnus Dei (in Liturgy)." *The Catholic Encyclopedia*. Vol. 1. New York: Robert Appleton Company, 1907. http://www.newadvent.org/cathen/ 01221a.htm, consulted 23 Feb. 2010.

– "Pange Lingua Gloriosi." *The Catholic Encyclopedia*. Vol. 11. New York: Robert Appleton Company, 1911. http://www.newadvent.org/cathen/11441c .htm, consulted 22 Feb. 2010.

Hess, Carol A. *Manuel de Falla and Modernism in Spain, 1898–1936*. Chicago, London: University of Chicago Press, 2001.

– *Sacred Passions. The Life and Music of Manuel de Falla*. Oxford, New York: Oxford University Press, 2005.

Holy Bible, rev. standard version. 4th ed. Toronto, NY, Edinburgh: Thomas Nelson & Sons, 1952.

Homenaje al eximio gaditano Manuel de Falla, Real Academia Filarmónica de Santa Cecilia de Cádiz, 1 May 1928. Program.

Huffman, Carl A. "Pythagoras." In *The Cambridge Dictionary of Philosophy*. Ed. Robert Audi. 2nd ed. Cambridge: Cambridge University Press, 1999. 760–1.

Hugo, Victor. *Les Orientales*. Brussels: E. Laurent, 1832.

Huidobro, Vicente. *Obra poética*. Madrid: Unigraf, 2003.

Inzenga, José. *Ecos de España: colección de cantos y bailes populares*. Barcelona: Andrés Vidal y Roger, 1900.

Jaensch, Erich. "*Über die Wahnehmung des Raumes*." *Zeitschrift für Psychologie und Physiologie der Sinnesorgane* 6 (1911): 1–488.

Jiménez, Juan Ramón. *Segunda antolojía poética (1898–1918)*. Madrid: Espasa-Calpe, 1959.

Karageorgou-Bastea, Christina. *Arquitectura de voces. Federico García Lorca y el Poema del cante jondo*. México: El Colegio de México, 2008.

Kennedy, Michael. *The Concise Oxford Dictionary of Music*. 3rd ed. Oxford, New York: Oxford University Press, 1980.

Klein, Dennis. "The Influence of Manuel de Falla on García Lorca: A Note." *García Lorca Review* (1976): 115–19.

– "The Possible Influence of Falla's *La vida breve* on Lorca's Later Plays." *García Lorca Review* 9 (1981): 91–6.

Lapesa, Rafael. *Historia de la lengua española*. 5th rev. ed. Madrid: Escelicer, 1959.

Lázaro Carreter, Fernando. "Lectura del 'Llanto' de García Lorca." *Los Domingos de ABC*, no. 848. 12 August 1984, pp. 8–9.

León, Luis de. *Exposición del Libro de Job*. Madrid: Pedro Marín, 1779.

– *Obras completas castellanas*. 5th ed. rev. Ed. Félix García. 2 vols. Madrid: Biblioteca de Autores Cristianos, 1991.

– *La perfecta casada*. Madrid: Compañía Ibero-Americana de Publicación, n.d.

– *Traducción literal and declaración del Libro de los Cantares de Salomón*. Salamanca: Oficina de Francisco de Toxar, 1798.

León, Luis de, and Saint John of the Cross (San Juan de la Cruz). *Poesías*. Madrid: Hernando, 1923.

Loughran, David. "Myth, the Gypsy, and Two 'Romances históricos' in Lorca's *Romancero gitano*." *Modern Language Notes* 87, no. 2 (March 1972): 253–71.

Lucas, Louis. *L'Acoustique nouvelle. Essai d'application à la musique d' une théorie philosophique*. París: Louis Lucas, 1854. With Falla's notes.

M., R.H. "*La Notion d'arabesque chez Debussy*. By Françoise Gervais." *La Revue Musicale*, No. 241. (Richard-Masse, Paris, 1958, Fr. 600). 188.

Macdonald, Hugh. "Manuel de Falla. Suite from 'Atlàntida' and Brahms." Boston Symphony Orchestra, 2010–2011 Season, Week 5. November 4–9, 2010. Program Note. 31–5. http://archive.org/stream/ bostonsymphonys2010111bos#page/n437/mode/2up.

Machado, Antonio. *Campos de Castilla*. Ed. Geoffrey Ribbans. Madrid: Cátedra, 1989.

– *Soledades. Galerías. Otros poemas,* 14th ed. rev. Ed. Geoffrey Ribbans. Madrid: Cátedra, 1997.

Machado, Manuel y Antonio. *Obras completas*. Madrid: Plenitud, 1967.

Machado y Álvarez, Antonio. *Cantes flamencos: Colección escogida*. Madrid: Impr. popular a cargo de T. Rey, 1880–9(?).

Manrique, Jorge. *Obra completa*. 8th. ed., Prol. Augusto Cortina. Buenos Aires: Espasa-Calpe, 1966.

Marcilly, C. "Il faut passer les ponts ..." *Europe* 616–17 (1980): 29–50.

– "Notes pour l'étude de la pensée religieuse de Federico García Lorca." *Les Languages Neo-Latines* 141 (1957): 9–42.

Martín, Eutimio. *Federico García Lorca, heterodoxo y mártir. Análisis y proyección de la obra juvenil inédita*. Madrid: Siglo Veintiuno de España Editores, 1986.

Martínez Nadal, Rafael, *Federico García Lorca and* The Public. New York: Schocken, 1974

Martínez Ruiz, José. *La voluntad*, 2nd ed. Ed. J. Inman Fox. Madrid: Castalia,1972.

Martínez Sierra, Gregorio (pseud. María Lejárraga). *Granada (Guía emocional)*. París: Garnier Hermanos, 1911.

– (pseud. María Lejárraga). *La pasión. Los románticos*. Madrid: Renacimiento, 1914.

Martínez Sierra, María (Lejárraga). *Gregorio y yo*. Mexico City: Biografías Gandesa, 1953.

Maurer, Christopher. *Federico García Lorca y su Arquitectura del cante jondo*. Granada: Comares, 2000.

– "Lorca y las formas de la música." *Lecciones sobre Federico García Lorca, Mayo de 1986*, 237–51. Ed. Andrés Soria Olmedo. Granada: Ediciones del Cincuentenario, 1986. 235–50.

– "Two Critical Editions of Lorca's Early Poetry." *Anales de la Literatura Española Contemporánea* 14 (1989): 223–37.

Mendelssohn-Bartholdy, Felix. *Liede ohne Worte. Für Pianoforte solo*. 2nd ed. rev. Ed. Theodor Kullak. Leipzig: Editions Peter, [189–]. Score.

Menéndez Pidal, Ramón. *Flor nueva de romances viejos*. 16th ed. Buenos Aires: Espasa-Calpe, 1967.

Miller, Norman C. *García Lorca's* Poema del cante jondo. London: Tamesis, 1978.

Molina Fajardo, Eduardo. *Manuel de Falla y el "Cante jondo*. Granada: Universidad de Granada, 1962.

Moliner, María. *Diccionario de uso del español*. 2 vols. Madrid: Gredos, 1967.

Mora Guarnido, José. *Federico García Lorca y su mundo. Testimonio para una biografía*. Buenos Aires: Losada, 1958.

Morris, C. Brian. *Son of Andalusia. The Lyrical Landscapes of Federico García Lorca*. Nashville, TN: University of Vanderbilt Press, 1997.

Nandorfy, Martha J. *The Poetics of Apocalypse: Federico García Lorca's Poet in New York*. Lewisburg, PA: Bucknell Press/London: Associated University Press, 2003.

Navarro Tomás, Tomas. *Arte del verso*. 3rd ed. Mexico City: Compañía General de Ediciones, 1965.

– *Estudios de fonología española*. Syracuse, NY: Syracuse University Press, 1946.

– *Manual de pronunciación española*. 5th rev. ed. New York: Hafner Publishing Company, 1957.

Neenan, Professor Tom. "Beethoven's Missa Solemnis. Mass in D, Op. 123." http://www.its.caltech.edu/~tan/BeethovenMissaSolemnis/analysis_of_missa_ solemnis.html#Agnus Dei, last updated 29 May 1996 and consulted 15 April 2011.

Newberry, Wilma. "Aesthetic Distance in García Lorca's *El Público*: Pirandello and Ortega." *Hispanic Review* 37, no. 2 (1969): 276–96. http://dx.doi.org/ 10.2307/471736.

Niemöller, Klaus Wolfgang. "Der Gedank einer nationalen Musik im europäischen Raum und der musikalische Hispanismus," ed. Susana Zapke, 25–36. In *Falla y Lorca*.

Nommick, Yvan. "Día de Reyes en casa de los Lorca. Muñecos en busca de maese." *La Opinión de Granada* (2 January 2005): 62.

– "Un ejemplo de ambigüedad formal: El *Allegro* del *Concerto* de Manuel de Falla." *Revista de musicología* 21, no. 1 (1998): 11–35.

– *Jardines de España de Santiago Rusiñol a Manuel de Falla*. Granada: Ayuntamiento de Granada, 1997.

Ochoa Penroz, Marcela. "Federico García Lorca o la palabra que gime." *Hispanic Poetry Review* 3, no. 2 (2001): 57–70.

Orozco, Manuel. *Falla. Biografía ilustrada*. Barcelona: Destino, 1968.

Orringer, Nelson R. "Absurd Un-forgetting in García Lorca's 'La viuda de la luna'." *Hispanic Journal* 27, no. 2 (2006): 43–56.

– "El impacto del creacionismo en *Canciones* de García Lorca," *Rilce* 24, no. 2 (2008): 357–74.

– *Ganivet (1865–1898)*. Madrid: Ediciones del Orto, 1998.

– "El diálogo con dos bucólicos griegos en el *Llanto por Ignacio Sánchez Mejías*." In *La tradición clásica en la obra de Federico García Lorca*. Ed. María Camacho Rojo José. Granada: Universidad de Granada, 2006. 199–207.

– *El diálogo entre Falla y Lorca sobre la creación folklórica*. Santander: Real Sociedad Menéndez Pelayo, 2011.

– "García Lorca's *Romancero gitano*: A Dialogue with Baudelaire." *Anales de Literatura Española Contemporánea* 27, no. 2 (2002): 221–44.

– "Introduction to Hispanic Modernisms." *Bulletin of Spanish Studies* 79, nos. 2–3 (March-May 2002): 133–48. http://dx.doi.org/10.1080/147538202317344952.

– "Married Temptresses in Falla and Lorca." *Bulletin of Spanish Studies* 88, no. 7–8 (2011): 201–17. http://dx.doi.org/10.1080/14753820.2011.620317.

Ortega y Gasset, José. "Introducción a un 'Don Juan'." In *Obras completas*. 12 vols. Madrid: Revista de Occidente, 1983. 6:121–36.

– *Meditaciones del Quijote*. In *Obras completas*. 1:311–400.

– *La rebelión de las masas*. In *Obras completas*. 4:113–285.

Oxtoby, Willard G. "Zoroastrianism." *The Cambridge Dictionary of Philosophy* 2nd ed. Ed. Robert Audi. Cambridge: Cambridge University Press, 2001. 988–9.

Pabanó, F.M. *Historia y costumbres de los gitanos*. Barcelona: Montaner y Simón, 1915.

Paco, Mariano de. "El auto sacramental en el siglo XX: Variaciones ascéticas del modelo calderoniano." In *Calderón, sistema dramático y técnicas escénicas: actas de las XXIII Jornadas de teatro clásico, Almagro, 11, 12 y 13 de julio de 2000*. Ed. Elena Marcello, Felipe B. Pedraza Jiménez and Rafael González Cañal. Cuenca, Universidad de Castilla-La Mancha, 2001. 365–88.

Pahissa, Jaime. *Vida y obra de Manuel de Falla.* 2nd rev. ed. Buenos Aires: Ricordí Americana, 1956.

Parker, A.A. "The Devil in Calderón." In *Critical Essays on the Theater of Calderón.* Ed. Bruce W. Wardropper. New York: New York University Press, 1965. 3–23.

Pedrell, Felipe. *Cancionero musical popular español.* Valls: Eduardo Castell, n.d.

– *Por nuestra música.* Bellaterra: Publicacions de la Universitat Autónoma de Barcelona, 1991.

Persia, Jorge de. "Lorca, Falla y la música. Una coincidencia intergeneracional." In *Falla y Lorca,* ed. Susana Zapke, 67–81.

– *I Concurso de Cante Jondo, 1922–1992.* Granada: Archivo Manuel de Falla, 1992.

Pino, Rafael del. "Gerardo Diego en apuntes." *La Opinión de Grenada* (24 April 2005): 34.

Plato. *Euthyphro. Apology. Crito. Phaedo. Phaedrus,* 18th. ed. Tr. Harold North Fowler. Cambridge, MA/London, UK: Harvard University Press, 1995.

– *Republic* 1–5, 10th ed. Tr. Paul Shorey. Cambridge, MA/London, UK: Harvard University Press, 1994 .

Pliny the Elder. *The Natural History.* In *Lacus Curtius,* Copyright Bill Thayer, 22 February 2002. http://penelope.uchicago.edu/Thayer/L/Roman/Texts/Pliny_the_Elder/12*.html.

Quance, Roberta A. "'Burla de Don Pedro a caballo': The Modern Ballad's Dismal Hunt." *Romance Quarterly* 33, no. 1 (Feb. 1986): 79–87. http://dx.doi.org/10.1080/08831157.1986.9925762.

– *In the Light of Contradiction: Desire in the Poetry of Federico García Lorca.* Oxford: Legenda, 2010.

– "The Trouble with Gender in Lorca's Suites: 'Surtidores'." *Hispanic Review* 74, no. 4 (2006): 397–418. http://dx.doi.org/10.1353/hir.2006.0038.

Renallus Grammaticus. Doctor Barchinonensis. *Vita vel Passio Sanctae Eulaliae.* In Henrique Flórez. *España sagrada. Teatro geográfico-histórico de la Iglesia de España.* XXIX. Madrid: D. Antonio de Sancha, 1775. 375–90.

Ribas, Pedro. *Para leer a Unamuno.* Madrid: Alianza, 2002.

Río, Ángel del. *Federico García Lorca (1899–1936).* New York: Hispanic Institute in the United States, 1941.

Ross, Alex. "Deep Song: Lorca Inspires an Opera by Osvaldo Golijov." *New Yorker.* 1 September 2003. 128–9.

Rotenstreich, Nathan. "Volksgeist." *Dictionary of the History of Ideas.* 2nd ed. New York: Charles Scribners, 1973. 4:490–6.

Sahuquillo, Ángel. *Federico García Lorca y la cultura de la homosexualidad.* PhD diss., U. Stockholm. Edsbruk, Sweden: Akademitryck, 1986.

Saint John of the Cross (San Juan de la Cruz). *Obras de San Juan de la Cruz.* Madrid: Apostolado de la Prensa, 1926.

- *Poesías completas.* Ed. Cristóbal Cuevas. Barcelona: Brugueras, 1981.

Saint Teresa of Avila (Santa Teresa de Jesús). *Las Moradas.* Madrid: La Lectura, 1922.

- *Moradas del castillo interior.* In *Obras completas.* 2nd rev. ed. Ed. Efren de la Madre de Dios and Otger Steggink. Madrid: Biblioteca de Autores Cristianos, 1967. 363–450.

Salazar, Adolfo. *Textos de crítica musical en el periódico El Sol (1918–1936).* Intro. and ed. José María García Laborda and Josefa Ruiz Vicente. Seville: Editorial Doble J, 2009.

Salinas, Pedro. *Ensayos de literatura hispánica.* 2nd ed. Madrid: Aguilar, 1961.

- *La poesía de Rubén Dario.* 2nd ed. Buenos Aires: Losada, 1957.

Salvador, Gregorio. *Glosas al "Romance sonámbulo" de García Lorca.* Granada: Universidad de Granada, 1980.

Sánchez Mejías, Ignacio. *Escritos periodísticos.* Ed. Alfonso Carlos Saiz Valdevieso. Bilbao: Laida, 1991.

- *Teatro.* Ed. Antonio Gallego Morell. Madrid: Espasa-Calpe, 1988.

Schenker, Heinrich. *Die Meisterwork in der Musik.* Munich: Drei Masken Verlag, 1925–30. http://www.schenkerdocumentsonline.org/profiles/work/index.html.

Scobie, Alex. "Lorca and Eulalia." *Arcadia* 9, no. 1–3 (1974): 290–8.

Segal, Peter. "Truth Without Authenticity: Origins of Manuel de Falla's Homenaje: 'Le Tombeau de Debussy'." *Guitar Review* 88 (1992): 18–23.

Singer, Deborah Pava. "Present in Spirit: Cante Jondo in Selected Works by Debussy, and the Influence of these Works on Manuel de Falla's Homenaje. Pièce de guitare écrite pour "Le Tombeau de Claude Debussy." MA diss., University of Iowa, 2006.

Soanes, Catherine, and Angus Stevenson. *The Concise Oxford English Dictionary,* 11th. ed. rev. Oxford: Oxford University Press, 2009.

Solomon, Maynard. *Beethoven.* New York: Schirmer; London: Prentice Hall, 1998.

Southworth, Eric. "On Lorca's "San Rafael (Córdoba)" and some other texts." *Modern Language Review* 94, no. 1 (1 January 1999): 87–101. http://dx.doi.org/10.2307/3736001.

- "Religion." In *A Companion to Federico García Lorca.* Ed. Federico Bonaddio. London: Tamesis, Woodbridge, 2007. 129–48.

Stanton, Edward F. *The Tragic Myth. Lorca and Cante Jondo.* Lexington: University of Kentucky Press, 1978.

Tinnell, Roger D. *Federico García Lorca y la música: Catálogo y discografía anotados.(Biblioteca de música española contemporánea).* Madrid: Fundación

Juan March in collaboration with the Fundación Federico García Lorca, 1993.

Torrecilla, Jesús. "Estereotipos que se resisten a morir: el andalucismo de *Bodas de sangre*." *Anales de la Literatura Española Contemporánea* 33, no. 2 (2008): 229–49.

Torres Clemente, Elena. "Manuel de Falla, del cisne al búho. Estudio de los borradores y manuscritos de El retablo de maese Pedro como tentativas para la construcción de un nuevo lenguaje." In Manuel de Falla, *El retablo de maese Pedro. Adaptación musical y escénica de un episodio de "El ingenioso caballero D. Quixote de la Mancha" de Miguel de Cervantes*. Edición facsímil de los manuscritos fundamentales. Granada. Junta de Andalucía. Centro de documentación musical de Andalucía. Ayuntamiento de Granada. Manuel de Falla Ediciones, 2011. Pp. XI–XLI.

– *Manuel de Falla y las cantigas de Alfonso X el Sabio: Estudio de una relación continua y plural.* Granada: Universidad de Granada, 2002.

Trend, J.B. *Manuel de Falla and Spanish Music*. New York: Alfred A. Knopf, 1934.

Turina, Joaquín. *Enciclopedia abreviada de música*, 2 vols. Madrid: Renacimiento, 1917. With Falla's annotations.

Umbral, Francisco. *Lorca, poeta maldito*. Madrid: Biblioteca Nueva, 1968.

Unamuno, Miguel de. *Del sentimiento trágico de la vida en los hombres y en los pueblos y Tratado del amor de Dios*. Ed. Nelson R. Orringer. Madrid: Tecnos, 2005.

– Miguel de. *Niebla*. In *Obras completas.* 9 vols. Madrid: Escelicer, 1966. 2:543–682.

Valbuena Prat, Ángel. "Introducción." In Pedro Calderón de la Barca. *Autos sacramentales*, with prologue, edition, and notes of Valbuena Prat. 2 vols. 1:9–36; 2:IX–XXII.

Verlaine, Paul. *Œuvres poétiques complètes*. Ed. Y.-G. LeDantec. París: Pléiade, Gallimard, 1954.

Viera, D.J. "El caballo negro en Antero de Quental y en García Lorca, y el tema amor-muerte." *Thesaurus* 36 (1981): 71–89.

Viñes Millet, Cristina. *La Alhambra que fascinó a los románticos*. Granada: Patronato de la Alhambra y Generalife, 2007.

Walsh, Michael. *A New Dictionary of Saints: East and West*. Collegeville, MN: Liturgical Press, Saint John's Abbey, 2007.

Walsh, Stephen. *Stravinsky: A Creative Spring: Russia and France, 1882–1934*. Berkeley: University of California Press.

Walters, D. Gareth. "Parallel Trajectories in the Careers of Falla and Lorca." In Federico Bonaddio and Xon de Ros, *Crossing Fields in Modern Spanish Culture*. Oxford: Legenda, European Humanities Research Center, 2003. 92–102.

Weber, Eckhard. *Manuel de Falla und die Idee der spanischen Nationaloper.* Frankfurt, New York: Peter Lang, 2000.

Weber, Eckhard. "Misterio para voces y orquesta: Pedro Calderón de la Barca, libretista del teatro musical del siglo XX." In *Calderón 2000: homenaje a Kurt Reichenberger en su 80 cumpleaños: Actas del Congreso Internacional, IV centenario del nacimiento de Calderón.* 2 vols. Pamplona: Universidad de Navarra. Sept. 2002. Vol. 1:905–18.

– "Los *Títeres de Cachiporra* und *El retablo de maese Pedro*: Manuel de Fallas Beschäftigung mit dem Puppentheater und die neuen Tendenzen im Musiktheater seiner Zeit." In *Falla y Lorca*, ed. Susana Zapke, 117–53.

W(hite), R. "Ayer en el Ateneo: Homenaje a Debussy." El Universo (Madrid) (28 April 1918): 1–2.

Wilde, Oscar. *Salomé: a tragedy in one act.* London: John Lane, 1912.

Zapke, Susana. "Presencia de la música antigua en la obra de Falla." In *Falla y Lorca*, ed. Susana Zapke, 39–64.

– "Presentación." In *Falla y Lorca*, ed. Susana Zapke, 3–7.

"Zarzuela.net *La montería*." © Christopher Webber, Blackheath, London, 2 January 2002. http://www.zarzuela.net/syn/monteria.htm, consulted 5 June 2010.

Zorrilla, José. *La leyenda de Don Juan Tenorio.* Barcelona: Montaner y Simón, 1895.

Index

TORONTO IBERIC

1 Anthony J. Cascardi, *Cervantes, Literature, and the Discourse of Politics*

2 Jessica A. Boon, *The Mystical Science of the Soul: Medieval Cognition in Bernardino de Laredo's Recollection Method*

3 Susan Byrne, *Law and History in Cervantes'* Don Quixote

4 Mary E. Barnard and Frederick A. de Armas (eds), *Objects of Culture in the Literature of Imperial Spain*

5 Nil Santiáñez, *Topographies of Fascism: Habitus, Space, and Writing in Twentieth-Century Spain*

6 Nelson R. Orringer, *Lorca in Tune with Falla: Literary and Musical Interludes*